# Blackstone's Policing for t

Third Edition

# Blackstone's Policing for the PCSO

Edited by
Dr Bryn Caless

Contributors
Barry Spruce, Robert Underwood, and Steven England

OXFORD
UNIVERSITY PRESS

# OXFORD
UNIVERSITY PRESS

Great Clarendon Street, Oxford, OX2 6DP,
United Kingdom

Oxford University Press is a department of the University of Oxford.
It furthers the University's objective of excellence in research, scholarship,
and education by publishing worldwide. Oxford is a registered trade mark of
Oxford University Press in the UK and in certain other countries

© Oxford University Press 2014

The moral rights of the authors have been asserted

First Edition published in 2007
Third Edition published in 2014

Impression: 1

Published in the United States of America by Oxford University Press
198 Madison Avenue, New York, NY 10016, United States of America

British Library Cataloguing in Publication Data

Data available

Library of Congress Control Number: 2014950235

ISBN 978-0-19-870454-6

Printed and bound by
CPI Group (UK) Ltd, Croydon, CR0 4YY

# About the Authors

**Dr Bryn Caless** was formerly Head of Human Resources for Kent Police and Director of Kent Police College and is now Senior Lecturer in Policing (School of Law and Criminal Justice) at Canterbury Christ Church University. He has extensive experience of the strategic management of police and PCSO training, having worked with Professor Robin Bryant on establishing the IPLDP training model in the force and, with Robin, devising and delivering an innovative European postgraduate professional qualification for senior police officers. Prior to this, Bryn worked at the Ministry of Defence. He was also a contributor to the *Blackstone's Student Police Officer Handbook* and to *Blackstone's Police Operational Handbook: Practice & Procedure* (ed. Harfield, 2nd edition, 2011). He edited the 'companion' *Blackstone's Policing for the Special Constable* (2013). He has written *Policing at the Top* (2011) on chief officers, and, with Dr Steve Tong, *Strategic Police Leadership across Europe; an empirical study* (2015), both published by Policy Press. He is currently working with Barry Spruce on a book about police crime commissioners.

**Barry Spruce** is an experienced PCSO trainer and formerly taught with Kent Police. He was Head of the Extended Police Family Department for Kent Police and now works in the Extended Partnership Team. He is joint author, with Bryn Caless, of the 'Neighbourhood Policing' section of *Blackstone's Police Operational Handbook: Practice & Procedure* (ed. Harfield, 2009). He contributed to *Blackstone's Policing for the Special Constable* (2013) and is currently working with Bryn on a book about police crime commissioners.

**Robert Underwood** is a former Kent Police officer, who helped to devise the Kent Student Officer Programme. Together with colleagues, he was jointly responsible for the design of the Foundation Degree in Policing which formed the basis of initial police learning in Kent. He is also a contributor to the *Blackstone's Handbook for Policing Students* and to *Blackstone's Police Operational Handbook: Practice & Procedure* (ed. Harfield, 2012), as well as working with Bryn and Barry on *Blackstone's Policing for the Special Constable* (2013). Robert is now Senior Lecturer and Programme Director of Policing Studies/Policing at Canterbury Christ Church University.

**PCSO Steven England**, formerly a student at Canterbury and winner of the Ruxton Prize for the outstanding policing student of his year, is now with Kent Police. We are grateful to Kent Police for allowing Steven to work with us on this third edition, bringing as he does valuable front-line knowledge to the role of PCSO.

**Notes:** The Editor is grateful to former PC David Morgan (Heddlu Dyfed-Powys) and to Professor Robin Bryant who both contributed to the first edition of *Blackstone's Handbook for the PCSO* (2007), and again to Robin who also contributed to the second edition (2010).

# Foreword

I am delighted to provide the Foreword to this excellent book. I have worked with the Editor, Dr Bryn Caless, for many years. Without question he is a leading authority in police and PCSO training; he talks good, solid, down-to-earth common sense and is someone always worth listening to. I couldn't have thought of a better choice of Editor. On this basis alone I would recommend the book unequivocally. Having actually read it, doubly so!

The role of Police Community Support Officer (PCSO) marks a significant shift in practical community policing, allowing greater numbers of officers to be deployed, more visibly and with excellent (and so vital) connections in their local communities. They now form a valuable asset for their police forces. However, their arrival has also had a couple of unexpected benefits too. As one example: the number of minority ethnic officers joining as PCSOs is roughly ten times the number joining as Constables. This is helping to engage with ethnic communities in a whole new way—to great benefit generally, and in countering modern terrorism in particular. You can see, therefore, that the job of a PCSO affects the 'sharp end' very directly.

Many PCSOs now want to progress to full Constables and go on to pursue a very worthwhile career in policing. Skills for Justice has ensured that the competences required of a PCSO dovetail exactly with the somewhat broader set of a Constable, which would allow seamless progression. Modern, forward-looking police forces such as Kent are now taking advantage of this (there's Bryn's work again!), saving some 30 weeks of initial training, and a whole lot of taxpayers' money.

The book is primarily for PCSOs, prospective PCSOs, and all officers responsible for the training and development of PCSOs, including tutor constables and divisional managers. Its coverage of neighbourhood policing may also be of interest to other practitioners involved in this vital area. Good luck! PCSOs are making a big difference in the challenging world of modern policing: go for it!

Dick Winterton
Former Chief Executive
Skills for Justice, now CEO of City & Guilds

# Acknowledgements

**The Editor wishes personally to thank:**

Those organizations that gave ready permission to quote extensively from their work, particularly the **Association of Chief Police Officers** (ACPO) and **Skills for Justice**; his former colleagues in **Kent Police**, particularly the PCSO trainers in the Personnel and Training Directorate, and all those many PCSOs in the wider world who shared their experiences and insights with the writing team.

**Peter Daniell** and the Law editorial department of Oxford University Press, especially Lucy Alexander.

**Dick Winterton**, former Chief Executive of Skills for Justice and now CEO of City and Guilds, for many conversations, friendship, and permission to quote extensively from the National Occupational Standards and the behavioural competences for PCSOs.

Extra special thanks go to esteemed colleagues **Barry**, **Bob**, and **Steve** who put up with my demands, tolerated my enthusiasms, delivered against a tight deadline, and whose support I value very much.

Most of all, my love and thanks to my darling wife **Clare** and my super family—**Helen**, **Wez**, **Sally**, **Johnny**, **Kit**, **Meghna**, and **Maddy**—for good-humouredly accommodating a phantom PCSO for many more years than any of us believed possible.

**Barry Spruce** thanks especially **Emma**, **Phoebe**, **Joseph**, and **Ethan** for their much needed support.

**Robert Underwood** thanks his wife **Vuka** for her continued support, understanding, and patience.

**Steven England** thanks Jeff, Pam, Chris, and Hannah, for their direction, love, and support and Paul Hollier of Kent Police; always on hand with insightful advice, encouragement, and friendship.

*Chapter 4*

We are grateful to Skills for Justice, the Skills Sector Council which owns and develops the NOS and Competences in the Justice sector, for permission to quote extensively from the NOS and other SfJ publications. Parts of the commentary under 4.2 are adapted from descriptors in C Naseby, Consultation Guidance for the Justice Sector (SfJ, 2006).

The Editor and Contributors thank Professor Robin Bryant and Sarah Bryant (editors) for their kind permission to use material from *Blackstone's Student Hand-*

*book* which underpins parts of Chapter 3 and which generally informs the world of student policing. It is a quarry in which all writers about policing practice wield a pick.

The authors of this book have taken care to ensure the accuracy of the information it contains, but neither the authors nor the publisher can accept any responsibility for any actions taken or not taken as a consequence of the information it contains.

No endorsement is implied in this book for the College of Policing's Wider Police Learning and Development Programme (WPLDP), any College of Policing Examination or Assessment, or any other CoP product, nor is any endorsement expressed or implied by Central Authority Executive Services.

# Preface to the Third Edition

When this book was first suggested in 2005–2006, PCSOs were still very much a novelty: the media coverage was (with uncharacteristic caution) hostile, the Labour Government in power, more in hope than expectation, thought that the scheme might work outside London, keen-eyed academics planned research projects on this new development, the criminal justice system heaved a sigh and went back into its sluggish inertia, the Police Federation sharpened its knives, the police service looked puzzled—and the public took the PCSO straight to its heart. Seldom has so unpromising a national beginning blossomed so quickly into such widespread community acceptance: people wanted to see PCSOs on patrol, were reassured by their accessibility, were (mostly) prepared to talk to them, and quickly concluded that the experiment had already worked. Vandalism seemed to be reduced, theft was halved, nuisance was suppressed, those made miserable by anti-social behaviour now seemed to have a champion in uniform: what was not to like?

As we will show you in the pages that follow, it has not all been plain sailing—often because the authorities are not quite sure what a PCSO is or can be—and there have been occasions when PCSOs have taken on tasks for which they are neither fitted not trained. Now, eight years later, PCSOs are a solid fact of Neighbourhood Policing life. Special Constables work alongside PCSOs all the time, and the police as a body has moved from reluctant acceptance to ungrudging admiration, acknowledging that PCSOs bring an extra dimension to the job of policing communities. The Federation is still hostile, but that's par for most of its responses to change. Its days are numbered anyway. The public still seems to like PCSOs, their impact on community policing is tangible, and perhaps most important of all, a new champion of the PCSO concept has arrived in police headquarters—the Police and Crime Commissioner, elected to hold the police to account and responsive to the twitches and concerns of the communities that elected the PCC in the first place.

It would now be a bold person who suggests that the PCSO has had its day: in many ways that day is just beginning. So this book, the third on PCSOs that we have written, updates the recruitment process, describes the PCSO's daily work, refreshes the referential detail about the powers and duties, tests the reader's knowledge periodically, and gives a new and sharply focused context to the police world in which the PCSO operates. After more than a decade, it seems clear to us that the PCSO is here to stay. We hope that this new edition will help them do their worthwhile and necessary job.

Bryn Caless
Editor

# Contents

Contents

Contents

# List of Photographs

# Glossary of Terms Used in Policing

The following is a list which explains many of the common terms in use in policing. It is not exhaustive but this 'Jargon Buster' is designed to help you to get a grip on the acronyms, abbreviations, mnemonics, and other linguistic contortions which form the often impenetrable language of the police 'family'.

**ABH**   Actual bodily harm

*ACC*   *Assistant Chief Constable,* command rank

**ACPO**   Association of Chief Police Officers; sometimes used as a vernacular proper noun for a Chief Officer (qv)

***actus reus***   Latin: 'criminal act', part of the proof of criminal liability, coupled with 'guilty mind' or ***mens rea*** (qv)

***ad hoc***   Latin: 'for this special purpose', but has elided to mean 'off the cuff' or 'unrehearsed'

**ADQ**   Assessor-Directed Questions (for evidence of competence in meeting the NOS, qv in your **SOLAP**, qv)

**ADVOKATE**   mnemonic to help with gathering evidence. Its principles were formulated in the wake of the famous case of *R v Turnbull* (1976). The mnemonic is: A = Amount of time you or the witness had the suspect under observation, D = Distance between you or the witness and the suspect, V = Visibility in the vicinity at the time, O = Obstructions between you or the witness and the suspect, K = Known or seen before, A = Any reason for remembering the suspect, T = Time lapse, E = Errors

**AIRWAVE**   National police radio communication system

**Analyst**   A professional police staff member whose role (usually) is to analyse and assess crime intelligence, and to present research

**ANPR**   Automatic Number Plate Recognition system; cameras linked to police and DVLA computers can identify or 'ping' registration plates on vehicles of interest

**ASBO**   Anti-social behaviour order

**BCU**   Basic Command Unit (Area, Division)

**'bilking'**   Vernacular term; means making off without paying (such as at petrol stations)

**'Biometrics'**   The use of unique physical characteristics as identifiers, such as the iris of the eye

**BMI** *Body mass index*, a determination of the fat ratios in the body and their relationship to obesity. Used by forces to determine propensity for things like diabetes and heart problems. Now largely replaced with 'waist/height measurement' indicators

**'Border Agency'** A term to describe the UK's Immigration and Nationalities Department, in its role of safeguarding the UK's international frontiers , often rendered as 'UKBA'

**'brought to justice'** [Often rendered as '**btj**'] a government term to describe the complete process from criminal act through detection to arrest and arraignment for trial. Clearly, to be meaningful, 'btj' ought to include a finding of guilt and a punishment, but purists and jurists argue that 'not guilty' and 'no punishment' equally represent 'btj' outcomes

**byelaws** Local laws (such as restrictions on parking) enforceable only in the local area itself

**CAP** Common approach path to a crime scene

**case law** Precedents set by court decisions

**Caution** The formal warning to a suspect under PACE 1984, in three parts, depending on the stage the investigation has reached:

1. *You do not have to say anything*
2. *but it may harm your defence if you do not mention* (**a**) *'when questioned'* or (**b**) *'now', something which you later rely on in court.*
3. *Anything you do say may be given in evidence.*

**CCTV** Closed-Circuit Television (note the '**d**'; it is *not* 'close-circuit')

**CDRP** Crime and Disorder Reduction Partnership, old term for Community Safety Partnership (CSP)

**chemical cocktail** The combination of chemicals and hormones in a person's body at moments of high tension or stress. Such chemicals as adrenaline and hormones such as cortisol prepare the body typically for *'flight or fight'*

**Chief Officer** A police officer with the rank of *Assistant Chief Constable* and above; Command rank

**CHIS** Covert Human Intelligence Source (informant)

**'CJ'(S)** A common acronym, referring to some process or unit concerned with Criminal Justice (Systems)

**'collar'** An arrest (vernacular)

**College of Policing** Established in 2012, has taken over most of the learning and training functions of the old National Policing Improvement Agency (NPIA), together with some representational functions previously the province of ACPO (qv) and new roles such as commissioning research

**common law**   The old (then unwritten) law of the land covering such basic crimes as murder, theft, and rape. Much common law is still **extant** (*alive and working*).

**'continuity'**   (of evidence): an audited and continuous trail from crime scene or suspect to court, such that evidential items can be accounted for at all times en route, to obviate interference or contamination

**CPIA**   Criminal Procedure and Investigations Act 1996

**CPS**   Crown Prosecution Service, now officially replaced with the Public Prosecution Service, but the change has been slow to catch on

**'CRAVED'**   A neat mnemonic which reminds us what items are 'stealable', that is, attractive to a thief or burglar. The mnemonic is:

Concealable
Removable
AVailable
Enjoyable
Disposable
(see Clarke, 1999)

**crime scene**   That place where a crime is known to have happened, or where it is suspected of having taken place

**CSI**   Crime Scene Investigator (forensic)

**custody, or custody suite**   A designated area in a police station (usually where the cells are located), where arrested persons are logged and processed by trained custody staff, usually led by a sergeant

**DC**   *Detective Constable*

**DCC**   *Deputy Chief Constable, number two in the Force*

**DCI**   *Detective Chief Inspector*

**DCS**   *Detective Chief Superintendent;* command rank

**de minimis**   At the least risk (Latin: from the phrase *'de minimis non curat lex'*, meaning 'the law is not concerned with trifles')

**Designation**   The process whereby a chief constable confers powers on PCSOs (we use a capital '**D**' to distinguish this specialist use of the word throughout the Handbook)

**DI**   *Detective Inspector*

**digital**   Referring to any computer-based equipment which uses binary digits as an encoding process

**direct speech**   The *verbatim* (word-for-word) recording of what someone actually said. The opposite is 'recorded speech'. You should record all things said to you and needed in evidence in direct speech in your **PNB** (qv)

**DNA**   Deoxyribonucleic Acid (genetic 'fingerprint')

*DS*   *Detective Sergeant*

**DVLA**   Driver & Vehicle Licensing Agency

**DWP**   Department of Work and Pensions

**ECHR**   European Convention on Human Rights, which led to European countries adopting common legal principles in defence of individual liberty. It underpins our own **Human Rights Act 1998**

**'either way'**   An offence triable at *either* a magistrates' court *or* the Crown Court depending on its seriousness (such as a financial limit for theft)

**EVA**   Environmental Visual Audit, sometimes known as the 'structured patch walk'; it is a way of noting all the problems in a patrol area, such as drugs paraphernalia, abandoned vehicles, graffiti, litter, and vandalism

**Federation**   Police 'Union', strictly a Staff Association, covering ranks from Constable to Chief Inspector

**5x5x5**   An intelligence report (**NIM**, qv). The numbers refer to the reliability, access, and other factors about the source providing the intelligence

**FLO**   Family Liaison Officer

**FOA**   First Officer Attending (a crime scene)

**FPN**   Fixed Penalty Notice, a fine for an offence, such as speeding, instead of going to court, in an attempt to speed up the criminal justice system. See also **PND**

**GBH**   Grievous (note *not* 'grievious') Bodily Harm

**HATO**   Highways Agency Traffic Officer, steadily replacing police major roads patrols in characteristic 'battenberg' vehicles in black and yellow

**'hit'**   A DNA sample which can be 'matched' with an identified person (not always criminal)

**HMIC**   Her Majesty's Inspectorate of Constabulary

**HO**   Home Office

**'hot spot'**   A location where there is a high incidence of current volume crime and criminality (linked with crime analysis, also 'hot victim', etc)

**indictable-only offences**   Serious offences tried at Crown Court

**informant**   See **CHIS**; an informant passes criminal intelligence to a police source handler

**intranet**   Police *internal* electronic information system

**IPCC**   Independent Police Complaints Commission, replacing the old Police Complaints Commission, made statutory in Police Reform Act 2002. The IPCC investigates complaints against the police, especially in shootings or deaths in custody

**JRFT**   Job-Related Fitness Test: a means to determine if a person is able to undertake a job with high physical demands (such as patrol or firearms)

**LOCARD**   Forensic database system, named after a renowned scientist

**MAPPA**   Multi-Agency Public Protection Arrangements (part of the joint agency approach to child protection, violent and sex offenders, rehabilitation, managed return of prisoners to the community, etc)

***mens rea***   Latin: 'guilty mind'—one of two things you must prove to show criminal liability (the other is the 'criminal act', or ***actus reus***, qv)

**MISPER**   Missing person

**MO**   Latin: '*modus operandi*', 'a (characteristic) way of doing something'

**MOD**   Ministry of Defence

**MOU**   Memorandum of Understanding

**MPS**   Metropolitan Police Service (the 'Met')

**NB**   Take especial note of (Latin: '*nota bene*', 'note well')

**NCA**   National Crime Agency, replaced Serious and Organised Crime Agency (SOCA) in 2013

**Neighbourhood Policing Teams**   Small, local policing unit, consisting usually of a police sergeant, up to two or three constables and three or more PCSOs, sometimes with Special Constables and partner agencies too; all working to local targets and agendas, but integrated with overall **BCU** targets and priorities

**'Nexus'**   A combined computer database system, linking, for example, local intelligence requirements, a criminal database such as the Police National Computer (**PNC**, qv), the Driver and Vehicle Licensing Agency's database of vehicle ownership, and a targeting computer system, such as **ANPR** (qv)

**NO ELBOWS(S)**   Mnemonic to help you to remember the rules for your Pocket Note Book (**PNB**, qv); stands for

NO
Erasures,
Leaves torn out or lines missed,
Blank spaces,
Overwriting,
Writing between lines,
Spare pages, and
Statements must always be recorded in direct speech

**NOS**   National Occupational Standards (held and developed by **Skills for Justice**, qv)

**PACE**   Police and Criminal Evidence Act 1984, PACE 'Codes' are additions for police guidance

**PACT**   Partners And Communities Together, an arrangement where key people in a community have regular meetings and agree plans for the neighbourhood with the police

**PC**  *Police Constable*

**PCC**  Police Crime Commissioner, an elected person who has replaced Police Authorities in all English and Welsh constabularies with the exception of London. PCCs, like the old volunteer Police Authorities, can 'hire and fire' chief constables and call the police to account. The PCC, who is highly paid, has an entourage of advisers and staff usually located at Police HQ in the constabulary in which PCSOs work. The PCC determines policing priorities but does not have any operational role. The first elections took place in November 2012. New elections will be held in May 2016 when the PCC's four-year appointment ends

**(P)CSO**  (Police) Community Support Officer, a title which signifies that the individual CSO is part of the police force, not a community, rural, or parish warden, or any of the associated designations, such as traffic (or parking) warden. PCSOs have standard powers on a national basis, but may have additional powers designated or conferred by the chief constable of the force in which they operate. PCSOs are under the operational command of their chief constable or Commissioner, but are employed by the Police Authority

**PDR**  Performance Development Review (annual 'appraisal')

**PLAN**  Acronym acts as a reminder that police and PCSO actions must be Proportionate, Legal, Authorized, and Necessary.

**PNB**  Pocket Note Book

**PNC**  Police National Computer

**PND**  Penalty Notice for Disorder, similar to Fixed Penalty Notice (**FPN**, qv) for low-level public nuisance

**police caution**  A formal warning given by a senior police officer to an adult who has admitted his or her guilt (do not confuse this with a **Caution** with a capital 'C', such as under PACE to a suspect)

**Police Staff**  Official designation of support ('civilian') staff, some of whom are operational but who do not have warranted powers like police officers. PCSOs are police staff

**PRA(02)**  Police Reform Act 2002, which gave the statutory basis for PCSOs, and helped to define their powers. Rendered in our text as 'PRA02'

**PS**  *Police Sergeant*

**PSNI**  Police Service of Northern Ireland (was the RUC, Royal Ulster Constabulary, GC). PSNI began recruiting PCSOs in 2007

**reprimand**  A formal warning given to a juvenile by a police officer, on admission of guilt for a first and minor offence

**RIPA**  Regulation of Investigatory Powers Act 2000

**risk assessment**   A process of understanding that hazard plus (or 'times') likelihood = something going wrong. Assessing the risk may help you to do something positive about it

**'sanitized'**   Intelligence with identifying features and origins omitted

**sic**   Latin: as it is written ('*sic*' = 'thus')

**'signal crime'**   The notion that some kinds of crime act as warning signals about the security of everyday life. Some crimes matter more than others in 'signalling' people's concerns. The theory behind signal crimes is also referred to as 'Broken Windows Theory'

**Skills for Justice (SfJ)**   Developed from the old 'sector skills councils', this is the learning standards and skills 'guardian' for the criminal justice system. As well as devising means whereby the professionalism and qualifications of staff in the criminal justice sector may be recognized, Skills for Justice (sometimes rendered as **SfJ** or **S4J**), holds all **NOS** for the sector and all behavioural competences

**SOCO**   Outmoded term ('Scenes of Crime Officer') largely replaced by **CSI** (qv)

**SOLAP**   Student Officer Learning and Assessment Portfolio initially used for police officers' learning; now the principles, if not all the content, are applied to PCSOs. You will be expected to sustain a reduced form of SOLAP after training, because a portfolio of evidence of your competence is needed to appraise your performance (see **PDR**, qv) annually

**SOLO**   Sex Offender Liaison Officer

**Statute law**   Modern, written legislation

**Statutory Instrument**   Legislation introduced by a government on the back of other Acts. The purpose is to avoid going through the consultation and debate process in Parliament for relatively minor things

**summary offences**   Offences which are dealt with at a magistrates' court

**TICs**   'Taken into consideration' offences by a court. These are crimes to which an offender admits, rather than face further charges. Always referred to in the plural

**Unison**   Police Staff ('civilian') Association, represents PCSOs, but also much larger representation of workers in the public service generally, such as hospital workers

**WPLDP**   Wider Police Learning and Development Programme—a particularly elephantine collection of letters to cover College of Policing learning and development programmes in the extended policing 'family', part of the 'mixed economy' of modern policing

**YOT**   Youth Offending Team; often a partnership group between police and other agencies, in which PCSOs can be involved

*The phonetic alphabet*

The purpose of the phonetic alphabet is to ensure that there is no confusion over similar sounding letters such as 'p' and 'b' and 'd'; or, more subtly 's' and 'f', or 'm' and 'n', when spelling something out over the radio or phone. The accepted '*sound form*' for each letter in English is as follows:

| | |
|---|---|
| A | Alpha |
| B | Bravo |
| C | Charlie |
| D | Delta |
| E | Echo |
| F | Foxtrot |
| G | Golf |
| H | Hotel |
| I | India |
| J | Juliet |
| K | Kilo |
| L | Lima |
| M | Mike |
| N | November |
| O | Oscar |
| P | Papa |
| Q | Quebec |
| R | Romeo |
| S | Sierra |
| T | Tango |
| U | Uniform |
| V | Victor |
| W | Whisky |
| X | X-Ray |
| Y | Yankee |
| Z | Zulu |

*Numerals*

Only two numerals sound similar '5' and '9'. These are distinguished in speech by saying '**FIFE**' for 5 and '**NINER**' for 9. This is important when spelling out a car registration such as **BD59 SFE** (try it and see). However, you need to know other sounds for numbers: '**0**' is always **ZERO** in the Phonetic Alphabet (to distinguish it from letter **O Oscar**). The best way to represent the sounds of the numbers is like this:

| | |
|---|---|
| 0 ZERO | 5 FIFE |
| 1 WUN | 6 SICKS |
| 2 TOO | 7 SEV—UN |
| 3 THUH—REE | 8 ATE |
| 4 FORE | 9 NINER |

Numbers are always given separately in speech. You don't say for 57, 'fifty seven' but 'Fife Sev-un'; you don't say for 103, 'a hundred and three', but 'Wun Zero Thuh-ree'. So the motorway 'M 62' would be 'Mike Sicks Too' in radio speech.

No confusion of the sounds is possible if this pronunciation is followed. This system is in universal use where English is the first or primary language (apologies to our Welsh colleagues); all the emergency services and armed forces in the UK use this phonetic alphabet. Don't worry about some odd spellings which you might see, such as 'Whiskey', because the point about the phonetic alphabet is that it is spoken not written. What you have to do is learn this alphabet by heart and practise it as much and as often as you can, in conjunction with the 24-hour clock.

---

**Task**

Get friends or family to help you by testing your spelling out of words and numbers (the 'alpha-numeric') in the phonetic alphabet. Practise relaying information to friends or colleagues on the phone or radio. Try using cards with the letters on one side and the phonetic name on the other, to test yourself.

---

You are expected to be proficient in the use of the phonetic alphabet and numbers without delay.

# Special Features

The book has been written from a PCSO's point of view in order to help you access more easily the information contained within it. Each chapter is laid out in broadly the same manner and contains all or some of the following features:

*Key point box*

Where it has been felt appropriate to reinforce an important or pertinent point which has been covered within the text of the chapters, a key point box has been included to reinforce the information or provide further context.

*Discussion points and Task boxes*

Both discussion points and task boxes explore issues around a certain area, as well as offering opportunities for discussions with colleagues.

*Flow charts*

Some chapters include flow charts to support points made within the text. Flow charts often make the interpretation of sometimes-complicated information much easier to understand.

*Knowledge checks*

Short tests are presented at the end of each substantive section, reflecting standard police training practice. A self-test should be carried out honestly, checking your answers against those provided at the end of the book. Completing these will show you how much you have absorbed and understood.

# Introduction

*How to use this book and how to test yourself*

Welcome to Policing for the PCSO! As you read through this book, you may notice that it is sometimes as much about the context of policing, what is driving your Force, and what your police colleagues may be doing, as it is about your role. This is because we did not want the book to be merely a reference manual (there are plenty of those).

Your job has meaning only in the context of what your individual Force is doing and specifically what the Neighbourhood Policing Team alongside you is doing in your community. The role of the Neighbourhood Policing Team itself needs to be understood in the context of where the police service is going and what constitutes 'policing' in the twenty-first century. We try to give that context throughout.

*How the book is organized*

The book consists of a number of stand-alone sections. Their importance to you as a PCSO will vary according to the job you are doing and the problems that you have to solve. **Each section is divided according to numbered headings**. Each of these heading numbers is referenced in the Index. This means that you can read 'thematically' as well as logically, with close, detailed, textual reference to the nuts and bolts of the job of PCSO. We begin with joining the police. This is not for the PCSO who is already employed and busy in a community; rather it is for the person who wants to know what being a PCSO involves and how to go about applying. **We test your understanding of what we have told you and offer particular points for you to note, as well as topics you may care to discuss with colleagues, trainers, and assessors.** These are recurrent features throughout the book—because we have *not* designed this book only for the student PCSO or the new joiner. We have designed it for the PCSO who is serving just as much as for the new entrant. You may want to refresh your knowledge of your powers (Chapter 3), or check which National Occupational Standards you have to complete (Chapter 4), the nature of 'Designation' (2.6); understanding the community's fear of crime (6.4); what is meant in practical terms by human rights (2.11); or what the difference is between 'common law' and 'statute' (3.1.2).

**Each section of each chapter is complete in itself**, but inevitably there is much cross-referencing between the parts of this book. When you come across a term you don't understand, or an acronym you are not sure about (such as **JRFT**—the job-related fitness test), we have provided (earlier in this part) a basic **Glossary of police terms**. Your own Force is also likely to have a 'jargon buster', so check how to access your local word crib. Note also that at the end of each substantive section, we have a **'knowledge check'**. This is a police term used extensively in training to mean that you need to check that you have understood something. For example, if you do not learn the Caution thoroughly in both its forms ('when questioned' and 'now'), you will not understand when it should be used. The answers to all the knowledge checks are given in numbered sequence at the end of the book.

Whilst **this book is the most comprehensive tool, the most exact explanation, the clearest description, and most rigorous analysis of the role of the PCSO in existence**, we never stop learning. The Reference List helps you to focus where you want your research and learning to develop. A comprehensive **Index** lets you find easily where everything is.

This, the third edition of the only context-specific book designed for PCSOs, is simultaneously a context for policing, an insight into the meaning of what you do, a detailed reference guide to powers and competences, a resource to explain the law, a means of helping you to learn, a challenge for the future, and a friendly, informal, but authoritative depiction of what it is like to put on the uniform and go out into the world as a Police Community Support Officer.

*Police ranks*

The Police is a disciplined service, with an established hierarchy or 'rank structure'. The ranks, shown below, are designated on the **epaulettes** (*shoulder boards*) of officers' uniforms. The general rule is that the greater the amount of embroidery on the epaulette, the higher the rank (but note the single crown of the Superintendent). This is matched by the peaked hat or bowler worn by uniformed officers. Senior ranks are depicted by the amount of braid, black or silver, on the cap's peak or bowler's brim. Again, the more silver you see, the higher the rank. You will be expected to show formal or 'due' deference to higher rank. Whether or not you salute the higher rank in uniform depends on your individual Force policy. Certainly, you should come to attention when addressed. One of our PCSOs had this comment:

> From my experience many trainees neglect the etiquette and culture of the police, and furthermore do not realise the importance of 'due deference' in a quasi-military organisation such as the police. Boot 'bulling' (polishing) is now expected even of PCSOs, as is drill practice and weekly inspection by a senior rank.

In other words, you are expected to take the formalities of rank seriously, and to give serious attention to what the police culture regards as proper presentation of the self in uniform.

Whilst the Police is structured hierarchically and has ranks like the Armed Services, don't expect discipline to be robotic in any sense, because you are, and will always remain, accountable at law for your own actions. What you do is always down to you to defend or justify, and you cannot hide behind orders, ranks, or silver braid if your judgement was poor.

*Some differences from the standard*

In the Metropolitan Police and the City of London Police, there are different ranks at the top end of the hierarchy. Broadly, in the 'Met', a Commander ranks as an Assistant Chief Constable (ACC), a Deputy Assistant Commissioner (DAC) ranks as a Deputy Chief Constable, and an Assistant Commissioner (AC) ranks as a Chief Constable (as does the Commissioner of the City of London Police). The Deputy Commissioner and Commissioner ranks in the Metropolitan Police are above Chief Constable rank in terms both of salary and the resources which they command. The Commissioner rank dates from the very first 'commissioners of police' in London's New Police in 1830. **Do not confuse these police ranks with 'Police and Crime Commissioners' (PCCs)**, elected individuals who hold police forces accountable for what they do and, by the way, employ you.

*Detective ranks*

You'll be aware that detectives don't wear uniform. They have the same ranks as their uniformed counterparts with the difference that their ranks are always preceded by the word 'Detective' from Constable to Chief Superintendent, so: 'Detective Sergeant' or 'Detective Chief Inspector'. You will be smartly corrected if you get the designation wrong; police officers are always very exact about their ranks and titles. Chief Officers of police, that is Assistant Chief Constables (ACC), Deputy Chief Constables (DCC), and Chief Constables (CC) are always regarded as 'uniformed' and do not use the title 'detective'.

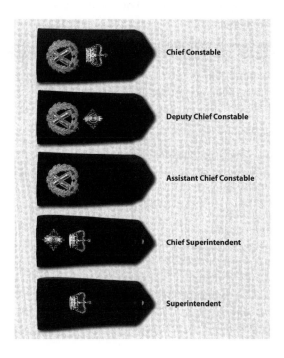

Chief Constable

Deputy Chief Constable

Assistant Chief Constable

Chief Superintendent

Superintendent

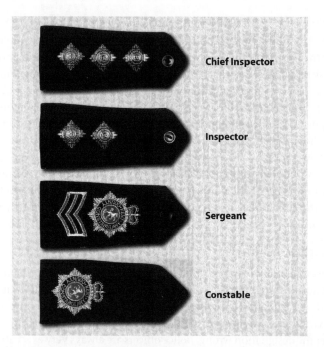

The point for you at the outset is to understand the formal designation of rank in the service you are joining. Being able to quickly identify the rank and how it should be addressed can certainly save you from embarrassing mistakes. Remember that supervisory ranks above you are addressed—according to gender—as 'sir' or 'ma'am'.

## DISCUSSION POINT

How would you structure PCSO 'ranks' in harmony with police ranks so that (a) different ranks are clearly marked and (b) there is no confusion with police ranks?

*The organization of a typical police force*

We have to note that organizational structures vary from police force to police force, and very few are identical. However, in the structure which we show below, the basic functions of:

- BCU level policing
- Neighbourhood teams
- Specialist crime investigation, including serious organized crime and major crime
- Specialist crime techniques, including forensic investigation, surveillance, and covert technical operations
- Information technology
- Force communications

- Finance, administration, engineering (vehicle fleet), and estates
- Human Resource Management
- Learning and Development (Training)
- Traffic
- Firearms and tactical operations
- Public Order
- Dogs
- Helicopter, boat, fixed-wing aircraft, or other specialists such as divers and searchers, cavers, mountain rescue, river police, and 'mounted' (horse) division (for example the City of London)

have to be brigaded together somehow. The standard method for doing this is by creating 'Directorates' commanded by an ACC or equivalent. A smallish police force of fewer than 4,500 might have three directorates such as **Divisional or Territorial (BCU) Operations**, **Central Operations**, and **Support Operations**. Larger forces, say of 6,000 or more, might have four or five Directorates organized as shown in our structure diagram below.

Don't ignore the 'impact drivers' on the chief constable of any police force: these are partners in the so-called 'Tripartite Arrangement' of the **Police Crime Commissioner** and the **Home Office** (the Chief makes up the other side of the triangle) but there are also the **Criminal Justice Inspectorate** which includes the Public Prosecution Service and HM Inspectorate of Constabulary, as well as the **media**, and the **public**. All or any of these can call the Chief Constable to account for the actions of his or her Force. If there is impact on the Chief, sooner or later there will be impact on you too.

---

**Task**

Look at our diagram (see below). How does your Force structure vary from what we describe? Note the differences.

---

*Matched funding and non-government funding*

Direct force-based funding is now the principal source for PCSOs, and, with rare exceptions, it is both the largest and the most common default option for police forces and PCCs. Centralized Home Office funding for PCSOs has ceased and constabularies are expected to fund the role from their own budgets. Arguably this makes the PCSO role vulnerable to the whims of the individual force and Police Crime Commissioner; however, many have come to recognize the importance of the PCSO role, public support remains high as there is increased understanding, and PCSOs themselves have created a 'niche' by adapting to the requirements of the community policing role. Not surprisingly, PCCs are keen to encourage other sources both of funding and of support, among which are local and county authorities, local businesses, consortia of city centre shops, local markets, schools, universities and colleges, local transport providers, and

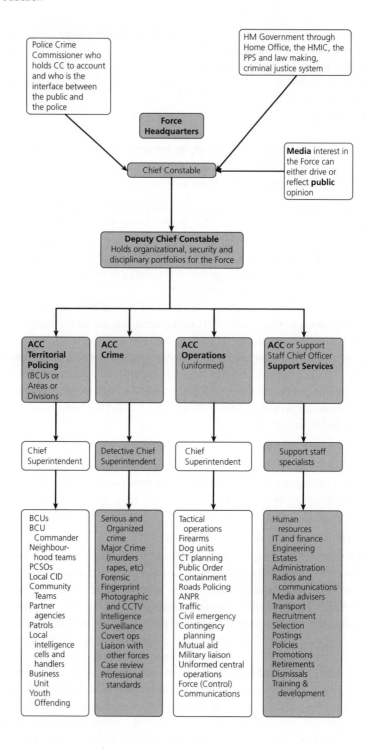

chambers of commerce. Not all of these groups and organizations could afford a full-time PCSO, in which case part-funding is sought, which can then be matched by the Police and Crime Commissioner. This is called **'matched funding'**. Advertising and sponsorship logos are also ways in which the business community is encouraged to invest in PCSOs, as is an appeal to their vested interests. A PCSO who patrols a bus station, say, at peak times, is likely to bring considerable reassurance value both to the travelling community and to the bus franchise operators. It is common for transport providers to sponsor PCSOs as a result. Indeed, we know of forces where there is an arrangement to carry police officers and PCSOs on the public transport network for no charge, provided that the officers are in uniform and that they will intervene if there is a problem. The incentive for the transport operators is obvious. But do not confuse this informal function with that of the British Transport Police Community Support Officer who travels the national railway system, and functions in the same way as PCSOs everywhere else. Finally, the support for locally-sponsored PCSOs need not be confined to ready cash and legal contracts with the police authority; it can be support 'in kind'. This means that, for example, provision of mobile phones, or of a vehicle or bicycle, of premises or accommodation, of lockers or venues for meetings, or use of CCTV can all help to sustain the viability of a PCSO.

---

**DISCUSSION POINT**

Can you think of any problems and downsides to sponsorship or matched funding?

---

Questions about sustainability arise from matched funding. At present, we have seen very few matched funding schemes which extend beyond four years. Yet government ministers and senior politicians frequently assure us that PCSOs are here to stay. Are they?

---

**DISCUSSION POINT**

Do you believe that there is a sustainable long-term future for PCSOs?
What do you base your opinions on?
What are the funding pitfalls, do you think?
Where else could funding come from?
What is the appetite for private funding?

---

*What happens if increased funding for PCSOs becomes hard to find or sustain?*

The short-term answer may be that fewer PCSOs will be recruited and 'natural wastage' (including application to police forces) may further thin the overall numbers. But the real and brutal truth is that police forces and their Police and Crime Commissioners are stuck with a bill—consisting of your wages, equipment, deployment costs, training, and pension—which they have to pay. Good for you, less so for the long-suffering council tax payer and the PCC who may have to seek an increase in the **precept** (*money raised locally from council tax to support the police force*). Failing that, or even as well as that, the likely recourse of your Force and PCC will be to slow down **police officer** recruitment. This may decrease further if the UK's economic crises multiply and deepen and police forces are strapped for cash (following the 25 per cent cuts of 2012–2013) and precepts are further capped. The shortfall will be seen in lower and slower recruitment of police officers and very probably a reduction in the number of PCSOs recruited and retained.

# 1

# Coming In

## 1.1  **So You Want to be a PCSO**

This chapter is largely addressed to the aspiring or enquiring person who is thinking about applying to be a PCSO—**it is not for the already serving officer**, who should press on now to whatever else in the book is directly relevant.

### 1.1.1  **To the person thinking of applying to be a PCSO**

Welcome to the only chapter in the book designed for you and you alone. This chapter will discuss with you your **motivation** for becoming a PCSO and then explore **what police forces are looking for**. This is followed by a detailed examination of the **recruitment** process and gives you the opportunity to consider how you should aim to perform in completing the **application**, attending **assessment**, and performing at **interview**.

### 1.1.2  **Other elements: ethics, diversity, fitness**

Then we look briefly at **ethics** and **diversity** (these are covered in much more detail later in the book), and consider the **physical fitness** and physical standards required of a PCSO. We hope that, by the time you have worked your way to the end of the chapter, you will have a clear idea of what is expected of you and whether or not you can meet those expectations. If you can, good luck with the application and subsequent stages and, if you are successful, we hope that you enjoy the job. If you don't get in, perhaps you need to consider some life choices, re-applying, or ask yourself whether this job is really for you.

## 1.2  **Why Do You Want to be a PCSO?**

We don't expect to be able to itemize all the individual motivations of PCSOs. This isn't intended to put you off, but to suggest that:

- It's not easy or automatic to become a PCSO.
- Lots of people try, but only the really well-prepared make it through the selection process.
- It's worth persisting because it is an important and challenging job.
- Because lots of people want to do it, we have a high standard against which to measure you and your motivation.
- The fact that you have bought this book (you have, haven't you?) means that you must be **serious about applying**.
- This book is a **guide**, not a crib—it suggests what you should think about, but doesn't give you the answers.
- If you really want to become a PCSO then this chapter will help to channel your determination into a strategy for success.

We asked one of our PCSO colleagues about his motivation for becoming a PCSO and he said that, when interviewed as an applicant:

> I recall that I was asked it (why did I want to be a PCSO?) three times in total at the various interview and application steps. Having a solid understanding of your motivation to join the role is essential as the interviewers will quickly pick any holes in your reasoning, and when you are trying to sell yourself to the police you need to convince them of your strong desire to serve in the role.

### 1.2.1 Motivation

Let's talk about motivation. Motivation, put simply, is what drives or encourages you to do something.

When people are motivated, it means that their interest in an activity or in what a group does is stimulated and they want to join in. Watch people listening to their favourite music; if their feet are tapping and bodies are swaying and they move with the rhythm, they are probably showing an interest in dancing. This is a very basic motivation and its behavioural manifestations are clear and simple. But motivations involving career choices are often very complex, made up of overlapping drives and desires, and may possibly involve sustaining all that interest over a long period. Think about becoming a doctor or a professional footballer or a pop idol or a classical musician. To succeed in any of these callings you have to have two things: the **drive** to achieve and the **potential** to achieve. We will talk about potential later when we look at what police forces want from you, the aspirant PCSO. We are here concerned with what drives you, what makes *you* want to become a PCSO.

#### 1.2.1.1 Reasons to be a PCSO

It may be that, at this stage, you are merely curious or you could be very motivated indeed and already starting to fill in the application form. Most of you will fall between the two extremes, but you may have a number of reasons for considering the job of PCSO.

---

**Task**

Write down the five main reasons why you want to be a PCSO. You may have more than five, but try to concentrate on the priority reasons for your application.

---

**DISCUSSION POINT**

What do you think:

(a) **motivates most people to become PCSOs** and
(b) **what motivates *you* to become a PCSO?**

The answers to (a) and (b) may not be the same. *Don't worry*. We all have different reasons for doing what we do and for entering the kinds of occupations which we choose. You need to be aware of **why people do things**, and most importantly (because you will be asked about it) **why you do things**. Look at the following list of statements. Do any of them match your own feelings and desires?

### 1.2.1.2 Behavioural statements

1. I really want to help people in my community because I can see what needs to be done to improve people's feelings of safety and civic pride, and I know that I am capable of helping them.
2. I want to make a difference; looking after people has always stimulated me, but I was never much good at biology and blood and things like that, so I didn't want to go into medicine!
3. I just like being with people and hearing what sort of things amuse them, infuriate them, interest them, and sadden them; I guess you could say that really I'm a people person.
4. What is really important to me is making people do what they should; there's so much sloppiness about with people not caring about the fabric of their community. I'd make them realize that there's a price to pay for ignoring the wishes of other people.
5. I have a strong sense of fairness and justice. I was bullied at school and I hated the helplessness that I felt then. I want to help the bullied to stand up and resist the intimidation or threat or whatever it might be, and to get some pride back, just as I had to.
6. Respect is what it's all about, isn't it? It's *not* to do with 'political' or any other kind of correctness; it's about understanding how people feel when they're treated as lower or inferior just because they are different. I don't just mean being black or lesbian, I mean respect for old people and their wisdom and experience, or respect for the young and their pride and hope, and it's respect for people who maybe can't always say what they feel or express how confusing life is to them. And respect isn't hard!
7. I was mugged for my new Tablet about six months ago and it made me feel sick and small, and very angry. There were three of them, and they just grabbed it and pushed me away. I felt like a little kid, but they were huge and threatening, and laughing at me. I couldn't get the Tablet back from them, and they walked away. Didn't run. They weren't scared, *I* was. I've been a victim and I know what it is like. I know what it means to feel frustrated and, you know, unable to do anything. I can understand how others like me feel; and I want to do something to help them. Not cups of tea and sympathy but really, REALLY doing something to stop this violence and make people aware of the jungle out there and how they need to cope with it.

8. My dad was in the army and he always said that a uniform makes people respect you. Well, I didn't get much respect at school or at work because I'm a bit, well, timid sort of thing and I'm basically shy. I didn't join in things, was never a football or cricket player. Did cross-country though, so I'm pretty fit. So I thought if I had a uniform on, people would look at that, at the police badge, and treat me better.

9. I wanted to be a cop but failed the selection thing and so this is next best.

10. I've never really thought about it much; I mean, my family has all been involved in public service in one way or another—my mum is a teacher, just as I was, and my dad is a staff nurse at the hospital, and my brother is a police officer in the Met in London. So I was always going to do something in the public service, doing things *for* people, and never going to go to the City and making pots of money or anything like that. I've been in lots of organized groups for sport and for charity and I don't think this is going to be that different—whatever you do, you have to work as part of a team and be part of a group—because that's how things get done.

11. My parents expected it and that's how it happened. I can remember when my father said that he thought that this was the sort of thing a woman could do with pride and so help all of us and I thought yes, he's right! I *can* do this and it won't matter that I'm a woman and I *can* be independent and make up my own mind.

You may be able to identify your own feelings and motivations with some of these, though probably not all. These statements are all based on comments made by past candidates when asked why they wanted to become PCSOs, but we now need to dig under them, and consider what each of the statements says about the person's ambition and motivation.

### 1.2.1.3 I really want to help people in my community because I can see what needs to be done to improve people's feelings of safety and civic pride, and I know that I am capable of helping them

This is an assertion that the person thinks s/he can make a difference in the community. Since this is fundamentally what a PCSO is about, the candidate is showing strong motivation, but s/he will have to go on and provide evidence that this is how s/he behaves and that the motivation is supported by clear achievements, perhaps through community projects in which s/he has participated, or some other tangible example of what s/he has done to help (or 'improve') the community. Simply making the assertion is not enough (because anyone can say that; the point is to prove it). The candidate would also be expected to explain what s/he means by *'feelings of safety'* and *'civic pride'*, because these are key concepts in understanding the police reassurance agenda and community/neighbourhood policing plans. Lastly, the candidate's comment that *'I am capable of helping them'* would be probed and s/he would be expected to be able to show some ways in which that capability had been demonstrated or evidenced. Perhaps you could think of examples?

### 1.2.1.4 I want to make a difference; looking after people has always stimulated me, but I was never much good at biology and blood and things like that, so I didn't want to go into medicine!

There is a mixture here of the positive and the negative in terms of motivation. The statement that the person wants to make a difference is positive and key to the effective role of the PCSO but s/he should expect to be asked precisely how s/he thought s/he could *'make a difference'*, and in what areas and why. In other words, a candidate should prepare specific evidence to support any general statement such as this. The person should also expect to be asked why *'looking after people'* has been stimulating and what experience s/he has of doing it. Some schools, for example, run activities where people in the community are aided by having small tasks done for them, such as shopping for the house-bound (of any age). Alternatively, candidates may have had a community support element in a previous or current job (teaching, local health administration, social work, and so on). A candidate would be expected to evidence that this *'looking after'* was more than a one-off; it should have happened consistently over a period. The comment on *biology, blood,* and *medicine* is refreshingly honest, but a bit negative in terms of motivation. Concentrate instead on the things which *do* stimulate and motivate you, except for brief illustrations of why you haven't done, or stayed with, other occupations. Besides, as a PCSO you may have to assist at accidents or road traffic collisions, or violent crime scenes where there may be an abundance of *'biology and blood'* and you'll have to cope as first on the scene, however squeamish you may feel. This is what we mean about thinking through the effect of your statements.

### 1.2.1.5 I just like being with people and hearing what sort of things amuse them, infuriate them, interest them, and sadden them; I guess you could say that really I'm a people person

This is actually a coherent and endearing statement from someone who clearly enjoys being with people and is stimulated by their company. Being a good listener and enjoying meeting people are key attributes for the successful and effective PCSO, but you also need to bear in mind that the role is not simply a refuge for the inveterate gossip. Try to avoid using such flat clichés as *'people person'*, which makes you sound a bit artificial or derivative. That said, this person was trying to explain that being with and around people was highly stimulating and enjoyable. There is nothing wrong with that at all and you'll be a poor PCSO if you don't like people. But, and it is a big 'but', as a PCSO, you have to maintain a degree of separation and objectivity in your daily dealings with people. You must be able to stand back from problems and see ways through to solve them, rather than being immersed in the flood of emotions and feelings with which people in the community sometimes invest projects or difficulties. You may have to make judgements between disputing parties; you may have to seek compromises between factions in the community; and you may have to resolve disputes and arbitrate when tempers run high. Simply being a jolly type who enjoys a good chinwag isn't going to help you do any of these things. Indeed, your partiality for one side or another may actually get in the way of your being effective. This candidate would be questioned closely about matters like objectivity and dispassion, as well as about the evidence to support his or her social gregariousness.

### 1.2.1.6 What is really important to me is making people do what they should; there's so much sloppiness about with people not caring about the fabric of their community. I'd make them realize that there's a price to pay for ignoring the wishes of other people

This speaker is a bit of a 'control freak', it seems: *people don't know what the right thing is to do, so I'll make them do it.* This is a form of self-righteous self-importance which anyone wanting to be an effective PCSO (or, indeed, an effective police officer) should avoid. Of course, there are times when compulsion, or the reasonable use of force, is the only recourse, such as when you have to intervene to prevent an innocent person from being attacked or endangered. But as a PCSO you will spend much more time persuading, cajoling, and encouraging than insisting on the exercise of power. **There is no place in policing of any kind for the exercise of power for its own sake.** So, do not think that being a PCSO is about your ego. That said, the points about *people not caring for the fabric of their community* and that there is *a price to pay for ignoring the wishes of others* are telling and may be fundamental to the problems which a community is experiencing. Some anti-social behaviour orders (**ASBOs**) are made precisely because people ignore the obligations and responsibilities that come with being a member of a community. *Making people realize* . . . is not within a PCSO's remit and, although a large part of your behavioural competence (which we explain later) is about respect for the origins, views, and life choices of others, you cannot compel it by force; only by example. This candidate, had s/he made it through to the interview stage, would have been asked in detail about cooperation, negotiation, team work, group identity, and tolerance. Much evidence would have been needed to offset the negative and rather compulsive character depicted here.

### 1.2.1.7 I have a strong sense of fairness and justice. I was bullied at school and I hated the helplessness that I felt then. I want to help the bullied to stand up and resist the intimidation or threat or whatever it might be, and to get some pride back, just as I had to

This comment expresses a series of strong emotions and it is clear that the injustice of being bullied, with its attendant feelings of low self-worth, is still quite raw (we do not know how old this person is, nor how long ago this experience may have been). There is nothing amiss with having a well-defined sense of right and wrong, justice and injustice, fairness and unfairness—indeed, such feelings are probably part of the vocational complex which inclines people to public service in the first place—but we have to be careful that this doesn't become a kind of vigilantism. There is a danger that such a person might blind him or herself to the complexity of issues and reduce them to the simple level of good versus bad. Most of life actually consists of shades of grey, rather than this tempting simplicity, and a PCSO, in particular, is expected to be able to make objective judgements about situations and see ways through and around difficulties. This calls for clear vision, not the distorting lens of anger. Of course a PCSO must act decisively to confront bullying, and '*resist…intimidation or threat*' but, as we see later with attitudes to 'hoodies' and groups of young people 'hanging about', the tendency of the angry and self-righteous can be to demonize others and to label them unfairly. We're all prone to do this at times, which is why the behavioural competences address such thinking quite specifically. Certainly, this candidate would experience some thorough probing about anger management, tolerance, respect for others, and clarity of judgement, as well as limits to PCSO powers.

**1.2.1.8 Respect is what it's all about, isn't it? It's *not* to do with 'political' or any other kind of correctness; it's about understanding how people feel when they're treated as lower or inferior just because they are different. I don't just mean being black or lesbian, I mean respect for old people and their wisdom and experience, or respect for the young and their pride and hope, and it's respect for people who maybe can't always say what they feel or express how confusing life is to them. And respect isn't hard!**

This person understands one of the central behavioural competences of a PCSO: *respect for others' difference*, whether deriving from race or sexual orientation, or gender, or age, or disability, or belief. There is a maturity in this statement which suggests that the speaker has practical experience on which to draw, and is about celebrating difference rather than fearing it. Some might disagree with the candidate's last comment, that '*respect isn't hard*'. For many it is very hard indeed, and you may encounter this in the police service as well as in many other walks of life. Many of us have difficulties in accepting that *all* have a right to be treated with dignity. This is not to say that you condone the crime, but that even the worst people, who do horrendous things to others, *should still be treated by you with respect*. At the interview stage, this candidate could expect persistent investigation into evidence of his or her approach to diversity and how he or she would respond to other people with closed minds or entrenched attitudes.

**1.2.1.9 I was mugged for my Tablet about six months ago and it made me feel sick and small, and very angry. There were three of them, and they just grabbed it and pushed me away. I felt like a little kid, but they were**

huge and threatening, and laughing at me. I couldn't get the Tablet back from them, and they walked away. Didn't run. They weren't scared, I was. I've been a victim and I know what it is like. I know what it means to feel frustrated and, you know, unable to do anything. I can understand how others like me feel; and I want to do something to help them. Not cups of tea and sympathy but really, REALLY doing something to stop this violence and make people aware of the jungle out there and how they need to cope with it

There is a distressing story here which informs the speaker's attitude to all victims, but especially with compassion for those who have been subject to a violent assault, because the speaker has experienced this and can empathize with victims. However, the same caveats apply to this series of statements as applied to the speaker who commented on having been bullied at school: care must be taken to avoid distorting one's view of the world. There is something a bit messianic about the speaker's desire to 'stop...violence and make people aware'. Most people *are* aware of the daily jungle, where the predatory criminals stalk. They rely on people like PCSOs and police officers, as well as the huge 'private policing' industry, to keep them safe. Yet in another sense, the speaker is right to say that there is a responsibility on each of us to be aware of threats and dangers around us; no less from crime than from fire, flood, or other incipient hazards. As for the speaker's dismissive 'cups of tea and sympathy', in fact, being a PCSO is often about having a cup of tea and a chat with people, simply to reassure them that PCSOs are approachable and human. The speaker could expect to be challenged at interview on how much emotional baggage s/he is carrying as a result of being a victim of crime, lest it prejudices or inhibits the speaker's ability to be an effective PCSO. The speaker's behaviour would certainly be monitored when given training in self-protection, lest there is too much latent aggression.

### 1.2.1.10 My dad was in the army and he always said that a uniform makes people respect you. Well, I didn't get much respect at school or at work because I'm a bit, well, timid, sort of thing and I'm basically shy. I didn't join in things, was never a football or cricket player. Did cross-country though, so I'm pretty fit. So I thought if I had a uniform on, people would look at that, at the police badge, and treat me better

This person has some real problems about self-esteem and confidence. There is nothing wrong with being shy (all of us experience situations or social events where we feel a bit inhibited) but there is a general expectation that PCSOs have a sturdy, independent confidence and resilience which does not rely on the very tenuous authority of a uniform. In a real sense, this person expects to be able to hide his or her inadequacies behind a badge, and **it won't do**. There are plenty of people in the community who will have little or no respect for a uniform, unless the wearer of it has something of his or her own to bring to the equation. At the same time, there are suggestions here that s/he is a bit of a loner (not a team player) and there is a central illogicality in supposing that a uniform supplies what is lacking in character or experience. The speaker could expect some close questioning on his or her motives to become a PCSO and some detailed probing on 'teamworking'.

### 1.2.1.11 I wanted to be a cop but failed the selection thing and so this is next best

There is a blunt honesty about this comment, and indeed, many of those applying to become PCSOs want to go on to become police officers. However, there is a bit more to being a PCSO than second-best to a police officer. This person could expect to be asked a number of questions about his or her perceptions of the differences between being a PCSO and a police officer, and some probing behind the bluntness of (and lack of detail in) the statement itself. In particular, the speaker could expect to be asked about the PCSO role and how much s/he understands about communities, patrol, intervention, and communication. There is another point: what people say on joining and what they say six or eighteen months later, can be quite different. It is likely that the enjoyment of the PCSO job itself will satisfy many, whilst others (about 10 per cent) will have left policing altogether. In our experience (and also using the Special Constabulary as a rough guide) fewer than 15 per cent of those who join as PCSOs will end up as police officers within five years.

### 1.2.1.12 I've never really thought about it much; I mean, my family has all been involved in public service in one way or another—my mum is a teacher, just as I was, and my dad is a staff nurse at the hospital, and my brother is a police officer in the Met in London. So I was always going to do something in the public service, doing things for people, and never going to go to the City and make pots of money or anything like that. I've been in lots of organized groups for sport and for charity and I don't think this is going to be that different—whatever you do you have to work as part of a team and be part of a group—because that's how things get done

Many PCSOs used to be teachers, and this speaker is evidently part of that growing tradition. There is more; this person is imbued with the spirit of public service (with education, health, and the police service as influencing factors) and has acquired experience of working within a community through sport and charity events. The behavioural competency of 'teamworking' (in contrast to the speaker before last) is clearly strong and s/he understands the power of individuals doing things together. There is a strength and a maturity about this speaker which suggests that s/he understands the nature of the work. Now, that is not the same as having a clear motivation, and the fact that the speaker admits to not having *'thought about it much'* might lead to some digging about motive and drive rather than understanding or experience. The police service wants candidates for PCSO roles to have thought carefully about why they want to do the job and what makes them interested in police activity. This speaker could merely be following a family 'tradition' of service without much in the way of self-analysis or reflection. This would not debar the speaker from being a credible candidate as a PCSO, but acceptance and the consequent investment in training and operational deployment by a police force requires something more tangible than family tradition. The interview team would explore the candidate's experiences and evidence to ensure that the level of commitment was genuine and the drive both sustained and individual.

**1.2.1.13  My parents expected it and that's how it happened. I can remember when my father said that he thought that this was the sort of thing a woman could do with pride and so help all of us and I thought yes, he's right! I *can* do this and it won't matter that I'm a woman and I *can* be independent and make up my own mind**

This speaker seems to have an expectation of the role of PCSO as some sort of liberating, emancipating activity in the performance of which she expects to blossom as a person. It could be the case that she has unreal expectations of the nature of the work, or it could be that she is projecting on to the role her own hopes and ambitions. Either way, this could be disappointing for her. Alternatively, her father's comment that being a PCSO is '*the sort of thing a woman could do*' is true enough, but there is implicit in the father's comment an assumption that there is 'women's work' and there are other kinds of work, which might entail gender discrimination for which there is no place in the policing family. A PCSO is a PCSO: the officer may be a woman or a man, there is no substantive difference. It is the **person's qualities and skills** which matter. But it may be that we are reading too much into what could be a simple statement of surprised pleasure in the woman's discovery that this seems to be a job which she could do and in which she could assert her pride and independence. If that is the correct interpretation, well and good. However, the speaker would have to be prepared for some detailed investigation at interview and in other situations, where her motivations and drive in wanting to become a PCSO will be followed up. Becoming a PCSO is not something which should be embarked on lightly, certainly never just because one's parents '*expected it and that's how it happened*'.

### 1.2.2  **Summary analysis**

We hope that you can understand from our analysis of the 11 motivational (behavioural) statements, which are pretty typical of those who apply to become PCSOs, that candidates' assertions are questioned and their motives are explored. None of us has a single unblemished motive for doing anything; motives are always a messy mixture of conceits, desires, ambitions, hopes, and wish fulfilment, bound up with our relative understanding of the activity itself and its everyday reality. This mixture is always worth examining and teasing apart, so that the most dominant motives can be detected and assessed. We go into this in more detail later, but for the moment you can assume that your motives to become a PCSO will be looked at by assessors and you should prepare yourself thoroughly for the questions which will ensue. **Why do you want to become a PCSO?** is a perfectly reasonable place to start.

Now let's have a quick check that you understood this last section:

## Knowledge Check 1

1. How could you define motivation?

2. What is the difference between 'drive' and 'potential'?

3. Why would assessors at interview probe the PCSO candidate's assertion that 'I know I am capable of helping [people]'?

4. What is discretion, and why is it important to act proportionately when deciding on a course of action?

5. What is meant by 'demonizing' others?

6. Do you feel a person who is led by personal experiences and emotions is suitable for a PCSO role?

7. What matters more than gender in being a PCSO?

8. What is a 'messy mixture'?

## 1.3 **What Police Forces are Looking For**

You should have some sense of what police forces are looking for in their PCSOs from the analysis and discussion in the previous section. Also, you should have a look at the section where we discuss the competences which PCSOs are expected to attain in the National Occupational Standards (NOS) within their first year of service, and against which they are assessed thereafter (Chapter 4). You will see the important behavioural competences examined there too.

### 1.3.1 **Behavioural competences**

You should become well used to these, because large parts of the recruitment process are based on six behavioural competences (see 1.3.1.1). Each competence is tested twice during the assessment day's syndicate work (see 1.4.7), but it is important for you to understand that you are being assessed as a **potential** PCSO, not as one already in service.

### 1.3.1.1 **Six behavioural competences**

These are the six behavioural competences, now used across all 43 police forces, but you should note that No 4, **Community and Customer Focus**, is *not* tested in the national selection process (because it is unfair to expect those not yet in the job of PCSO to understand and participate in the delivery of neighbourhood policing plans, among other things):

---

**Six Behavioural Competences**

1. Resilience
2. Effective Communication
3. Respect for Race and Diversity
4. Community and Customer Focus
5. Personal Responsibility
6. Teamworking

---

We shall examine these in some detail in a moment, but you should know now that you will continue to be assessed against all six of these behavioural competences for the rest of your service: they are central to your performance as a PCSO and the bedrock of all police interactions with other people (including colleagues in your Force). Firstly though, let's define what the terms mean as far as the competences are concerned.

### 1.3.1.2 **Definitions of the behavioural competences**

---

**Resilience:** Can persist with a plan of action, even if circumstances and situations are difficult; not cast down by lack of success, persistent, dogged, able to withstand disappointment, can change to fit necessary circumstances, flexible under pressure.

**Effective Communication:** Can communicate instructions, decisions, requirements and needs clearly; has a good vocabulary and can adapt language to circumstances, can speak simply without being patronising, understands how people respond to authority and can adapt to fit the needs of the person or the larger audience; can write clearly and coherently and draft reports, plans and strategies appropriately.

**Respect for Race and Diversity:** Understands other people's points of view and takes those views into account when responding to them; treating all people, irrespective of their appearance, or what they may have done, with dignity and respect all the time, whatever the situation or circumstance.

**Community and Customer Focus:** Can see things from the point of view of those who are policed as well as from the point of view of those who do

---

the policing [empathy]; encourages others to empathize, building a good understanding and relationships with all parts of the community that is served.

**Personal Responsibility:** Makes things happen because of taking responsibility and achieves tangible results; shows motivation to succeed, is conscientious and committed to the role and to making a difference in the community; has a high degree of integrity in all actions and takes personal responsibility for own actions seriously, sorting out any problems that develop; focused on achieving outcomes which assist the community; always willing to learn new things, develop personal skills and knowledge; leads by example.

**Teamworking:** Works effectively as a team member, supporting colleagues and sharing burdens fairly; not shirking the humdrum or routine tasks, not one to bask in self-glory, a team player, where collective effort always exceeds the lone attempt; a keenly participative member of a team or group, quick to praise others, slow to blame; eager to share.

If you are accepted as a PCSO, these behavioural competences will form part of your **continuing professional development** (called CPD for short), when each competence is assessed at a particular level. You need not be concerned about that now, but the detail is at 4.8 if you want to understand what is involved. For the rest of this section, we shall look in more detail at the basic competences needed with the five behaviours (remember, we are excluding **Community and Customer Focus** for the time being) and suggest to you how you might evidence your potential in achieving them, as well as suggesting what other characteristics your assessors will be looking for.

### 1.3.1.3 Positive and negative behaviours

Each of these behaviours has **positive indicators and negative indicators**. The positive represents the sorts of things which police forces want to see, and the negative the sorts of things which they don't want to see. Study them carefully.

### 1.3.2 Resilience

You are expected to attain a Category B standard in this competence. The **positive indicators** include dealing confidently with members of the public, feeling comfortable with working alone (without direct and present supervision), being aware of and dealing with personal stress, but able to accept both criticism and praise. It is also expected that you will exclude your emotions from disputes and disagreements, and be patient in dealing with people who make complaints, although you can say 'no' firmly, when necessary. Above all, you take a 'rational and consistent approach to work'.

**KEY POINT—WORK–LIFE BALANCE**

What this means in effect is that you are a self-starter and can be relied on not to get emotionally hung up on issues. Work is important to you but not the be-all and end-all of life: having this in balance means that you do indeed have a rational and consistent regard for your duties.

### 1.3.2.1 Negative behaviours

By contrast, the **negative behaviours** involve you not seeing the wood for the trees, where you get upset easily; panic when you confront problems; and need constant reassurance, support, and the comfort of a supervisor in the offing. This can lead you to react inappropriately when faced with rude or abusive and foul-mouthed people, and your way of dealing with this can be aggressive. You moan a lot and give in when pressured. You spend a lot of time worrying about making mistakes which leads you to become risk-averse.

**KEY POINT**

You will not be much use as a PCSO if you cannot quietly and effectively get on with the job, referring upwards only when you cannot make that level of decision yourself. The kind of person described negatively here is a liability, always needing a supervisor as a kind of 'comfort blanket' and never making and standing by his or her own decision. Should you show these characteristics at assessment or during your probationary period of service, it is probable that you are not suited to being a PCSO. We describe elsewhere the salient characteristic of resilience in a PCSO as a '*sturdy imperturbability*', where very little can deflect you or put you off.

### 1.3.3 Effective communication

You are expected to attain a Category C standard in this behaviour. The **positives** include the ability and skill to speak clearly and concisely, without hiding behind jargon. You make sure that all your written and spoken communication is well constructed and understood, and you put your points across in a friendly and approachable way, making sure of your facts and trying to keep people's interest. You listen well and pay attention to what others are saying and you clarify issues through apt questions.

**KEY POINT—POSITIVE COMMUNICATION**

You should refer to any of the excellent books on the market on how to write English to help you communicate clearly in writing, if you are not already confident that you can do so adequately. Speech is less formal but still needs a structure and clarity to ensure that people understand you precisely. This means that you know what words mean, and what ambiguity entails; you know how to select words that people won't feel threatened by, or simply not understand. You do not fall into the trap of using acronyms (abbreviated terms which become words in their own right, like ACPO) to non-police audiences.

The **negative behaviours** are the polar opposites of engagement and clarity. This involves speaking without thinking; not understanding (or caring) about the needs of your audience; rambling, unstructured, diffuse, ambiguous, and inappropriate writing and speaking; ducking difficult questions; and being a poor listener. The most negative behaviour of all is to assume that people understand you without checking to see if they do.

### 1.3.4 **Respect for race and diversity**

You are expected to attain a Category A standard in this behaviour. We have already looked at some of the issues contained in this misleadingly mild title, and we refer you to 4.8.2 for fuller discussions and analyses of what this behaviour entails. We shall simply summarize here what the positives and negatives are, with brief commentaries. *Remember that not attaining the desired standard in this behaviour may result in your failure to be accepted into the police family, no matter what your other attainments or grades.* The police service takes positive behaviours in this subject very seriously indeed. It is worth noting that the Equality Act of 2010 gathers together the various strands for equality and calls them '**protected characteristics**'. They include age; disability; gender reassignment; marriage and civil partnership; pregnancy and maternity; race; religion or belief; sex and sexual orientation. This is further explained as:

Age
Where this is mentioned, it refers to a person belonging to a particular age (e.g. 32-year-olds) or range of ages (e.g. 18–30-year-olds).

Disability
A person has a disability if s/he has a physical or mental impairment which has a substantial and long-term adverse effect on that person's ability to carry out normal day-to-day activities.

Gender reassignment
The process of transitioning from one gender to another.

Marriage and civil partnership
Marriage used to be defined as a 'union between a man and a woman'. But same-sex couples can now get married (2014) in the same way as heterosexual couples, or they may have their relationships legally recognized as 'civil partnerships'. Civil partners must be treated the same as married couples on a wide range of legal matters.

**Pregnancy and maternity**

Pregnancy is expecting a baby. Maternity refers to the period after the birth, and is linked to 'maternity leave' in the employment context. Protection against maternity discrimination is for 26 weeks after giving birth, and this includes not treating a woman unfavourably because she is breastfeeding.

**Race**

Refers to the 'protected characteristic' of Race. It refers to a group of people defined by their race, colour, and nationality (including citizenship) ethnic or national origins.

**Religion and belief**

Religion has the meaning usually given to it but belief includes religious and philosophical beliefs including lack of belief (such as atheism). Generally, a belief should affect your life choices or the way you live, for it to be included in the definition.

**Sex**

A man or a woman.

**Sexual orientation**

Whether a person's sexual attraction is towards their own sex, the opposite sex, or to both sexes.

---

**Further Reading**

For more information, go to <http://www.equalityhumanrights.com/about-us/vision-and-mission/our-business-plan/race-equality/>, which explains the Equality Act 2010 in detail.

---

### 1.3.4.1  Other points of view

**Positive behaviours** include being able to see things from others' perspectives and understanding that there may be different views of the same thing, without threatening your independence of thought. Similarly, you will be polite, tolerant, and patient with people inside and outside the police, treating everyone with respect and according them dignity, especially when resolving disputes or dealing with people who feel vulnerable. You acknowledge and respect a broad spectrum of social and cultural customs, beliefs, and values within the law and you challenge inappropriate behaviour vigorously. The key words are sensitivity and respect in this behaviour, perhaps particularly when others' values clash with your own.

---

**KEY POINT—STRONG VALUES**

These strong values underpin the essence of behaviour in the police family, and especially so for you, the PCSO, with your daily contact with people in front-line neighbourhood policing. Your positive role model in showing respect and tolerance may impact on the behaviour of others.

---

**Negative behaviours** need spelling out, perhaps, so that you understand what actions and attitudes should be avoided. Such behaviours would ignore the feelings of others and deride or belittle their beliefs, customs, and cultures, and would be shown in such actions as not encouraging people to talk about what concerns them, being tactless, dismissive, or impatient with different points of view or attitudes, leading you to overemphasize power and control in inappropriate ways. This includes using humour inappropriately and showing bias or prejudice when dealing with people who are not like you.

---

**KEY POINT—NEGATIVES IN RACE AND DIVERSITY COULD BE DISMISSAL OFFENCES**

We have commented elsewhere that negative behaviours in respect for race and diversity could be dismissal offences. Should you exhibit any such behaviours at the assessment process, you will not be accepted into the police service. If you are serving, you may very well be dismissed. Some of these negatives are actually against the law (racism, sexism, homophobia, discrimination on any of the grounds of race, belief, age, disability, gender, or sexual orientation); which, we remind you, *you are pledged to uphold*. We make no apology then, for continuous reference to these standards throughout this book. It is a message that you must take on board, leading you to act positively if you are to serve the community as a PCSO.

---

### 1.3.5 Personal responsibility: doing a good job without supervision

You are expected to attain Category B in this behaviour. The **positive behaviours** in this competence have to do with your willingness to take responsibility for what you do and that, by extension, you can be trusted to get on with doing a good job without close supervision. You can be relied on to get results in a sensitive, determined, and effective way, mindful of the feelings of others but focused on what you need to do. You keep promises, you don't let people down, you are conscientious, take pride in your work, and you follow things through without having to be asked to do so. You are open, honest, and genuine, standing up for what is right and not being swayed by expediency or short-term gains at the expense of your integrity.

---

**KEY POINT—BEHAVING ETHICALLY AND RESPONSIBLY**

This is about behaving ethically and responsibly, showing others that you can be trusted and relied on; you deliver what is needed and go the extra mile to ensure that what is needed is what happens. To do this well, you need to be aware of your own strengths and weaknesses and know when you need the help of others and when you can go ahead on your own. Much of this has to do with confidence and a blend of experiences in the role, though you will be expected to deliver on this competence as soon as you join.

---

### 1.3.5.1 **Shirking personal responsibility**

**Negative behaviours** are found in people who are frightened or lazy and who don't want to accept that they are in charge of their own lives, work, and results. Such people ignore issues, hoping that they will go away, or duck issues, hoping someone else will cope, and they put in the minimum effort to get by. They are often cynical, give up easily, and have poor motivation or desire to learn.

> **KEY POINT**
>
> Showing behaviours of this kind during the recruitment process will probably result in your being screened out early. However, should you make it through selection and begin to exhibit these traits when you are in training or on patrol, you can expect to be challenged and your behaviours brought to your attention quickly and strongly. Persistence in refusing to take personal responsibility will almost certainly result in you being assessed as incapable of being an effective and efficient PCSO.

### 1.3.6 **Team working: supporting each other and pulling together**

You are expected to attain a Category C standard in this behaviour. Team working is a core activity in the work of a PCSO. For all that you take personal responsibility for what you do and for all that you are capable of working alone, it is with and through colleagues, and with and through partnerships, that you really get results. The **positive behaviours** are that you actively support the team and individuals within it to achieve the objectives and that in doing so you are cooperative and friendly with others, whom you support. You are always willing to help others, but not afraid to ask for help yourself, and you develop mutual trust and confidence in those with whom you work. You willingly take on unpopular or routine tasks and you take pride in any of the teams of which you are a member.

> **KEY POINT—THE IMPORTANCE OF TEAMWORK TO THE PCSO**
>
> This is another behaviour by which the success of the concept of PCSOs, and indeed of neighbourhood policing, stands or falls. Results are obtained through mutual and consensual effort, and this means that the effective PCSO is a member of many different teams, both inside and outside the police, and within communities and within partnerships working with those communities.

### 1.3.6.1 **Being selfish and in it for yourself destroys teamwork**

The **negative behaviours** show high degrees of selfishness and egotism, such as the individual who takes credit for success without acknowledging what others did to help. Such people only do the jobs which are interesting or which will bring them to notice and they have a personal agenda for success which ignores or bypasses teamwork and joint efforts. Such people show very little interest in working with others and are always scarce when a difficult or unpopular job is to be done.

---

**KEY POINT**

These negative behaviours disrupt teams and make joint ventures fail. The cynicism with which the person promotes his or her own interests is also a factor in destroying the best of cooperative intentions. Such behaviours are often hard to detect, particularly by a supervisor who may not spend prolonged periods with team members, but over time, such selfishness will emerge. If properly evidenced, such behaviours can result in disciplinary actions and in extreme cases, dismissal. It is much better not to employ such people in the first place, hence the importance of detecting any such behaviour at the initial assessment stages.

---

### 1.3.7 Summary

These are not the only characteristics that police forces will look for in those who want to become PCSOs, but they are the principal indicators and, between them, they capture many of the manifestations of positive behaviour that forces will look for. The **Community and Customer Focus** behaviours are expected to develop during your initial period of training and in your job performance, and you emphatically will be assessed on your positive achievements here. We talk about the behavioural competences at greater length at 4.8 but our purpose in covering the same ground now (though not in precisely the same way) is to ensure that all material relevant to those applying to become PCSOs is available in the same place. Before we go on to look more closely at the recruitment process itself, we have a knowledge check for you on section 1.3:

---

**Knowledge Check 2**

1. What are the five 'behavioural competences' that you will be tested on?

2. What is the sixth?

3. Define 'Respect for Race and Diversity'

4. What is CPD?

5. What kinds of indicator does each behaviour have?

6. What is an acronym?

7. What are 'protected characteristics'? Name five of them.

---

8.  Which behavioural competence requires a Category A attainment?

9.  What are the kinds of positive behaviour you would demonstrate to be competent in Teamworking?

# 1.4  **Applying to Join: the Recruitment Process**

We are grateful to the Home Office and the Office of Public Service Information (OPSI) for permission to quote from recruitment documents and summaries of assessments.

The application process is entirely computerized now and paper applications are no longer sent out. What normally happens is that the role vacancy will be advertised on the force website under 'recruitment/ jobs' and candidates will create a portfolio here which will be their application for the role. There will be information about the recruitment process including a mandatory briefing session, which all applicants who pass the online application sift must attend in person. (This is usually held at force headquarters, and may be attended by the head of recruitment, many of the recruitment team, and several senior police officers.)

On line there will also be a detailed PCSO role description and a description of the qualities being sought from applicants, typically including the competencies, qualifications, and previous experience that we noted earlier. You should also read the Guidance for becoming a PCSO, parts of which we have quoted in this and in the sections which follow, and which you can access on the 'Police Could You?' site at: <www.policecouldyou.co.uk/documents/Guide-pcso2835. pdf?view=Binary>.

You must pay close attention to these documents so that the examples you use in the application process clearly demonstrate your capability for the role (see 1.3). You will be asked to supply your personal details, a declaration of any convictions, and answer questions about your close family members for vetting purposes. Typically the 'window' for this online application is approximately two weeks, so you have time to get your competency examples polished and ready, rather than trying to think of them whilst you complete the application process. The use of the acronym STAR might be helpful to you here. This helps you focus an example as effectively as possible, both in your application and later at your interview:

- SITUATION
- TASK
- ACTION
- RESULT

Reflecting on the entire example is crucial in the application stage, simply recounting an incident is not sufficient. Police forces want applicants to self-evaluate and to show a detailed understanding of their actions. This 'outside the box thinking' is exactly what they are looking for in the application stage; one of our PCSOs learned during training that the most important quality in the early stages is that *an applicant is a socially rounded, developed individual*. There is even a desire with some forces that PCSOs have good public speaking experience, as it can be a very public role and you will be expected to contribute to community meetings. One of our contributing PCSOs received an entire input on effective public speaking during training and all students had to give a five minute presentation on a topic of their choice.

All applicants who pass the online application process will be invited to attend a briefing session, when you will also be measured for your uniform, exchange paperwork (vetting forms, doctor's form, passport identification, employment references etc), undergo your physical fitness test, and be provided with an assessment centre date (for your interview).

We now break this process down into the steps that a successful applicant will follow:

1. **Online application:** Usually a week/two after closing date you will find out if you have been successful.
2. **Briefing**, fitness test, paperwork exchange, uniform fitting, provided with an assessment centre date. (NB Applicants can have three attempts at the fitness test and may continue with their application if they fail; however it must be completed before they commence training.) The briefing is usually scheduled for about a month after the closing date for applications.
3. **Assessment Centre:** Usually two/three weeks after briefing. This gives you a very limited time to prepare, which is why it is important to have a firm grasp of your competency examples.
4. If you are successful, **routine checks** (medical test with the force Medical Officer, taking up and assessing your references, and beginning the vetting process) usually begin about a month after the assessment centre.
5. **Home visit** from an officer to confirm you are a suitable individual. This is usually much more informal than the assessment centre, and covers what you expect from the role and why you think you are appropriate to become a PCSO. Therefore, even after you have passed the assessment centre, you still have to be switched on about why you want to be a PCSO and what you can deliver in the job. This final stage is usually conducted two/three weeks after the medical or a month before starting training.

Many of the PCSOs we have talked to, as well as our own contributors, attest to how demanding the online application is, because there are numerous competencies to cover, and you have only have **a limited word count** to sell yourself. Therefore concise answers are a must. There is a considerable focus on personal responsibility, customer service, going beyond required expectations, team work, problem solving, community engagement and conflict management. At this stage there is very little reference to policing; rather it is a search for desirable characteristics. This is where any voluntary experience with the police or other organizations can be a real benefit, especially if you have a limited employment history.

It is also important to give serious thought to your answers. To give you an idea of the standard and range that would be expected, we have devised a 'model answer' for you to consider. The situation itself is a bit of a cliché, but see what use can be made of it:

> '*I observed an elderly female with a considerable amount of shopping attempting to cross a road which had a heavy traffic flow. I conducted a swift mental dynamic risk assessment and deduced that there was a potential hazard to the elderly lady and other road users as she was carrying a lot of shopping and there were many cars and lorries passing in both directions at that time. I politely asked the elderly lady if I could assist her in any way to which she replied yes. Hopefully this person will feel more comfortable asking for help in the future as she had a positive experience with a young person on this occasion.*'

This ticks a lot of boxes that the police are looking for in applicants—appropriate communication, awareness of risk and surroundings, willingness to help others, and a positive attitude. This is the biggest key to the recruitment process, getting the most out of the answers you give and showing yourself off as much as possible. We consider this in more detail in a moment.

One of our colleagues described his nerves and feelings about the recruitment process like this:

> Despite my strong academic background, extensive experience with the police as a Special, and having previously been successful with an application; I was incredibly nervous throughout the entire recruitment process and often felt that I would be unsuccessful because of the high demands expected by the police force and the sheer volume of applicants with which I was competing.

No-one should think that this is an easy process or one you can waltz through: the toughness of selection alone should tell you something about the sorts of people who are accepted to be PCSOs.

### 1.4.1 Guide to becoming a Police Community Support Officer

The important and obvious first point to make is that you must read the *Guide* before starting to fill in the application, because the *Guide* explains what a PCSO does. The on-line application form specifically requires you to provide examples of how you meet some of the competences, which will enable assessors to judge whether you are likely to have the skills and qualities to be 'an effective PCSO'.

### 1.4.1.1 **Thinking about your application: conveying 'the true you'**

Another thing that the *Guide* (available at <www.policecouldyou.co.uk/documents/Guide-pcso2835.pdf?view=Binary>) tells you is that if you are unsuccessful in your application, you cannot apply again within six months. This makes it all the more important that your application is carefully thought out and considered before you send it in. It would be a pity if your haste and carelessness resulted in your application being refused, when a little forethought and planning would have got you through. This is especially the case, as we shall see in a moment, when you are asked for examples of how you meet a competence. If your examples are poorly considered (they do not illustrate how you performed competently) and weakly expressed, you will not be helping yourself; whereas examples that clearly illustrate how you meet the competence will be effective indicators of your likely performance as a PCSO. It follows that better and more relevant examples mean that you are more likely to be invited to the assessment process.

### 1.4.2 **The recruitment process**

The **recruitment process** itself is in three parts:

1. **Applying to be considered as a PCSO**
2. **Attending an assessment centre**
3. **Passing medical, security, and reference checks.**

(Each of these stages has to be passed before you will be accepted by a police force as a PCSO.)

The *Guide* is quite clear from the outset, indicating that PCSOs must have special qualities and asking these questions:

• How would you deal with a group of binge drinkers dancing in the street?
• What would you do to win the trust of housing estate residents scared to give evidence about a violent assault?
• How would you handle kids using a shopping centre as an indoor cycle speedway?
• What would you do to rebuild the confidence of an elderly couple who were burgled last week?

### 1.4.2.1 **The nature of a PCSO's work**

We have quoted these examples in full, partly because they are eminently practical, but partly also because they go to the heart of a PCSO's work. You will not always be dealing with crimes, but sometimes you will be dealing with conditions that occur as a result of crimes, or actions and events which may precede a crime. Using the example above, the binge drinkers could quickly turn violent and cause damage or assault someone. The children cycling could crash through a shop window or knock someone down. A member of the public could try to restrain the children and be injured, or criminal damage could be caused when the children try to turn movable items in the shopping centre into ramps and obstacles. The other two examples are consequences in the wake of possibly serious crimes.

The *Guide* then tells you:

> You can't arrest anyone. You've got no handcuffs, no baton. All you've got is you. It's down to your ability to get on with some of the most challenging people in some of the most difficult situations. The way you win cooperation is through good-humoured persuasion.

It is difficult to imagine a more succinct and persuasive description of a PCSO's role than this, nor one in which the range of skills and qualities which a PCSO must have is so clearly and practically illustrated.

### 1.4.2.2 Structure of the application form

The application form consists of five sections:

1. **About you**
2. **About your employment**
3. **About your education and skills**
4. **Competency assessment**
5. **Declaration.**

#### Demonstrating all the competences

There is no presumption in section 2 that people cannot apply who have not worked (such as school leavers) but it is unlikely that all such candidates would have the life skills needed to be a PCSO. Candidates must be able to demonstrate potential for *all* the competences required of a PCSO, throughout the whole assessment process. That said, Thames Valley Police employed two 16-year-old PCSOs in 2007, commenting in the face of considerable media criticism that '*if you've got the skills, you can do the job*'. One or two other police forces have employed 17-year-old PCSOs, but such occasions are rare. The majority of PCSOs are mature people with extensive life experience.

### 1.4.3 Section 1: about you

#### 1.4.3.1 Personal information

##### Identifying particulars

The usual requirements for your full name, current postal address, and so on head this section, with the additional request for your National Insurance number (so make a note of it in advance). You must list all surnames (family names) by which you have been known because of the security and vetting checks that will be used to ensure that you are (a) who you say you are, (b) that you have no serious criminal convictions (see 1.4.3.3) and (c) that you are not associated with any criminal in such a way as to inhibit your proper function as a PCSO.

### 1.4.3.2  Right to residence in the UK

Your right to residence in the UK is a factor. If you can live in the UK free of restrictions then you can apply to become a PCSO, but your **written and spoken English** must be of an acceptable standard (ESOL level 5 for example) so that you could function effectively. If you come from the Commonwealth or if you are a foreign national, you will have to supply proof that your **residence in the UK is unrestricted**—for example you would not be eligible if you are only allowed to reside here as a student or if your work permit is valid only for six months. Foreign nationals or Commonwealth citizens need to take passports with them if called for assessment.

### 1.4.3.3  Have you been in trouble with the law?

There follows a section on **convictions and cautions** and it is important that we discuss what this is about. You are asked if you have ever been convicted for any offence or if you have had a formal caution by the police for any offence, or if any court has ever 'bound you over'. This category includes traffic offences and any cautions you may have had as a juvenile, or any appearances before a court martial if you have served in the Armed Forces.

### 1.4.3.4  Declaring convictions, cautions, fixed penalty notices, and so on

Having a conviction or a caution does not mean that you are automatically debarred from becoming a PCSO. It will depend on the circumstances of the offence and the nature of the offence. If, for example, you had a caution ten years ago at the age of 17 for under-age drinking, it *probably* will not disbar you, provided that the offence was not aggravated (made worse) by criminal damage or assault, or some other offence. Speeding offences, fixed penalties, and fines for disorder may also be discounted or regarded with a tolerant eye after a sufficient time has elapsed without re-offending. The really important point is that **you must declare on the application form any such convictions or cautions**. If you do not, your application will be rejected when any undeclared offences come to light—as they surely will. Equally, if there is a summons against you at the time of application or if you are facing any charge, you must declare it (as you must any 'spent' convictions under the **Rehabilitation of Offenders Act 1974**). Police records are extensively searched for applicants to the police family (in any capacity) and these may include details that you might have thought were no longer held, including 'spent' convictions. *Failure to disclose will lead automatically to your rejection as a candidate*. If in doubt, include the details and let the police decide whether they are relevant or not.

### 1.4.3.5 **Checks are also made on your family**

You should know that **the search doesn't stop with you**: there will be criminal record checks on members of your close family to find out if there are any convictions or cautions lodged against any of them, as in Figure 1.1. The application form specifically asks you to tell your family that this will happen. Under the **Data Protection Act 1998,** *the police can't disclose to you the results of enquiries into a third person*—even if the person concerned is your partner or your child. The last point to be made is that if you have had a conviction for a serious offence, such as a crime of violence, or dishonesty, no matter when it was, you are unlikely to be accepted in any capacity in the police.

In summary, the process of declaration looks like this:

**Figure 1.1  Flow diagram of declaration of convictions or cautions**

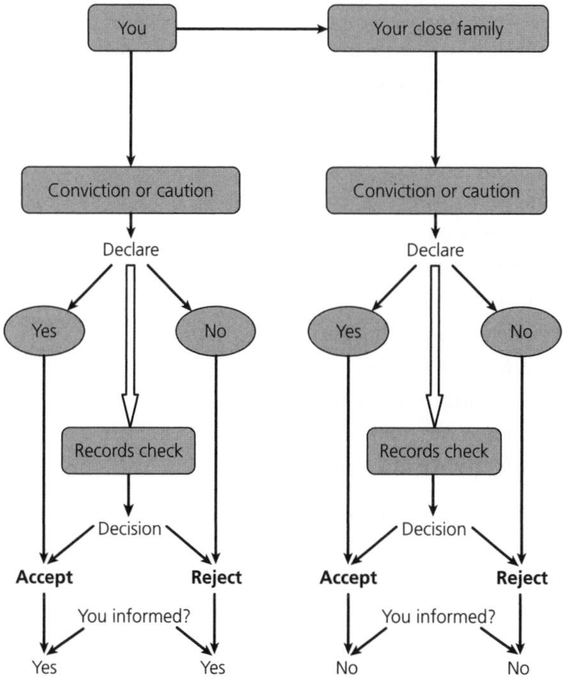

### 1.4.3.6 **Other parts: health, business interests, finances**

The remainder of the sections to be completed concern your health (including days absent from work or college), your business interests, especially whether there might be a clash of interests between your new job as a PCSO and your partner's involvement in running a pub or a gaming house (gambling) for example, together with a summary of your financial position. This last is of interest. In recent years, with the availability of credit made easier, some people have got into considerable debt. By this we don't mean standard mortgages, student loans, or other small-scale debts on credit cards or car finance, but really large debts such as the £374,000 gambling debt declared by one applicant in the North-East or the 27 credit cards owned by another PCSO applicant in southern England, the *average* debt on each of which was £16,857. This applicant's total debt in un-secured loans exceeded half a million pounds. Such indebtedness would almost certainly disbar you from acceptance as a PCSO, especially since the size of the debt might render you vulnerable to corrupt approaches by criminals. However, each case would be judged on its merits. Personal debt is likely to have increased as a result of the economic recession and this will be taken into account when applicants are assessed, but massive debts on the scale indicated above are none-theless likely to disbar such candidates from acceptance as PCSOs.

### 1.4.3.7 'Identifying particulars' of your family members

The final part of section 1 about yourself is a full-page table requesting the full names, dates and places of birth, and addresses of all members of your immediate family. **The immediate or close family** includes:

- **Your mother**
- **Father**
- **Stepfather or stepmother**
- **Mother's or father's partner**
- **Brother(s) and sister(s)—full, half, or step**
- **Your spouse or partner**
- **Your spouse's or partner's parents or step-parents**
- **Your children (over 10 years)**
- **Your partner's children (over 10 years)**
- **Any grandchildren or step-grandchildren (over the age of 10)**
- **Any other adults living at your address.**

If you are to have this information to hand when you fill in your application, then it does mean that you have to prepare yourself in advance and thoroughly. If you come from an extended family, it may take several days of enquiries to amass all the necessary details. A last point on the financial side: if you have any outstanding **county court judgments** against you or if you have been registered **bankrupt** (and your debts in bankruptcy have not been discharged), your appli-cation is likely to be rejected. Credit references are examined, as are any court records around your solvency, but if debts have been discharged together with any county court judgments, you may be considered after three years.

### 1.4.4 Section 2: about your employment

This is the record of the jobs you have done, or service you have had if in HM Forces, over the last ten years, including any period of unemployment or part-time work as well as full-time employment. If you are currently serving in

HM Forces, your application will only be considered if you are within 12 months of release or discharge. Incidentally, it will be up to your Chief Constable to decide if you remain on the Reserve List following discharge.

### 1.4.4.1 Previous employment details

What the police need to know about your employment is what sort of job it was and what position you held, who your employer was and the address of the organization or company for which you worked, and the period of your employment. You will also be asked to provide reasons why you left. You will need to provide a contact name at each company or organization, so that the police can verify the details that you provide, and ascertain that your employment there was unblemished. The only other characteristic of this straightforward provision of detail is that the process works in reverse order; in other words, you put your most recent or current employment first and work backwards from there.

### 1.4.4.2 References: the importance of using people who know you well

You will also be asked to provide contact details, including physical addresses, for two **referees**, noting the position held by each referee and indicating whether the referee can be approached immediately or not. (Nothing sinister: it is simple courtesy to ask someone if s/he would provide you with a reference.) Please note that **a reference is not a testimonial**, nor is it a mere record of work. It is a statement by someone who knew, or knows, you and who can attest to your attributes, skills, probity (honesty), and that you did indeed work in the role you described at the place referred to for the times stated.

(**NB:** If this intense desire to prove facts bothers you, you should think of another career choice. Attention to detail, and not taking statements on trust but seeking to corroborate them, are highly characteristic of all police work.)

One of your referees can be a 'character' referee (if, for example, you have not worked anywhere long enough to have more than one referee), but it is preferable to provide two, each of whom can talk about you as an employee. This is important because it may affect how the police will perceive you as a potential employee. The health declaration in Part 1 is also relevant here, since a poor attendance record *might* indicate unreliability. Referees are usually asked to confirm your diligent attendance at work. Finally, you will be asked to enter details of any service with HM Forces or in any previous capacity with a police force (for example as a Special Constable, a police cadet, or as a police staff employee). All this will be very familiar to those who have experience of applying for jobs in any sector. Do make a mental note to consider suitable referees—don't use someone who detested you, for example, nor the name of your best friend, who may not know you in a work environment. It is conventional to use a previous line manager, tutor, or commanding officer, but in addition, anyone who has known you in a professional or social capacity might do; such as your local charity organizer or sports club chairperson.

### 1.4.5  Section 3: about your education and skills

The difference between education and skills is simple, despite what some academics will tell you: **educational qualifications** are usually about **knowledge**, like GCSE Geography, whilst skills are about **what you can do**, such as creating PowerPoint slideshows on a computer. As individuals, we are composed of different attributes, which may include our education, training, skills, traits, and experiences. 'Traits' include characteristics of ours which determine our preferences, hobbies, interests and how we like to learn. Having examples of all of these attributes and understanding what they mean, will allow you to sell yourself more effectively both in the application and, if you are successful in passing the screening, at interview.

First, you are asked for a list of the schools or colleges, universities, or other institutions that you have attended in reverse date order (put the most recent first). Using the same principle, you are then asked to give your most recent educational qualifications first and then work backwards to your first (oldest). You will be asked for all of your qualifications, including **academic** (such as bachelor's or master's degrees), **vocational** (such as NVQs), and **professional** (such as CIPD or FCA), with dates and details of any examinations taken or about to be taken, short courses, in-house training, or any other relevant educational attainment (such as Grade 6 in playing a musical instrument).

#### 1.4.5.1  Skills, membership of civic bodies, charities, local groups

In the part of the application form which follows, you are asked to itemize your skills and to provide details of any voluntary or community activities in which you have been involved. Skills might include using a computer effectively (as noted above), or driving skills (you are expected to be qualified to drive), cycling proficiency, and so on, together with any **membership of organizations** such as Guides or Scouts, church or faith groups, Cadet Corps, the Duke of Edinburgh's Award Scheme, charities like Help the Aged or Shelter, or local community projects and such like, especially if you have had an organizational role or command role in any of these. If you have a **knowledge of languages**, then this should also be shown—not just your educational attainments such as GCSE German, but any periods of residence in the foreign country and any continuous learning, which would show that you have a grasp of idiom and contemporary speech, for example. It is clearly helpful for a PCSO to have some acquaintance with a language used by minority groups in the community and this can cover a wide range of languages from Urdu and Punjabi to Mandarin or Cantonese Chinese.

### 1.4.6  Section 4: competency assessment

We referred to this earlier. It is without doubt the most important part of your whole application because this will show to assessors whether or not you have the potential to become an effective PCSO. Indeed, your performance here will determine whether or not you are invited to Part 2 of the recruitment process, the assessment sessions (see 1.3.1). So read the following with care—we are providing you with pointers and suggestions, not model answers. Start thinking about experiences you have had which will help to illustrate your competences.

### 1.4.6.1 'Worked' examples

You will be asked to give **three** detailed examples from your recent (say, last three years') experience. The assessors are looking for the kinds of behaviours that both experience and research have shown to be integral to the role of a PCSO. Such competences are obvious if you stop and think about it: for example, being able to persuade somebody to do something differently is a generic competence that you will use on a daily basis as a PCSO. It calls for tact, a persuasive tongue, an understanding of logic, and the need to appeal to people's sense of belonging to a group or community. *What is really central to success in answering these kinds of question is that you use very specific examples and explain clearly what part you personally played and how you managed yourself to change things or achieve a desired outcome.* If you are woolly or vague, you will be marked down and could fail altogether. Each of the three questions has a series of prompt questions that focus you on detail; make sure you answer these specifically as you go. Above all, use examples from your personal experience (at work, or from your social, domestic or leisure life, or from your educational experience) which you found challenging or difficult and which show you to have had a bit of a struggle to get the result you wanted. The more challenging the circumstance you describe, and therefore the more difficult to get a 'good result', the higher it will be marked. Lastly, write clearly in fluent English, avoiding slang or jargon (specialized words) and use complete sentences. There are notes about this in the Guide:

> Remember that this is a formal application for an important and responsible job.

The section then goes on to ask you about your motivation (discussed at length in 1.2), what you think the job will entail, and what you have done already to prepare yourself for it (such as speaking to existing PCSOs or visiting your local police station, reading through the literature on the PCSO role, and so on). Let's look now at the kinds of question you will be asked.

### 1.4.6.2 Situation 1: competence is assessed against the service which PCSOs give to the public through problem solving

You are asked to:

> Recall a situation when you had to deal with someone who was unhappy with the service [s/he] had been given or the way [s/he] had been treated, and you helped [him or her] to resolve [the] problem.

### 1.4.6.3 Showing what you did to solve someone's problem

Remember that your example has to show *what you did, and how you personally contributed to solving the person's problem*. If you imagine that you may have been working in a shop when someone came to complain about something they had bought which did not work, your prompt referring of the complainant to a supervisor is not a good illustration of your ability to solve problems. It would be far better in such an example to show what *you* did proactively to replace the defective purchase or that you obtained expert advice on the operation of the equipment and helped the complainant to understand what s/he should do to prevent the problem recurring. In acting like this, you are taking the lead in solving the problem and demonstrating your resourcefulness. Perhaps now you can see how the assessors will examine your examples carefully in order to find evidence of your potential competence as a PCSO. However, if you choose a 'service' example like a shop, do make sure that it entails more on your part than simply replacing a faulty bit of kit.

### 1.4.6.4 Describing what you did

As you develop your example of how you personally did some problem solving, you are asked to do specific things in order. These are:

- **Briefly describe the situation, explaining why the complainant was unhappy.**
- **Tell us what you did and said to try to sort the problem out.**
- **When did you do these things?**
- **If you hadn't acted the way you did, what do you think the consequences for everyone involved would have been?**
- **How did you know that the person was happy with what you had done for him or her?**

Using these '**prompts**' helps you to structure a coherent and intelligible account of your problem-solving capabilities (and potential). Notice that the final pair of questions is actually quite searching in terms of what they ask you to do. The first effectively asks what would have happened if you hadn't taken responsibility for solving the problem, and invites you to project imaginatively the alternatives to your helpful action. Understanding what you need to do here will clearly impact on your role as a PCSO because it will show that you are aware of consequences to actions and, equally, consequences to you **not** doing something. The second (that is, the last) question is about **evaluation** of what you did. How do you know that the complainant was content with your attempt to solve the problem? You might cover both verbal and non-verbal (body language) responses such as a smile and the words 'thank you', but be careful not to exaggerate people's supposed gratefulness; complainants are often angry and may need to be calmed before matters can be resolved. How you dealt with that calming process (taking the sting out of confrontation) can often be an important part of your success in problem solving.

### 1.4.6.5 **What the examples are for**

We don't want to labour this: you should be able to see from the scenario and the prompts what sort of examples the assessors are looking for, and you should be experienced enough to be able to supply a good and complex example. We hope though that you've grasped the essence of the exercise: this approximates very closely to a PCSO's daily activities. One last point: we don't want you to think that somehow a PCSO is a superhero. Very few problems can be solved by a single person acting alone. It's perfectly acceptable to show, in your example, how you would make use of others, including the complainant once calmed, in your drive towards solving the problem. **The essential fact is that you were proactive, organized, and led the resolution**, whoever and whatever you called in to help.

### 1.4.6.6 **Situation 2: revolves around how a PCSO should show respect for the lifestyles of other people**

You are asked to:

> Think of an example of a situation when you have shown respect for someone who had an important part of his or her lifestyle that differed significantly from your own.

On-line you are offered the example of someone with a deep-rooted moral or religious belief which you don't share, but which you can understand. The scenario setting also suggests that what is important in this example is **your understanding and sensitivity to difference** between you and this other person, and how you changed what you said or did to meet their needs.

### 1.4.6.7 **Think of a real clash of values**

We advise you not to think in narrow or limited ways about this problem, but choose an example where there genuinely could have been a clash or substantial difficulty between you and another person because of the differences between you, except that what you did prevented that from happening. Think of experiences you have had such as dealing with someone who is profoundly deaf. People with disabilities of this degree will tell you that, often, other people talk as though the deaf person wasn't there, speaking only to the carer or another companion. This is sometimes called the *'Does he take sugar?'* syndrome and it is profoundly careless of the deaf person's feelings. What you would need to show, if you used an example from your genuine experience of this kind, is how you used sign language or ensured that the deaf person could lip-read what you were saying (some people can cleverly use both sign language and speech together to do this), and that you took time to find out what problem or difficulty the deaf person had and that, although *you* can hear, you showed sensitivity by your actions and speech to the other person's needs. Simple but telling things such as gently touching the person's forearm to attract attention, always speaking directly in the deaf person's line of sight (to your lips), and speaking more slowly and clearly than normal—but not patronizingly so—will demonstrate how you modified your behaviour to suit the person's need.

### 1.4.6.8 Don't make unsupported assumptions about people

You might argue that this example doesn't illustrate a genuine difference from you. It might be better if you asked a deaf person the same question and then you would find out more about the often-unthinking barriers which come between deaf people and others. Being deaf is simply a physical condition that impairs communication; it doesn't mean that communication can't happen, nor that the deaf person is stupid or unintelligible. The danger always is in unthinkingly making assumptions about other people.

The assessors offer four fairly straightforward prompts:

- **Tell us how the situation arose.**
- **Tell us in detail what you did and said.**
- **What did you learn about the other person from this experience?**
- **How were you able to adapt what you did to suit the other person?**

Remind yourself of the nature of race and diversity as we have set it out in a number of ways in this book, by reading the NOS and other observations in Chapter 4.

### 1.4.6.9 Respect for diversity is a key PCSO strength

Your responsiveness to difference, the breadth of your understanding, and the imaginativeness of your solutions are all key factors in the role of PCSO. You cannot, of course, police only one part of a community; you must police all and this may mean accommodating yourself to considerable ranges of difference (think of the yawning gaps between teenage culture and that of people over 75).

### 1.4.6.10 Choosing the appropriate example

The same principles apply in answering this question, founded as it is upon respect for race and diversity, as applied in the problem-solving question with which we began. The same principles of evidencing your active and effective role in the examples you choose, the clarity with which you express yourself, and the fluency of your writing will all be elements which you should aim to display as well as you possibly can. *Don't pay lip service*: assessors will see straight through it. Try if you can to find a situation which you found difficult. If you solve a difficult problem, or even show how you mitigated (*made a bit better*) the worst effects of the problem, you are likely to gain more credit from the assessors than if you choose a simple example which was easily handled.

#### 1.4.6.11 Situation 3: acting without being told what to do and attempting to do the best possible job as a PCSO

You are asked to:

> Tell us about a situation where you have acted without being told, gone beyond what was expected of you, and even gone further than others would have done.

'Going the extra mile'

Note that this is a two-pronged question: the first part is about your ability to **exercise individual initiative**—to do things which need doing without waiting to be told to do them—and the second part is how you **surpass the normal parameters for action** and how you have tried to attain a really excellent result; it's about going 'the extra mile'. Both are key elements in being a successful and effective PCSO and you need to follow the same careful planning here as you have done in the other two questions.

#### 1.4.6.12 Example where you gave the lead

Choose a specific example which illustrates your leading role in acting (without being prompted) for the good of the community or on behalf of someone in the community, and how your persistence in getting the best result you could went further than others would have done: *you weren't content with just doing enough, you wouldn't settle for less than the best.* There may be plenty of examples from work—if a teacher, how you turned a disruptive class into a supportive and focused group of young people; if a librarian, how you not only helped someone to research making a will, but found them examples, recommended low-fee solicitors for consultation, and offered to go with the person if s/he was nervous or shy. This would be acting outside the standard parameters, without waiting for someone else to stimulate you to action. Or your example could come from the community, where you establish a site for a skate park (see Figure 1.2), persuade the local or parish council to build the basic infrastructure there, and then you recruit a small army of volunteers to construct more sophisticated ramps and jumps, install lighting, and persuade the local media to cover the opening.

#### 1.4.6.13 Using prompts to keep focused

What we have offered earlier in the chapter are short but expandable examples that demonstrate in general terms what the assessors are looking for, but you need to be specific and detailed. The following are the prompts which the assessors have provided to help you structure your competence:

**Figure 1.2 Skateboard park and graffiti wall**

- What was the situation and why did you feel the need to act?
- Exactly what did you do and say?
- If you had not acted as you did, what do you think the consequences for everyone would have been?

### 1.4.6.14 Define and describe in detail what you did

You are familiar by now with these structures, and you should have a fair idea what the assessors are looking for. You need to put your actions and decisions in the forefront of the action, defining and describing in detail what it was that you did and said which demonstrates the competence. The final prompt is similar to that in Question 1 in that it encourages you to think what the consequences might have been if you had not acted. If you have something similar to our skateboard park example, it isn't enough for you to say that 'things would have stayed the same' because things don't. Tense situations invariably get worse; bored and disaffected youths get into trouble; streetlamps left broken and unrepaired continue to create hazards and to provide criminal opportunities in the darkness, and so on. The assessors expect you to be able to think through the course of events that would have developed if you had not acted: would someone have lost his/her life? Would someone have been put at risk? Might a vehicle have crashed? Could the community have split into factions and bred mistrust? Your alternative scenarios, which show that you understand the value of your intervention, need careful thought before you type anything on the screen.

### 1.4.6.15 Plan it first

One last general point: it always helps to rough your ideas out on screen before typing your 'fair copy' on the application. Think about the advice in the **Notes** which read, in part:

You are being assessed throughout this application form on your written skills. We also expect your examples to be focused, succinct [*brief and crisp*] and fluently written, as any police report or statement would need to be.

This is unequivocal (*crystal clear*), as is the instruction that **the application must be your own unaided work**. Since you should expect to be questioned during the assessment process on the answers you have given, it makes sense that you are the only author. Any evidence of collusion with another is an automatic fail anyway.

### 1.4.6.16 **Motivation and knowledge**

The final questions in the **Competency assessment**, as we noted above, concern **your motivation and your knowledge of the PCSO role**. We have already dealt with motivation in 1.2, and will not repeat the discussion here. Go back and re-read what we stated there. You need to be aware that the assessors' prompt for **Question 4** not only notes that '*we want to know why you want to be a PCSO*', but also what experience, skills, and abilities you have which you feel will make you suitable as a candidate PCSO. The final question, **Question 5**, is designed to find out how well informed you are about the work of a PCSO. [Read this book and you will be superbly prepared!] Specifically, the assessors want you to tell them what tasks you expect to carry out if appointed, to demonstrate to them that you know what the job entails. Importantly, the assessors will explore with you if you have properly considered whether the job really is for you.

### 1.4.6.17 **The sorts of task a PCSO undertakes**

Helpfully, the *Guide* details some of the PCSO tasks, which we reproduce here:

---

**What sort of things do PCSOs do?**

- Go on highly visible uniformed foot patrols
- Support Community Beat Officers and Community Action Teams in solving local problems
- Make house visits to gather intelligence and offer public reassurance after minor crimes or anti-social behaviour
- Get involved with key people in the community, such as community, religious, and business leaders
- Work with *Community Watch, Neighbourhood Watch, Business Watch, Pub Watch, Farm Watch,* and *Horse Watch* schemes
- Protect crime scenes until police officers arrive
- Collect CCTV evidence
- Provide low-level crime prevention and personal safety advice
- Carry out low-level missing person enquiries
- Act as professional witnesses, attending court when needed

---

- Support crime prevention
- Engage with youths
- Interact with schools
- Support the Mobile Police Station Partnerships.

Whilst this list is a helpful indicator of the range of a PCSO's activities, *it is not definitive* (it doesn't cover all PCSO activities) and you should not reproduce it wholesale and undigested in answer to **Question 5** (you'll get no marks if you do). Instead, think about these tasks and what they represent, and look at all aspects of the work of the PCSO, which of course we discuss at length in this book. Make a list of activities, bearing in mind the National Occupational Standards, perhaps dividing your notes for convenience into:

- **Support for the police**
- **Support for the community**
- **Support of the NOS**
- **Support of local partnerships and other agencies**

then your answer to **Question 5** will be in your own words and will show that you have a very good grasp of the PCSO role.

### 1.4.6.18 Can you do the job?

Finally, you need to ask yourself, very honestly, whether you have the necessary qualities to be a PCSO and whether you can cope with all the problems, frustrations, situations, confrontations, and obstacles that you will meet on a daily basis. Helpfully, the *Guide* notes some of the 'right qualities to be a PCSO':

- a confident, level-headed, positive and mature manner
- the ability to deal with difficult people and situations
- to be sensitive but objective
- good communication and listening skills
- good team-working skills
- stamina for long periods of foot patrol
- skills to deal with all types of people, some of whom may be drunk, hostile or upset
- to be accurate when completing paperwork
- an appreciation of the confidential nature of police work.

Again, you will appreciate that this is not an exhaustive list of the qualities, some of which we looked at in 1.2, when we discussed motivation, and in 1.3, when we talked about what qualities police forces are looking for in their PCSOs. Remember the key skills of:

- **resilience**
- **effective communication**
- **respect for race and diversity**
- **personal responsibility**
- **team working**

all of which we looked at in 1.3 when we examined the behavioural competences. (**Community and Customer Focus** is missing; this is because it is seen as something which you will develop as a competence once you are doing the job and implementing your local neighbourhood policing plan.)

### 1.4.7 Section 5: declaration

The final part of the application, **Section 5**, is a **declaration** (see Figure 1.3).

**Figure 1.3 The Declaration**

I declare that all the statements I have made in this application are true to the best of my knowledge and belief and that no relevant information has been withheld.

I understand that:

- I must inform the Recruitment Office without delay of any change in my circumstances;
- criminal conviction checks will be made against myself and my family members and I have informed them of this;
- financial checks will be undertaken to verify my financial status and all such information will be treated in confidence. I consent to these checks being made;
- formal disclosure of my Service Character Assessment (Armed Forces) will be sought and I consent to this;
- any offer of appointment will be subject to satisfactory references and vetting, a medical examination, continued good conduct and the maintenance of fitness;
- a member of a police force who has deliberately made any false statement or omitted information in connection with his or her appointment may subsequently be liable to misconduct proceedings;
- if I am appointed my fingerprints and a sample of my DNA will be taken and held on record for elimination purposes;
- successful candidates must serve wherever required to do so within the Force area;
- the Chief Officer retains the right to reject any application without giving reasons and
- the information I have provided may be held on manual filing and computer systems as part of the recruitment process and may be shared by other police forces.

I am not and have never been a member of the British National Party or similar organisation whose aims, objectives or pronouncements may contradict the duty to promote race equality.

.....................................................................................................................

Signature                                              Date

### 1.4.7.1 **Think about what the declaration entails**

Think about what you are signing up to here. There has been some critical public discussion about whether a specific political party should be mentioned as pro-scribed (*banned*) for members of the police family, or whether a simpler statement would be better, noting that any group espousing intolerance of others should not have police staff or police officers as members. The fact that the British National Party's or the English Defence League's views are repellent to many is not the point; it is the membership, public acceptance of, or the signing up to the aims of such organizations which is to be disavowed. But there is a simple test which you may apply to all this. Look again at the discussions about race and diversity at 1.3.1.2 and 1.3.4 and you will understand that **nothing may modify your duty to respect race and diversity.** Outlawing membership of any party holding views which run counter to that duty is therefore irrelevant. No one signed up to respect race and diversity could consider membership of such an organization for a moment.

### 1.4.8 **The assessment process**

Time passes. Your completed application has now been carefully scrutinized and, as a result of your breadth of knowledge and understanding (provided in major part by this book), you have impressed the initial assessors enough to receive an invitation to attend the assessment process. This section explains what is in-volved and offers you advice on how to prepare for the assessment and how to conduct yourself on the day.

### 1.4.8.1 **What and where and when**

The assessment process is run in regional assessment centres or sometimes, for larger forces, in force assessment centres and normally the national assessment takes place over five working days, usually a Monday to Friday. Candidates are assessed in syndicate groups of up to eight, often with three syndicates in the morning and three in the afternoon sessions. This allows for 48 candidates per day. Each of the sessions, morning and afternoon, lasts about three-and-a-half hours. Normally, morning syndicates begin at 08.30 and finish at 12.00, while afternoon sessions begin at 13.00 and finish at about 16.30 (get used to the twenty-four hour clock; all police forces use it all the time and so should you). A candidate will attend **one** session of three and a half hours. You will be informed about your results about three weeks (or 15 working days) after the final day of the assessment process. Therefore, if you were assessed on the Monday morning in the first syndicate, it might be 20 working days or four weeks before you hear how you got on. This is a tedious wait, but assessments have to be made judi-ciously and with care, so no parts of it can be rushed. Remember that much ac-tivity in terms of your assessment takes place after you have gone, with marking, cross-checking, research, moderation meetings between assessors, and a quality assurance team ensuring that the processes are rigorous and fair.

### 1.4.9 **Testing the competences and marking**

We explained to you in 1.3 what the police force that employs you will be looking for, and we spent some time examining the behavioural competences which underpinned the assessment. We pointed out to you that each of the competences is tested at least twice during the assessment process, both in written and in verbal (or 'oral' as the Framework Guidance erroneously insists) communication. To be successful, candidates must achieve at least:

- *50 per cent of the overall marks and*
- *50 per cent in Respect for Race and Diversity and*
- *50 per cent in verbal ('oral') communication and*
- *33 per cent in written communication.*

The assessment sessions for each syndicate consist of:

- a competence-based **interview**
- **two** competence-based written **tests**
- **two** competence-based interactive role-play **scenarios.**

### 1.4.9.1 **Preparing for the assessment process: Interview**

The obvious things that you have to do in advance of being interviewed are to think about your interview techniques, think how you would construct your answers to questions, and ensure that you have rehearsed with someone the examples you intend to use which demonstrate your competence and potential to be a PCSO. Your assessors are there to focus upon the job in hand—assessing you—not to gossip or pass the time of day. This means that you too have to be professional about the whole process, focused on what you need to do, and not diverted by other things (even by being nervous ...). The assessors are working from a script from which they do not deviate; this means that you have to concentrate as much as they do on what is being discussed. Watch things like talking for too long, wandering off the point, or getting sidetracked. If you don't give enough information, don't worry. The assessors can ask supplementary questions to draw out your knowledge and thoughts. Don't go to the other extreme either: avoid being monosyllabic, terse, or abrupt. Such attitudes can seem rude or aggressive. Steer a middle course between not giving enough information and giving too much. Practice with friends and family in explaining something simply and clearly—imagining that you are explaining something to someone who is not familiar with British society is a good exercise and discipline in this respect. **You cannot go wrong in your preparation if you think clearly and carefully about how you can show your abilities in each of the competences, using real-life examples which you can remember clearly and which had an effect on you.** One of our colleagues recalls the intensity of preparation before attending the assessment centre:

> I found it highly beneficial to run through practice questions in preparation for my assessment centre and this is where organisation is key. I thought about

what they were likely to ask, and prepared some talking points to discuss in response to reduce the possibility of being caught out and having to conjure an answer out of thin air. It can also be helpful to look on the police news to check current affairs and also look through the constabulary website to get some individual information about their priorities, such as the use of PCSOs' powers, to make you stand out as an applicant.

This is good advice: pay heed to it.

### 1.4.9.2 Written exercises

Whilst the content of what you are asked to write about is clearly very important to your success in these exercises, spelling and grammar are assessed as well. Currently, if you make *four or more* grammatical errors or *four or more* spelling mistakes you will fail the exercise.

---

## Guidelines to help you in your written work

**Keep it simple:** more errors are caused by being over-complicated than any other factor.

**Writing is a formal activity:** don't use the jargon words or slang that you employ in casual conversations.

**Every sentence has a** *subject* **and a** *verb* (a word which names something and a word which does something, such as The *cat purrs* or *I write* *notes*). Each sentence begins with a capital letter and ends with a full stop.

**Don't abbreviate words:** you are not sending a text message, you are writing formally. It helps to **plan out what you are going to write** first, even if this is only in the form of a few scribbles. This helps you to remember to put material in a logical order and to ensure that you have missed nothing.

**Read over what you've written** so that you can correct any inadvertent errors.

**Don't try to impress,** ever, by using words which sound impactive and serious but which you do not understand; such things are *egregious*.

---

### 1.4.9.3 Why written skills matter

In case you are wondering why so much emphasis is laid upon proper formal writing, presentation, and grammatical accuracy, it is because much of police work is in the form of formal records. It doesn't matter whether these are in your Pocket Notebook, or in a formal statement, or in a report, or in a plan, or in written submissions to partners: you will look inept, ill-educated, and slipshod if your writing is careless, strewn with errors, confused about the meanings of words, and badly spelled. This is particularly the case if your written work is produced in court or if it is widely copied outside the police force, such as a notice from you put up in a public place, or a plan that is put before a council meeting.

### 1.4.9.4 **The interactive exercises**

The two exercises concern scenarios (*little plays*) which are based in a fictional place. This is to give you a context in which you can make judgements and help you to understand or visualize what it is you have to do. The essence of the idea is to make the exercise practical rather than theoretical. Do read all the preparation material thoroughly before you go into the exercises, and make notes. When you go into the exercise scenario area, you will meet a role-player (an actor) who will play the part of one of the characters in the scenario, while you normally play the part of the PCSO. The role player will not step outside the part s/he is playing, so don't expect the actor to say that you are doing well, or whisper an aside such as '*Don't forget to say ...*'. You are expected to play your role seriously too, so if, for example, you are asked to play the part of a PCSO meeting a distraught lady in a shopping centre who has lost her small son aged four, you are not expected to laugh and joke but to act as you would if the scenario were a real one and you were really on duty. The role-player will be convincingly distraught, or angry, or distressed, or whatever else it is that is required by the scenario.

### 1.4.9.5 **Playing the part**

Listen carefully to what the role-player says to you. Respond appropriately to what you are being told. One last, but very important, point is that if you are awarded a D grade (fail) for Respect for Race and Diversity in either the written exercises or the interactive exercises, you may fail the entire process, irrespective of the grades you obtained in other parts of the assessment. If you think about this for a moment, you will see why, and we refer you again to the earlier discussions. Respect for race and diversity is at the core of what you will do as a PCSO and to fail to attain this as a competence because of inappropriate behaviour or comments suggests that you will not make it as a PCSO either.

### 1.4.10 **Medical, security, and references check**

These are all straightforward matters, very much linked to you as an individual and we cannot see much point in discussing any of the factors in detail. We have in any case covered many of the elements earlier in this section. Here they are in brief:

### 1.4.10.1 **Medical**

You know that you must be:

**in good health, of sound constitution and able both mentally and physically to perform the duties of a PCSO once appointed.**

PCSOs, like all other members of the police family, are covered by the **Disability Discrimination Act 2003** and employers must make reasonable adjustments if a disability is declared. Disability is defined as '*a physical or mental impairment that has a substantial and long-term adverse effect on the ability to carry out normal day-to-day activities*'. It is your responsibility to bring to the attention of your employer, or potential employer, any disability in order that reasonable adjustments may be made to accommodate you. All applicants will fill out a medical questionnaire and have a medical examination prior to appointment. You will have your eyes tested at the medical examination and there are restrictions around colour blindness and eye surgery which you need to read and understand (look at the notes at the back of the application booklet).

### 1.4.10.2 **Security**

There will be vetting checks on your background and that of your family, including the criminal records and financial checks which we discussed earlier. You may expect to undergo re-checks every five years or so, or whenever your circumstances change (such as moving in with a new partner, changes in your financial status, and so on). Because you will continue to have access, in the course of your duties, to confidential police information, including to criminal records databases, your security status is of continuous importance.

### 1.4.10.3 **References**

We have discussed this in relation to the application and need not discuss it further now. Your referees may be approached at any time, depending on your indications, after receipt of the application. References will have been taken before a job offer is confirmed.

The general point about this part of the recruitment process is that you will probably have been given a conditional offer of employment, which means that all other things being equal, you will soon be appointed as a PCSO. The 'other things being equal' are clearance of all conditions which might disbar you, but which emerge only after the specific medical and security checks, and what your referees have to say about you. Unlike medical and security checks, what your referee may say about you is not a reason on its own to disbar you. In other words, if one of your references asserts that you are dishonest and not to be trusted, we would expect independent evidence to corroborate what was said.

### 1.4.11 **Summary**

The comments and discussion in this section are no substitute for your careful reading and understanding of the guidance notes for prospective PCSOs, nor for your careful perusal of the application, including the useful Notes. **We would strongly advise you to talk to serving PCSOs and police officers before you commit yourself** to a thorough and painstaking process. Your motivation and commitment must be strong and unwavering even though it only gets you through the door. The key to success in applying to become a PCSO is **assiduous preparation, prior thought, and planning**—just like being a PCSO for real.

Now a knowledge check on this section. It's a bit longer than the first two, because this section is longer and because it's about your application, it's very important too:

## Knowledge Check 3

1. In terms of 'proving' the competences, what will the on-line application ask you to provide?

2. What are the three parts of the recruitment process?

3. What personal reference item is required for the application?

4. What non-financial matters *must* you declare?

5. What is 'immediate or close family'?

6. What financial matters *must* you declare?

7. In what order do you record your education, qualifications, and employment?

8. How many referees do you need? Distinguish between them.

9. What is the difference between education and skills?

10. Why should thinking about an example of a 'clash of values' help you in responding to a question about respect for others?

11. What specific example did we use?

12. What are 'prompts'?

13. Name **four** things PCSOs do.

14. What is the last section (5) of the application?

15. How long does the average assessment session last?

16. What does each 'syndicate' session consist of?

17. What are 'scenarios'?

18. What is a 'role-player'?

19. What medical standards should you have?

20. Why is there an emphasis on physical fitness?

## 1.5 Ethical Standards in Brief

**Ethics is about right behaviour.** You are joining an organization that prides it-self on the maintenance of professional standards of behaviour and integrity. As a PCSO, you will be expected to sign up to the police codes of practice, ethical and professional standards, and your Force's internal standards.

### 1.5.1 The importance of ethical standards

We have already seen something of this in the discussions about behavioural competences (at 1.3.1), which we don't propose to repeat here. The point is that **there are acceptable behaviours and unacceptable behaviours**. These now need to be set in a wider context and used in a broader discussion with you about what ethical standards are and why they are important.

### 1.5.2 Defining ethics

A working definition of 'ethics' is:

**Ethics are the values and standards of behaviour by which individuals govern their conduct and organizations regulate their members and soci-eties manage the actions of their citizens.**

### 1.5.3 Principles

Such principles as respect for others, honesty, integrity, fairness, and treating people equally, can all help to define ethical behaviour and will find their way into various codes of conduct to which organizations, particularly the police, are publicly committed. You are joining the police service, and there exists a frame-work for ethical behaviour in **Police Regulations**. These govern the activities of police officers in the discharge of their duties and whilst you, as a PCSO, are not subject to Police Regulations, your police colleagues are and this will impact upon you.

### 1.5.4 Ethical standards for police officers

**Police (Conduct) Regulations 2012, 'Standards of Professional Behaviour'** set out the acceptable behaviours, attitudes, and conduct which are expected of police officers, building on an original 'Code of Ethics' in the 2004 Regulations. This is a summary:

- Officers should respect confidentiality—they must not disclose confidential information unless authorized and they should not use confidential informa-tion for their personal benefit.
- Police officers must act with fairness and impartiality in their dealings with the public and their colleagues.

- Officers should avoid being 'improperly beholden' to any person or institution.
- They should be open and truthful in their dealings.
- They should discharge their duties with integrity.
- They must obey all lawful orders.
- Officers should oppose any improper behaviour, reporting it where appropriate.
- Officers should treat members of the public and colleagues with courtesy and respect, avoiding abusive or derisive attitudes or behaviour.
- Officers must avoid favouritism of an individual or group; all forms of harassment, victimization, or unreasonable discrimination; and overbearing conduct to a colleague, particularly to one junior in rank or service.
- Officers must never knowingly use more force than is reasonable, nor should they abuse their authority.
- Officers should be conscientious and diligent in the performance of their duties.
- They should attend work promptly when rostered for duty.
- Officers on duty must be sober.
- Officers should always be well turned out, clean, and tidy.
- Whether on or off duty, officers should not behave in a way which is likely to bring discredit upon the police service.

### 1.5.4.1 A flavour of ethical standards and 'right' behaviour

Some of these issues, and the words used to express them, should be familiar to you, especially concepts such as 'respect', 'courtesy', 'open', 'truthful', 'impartial' which we encountered when examining the behavioural competences (1.3.1.1). Other phrases may be less familiar: 'improperly beholden' is an example. This means that police officers should never be in a position where they have an obligation to someone which gets in the way of their duty. The idea that you owe anyone a favour has no place in policing. There are some interesting negatives too, such as not being overbearing (oppressive) because of one's authority, avoiding favouritism, and avoiding abuse of, or being derisive about, others.

### 1.5.4.2 Smartness is part of the maintenance of standards

We doubt that there is anything here which you and the public would not sign up to as **preferable behaviour**. There may be some eyebrows raised about the need to be 'well turned-out, clean, and tidy' in these more permissive and relaxed days, but in fact such punctiliousness has its place in policing, because a smart, groomed officer commands attention in ways that a dishevelled or untidy person would not. It is part of the image of the police officer and applies to anyone, such as a PCSO, acting on behalf of or with the police.

### 1.5.5 **New code of ethics for police officers and staff**

Following a series of events from 2012 to date, in which the police did not show to best advantage (including the outcome of the 2012 Report into the Hillsborough Disaster (1989), the 'Plebgate' scandal of 2013 in which a senior Conservative politician lost his post for swearing at police officers, that some police inaccurately recorded and others lied about; and the 'phone-hacking' affair, 2010–2012 in which police officers passed information to journalists working for among others *The News of The World*), the Home Secretary in 2013 determined that there would be a new **National Code of Police Ethics** that applied to everyone employed by the police and to police officers themselves. The National College of Policing drew up the Code and it is reinforced by new powers for the Independent Police Complaints Commission (IPCC). HMIC also plays a role in 'enforcing' police ethical standards. As we note later, the College of Policing had not published the Code at the time of writing, but we note at 1.3.1.1 and in Chapter 6 among others, the kinds of behaviour expected of you.

#### 1.5.5.1 **Accountability**

Part of the National Code of Police Ethics covers the police 'contract' with the public and concerns **accountability**. This is an ethical dimension which is not often discussed, but should be, not just because of the police related activity you are applying to join, but because, as a citizen, it should matter to you that the police are accountable for what they do. The code establishes the means by which the ordinary citizen can achieve redress for wrongs, injustices, unfair treatment, rudeness, incivility, or discrimination from police officers. What is more, it sustains the notion of the police as a 'public service product' of society, working for the good of society rather than a force imposed by the unchallenged rulers of a tyrannical regime. We should note too that although poor police behaviour receives perhaps a disproportionate amount of media attention, nonetheless it is properly part of police accountability to the public that a light is shone on unsavoury acts. These can impact on the majority of police and police employees who, we should emphasize, act entirely ethically and properly in the discharge of their duties. As ever, a small amount of wrong-doing can reflect upon the majority—as MPs should be only too aware following their expenses scandal of 2009–2010.

### 1.5.6 **Who watches the watchers?**

You might argue ethics and codes are all very well, but do they work? Are police officers and police staff really accountable for what they do? If they are, who or what makes them so? There are a number of mechanisms of which you should be aware, which hold the police (and anyone who works for the police, so including PCSOs) accountable for their actions. These are some of them:

- The Independent Police Complaints Commission (national)
- Her Majesty's Inspectorate of Constabulary (national)
- The Force's Police and Crime Commissioner (PCC)
- The Force's Professional Standards Department—PSD (many PSDs now have the remit to investigate complaints and allegations against police staff as well as against police officers).

## 1.6  Race and Diversity Issues in Brief

### 1.6.1  Why we repeat information on race and diversity

We know that you will dip into this book in different places, depending on your need at the time; you won't sit and read the book through like a novel. Rather than risk you not knowing about the importance of **respect for race and diversity**, we have included it in key places, such as in the recruitment process earlier in this chapter, and in the behavioural competences in 4.8, or discussing *Professional Standards* in 6.7. We shall continue to do this throughout the book where it is relevant and where we think you need to be alerted to its importance.

### 1.6.2  Policing a diverse community

This time, though, we are going to look quickly at some of the main headlines concerning race and diversity and glance at the legislation and the obligation which all this places on you, the PCSO. You police a diverse community, with many different needs and viewpoints, and we discussed earlier (at 1.3) how that means that your duty obliges you to respect the, beliefs, customs, and practices of others. You have to provide the same high standard of service to everyone, regardless of their backgrounds, origins, beliefs, and personal or social circumstances. This is often shortened to calling your attitude 'an even-handed approach', where everyone is accorded the same impartial respect. That extends to the workplace as well, where you have every right to be treated with respect by your colleagues and to have a working atmosphere free from discrimination of any kind, harassment, bullying, or victimization. It follows that your attitudes, if you discriminate against people, or harass, bully, or victimize others, will not be tolerated. Remember, you may be the only visible boundary which some people see between their beliefs and cultures and other people's prejudiced discrimination.

#### 1.6.2.1  Ethical behaviours and diversity

We have just discussed, in 1.5, the sorts of things involved in ethical behaviour. Here is a quick summary of the sorts of ethical behaviour in your day-to-day exchanges with the public and with colleagues, which relate to race and diversity:

- Improve trust and confidence in policing among all members of the community, especially the vulnerable
- Always lead by your own unprejudiced, non-discriminating example
- Understand the value and strength of diversity, know why respect is important, and accept the rights of all to personal dignity
- Engage with local partnerships and agencies to enhance the sense of safe community
- Apply your powers sparingly, proportionately, and justifiably
- Aim for and achieve consistently high standards in the quality of your interventions with the community
- Be open-minded and flexible in responding to people's needs: don't stereotype them, or stereotype your responses.

This is not hard—thousands of police officers, PCSOs, and public sector workers do this all the time without evident difficulty. It is a mind-set, not a gymnastic contortion. There is no reason why you cannot do the same.

### 1.6.2.2 Six diversity strands

There are nine 'protected characteristics': age, disability, gender reassignment, marriage and civil partnership, pregnancy and maternity, race, religion or belief, sex and sexual orientation and the Equality Act of 2010 makes it unlawful to discriminate against people on any of these grounds. You should familiarize yourself with the provisions of the Act. Look too at 4.8.2 where we discuss this in greater detail.

### 1.6.2.3 Allport's scale

In 1953, an American psychologist called Gordon Allport published a book called *The Nature of Prejudice* (now long out of print) in which he described a rising scale of prejudicial treatment of people, based on his studies of the ways in which the Nazis treated the Jews in Germany. **Allport's scale**, as it is called, is a familiar model to use when discussing the ways in which discrimination can develop and intensify.

### 1.6.2.4 Forms of discrimination

We have had to modify some of the steps, such as level 5 'extermination', where Allport clearly had the Holocaust and the Nazis' deliberate genocide of the Jews in mind, by saying that forcing someone out of a job, or making a family pack up and move away, would be the community equivalent (see Figure 1.4). Remember, we are discussing *all* forms of discrimination not only racial discrimination. Allport's scale applies as much to prejudiced activity against old people (or young 'hoodies') or gays or Muslims or blind people, as it does to gender or race. The Scale can be used to test for discrimination against any of the 'protected characteristics' of the Equality Act 2010. It follows generally that a determined interven-

**Figure 1.4 Adaptation of Allport's scale, 1953**

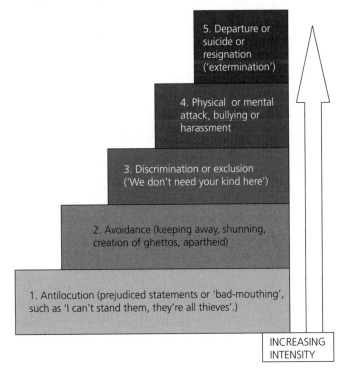

tion at level 1 (**antilocution**), when you hear racist chanting or snide remarks about minority groups, may prevent escalation to any of the other levels. But prejudices, born of fear, envy, or bad experiences in the past, run very deep within society and inevitably you will encounter many instances of discrimination in the course of your work as a PCSO.

At this point we think it helpful for you to check how much of the ethics and diversity sections you have understood:

## Knowledge Check 4

1. What are ethics?

2. In which legal statutes would you find a scheme of ethical values for the police?

3. Name five of those ethical standards

4. What does 'improperly beholden' mean?

5. Who drew up the 2014 National Police Code of Ethics?

6. Which two bodies will be most involved in enforcing the Code?

7. What is meant by 'an even-handed approach'?

8. Name five of the 'protected characteristics' (again)

9. What is Allport's Scale?

10. What does 'antilocution' mean?

## 1.7 Physical Fitness and Standards

### 1.7.1 Why fitness and good physical standards are important

For those considering embarking on a career as a PCSO, one of the factors that needs to be considered is physical fitness. Many PCSOs are engaged on daily foot patrols that can often encompass anything up to 15 miles in distance travelled, and for those on cycle patrols this figure will be even higher. This figure will vary enormously from PCSO to PCSO, from one Basic Command Unit (BCU) to another, and of course from force to force. The sheer physicality of the job is something you need to take into account when thinking of community policing as a career. Nor is this just a random consideration. This book explores the role of the PCSO in providing a highly visible patrol presence within a community, because it is this presence that is precisely a reassurance factor for that community. This reassurance is better evidenced when a PCSO is on foot or on a bicycle, because it allows the opportunity for the officer to stop and communicate with members of the public. Think how much harder it is to feel reassured by a police or liveried 'community team' car going past you, often at speed, as its anonymous and unreachable occupants move on to the latest in a series of calls.

### 1.7.2 Not an Olympic athlete

Many PCSOs gain important community intelligence from having conversations with community members and they attest to the powerful effect that being seen to be approachable, unthreatening, and on foot or pushbike, has upon members of the community. Therefore, physical fitness is important in attaining and maintaining this role.

### 1.7.3 Fitness tests vary, but the need to measure fitness is constant

- The fitness tests on entry or at selection may vary from force to force in terms of the actual test and the exercises used, but the need for some means to assess physical standards is universal. The national recruitment process requires the new entrant to undergo a medical test and the job-related fitness test (JRFT) is a corollary of this. The officer safety training that you will undertake as part of your overall induction training will require that a basic fitness level be established and sustained. One of the most commonly used fitness tests involves: **Endurance**—this involves running back and forth along a set length of track in a measured time-period, indicated with a series of bleeps, which become faster as the test goes on.

### 1.7.3.1 Find out what your preferred police force requires in terms of fitness standards

You should look at your individual force requirements for further information on both the fitness tests and the performance indicators required, as well as the procedures should you fail the fitness test. It is worth mentioning that in many cases a failure at this stage will *not* result in your failing to get the PCSO job. You will have the chance to get yourself fit to retake the test, even whilst you are on your induction training course. There is, though, a requirement to pass the fitness test within an allotted period of time.

We asked one of our PCSO colleagues what the fitness test was like. He replied:

> The fitness test requires that you reach level 5.4 on the bleep test, however the pressure of the day and nerves can easily affect your performance. This is why your physical condition is important, just scraping through in practice may mean you fail on the day of your fitness test. It is also important to practise the bleep test before the real thing to familiarize yourself with the process. I had people fly out of the blocks at the start despite it only being walking pace, and then they were really struggling at the end.

The experience is not the same for everyone of course, especially as some forces will not ask you to do the 'dynamic strength' test, but only the 'endurance'. So check carefully what you will be tested on before you start your fitness programme.

A selection of constabularies are also now requiring trainee PCSOs regularly to participate in mandatory PT sessions throughout their initial training. Applicants are expected to improve their physical capabilities, and demonstrate their resilience and determination when pushed. This helps the force to ascertain if the trainees have a good team ethic and whether they support their colleagues to perform to their best. This highlights that the element of physical conditioning goes well beyond the application stage.

### 1.7.4 The 'honest reflection' test

Assuming that the thought of a fitness test, or of a daily foot patrol, or sessions of keep-fit in the gym, has not put you off applying to be a PCSO, then there is much that you can do to be in a position to pass the test first time. Much of this revolves around your honest assessment of your physical fitness and so this should be your first task—**ask yourself unflinchingly if you are fit enough to pass the test**. If the answer is yes, then all you have to do is to maintain your levels of fitness in preparation for the test. If your answer is an equally honest no, then you must look at ways of improving your fitness to optimize your chances of passing first time round. Methods will not simply include training or physical effort, you should look at basic principles in fitness and the nature of **your nutrition, diet, and lifestyle**. Consider the effect of that chocolate craving on Mondays or the few beers with your friends on a Saturday night. Are you eating lots of fried food? How many portions of vegetables and fruit do you have each day? Is it seven or more? And are you exercising regularly, sleeping well, not stressed by other factors which may inhibit your fitness? Are you balancing your working life with home and leisure time? This book will not provide a 'how to get fit' guide, because there is already a wealth of information in any bookshop on that very subject. You should know that some forces are lobbying to use a lower standard of fitness for PCSOs, to match the physical demands of the PCSO patrol role rather than the more confrontational role of the police officer in obtaining compliance. At present, there is no national agreement on how to design a PCSO fitness test, nor any national fitness standard. At the moment, you have to do what others do for police job fitness.

### 1.7.5 **Staying fit**

Passing the existing fitness test to become a PCSO is one thing, maintaining that fitness during your career is another. The daily patrols will help with that in part (you could wear a pedometer to 'clock' your daily patrol miles, for example), but looking at your overall fitness will help to ensure that your health is maintained in a holistic manner. Many police forces will have information on maintaining a healthy work–life balance as part of the internal information available to all staff. Various initiatives may be held in your Force throughout the year to improve staff fitness levels, not least to reduce absenteeism through sickness. Many police stations also have gyms or corporate membership at private gyms, so that staff can maintain and improve their fitness levels.

$\boxed{2}$

# Joining Up and Staying On

## 2.1 **Impacts on PCSOs from the Start**

This chapter looks at issues which will impact on you from the time that you join a police force and put on the PCSO uniform, covering the following areas: the nature of the PCSO uniform itself, what your training will probably include in the first few weeks, your 'rules of engagement' as a PCSO, and the calls in some quarters for PCSOs to have even more powers.

### 2.1.1 **What the job entails**

#### 2.1.1.1 **'Designation' and its importance**

We glance at the nature of Designation and documents which you carry, before looking at what a typical tour of duty might entail, together with a discussion of PCSO duties and obligations. This is followed by a discussion about some hostility towards the PCSO concept from within policing itself, and we look at associated elements such as 'mission creep' and argue the need to keep PCSO work distinct from policing, even when neighbourhood management is shared between the two roles of police officer (regular or Special) and PCSO. We examine carefully some of the research into, and evaluation of, the PCSO role across the country.

#### 2.1.1.2 **The courts system in England and Wales**

This leads us naturally enough to examine the outcome of the work you do in bringing offenders to justice, and we look at the courts system in England and Wales, examining the characteristics of the criminal justice system and what is entailed in both magistrates' courts and Crown Courts.

#### 2.1.1.3 **Human rights and criminal justice**

This is followed by a short analysis of human rights and how these relate to your work as a PCSO, but also more generally in the way that human rights and the Human Rights Act 1998 impact on criminal justice.. As usual, there are discussion points, key points, and Knowledge Checks throughout the chapter to reinforce your learning and understanding.

## 2.2 **Joining Up**

### 2.2.1 **Typical induction for a PCSO**

We must emphasize at the outset of this section that what we describe and comment upon is a typical induction into a typical police force. There may be something like 44 minor variations on what we describe as typical, and the chances are that your own induction, whether several years ago or next month, may have had or will have differences. Please bear that in mind: we are not offering a template of how induction should be handled, but describing what we have seen to be common practice across the police service of England and Wales. We have already examined in depth the recruitment process and talked about your fitness and physical standards in Chapter 1. Now is the time to discuss joining the police.

### 2.2.2 Starting as a PCSO

When you receive your letter of appointment as a PCSO, you will have contained within it your start date for training and instructions to 'parade' or to arrive in time for your uniform fitting.

#### 2.2.2.1 Uniform

The PCSO uniform is described in the Designation by some forces and often a distinction is made between <u>Police</u> CSOs and any other kind. Some rural community support officers, or those who patrol a country beat, may have green facings, green hat bands, and green-embroidered epaulettes to distinguish them from the royal blue colours associated with the standard PCSO uniform. Other CSOs may have the standard uniform which we itemize at 2.2.2.2, with the omission of the word 'police'. Some forces will not use the 'police' designation for fear of further confusing the separate identities of community support officers and police officers. The standard description is, as we adopt throughout this book, *Police* Community Support Officer; the distinction made by ACPO is entirely sensible: PCSOs have the 'Police' prefix if their appointments are made by the Chief Constable, under section 38 of the Police Reform Act 2002. If the officer is funded by a partnership or through non-police agencies, then the words 'Community Support Officer' or CSO suffice.

#### 2.2.2.2 The uniform's components

The PCSO uniform typically consists of:

- Police-type flat cap (male officers) or bowler (female officers) with a reflective hat band in royal blue or edged in royal blue (a lighter blue than that associated with police officers)
- Blue enamel hat or cap badge with 'Police Community Support Officer' (or sometimes 'Community Support Officer' only); sometimes with the local Force badge
- Blue epaulettes embroidered with 'Police Community Support Officer' and the officer's number (or sometimes with 'Community Support Officer' only and the Force number), sometimes with the Force badge
- Because of the Welsh Language Act, all public authorities in Wales must produce a Welsh version of whatever they do, so PCSO is rendered as

SCCH—Swyddog Cefnogi Cymuned yr Heddlu. Both English and Welsh versions are printed on blousons, high-visibility jackets, Gore-Tex (trade-marked description of the waterproof material) anoraks, epaulettes, cap badges and so on, much the same as is done for police (Heddlu) designations in Wales
- White shirt with epaulettes and radio loops, though some forces have issued light-blue or grey shirts to distinguish them from those issued to police officers
- Blue or black tie (plain) with collar inserts
- Trousers (black heavy duty); plus all-weather or waterproof black trousers (see kit 'table' [at 2.2.2.3])
- Black leather belt
- Blue sweater (jumper or pullover) with an embroidered badge with 'Police Community Support Officer' (or sometimes 'Community Support Officer' only) and the individual Force badge
- Black *Gore-Tex* type anorak, with epaulettes, radio loops and a badge embroidered with the words 'Police Community Support'

## Variations on a uniform theme

Some forces issue black 'blouson'-type jackets, embroidered or printed with the words 'Police Community Support Officer' and the Force badge. Many forces additionally issue high-visibility yellow tabards or 'gilets' to go over the uniform jacket or anorak, and nearly all forces will incorporate a reflective panel in the rear of the anorak or blouson which reads 'Police Community Support Officer' or 'Swyddog Cefnogi Cymuned yr Heddlu' (or sometimes 'Community Support Officer' only). There is also a suggestion that the 'collar and tie', or cravat, will disappear in time, to be replaced by a roll neck or similar. Even if this proposal is accepted by the police service at large, it will be some time before it is universal.

## Document pouch

Note that the document pouch is similar to the type issued to traffic wardens or parking attendants, and is often used to hold fixed penalty notices or penalty notices for disorder (FPNs and PNDs), though increasingly, PCSOs are carrying their Pocket Note Books (PNB) in the document pouch rather than in the blouson or anorak top pocket, assuming that their uniform has such pockets. Police officers, too, increasingly find that the newer blouson is not as useful for housing the PNB as the old-style tunic with two chest pockets.

### 2.2.2.3 Specifying equipment

Many forces additionally specify the uniform and the amount of equipment issued to male and female officers respectively as we show in the table below.

| Male PCSO issue | Female PCSO issue |
|---|---|
| 1 × Anorak with lining | 1 × Anorak with lining |
| 1 × general service (GS) over-trousers | 1 × general service over-trousers |
| 1 × hard-wearing trousers | 3 × skirt or trousers (choice of the individual officer) not usually issued AW trousers |
| 2 × all-weather trousers | 7 × shirts white (but see 2.2.2.2) |
| 7 × shirts white (but see 2.2.2.2) | 1 × bowler hat |
| 1 × cap (police-type) | 1 × hat badge numerals |
| 1 × cap badge numerals | 2 × epaulettes |
| 2 × epaulettes | 1 × document pouch |
| 1 × document pouch | 1 × leather belt |
| 1 × leather belt | 2 × pullover (unlined) |
| 2 × pullover (unlined) | 2 × cravat or clip-on tie |
| 2 × ties (clip-on type) | 1 × gloves black leather |
| 1 × gloves black leather | 1 × woollen scarf |
| 1 × woollen scarf | 1 × 'Hi-Viz' over-jacket |
| 1 × 'Hi-Viz' over-jacket | |

We are not making a gender point here; it is enough to note that female PCS officers have different headgear from their male colleagues, different trousers, and they can opt for a cravat rather than a tie, if they wish.

### 2.2.2.4 Uniformity

A report in July 2008 noted that there was no consensus for a national uniform for PCSOs and that to set a standard uniform for PCSOs was unrealistic. It added that the cost would be prohibitive, but went on to recommend consistency of uniform, in particular a common approach and appearance:

- The uniform should be of good quality, fit for the duties performed, and ensure the health and safety of the wearer.
- It must be distinct from that of a police officer.
- It should identify the wearer as a 'Police Community Support Officer' or 'Community Support Officer'.
- The uniform should identify the wearer as a member of the wider police force they belong to.
- The PCSO identifying features should be nationally consistent:
  - Plain blue hat band
  - Plain blue epaulettes
  - Plain blue tie.
    [adapted from NPIA's PCSO Review, July 2008, Recommendation 14, p. 19]

**59**

> **KEY POINT**
>
> It is a matter for individual forces whether footwear is issued or not, but in many forces, PCSOs have to supply their own black shoes or boots.

### 2.2.3 **PCSO training**

We cannot prescribe for you the training you will receive; not only will the content of your training vary from force to force, but its length and intensity will also be a matter for each individual force within the broad framework of **Knowledge, Understanding, Skills, Attitudes and Behaviours** (KUSAB). There is also variation in *when* you may receive particular training; some forces concentrate on 'core' training, others have a broader programme which includes some of the National Occupational Standards at the outset. The extent of this training is not prescribed, merely advised.

#### 2.2.3.1 **Components of training**

However, there are elements of PCSO training which are almost certain to be covered in the first year. A list might include most of these elements that follow, which we have split into KUSAB headings for convenience of presentation [and to show you how important all parts of your learning are to your effectiveness as a PCSO]. The capital 'C' shown against some learning elements denotes that the element is considered as 'core' to the learning for a PCSO:

> **Knowledge**
>
> - Introduction to the National Occupational Standards: what they are, how you achieve them, and over what time-frame
> - Police ranks C
> - Police stations: locations, staffing, and how they function C
> - Structure and organization of your police force C
> - The criminal law, including law to define PCSO powers, sex offenders, RIPA, etc
> - The criminal justice system; going to court, giving evidence
> - Your powers (the standard powers and any powers specified by your Force, such as powers to issue additional fixed penalty notices (FPNs), or to have the powers of a traffic warden) C
> - Professional qualifications
> - Personal issues: welfare, shifts, pay, benefits, sickness, and counselling
> - Criminal intelligence and how to report it
> - Attending a crime scene C
> - Gathering evidence; the 'continuity of evidence' C

- Making dynamic risk assessments
- Forensic evidence and scene-preservation C
- Sudden deaths
- Laws relating to property; 'lost and found'
- Pocket Note Book C
- Drugs and solvent abuse
- Missing persons and searches

## Understanding

- Your powers C
- Learning opportunities provided by tutors, assessors, supervisors, and managers
- On-the-job assessment
- The criminal justice system; going to court, giving evidence
- Anti-social behaviour (including ABCs and ASBOs) C
- Your status in law
- Criminal intelligence and how to report it C
- Attending a crime scene C
- Major incidents
- House-to-house enquiries
- Searches
- Pocket Note Book C
- Gathering evidence; the 'continuity of evidence' C
- How you learn
- Your community and how it works C
- Partnerships and how to develop them C
- Understanding victims' needs
- Missing persons
- Personal development (advancement, appraisal, moving on, or moving up)

## Skills

- Safety awareness training (sometimes called by different names: 'personal safety programme', 'self-defence', 'aggression-handling', 'unarmed combat', 'empty-hand skills', and the like) C
- Chairing meetings
- Negotiating and persuading
- Running a public assembly meeting
- Dealing with disputes, arguments, and differences
- Fitness training C
- Making dynamic risk assessments
- Interviewing and questioning
- Communications C

- First aid training **C**
- Forensic evidence and scene-preservation **C**
- Writing and self-expression (including making entries in the Pocket Note Book)

### Attitudes

- Human rights and the police **C**
- Race and diversity **C**
- How you respond to your community
- Ethical and professional standards
- Portfolios of evidence (SOLAP)
- Dealing with disputes, arguments, and differences
- Dealing with the vulnerable
- Partnerships and how to develop them
- Communication **C**

### Behaviours

- Race and diversity **C**
- Relations with the community **C**
- How you respond to your community **C**
- Dealing with the vulnerable
- Communication **C**
- Working with colleagues
- Partnerships and how to develop them

### 2.2.3.2 Applied learning

You don't need to be an Einstein to realize that many aspects of KUSAB inter-relate and overlap, which is why we have put some learning elements twice under different headings. **This has to do with possible differences between what you know and what you do**. For example, you may think that you understand all the elements around diversity, and genuinely believe that you are tolerant of others' points of view and non-judgemental in your approach. Yet your behaviour out on the street may signal something very different, if you patronize the elderly, dismiss their concerns, always plead the cause of the 'misunderstood young', and fail to preserve balance and fairness in your dealings with all members of the community. Another instance might be that you have learned and noted down what to do when you are first to arrive at a crime scene, but, in the heat or stress of the moment, you forget important matters such as a 'common approach path' (CAP); as a result, vital evidence is lost. In other words, there may be a gap be-tween how you *think* you come across and how in fact you impact on others, or between what you know you should do and what you actually do.

### 2.2.4 **Outcomes**

Your trainers and tutors will properly emphasize that you will do a great deal of learning 'on the job'; that is, out on patrol and engaging with members of the community. This is when you will understand the value, for example, of a persuasive tongue and you will learn how your effectiveness may be enhanced by your knowledge. The outcome of a particular negotiation might confirm your (perhaps) newly acquired skills, whilst a public meeting in which the community starts to create a unified approach to its problems may testify to your skills as an organizer of such activities. These are the outcomes of applying your learning, exemplifying that old military dictum that 'the battle is the pay-off' for all the hard work which went into preparation for, thinking about, and understanding the terrain in which to operate. (Incidentally, it should also be clear to you that many of the learning items and outcomes which we list above form the basis of this book, and thus we try to contribute directly to your KUSAB as a PCSO.)

### 2.2.5 **Concerns about 'mission creep'**

We discuss in 2.8 the possible hostility which you may encounter when you join, from colleagues within the police service. We do not exaggerate this potentially negative reaction to you and to PCSOs in general, but we certainly should not ignore it either. The hostility is there and it is tangible and, inside the job at least, has much to do with impressions that PCSOs are blurring the distinctions between police support staff and police officers. The perception that, slowly and with deliberation, forces are giving PCSOs more of the traditional constable's role to perform, has been described as '**mission creep**'. The Association of Chief Police Officers (ACPO) acknowledges that this hostility exists, and that it was marked when PCSOs first began:

> The role of the PCSO in comparison to [sic] that of the police officer is still relatively new. It is clear that there is still some lack of understanding of the role of the PCSO....It is imperative that all those in the police service are aware of the importance of the role, what the role actually entails [and] ensuring that there is no mission creep, nor abuse of authority.

### 2.2.5.1 **Potential and actual confusions between PCSOs and police officers**

ACPO has asserted also that the successful deployment of PCSOs in non-police roles has mitigated much of the initially negative response and that criticism of PCSOs is slowly ebbing. This may be true, though we continue to obtain evidence of the continued hostility to PCSOs in some quarters, and the Police Federation has remained implacably opposed. What is painfully evident is that the distinction between the roles of police officer and PCSO must continue to be tightly and publicly distinguished. We should inform you at this point that ACPO has made very clear the distinction in practice between the role of a police officer and that of a PCSO. ACPO defined the 'preserve of sworn police officers' as:

- Whenever there is a clear likelihood that a confrontation will arise
- When there is scope for [the] exercise of a high degree of discretion
- Where police action is likely to lead to a higher than normal risk of harm to anyone
- Where there is a clear likelihood that police action will include any infringement of a person's human rights
- Where the incident is one which is likely to lead to significant further work.

### 2.2.5.2 Rules of Engagement

In the British Army, and especially when 'policing' a hostile area, soldiers are issued with a yellow card on which are printed the rules under which they may open or return fire. These are called '**Rules of Engagement**' and the idea has been transferred to police practice. We offer the following as the PCSO version (you will note, of course, that there will be the inevitable minor variations from force to force):

---

**This framework governs all interventions, including the exercise of powers, and draws on risk assessments for the particular location where the PCSO or SCCH will patrol or be engaged.**

- There will be no expectation that PCSOs will be engaged in activities assessed as 'high risk'.
- The decision by a PCSO to withdraw, observe and report is a valid tactical option and will be supported by the Force.
- There is no positive duty for PCSOs to intervene: they are not police officers.
- The PCSOs' main purpose is to support police officers by performing (primarily) observation and reporting activities.
- PCSOs' actions will support the human rights of individuals according to PLAN guidance to ensure that actions are proportionate, legal, authorized and necessary.
- PCSOs are expected to use their judgement in determining what the benefits and risks are in any given situation.

---

### 2.2.5.3 Safe working

We look at making **dynamic risk assessments** in greater detail in 5.7, but it is worth noting at this point in the book that a 'safe working' flow diagram has been developed by forces (notably Lincolnshire) in the *ACPO Guidance* to forces. (See figure 2.1.)

### 2.2.6 **Conclusions**

We have examined several matters which relate directly to your entry into the PCSO ranks and to your deployment by your police force. We have looked at the way you will dress and the close association between your uniform and that of a police officer, whilst noting that distinctions between the two are sustained. There is a distinction too between your uniform and that of CSOs in other partnerships or arrangements. We examined the probable content of your training, within KUSAB, and noted which elements may be denoted as 'core' and which might follow later. We looked finally at the 'Rules of Engagement' for PCSOs. Debates about all these issues will not end with this book, but will probably continue to take place as long as there is a central confusion about what a PCSO is and how that is different from, or increasingly identical to, the role of a sworn police officer.

**Figure 2.1 Safe working—risk-assessing PCSO work**

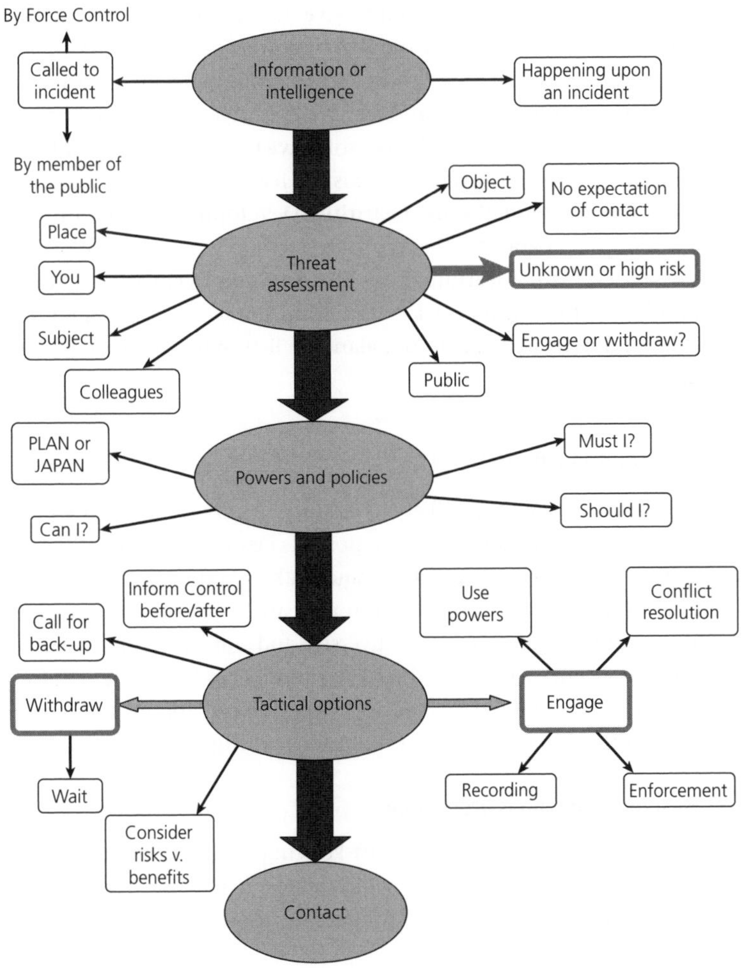

**Knowledge Check 5**

1. Who wear green facings, hat bands, and epaulettes?

2. What distinguishes PCSOs from other CSOs?

3. What is the Welsh for PCSO?

4. What does KUSAB stand for?

5. Name four 'Core Skills'.

6. What is 'mission creep'?

## 2.3 **Teaching and Learning**

As soon as you enrol as a PCSO you will receive training. To some extent the content of your training will reflect the number of powers designated to you by your Force. You may be aware that there is now a standardized agreement on a common set of powers for all PCSOs in England and Wales (differences persist concerning powers to *arrest, detain, and report*). Forces still have the autonomy to add to those 'standard' powers if they wish, based on existing legislation. Increasing standardization is in the **Wider Policing Learning Development Programme** (the WPLDP), a learning programme that outlines the core elements of initial training for PCSOs, underpins the learning from the National Occupational Standards (NOS), and looks at continuous learning within the wider policing family. We touched on this briefly in 2.2, with our glance at lists of topics which PCSOs will have to know.

### 2.3.1 **Basic training components**

Typically your initial training is likely to last anything between three weeks and two months and will include a combination of classroom and supervised practical activity. In some forces you may be undertaking some training in common with trainee police officers. You will certainly learn about the **community** that you will support (including issues of diversity and human rights), **health and safety** (including your own personal safety), a number of **basic offences** (such as theft, assaults, and criminal damage), and your **powers**. You may also be given some instruction in interviewing and **statement taking**.

#### 2.3.1.1 **'Bespoke' training is preferable**

This might involve the use of College of Policing-designed learning materials (old police training materials, some of which appear to have been rather clumsily adapted from existing police training manuals; there is nothing wrong with doing this except that the learning for PCSOs would be better, we think, if specifically designed or 'bespoke'). You could well receive follow-up training at later dates, particularly if your number of designated powers increases.

### 2.3.1.2 Controversy and good practice

Although the format and content of your training is largely a matter for your Force, the Home Office (2002) does recommend the following:

- That it is locally delivered.
- That your trainers are appropriately qualified to train, particularly in specialist areas such as health and safety.

There has been some controversy in the past concerning the appropriateness of PCSO training, some of which was fuelled by a *Daily Mirror* article by an undercover journalist in May 2005 (Sampson, 2005). The undercover reporter claimed that his four weeks' training left him unprepared for and 'terrified' of the role as a PCSO. However, some at least of his claims were refuted by the then-Commissioner of the MPS, Sir Ian Blair, and others (Blair, 2005). Other concerns on training were reported in the Home Office Research Study 'A national evaluation of Community Support Officers', particularly with regard to IT and use of radio training (Cooper *et al*, 2006). Good practice was also identified by the evaluation, particularly in terms of PCSO trainees' induction into both their Force (specifically their BCU) and their local communities (Cooper *et al*, 2006).

## 2.4 **Tutoring, Assessing, and Mentoring**

About 60 per cent of trainee PCSOs are allocated a tutor or assessor after basic training (Cooper *et al*, 2006). As in many other aspects of training, whether you are allocated an assessor or a tutor or not will be down to your Force policy. If you are tutored, then the tutorship period will probably last about two months after your basic training. Your tutor is likely to be either a police officer or a more experienced PCSO (some undertake a PCSO tutorship course before going on to become assessors or mentors). The role of the tutor or mentor (meaning 'trusted adviser') is to provide you with support, guidance, and advice in your first few months.

---

**DISCUSSION POINT**

What are the qualities which you would look for in a tutor or mentor?

Do you think that the roles of tutor and mentor are different?

Would there be a wide variation, do you think, between people's needs for tutoring or mentoring? If so, what might they be?

---

## 2.5 **What Does the PCSO Need in Terms of Qualification?**

What is clearly needed for PCSOs is a national qualification linked to the attainment of competences through the National Occupational Standards (NOS, dealt with in more detail in Chapter 4). There is at present no national acceptance of the need for or structure of any such award and it is left to individual police forces to devise, arrange, or commission their own. The College of Policing currently recommends that forces consider adopting an NVQ route for training of PCSOs. However, the College also suggests the Chartered Management Institute (CMI) 'Introductory Certificate in Neighbourhood Management' as an alternative. Others suggest that the Certificate of Police Knowledge (CPK), a Level 4 short course introduced in 2013 for new entrant police officers, would also be suitable for PCSOs; while critics of the CPK demur and suggest a university-related degree or diploma instead. We are unlikely to have a resolution of this incoherence for some years.

## 2.6 **Designation**

### 2.6.1 **Carrying the 'Designation'**

In something like the way that a police officer carries a warrant card, you carry your PCSO Designation from your Chief Constable, the possession of which, whilst you are on duty and in uniform, gives you the legal right to exercise your PCSO powers.

### 2.6.2 **No uniformity for the Designation**

The manner of the Designation varies from police force to police force; there are no hard and fast rules as to what the document should look like. That said, common features should specify the powers which you have within the law and carry your Chief Constable's name and signature. Look at the example in figure 2.2.

### 2.6.2.1 **The meaning of the Designation**

Notice how the authority of the Chief Constable over PCSOs derives from the Police Reform Act 2002, which we look at in more detail in Chapter 3. The essential point is that the bearer of the Designation is under the 'direction and control' of the Chief Constable, and acting with his or her authority. This is supplemented by specifying which of the powers designated under the Police Reform Act 2002 are applied by the Chief Constable. In some forces, each of the powers is specified and in others a summary of the powers is provided. The Designation is not an identity document (that is supplied separately as a police staff identification,

**Figure 2.2 Designation of a PCSO in Gloucestershire Police**

---

**DESIGNATION**

**(Sections 38 & 42 & Schedule 4, Police Reform Act 2002)**
**This is to certify that ..................... who is an employee of**
**Gloucestershire Police Authority and is under my direction and**
**control, is designated \*POLICE COMMUNITY SUPPORT OFFICER**
**with powers and duties set out in Paragraphs 1 (excludes 2(a)**
**disorder) 2,3,5,6,7,8,9,10,11,12,13,14,15,16 of Part 1 (Paragraph 4**
**is currently suspended) of Schedule 4 to the Police Reform Act**
**2002.**

**Chief Constable** *Timothy Brain*. Timothy Brain QPM BA PhD

**Date ................................................**

The Chief Constable may at any time by notice to the Police Community
Support Officer modify or withdraw this Designation.

This Certificate of Designation is to be retained by the Police Community
Support Officer. When producing this Designation upon request in accordance with s.42 of the Police Reform Act 2002 the Community Support
Officer shall produce the Constabulary Identity Pass bearing a photograph of the holder.

A copy of this Certificate of Designation will be retained with the Police
Community Support Officer's personal file.
If this Certificate is modified, withdrawn or replaced it shall be surrendered immediately to Gloucestershire Constabulary Personnel Department and retained within the Police Community Support Officer's
personal file.

*s.38(7)(a)*

---

which, again, varies from police force to police force) and possession of the Designation paper simply confirms that a PCSO can exercise specified powers, in
uniform and on duty. Production of the Designation (under section 42 of the
Police Reform Act 2002) is likely only in circumstances where the PCSO's authority is challenged or questioned. Note that production of the Designation is
'upon request': it is not used like a warrant card.

### 2.6.2.2 Distinction between PCSO and police officer

PCSOs are support staff, employed by their Force Police and Crime Commissioner and are not subject to the discipline requirements of police regulations or
sworn authority. In fact, police support staff, including PCSOs, are subject to and
protected by employment legislation in ways that police officers are not. This is
why the Chief Constable's 'direction and control' are specified. The Chief Constable does not employ you but he or she does have **operational command**,
which means that he or she can tell you what to do, where to go, and how to
discharge your duty in accordance with the operational priorities and directions
established for your police force.

### 2.6.2.3 **Your authority**

In summary, then, the Designation sets out the legal authority and conditions under which you are deployed and specifies your powers. The Designation is signed by the Chief Constable of your Force and is your legal entitlement to be a PCSO and exercise the powers of a PCSO whilst on duty. There are important differences in this from being a sworn police officer, which we should glance at briefly.

---

**DISCUSSION POINT**

Can you enumerate the differences between a police officer and a PCSO in terms of powers and 'office'?

---

## 2.6.3 **Differences between PCSOs and police officers**

The differences are quite profound, and the police officer's greater extent of powers, the wide exercise of them, the use of discretion, and the ability to use force to ensure compliance means that police training, both in terms of physical training, skills for the job, and in knowledge of the law, is much more extensive and thorough than a PCSO's (about 6 months as against a maximum of eight weeks).

### 2.6.3.1 **The powers of 'the office of constable'**

A police officer is attested (or 'sworn') before a magistrate, whereupon the powers of **the office of constable** are conferred upon the individual officer, who may now act in the name of the Crown. S/he is issued with a warrant card which identifies the holder by name, photograph, and rank, and which is signed by the Chief Constable or Commissioner of his or her Force. The warrant card is an important form of identification for a police officer, but s/he can continue to exercise his or her powers whether or not actually holding the card physically. The powers of the 'office of constable' are available all the time, whether or not the police officer is on duty and whether or not the officer is in uniform. In practical terms, however, a police officer usually carries his or her warrant card at all times, and, of course, especially when on duty. Also, in practice, he or she is unlikely to exercise police powers in another force or in another part of the country unless participating in a joint police operation of some kind, in which case arrangements for the inter-operability of powers will have been made.

### 2.6.3.2 **PCSO powers**

All this is a far cry from being a PCSO. You can see that the powers for a PCSO are much more limited:

---

**KEY POINT—PCSO POWERS AND JURISDICTION**

- Limited to the powers designated by a chief constable (irrespective of the 'standard powers')
- Operable only when on duty
- PCSOs must be in uniform
- PCSOs must carry their Designations. In any law-enforcement or crime situation where police officers are present, PCSOs are always subordinate to police officers in terms of powers and jurisdiction.

---

#### 2.6.3.3 Function of the Designation

Those of you about to enter service as PCSOs should now have an appreciation of how your Designation serves as the legitimation of your function, as well as being a handy form of reference for your legal powers. For those of you already with some service in, you may wish to note that Designations vary from force to force. It is worth comparing your Designation with others, since there may be elements in yours which could assist or clarify the Designation used in another force, and vice versa. For the foreseeable future, the Designation paper will continue to act in the 'standing' of a police warrant: it is simultaneously the PCSO's authority and the means of defining that authority.

---

**Task**

Compare your Designation with that of two of your neighbouring forces.

What points are there in common between Designations?

Are any of the differences worth importing to your Force? How would you go about that?

---

## 2.7 What Do You Do? Varieties of PCSO Deployment, Variations from Force to Force: A Typical Tour of Duty

The difficulty in producing a PCSO book whose guidance and information apply across all police forces and circumstances in England and Wales is that some of the topics we cover will vary in emphasis, utility (whether it works or not), and popularity from force to force, from BCU to BCU, from neighbourhood team to neighbourhood team, and even from PCSO to PCSO. *None will vary more than what you actually do.* The strength of the PCSO role, of course, is that it adapts to the local community in which it is placed and, in terms of community engagement and problem solving (two of its chief functions), it takes its cues from the people in the community themselves. Therefore, a definitive guide to what you do on a daily basis is impossible to compile and could actually take you down a wrong path, especially if what you attempt (because you saw it here) is at odds with what your community wants and expects.

### 2.7.1 Generic and specialist roles

This section will look at some generic roles that would probably be included in a PCSO's daily duty, as well as looking briefly at some of the specialist *roles* that a PCSO could play. We are not providing a 'to-do list', rather we are suggesting a guide to some of the common areas of work undertaken by a PCSO. The National Occupational Standards (NOS, see Chapter 4) determine the standards you must attain to demonstrate competence, but the NOS don't tell you *what* to do or *how* to do it. We make some suggestions about what we know works, what we have tried ourselves, what we have observed, what has worked elsewhere as 'best practice' in policing, and what we have been informed about as having been effective and productive in other places. The way forward is for you to try out such ideas or suggestions in your own area and then see if they are suitable for that neighbourhood or that community.

---

**DISCUSSION POINTS**

What work would you consider to be in the daily routine for a PCSO?

Make a note of the tasks you identify and see if they crop up in the following section or perhaps elsewhere in the book. However, do not neglect or forget your own ideas because they could be really suitable for your BCU and worth trialling.

---

### 2.7.1.1 What would be likely to occur on a 'standard' PCSO shift?

---

**Task**

Using the table below identify which of the following tasks you think would occur on a 'standard' PCSO shift.

---

| Task | Yes or No |
| --- | --- |
| Visible foot patrol | |
| Intelligence gathering | |
| Organizing a road safety event at a local school | |
| Community surgery at the local library | |
| Dealing with anti-social youths, or anti-social behaviour by any age group | |

| Task | Yes or No |
| --- | --- |
| Issuing 'tickets' for littering | |
| Chairing a public meeting | |
| Attending a multi-agency meeting | |
| Seizing a mini-motorbike | |
| Taking part in a truancy sweep | |
| Manning a police cordon in the event of a terrorist incident | |
| Mediating in a neighbour dispute | |
| Meeting local business owners | |
| Directing traffic at the scene of an accident | |
| Administer first aid to a casualty | |
| Taking a statement from a victim of crime | |

### A varied day

As you know, of course, *all* the above are events that could occur in a shift and are ones that a PCSO could deal with at any time. The likelihood of them all occurring on the same day is remote unless you happen upon the shift from hell. This simple table demonstrates the wide variety of work within the PCSO remit but it is far from definitive and you will very probably have thought of more.

### 2.7.1.2 Core purpose of a PCSO

What we have shown you here is that there is a breadth and a 'complexity of exchange' within the PCSO role that is hard to replicate on a page or even in a sustained exercise. We do know, though, what is expected of you and what you may be called upon to do. The core **purpose** of a PCSO has been articulated well by ACPO:

> The fundamental role of the PCSO is to contribute to the policing of neighbourhoods, primarily through highly visible patrol with the purpose of reassuring the public, increasing orderliness in public places and being accessible to communities and partner agencies working at local level. The emphasis of this role, and the powers required to fulfil it, will vary from neighbourhood to neighbourhood and force to force.

This description provides us with a handy basis from which to look at a typical PCSO day, as well as containing the useful caveat that the role does vary dependent on location, circumstances, and the composition of the community with which you engage. It will also vary according to your temperament, your inclinations, your strengths, and your sense of purpose. That said, and allowing for local variability and the peculiarity of circumstances applying at any particular time and place, the key themes in the ACPO Guidance are clear—

**policing**
**reassurance**
**increasing orderliness**
**accessibility.**

These elements would therefore form the core of any PCSO day.

### 2.7.2 **The four basic themes**

We can take these four basic themes and begin to build a perspective on how they modulate and clarify the daily work of a PCSO.

#### 2.7.2.1 **Policing: Peel's 'Principles'**

In 1829, Sir Richard Mayne, one of the first Commissioners of the Metropolitan Police, may have provided a definition of policing that has stood the test of time even in today's more complex and fragmented world, though it is now popularly attributed to Sir Robert Peel, Home Secretary at the time, and responsible for introducing the 'new police' in London:

> The primary object of an efficient police is the prevention of crime: the next that of detection and punishment of offenders if crime is committed. To these ends all the efforts of police must be directed. The protection of life and property, the preservation of public tranquillity, and the absence of crime, will alone prove whether those efforts have been successful and whether the objects for which the police were appointed have been attained.

> [Note: the latest theory is that the commonly-accepted version of 'Peel's 9 Principles' may have been a twentieth-century embellishment of this basic text; see Reiner, 2013]

This vision of what policing a community entails and what should be the measure of success still has a resonance for PCSOs, as it does for police officers. With the addition of the concept of **community engagement policing**, we can still look at 'protecting life and limb', maintaining 'tranquillity' (or 'keeping the peace'), and 'prevention of crime' as primary objectives for any PCSO, engaged with any community anywhere in the country. It is also of equal contemporary importance that the description proffered by Mayne for success is found in the community's judgement of the police on these issues. It is not only a key facet of neighbourhood policing and therefore a core part of your work, but it also shows that the essence of policing has not changed, because the fundamentals of human nature have not changed. Sir Richard was a far-sighted man, but even he could not have foreseen how, in the 1980s and 1990s, the police would become divorced from the communities they were sworn to protect, and how it is through the 'reinvention' of the neighbourhood team concept, including introducing the PCSO, that the police now seek to recapture the lost ground.

### 2.7.2.2 **Reassurance**

ACPO has identified reassuring the public as a crucial part of PCSO responsibilities and this has itself evolved from the **National Reassurance Policing Programme**, a project designed to assess the impact of neighbourhood policing within communities. Reassurance policing is a model of neighbourhood policing which seeks to improve public confidence in policing. It involves local communities in identifying priority crime and disorder issues in their neighbourhood, which they can then tackle together with the police and other public services and partners.

Listening to what the community wants, in terms of its feelings of safety, security, and reassurance, has become a key theme for successive governments, with special emphasis on the notion that all public services, not just policing, should have a 'citizen focus'. As we note elsewhere in this book (for example at 6.5), the annual publication of the **British Crime Survey** records people's responses to crime and to what the police do. Consistently, over a number of years, such surveys have said in summary that **no matter what the crime statistics tell you about falling crime or the decreasing likelihood of theft or robbery, people judge the effectiveness of their police forces [in part at least] by whether they can go out safely at night and whether they can live in their communities without the constant fear of being mugged, burgled, robbed, assaulted, or subjected to anti-social or low-level criminal behaviour.** Taking the need to reassure the public as a central strand of police work, it is very much the neighbourhood teams, of which you are a part, which will deliver on this reassurance. Being there and being seen, being approachable and being effective, are thus very important components of what you do.

What is evident is that, political imperatives aside, the community of residents and commercial property owners in towns and villages overwhelmingly want to be able to go about their business safely, in orderly tranquillity, free from disorder, interference, or crime. Whilst some commentators on the police and policing tend to dismiss the importance of orderliness, it is a real enough aspiration for most people and a fundamental aspect of the reassurance agenda.

### 2.7.2.3 **Accessibility**

This role requirement extends to both the public and the partnership agencies with which the police work. The PCSO needs to be accessible on a practical level; that is, known to the public and available to consult on a regular basis, as well as on a perceptual level where the individual officer is amenable and open to new ideas or new opportunities. How accessible you are depends very much on what sort of person you are, as well as what sort of training you have had. You will see in Chapter 4, where we look at the National Occupational Standards, that there are expectations about people in the community feeling confident about approaching you, and that you will be a focus for them in doing something about their problems. You are expected to be a good listener with a bent for practical resolutions (that doesn't mean, by the way, that you have to suffer fools gladly, but you do have to show 'imperturbable impartiality'). Your competence is judged on a recurrent basis, as those of you with service will acknowledge. This is part of the central 'toolbox' of your skills and effectiveness, whether working with hard-to-reach groups in the community, influencing partners and partner agencies to help you, or influencing your superiors to undertake a sustained policing operation to assist the community. It all begins with members of the community seeking access to you.

### 2.7.3 **The PCSO's daily job**

Your daily PCSO job will revolve around the four themes of:

- Policing
- Reassurance
- Increasing orderliness
- Accessibility.

You would probably start your shift by accessing the latest briefings in regard to your BCU, such as intelligence reports, crime reports, operational activities, and so on (**policing**) and deal with any correspondence from the public or partner agencies (**reassurance, accessibility**). Having then left the station or office where you are based, visible patrolling will be a large part of your role as you walk, cycle, or drive around your patch (**reassurance**). In providing this high visibility you will be meeting residents, business owners, young people, schoolteachers, parents, and other members of the community as you make your way around. This will allow you to talk to people and give them the opportunity to talk to you (**accessibility**). You will conduct an 'Environmental Visual Audit' (this means, briefly, that you make careful note of what has physically happened or changed as you patrol), and that will allow you to identify problems within a community that need solving and highlight which partners would be best to work with to achieve this (**accessibility, policing, reassurance, increasing orderliness**).

You will deal with any relevant matter within your remit, such as calls from your Force Control Centre with regard to your BCU (**policing**) and deal with any spontaneous events that occur whilst you are out on patrol (**policing, reassurance, increasing orderliness**). Throughout the whole shift you will collate community intelligence that you discover or that comes your way and which can be reported in the appropriate manner on return to your station or office at the end of the shift (**policing**).

**DISCUSSION POINTS**

What do you feel about this daily work pattern?

Is it what you thought the job would involve?

Does it correspond to the Home Office adverts which brought the job to your attention (if they did)?

How does your daily experience of doing the job accord (or not accord) with what we have described?

### 2.7.4 **Variable tasks**

Within the police forces of England and Wales there are many variations in PCSOs' tasking and we have already said that we cannot provide a comprehensive guide to all the permutations which may be devised or pieced together, as local circumstances, partners, and funding dictate. In whatever way these tasks are constituted, and whatever the PCSOs' described roles in the community, at the core are these four themes. There is, though, a further permutation which builds on the core themes, and adds a specialism. Some PCSOs may have been allocated to 'specialist' positions because of the needs of their individual force or area. Such positions include:

- **Schools PCSOs**—based in a school, often joint-funded with that school and working with that school (this can be popular with PCSOs who want to work 'term-time only', but watch dictatorial head teachers who want you there all the time, acting as a super-caretaker). Your working day will almost exclusively concern young people and the problems which beset them, but your crime prevention and detection skills will not be neglected and you may become an invaluable source to the sworn police, for example in detecting or gaining intelligence on drugs dealers.
- **Family projects**—working with 'problem' families to ensure that low-level anti-social behaviour does not escalate into full-blown criminality. This role can entail very close liaison with social services (indeed some have criticized this use of PCSOs as being 'social workers on the cheap'—sometimes you can't win), but in places it has proven most effective in 'straightening' someone who otherwise might have drifted into criminality.
- **Prisoner resettlement programmes**—this can involve working within **Multi-Agency Public Protection Arrangements** (MAPPA), which deal with the complexities of staging the return from prison to communities of violent or sex offenders. In our experience, MAPPA tends to be highly specialist and the PCSO's role in it tends to be minor. You are much more likely to be partnering the Probation Service and Social Services in resettling those who have served prison sentences for non-violent crime such as theft, burglary, or deception.

- **Missing persons programmes**—our research shows that PCSOs have enjoyed the challenges of 'misper' work and have rapidly accumulated both specialist knowledge and credibility, but do not expect that, by playing this role, you will necessarily be involved in exciting murder investigations. Most of the time you will be involved in tracing runaways—which is valuable in its own right—or bringing family members back into contact with each other, with any potential for conflict modulated through you. It can be a long-haul job, with many people choosing to cover their traces when they opt to disappear, and may include some who wish to remain undiscovered to their families, which can be frustrating. On the other hand, there are huge psychological and professional rewards in finding unharmed a child who has strayed, or in returning a vulnerable adult to the protection of the community.
- **Road Safety programmes**—these are primarily aimed at young people, and may involve coordination with cycling safety schemes and other established ways of raising safety awareness, but it may also have to do with schools' visits, work with local environmental groups, and liaising with your Force's roads-policing staff. The work can also entail raising road safety awareness among the frail and elderly, or among those with mental disorders who need gentle instruction in the safest places to cross the road or how to be visible at night.

### 2.7.5 What next? What of the future? Where is the PCSO role going?

It seems that the opportunities for PCSOs over the coming years may grow to encompass further projects or specialist positions. Although the core role for most PCSOs will always be in neighbourhood policing on the street (which is where the 'reassured' community wants you to be), it is not difficult to propose where future challenges may arise. Perhaps new housing estates will have a dedicated PCSO working and living within that defined geographical community. Maybe the PCSO will become a fixture in the community with an office in the doctor's surgery or in the local library as a 'one-stop' community approach is adopted. There is a strong possibility that PCSOs could work in hospitals in a visible reassurance capacity (such as in Accident and Emergency departments) as well as assisting with other community and social problems that exist within hospitals. We will see more PCSOs 'embedded' in schools and having a patrol beat among the children and on the school premises; this is a specialist role that is certain to expand. Finally, though, the role of the PCSO will change and adapt largely because of the success of the work you do in your area, and will expand through the innovation, tolerance, and adaptability which you bring to the role. It is very much a case of **the job is what you do.**

> ### Knowledge Check 6
>
> 1. How long will your initial training last?
>
> 2. What is 'Designation'?
>
> 3. Give three examples of typical activities on a standard PCSO neighbourhood shift.
>
> 4. What are the four 'basic themes' in PCSO work?
>
> 5. What is 'misper'?

## 2.8 Pitfalls and Problems: Potential Hostility in the Job and How to Deal With It

**Hostility to PCSOs does exist, but not everywhere and not all the time.** You may well be prepared, at least mentally, for displays of open or concealed hostility to you in the exercise of your function as a PCSO and in the discharge of your duty. You will assume that parts of the community will not welcome your presence, and those people who may previously have got away with anti-social behaviour may be actively hostile to you and to your neighbourhood team colleagues.

### 2.8.1 There can be hostility from those who don't understand your role

What you may be less prepared for is open or concealed hostility from among some of your 'police family' colleagues. Yet it exists, and we would be failing in our duty in writing this book if we glossed over the fact that some police officers think that you are a threat to them, or think that, by some weird alchemy, you represent the end of policing as we know it (Caless, 2007). *Why this has happened and what you can do about it are the themes for this section.* It may be that you never encounter, by look or action, the slightest resentment or hostility towards you and what you do. If so, congratulations and you can move on. If, however, you are one of the majority of PCSOs who has encountered precisely this sort of behaviour, then read on.

---

**DISCUSSION POINTS**

Why would your police colleagues feel hostility towards the PCSO role?

What sort of threat do you pose to your police colleagues?

---

Don't expect to find much written about this hostility in your training notes: publicists for the PCSO concept will not allow themselves to be diverted by what they see as a 'bedding in' or adjustment between the two sides, and those who oppose the whole concept of the PCSO are warring on a different political plane.

### 2.8.2 **The Police Federation's open hostility**

The Police Federation has led criticism of the PCSO concept. Much of the commentary from the Federation, particularly over the potential and actual confusions of role between PCSO and police officer, has been reasoned and intelligent, but sometimes the language used by Federation leaders reflects the emotional aggression which is sometimes used on the ground by police officers, such as calling PCSOs *'numties in yellow jackets'* (Caless, 2007), when the concept was first introduced on the streets in 2002; whilst in 2006, the Federation chairman of the Metropolitan Police's constable branch board said this:

> [there is] a growing army of community support staff who walk around like gaggles of lost shoppers [recruited to take the place of constables on the street].

Paul Kelly, Chairman of the Police Federation in Manchester is reported as saying in 2007 that 'PCSOs […] are a failed experiment' and calling for them to be 'done away with'.

The Police Federation in London took out full-page advertisements in south-east London newspapers in late June 2006 in an attempt to influence public opinion about PCSOs and the perceived threat which they pose to traditional policing. Two pictures were shown in the advertisement, one of a police officer and one of a PCSO. Each picture was surrounded by a dotted border and the image of a pair of scissors. The Federation is reported as saying: 'real officers are being replaced by the new breed.' Readers were invited to choose which they would 'cut out', a police officer or a PCSO.

---

**DISCUSSION POINTS**

How helpful is this 'either/or' choice?

Why is the Federation trying to harness public opinion in this way?

How might this hostility affect your work in the community?

---

### 2.8.2.1 **PCSOs: Policing on the cheap?**

The Federation's argument is essentially in defence of its members in police ranks (constable to chief inspector). Within that membership there is widespread unease that PCSOs *are* policing on the cheap; that the increase in the PCSO numbers threatens the recruitment of more police officers; and that there may be a withering of the need for fully-warranted police officers to perform core neighbourhood 'policing' tasks. However, what the Federation appears to miss, or ignore, is that there are fundamental changes afoot in the nature of policing which have very little to do with the role of PCSO or any other community support officer or rural warden. **It has everything to do with the rise and rise of 'private policing'** in which many of the functions of the traditional police are being contracted out to private companies, to security firms, or to people, more or less skilled, who undertake patrol, engage in prevention, and collect evidence for the prosecution of offenders. The point we want to make here is that policing in England and Wales is already in flux, it is already changing in profound ways, and PCSOs are merely one among many manifestations of that change.

---

**KEY POINT**

Think about private policing, commercial security companies, 'gated communities', roads policing with the Department of Transport, 'immigration police' in the UK Border Agency, the Security Industries Authority, which licenses 'door stewards' among others, rural wardens, community support officers paid for from local authority funds, schools security officers, police staff, police and crime commissioners, and public/ private investment schemes (PPIs). The 'wider police family' can only expand.

(See Reiner, 2013.)

---

### 2.8.2.2 Unison, not the Police Federation, represents the PCSO

This gives a context for some of the organized hostility that PCSOs have faced, and which they may continue to face, but of equal importance is the likely reaction to PCSOs on the ground, especially as they feature in Neighbourhood Policing Teams in increasing numbers. Perhaps what happens is that people distrust statements from politicians, both national and local, when the latter try to say what it is that PCSOs will do. Certainly the Police Federation was so disenchanted with the whole PCSO concept that, in June 2006, its members voted 'overwhelmingly' against a proposal to extend membership of the Federation beyond sworn officers. The union which represents police staff, Unison, was swift to move into the vacuum and promptly offered membership to PCSOs. The response from PCSOs themselves was equally rapid, and by the late summer of 2006, Unison reported the formation of a PCSO National Working Group under its auspices. For all that, in February 2007, PCSOs were being described contemptuously in print, as '*minimally-trained auxiliaries who, despite their best intentions, are not up to it*' (Caless, 2007). Some grudging acceptance of PCSOs within policing was implied in a website entry in 2014, but the warning was still posted firmly that they were not a '*substitute* [for] *a fully warranted police service*' (Police Federation, 2014, available under 'PCSO' at <http://www.polfed.org/aboutus/223.aspx>; accessed 4 June 2014). It is quite something to accuse the PCSOs of being something they have never claimed and could not be.

### 2.8.3 How good are PCSOs? Public perception and public survey

Research carried out in West Yorkshire by Adam Crawford, Deputy Director of the Centre for Criminal Justice Studies at the University of Leeds, and a team of his colleagues suggested that PCSOs were a popular innovation within the community. The results were published as *Patrolling with a purpose*. Among the survey results analysed by Crawford's team, we might note the following:

- 69 per cent of those surveyed perceived an increase in the number of officers patrolling the city centres.
- 22 per cent saw a community support officer more than once a day while 40 per cent saw a community support officer at least once a day.
- 96 per cent of those who had encountered a community support officer reported high levels of satisfaction with how their problem had been dealt with.
- 82 per cent agreed that the presence of visible patrol personnel makes [the city centre] a more welcoming place to work, shop and visit.

Interestingly, the report came to this conclusion:

> [West Yorkshire Police] successfully shielded CSOs from the normal demands of policing, such as dashing from incident to incident and dealing with a backlog of incident enquiries, which have traditionally served to undermine locally-tied foot patrol. *Furthermore, community support officers have demonstrated that they can deliver effective patrols and engage with different communities without the need for the full range of powers vested in constables*. [Our italics]

### 2.8.3.1 Reassurance and impact on fear

A detailed study of the effect of PCSO patrolling, in concert with a carefully developed neighbourhood policing plan, suggests that the impact on the community's sense of safety and security is out of proportion to the numbers involved. Additionally, there was a measurable effect on crime; the report suggests that in Leeds city centre, theft of vehicles fell by almost half, theft from a vehicle declined by a third, and tampering or interference with a vehicle fell by more than half. These are spectacular figures, even in a high crime-rate area, and the falls are confirmed by similar results in Bradford city centre, where theft from a vehicle fell by nearly a quarter, theft of vehicles was reduced by a quarter, and vehicle interference and tampering dropped by almost a quarter. The proportions are remarkably consistent, matched by the decline in personal robbery (down 47 per cent in Leeds and down 46 per cent in Bradford). That most reductions occurred in 'hot spot' areas suggests too that the PCSOs were appropriately deployed.

---

**DISCUSSION POINTS**

What does this tell you about the need for accurate targeting and focused deployment?

Are you surprised by the survey results?

Will they change the minds of your critics?

---

### 2.8.3.2 PCSO survey in Kent

At the other end of the country, a similar survey of public opinion, conducted in Kent, came to very similar conclusions. PCSOs tackle 'real crime', the public said, and are not simply a visible presence, reassuring though that is. Vehicle crime fell by a fifth in the 'control sites', which was more than double the rate in other areas where PCSOs were not deployed. There was a reduction in criminal damage three times that of the areas outside the control site. There was an increased perception of safety by residents, especially walking alone in the dark, or at home alone during the day and during the night. The Kent report went on to note that two-thirds (62 per cent) of residents had contact with a PCSO and nearly 90 per cent noted that their expectations of PCSOs regarding community involvement had been fulfilled. Three-quarters of those surveyed (76 per cent) agreed that their PCSO represented 'good value for money'.

### 2.8.3.3 The first national evaluation of the PCSO

In 2006, a national evaluation of the work of Community Support Officers was published by the Home Office and for the first time gave us a picture of the effectiveness of PCSOs on a national scale. The findings which emerged were relatively straightforward and may be summarized like this :

- PCSOs were seen as more accessible than police officers. Members of the public were more likely to report things to PCSOs which they would not bother a police officer with.
- The public valued the role of PCSO and there was strong evidence from two of the 'case study areas' [Merseyside, Sussex] that, where PCSOs were known in their communities, there was a perception that PCSOs had made a 'real impact' in their areas, 'especially in dealing with youth disorder'.
- More than 40 per cent of PCSOs said that they joined as a stepping-stone to becoming a sworn police officer.
- The diversity of PCSOs, particularly in terms of ethnicity and age, has been a marked feature of the implementation.
- The survey found that there was no evidence that PCSOs were having a measurable impact on the level of recorded crime or incidents of anti-social behaviour in the areas where they were deployed.

### 2.8.3.4 Opinion surveys may confirm the value of the PCSO

Some of the conclusions are a little suspect, or may be predicated on too little data. It seems axiomatic that the presence of PCSOs will have a deterrent effect on low-level criminality and on anti-social behaviour over time, as we saw illustrated quite dramatically in the force-level studies in West Yorkshire. The best comparators will be found when results are quantified on a neighbourhood (and thence a BCU) level. Any appreciable or measurable effect on national crime figures is probably still some distance away. Meanwhile, should we be content with the positive effect which PCSOs are having on public opinion?

By contrast, there have been a number of stories in the media which have criticized the so-called 'disengagement' role of PCSOs. One occurred on 3 May 2007 when two Lancashire PCSOs turned up at a lake near Wigan after reports of a boy,

Jordon Lyon, getting into difficulties in the water. The boy was nowhere to be seen and the two PCSOs did not enter the lake and dive to search for him, leaving this to a police officer who was trained to do so. The boy's body was later recovered. When the matter came before a coroner's inquest some months later, there was much media comment on the apparent supineness of the PCSO role. An Assistant Chief Constable from Lancashire Police, Dave Thompson, publicly defended the actions of the PCSOs, noting that they had not been trained to perform such rescues and that observing and reporting were valid tactical options. The public grumbling continued, and surfaced again with reports in November 2007 that two Metropolitan Police PCSOs did not go to the aid of a man being attacked by three girls. A female member of the public went to his help and she led the subsequent media criticism, in which the PCSO's were labelled as 'plastic policemen'. An internal enquiry was launched by the Metropolitan Police, but the outcome was not made public.

### 2.8.3.5  Other evaluations of the PCSO role

An NPIA report into the effectiveness of PCSOs was published in July 2008, as part of an evaluation of the Neighbourhood Policing Programme. We note from the report that 'neighbourhood policing can increase public confidence in policing, feelings of safety, and reduce crime and anti-social behaviour'; self-evidently, PCSOs have a major role to play in the delivery of such reassurance. The report identified that there was an element of PCSO 'role drift' in some forces where PCSOs were taken away from NPT duties and set to do other things, for some of which they had not been trained, and for others their duties played no part in public reassurance.

Another report in 2010 in the *Daily Telegraph* suggested that PCSOs were still regarded negatively:

> critics – including many regular officers – have branded them 'plastic policemen' or 'CHIMPS', which stands for 'completely hopeless in most policing situations'.

> [Barrett, March 21 2010]

By contrast, a sober academic study by Craig Paterson and Ed Pollock in 2011 concluded broadly that PCSOs were a positive contribution to neighbourhood policing and reassurance, despite their lack of real policing power. Another, more recent, review, this time by Cambridgeshire Constabulary, was published in February 2014 and noted:

> PCSOs have been the visible face of the Constabulary for more than a decade. They have become interwoven in the social fabric of communities, built lasting relationships with partners, elected representatives and individual members of the public.

> [Sutherland, 2014]

**DISCUSSION POINTS**

What evidence do you have locally for the effectiveness of PCSOs in driving down crime?

What performance indicators on your BCU do you directly affect? How 'effective and efficient' do you think PCSOs are in their contribution to Neighbourhood Policing?

### 2.8.3.6  Reponses to criticism of PCSOs

What should you do if you encounter some or any of the criticisms which we have looked at above? There are a number of tactics which you can use. The most obvious is to ignore the sniping and carry on doing your job as well as you can. Another tactic is to ensure that *your* work is singled out for praise because you have indeed 'gone the extra mile'. Again, you can use feedback from the community to evidence your effectiveness (you will be collecting all of this to demonstrate that you continue to meet the NOS Competences), ensuring that good news stories get as much prominence as the bad ones. You could use some of the statistics we have referred to, from West Yorkshire (2004), Kent (2005), the national evaluation study (2006), and the 2008 NPIA Review as well as Paterson and Pollock in 2011; or Sutherland in 2014 to prove that **the popularity and effectiveness of PCSOs is growing exponentially year by year**. ACPO Guidance states that '*the fundamental role of a PCSO is to contribute to neighbourhood policing, primarily through highly visible patrol in order to reassure the public, increase public order and be more accessible to communities and partner agencies at the local level*'. Home Office findings confirm that PCSO activity corresponds well with ACPO Guidance, since PCSOs spend the majority of their time being highly visible within the community, dealing with minor offences, and supporting front-line policing.

Ultimately, it is by *your* effectiveness that you will prove the doubters wrong. You can probably empathize now with those first women police officers struggling to be taken seriously by their male colleagues. Then and subsequently, the female officers were patronized, belittled, ignored, or expected only to deal with lost children and female suspects. Seldom were they seen as police officers who could handle whatever was thrown at them. The same unthinking prejudice is founded on insecurity and a lack of understanding about what PCSOs do.

### 2.8.4  **Weather the storm**

The message we want to leave you with is a simple one: if you encounter hostility at work from your police colleagues, it is likely to be from ignorance of your role and its value. As long as you have the support of your neighbourhood colleagues, and the community you serve, you can safely ignore the sniping from the side-lines. Most NPTs staunchly support the work of their PCSO colleagues and would not be without them. The criticism will diminish in time. After all, the Police Federation finally admitted women to membership in 1948, only fifty years after female police officers began service. Maybe, by 2052...?

---

**Knowledge Check 7**

1. What might be included in the 'wider police family'?

2. Which union represents PCSOs?

3. Where was it shown that PCSOs are 'more accessible' than police officers?

4. To what two outcomes do PCSOs contribute?

---

## 2.9 The Criminal Justice System in England and Wales: Magistrates' Courts, Crown Courts, and Coroners' Courts

You will almost certainly have visited a court to watch what happens as part of your initial training as a PCSO. You might have been able to visit a **Crown Court** (see 2.10) where criminal trials take place, or a **coroner's court**, which is convened (usually) to determine how someone died, but it is more likely that you attended a **magistrates' court**. You may be familiar from your local paper or news broadcasts with the role of the magistrates' court (the fines and appearances there of local people fill many column inches in local newspapers, or air time for local radio and TV, for example). The Crown Court deals with serious criminal cases, and will attract national media attention sometimes. We're going to discuss now how these courts and the appeals processes in criminal law make up the **criminal justice system** of England and Wales.

### 2.9.1 **Magistrates' court**

This is the lowest level of '**judicial process**' (meaning *the working of the law*) in England and Wales and the first court for any criminal proceedings. Magistrates are ordinary, worthy, local people who apply to become magistrates and who are given some minimal training in the law. At the end of this process and after 'sitting' in judgement for a time, they are appointed by the Lord Chancellor on behalf of the Crown and are then styled as **Justices of the Peace or JPs**. Such people are **lay magistrates**—they do not get paid—and usually work part-time as a civic duty. If you talk to magistrates you will often find that they are experienced, mature people who are as concerned about society and community as anyone else, and that they have a strong sense of communal duty, keen to 'put something back' into the society which nurtured them.

### 2.9.1.1 Unpaid magistrates

This is all very good and very laudable, and we can be proud that the amateur tradition which has persisted in our justice system for a thousand years is still going strong. But the sorts of people who can become magistrates and devote time to hearing cases during the working day, are either those who have retired or those who do not have to work. A *very* small number of the current magistracy in England and Wales also have full-time jobs. It's possible to juggle full or part-time jobs with the demands of sitting as a lay magistrate, but it isn't easy and not many do it.

---

**DISCUSSION POINTS**

Why should it matter that magistrates are drawn from those who don't work or who have retired?

Shouldn't we be grateful that people want to do it at all?

---

### 2.9.1.2 Some responses

Of course, we should be grateful that ordinary people volunteer to give up their time to assist the community. This is not just a carping from the side-lines about people who can afford the time to sit as magistrates, but a concern about how representative they may be of the community. If the magistracy is drawn overwhelmingly from the white majority and professional occupations (which they are), what kind of handle will such people have on the tensions and problems of, for example, minority ethnic communities? How well will they understand the boredom of young people with nowhere to meet and nowhere to let off their exuberant energy? We are *not* saying that there is a permanent barrier of incomprehension between magistrates and those upon whom they sit in judgement, but we are saying that there is a danger that drawing magistrates from a rather restricted stratum of society may lead to their being unrepresentative.

### 2.9.2 Stipendiary magistrates

There exists a kind of compromise between the points we have been making above and the higher courts, and that is the **stipendiary magistrate**, now more commonly called 'District Judge'. 'Stipendiary' means that the office holder receives a '*stipend*' or payment. In other words, the stipendiary magistrate (District Judge) is paid and is always a person trained in the law. The incumbent could have been either a solicitor or barrister, but his or her experience of practising law, for at least seven years, is a prerequisite. The stipendiary magistrate usually sits alone in judgement, whereas lay and unpaid magistrates usually sit in a panel or 'bench' of three, but there can be any combination between two and seven. Lay magistrates are always advised on matters of law by the **magistrates' clerk**, who is also a paid professional lawyer with at least five years' experience of practising law. In most magistrates' courts, the Clerk sits immediately in front of the bench of magistrates, and in some courts the Clerk will wear a black gown, even a little wig made of horsehair. It is worth noting that, as a professional lawyer, the stipendiary magistrate is likely to be even less representative of society at large than the lay magistracy, but the public appears to care less about the stipendiary District Judge, probably because s/he is paid and therefore a 'servant of the state', than about those who volunteer to become JPs and who cost us very little. It is a characteristic hypocrisy which underlies much to do with public justice.

### 2.9.2.1 **Role of magistrates**

Magistrates make judgements about guilt or innocence in **petty offences**. These are offences which, characteristically, attract fines or community service rather than imprisonment. This has caused controversy, because magistrates are concerned about what they see as increased police use of fines at the expense of the 'transparency of justice' in the magistrates' court. The police use of summary fines is reported to extend now to some forms of violent behaviour, but a proposal by the Justice Ministry in February 2009 to add a further 21 offences which were to be punishable by fines (including 'drunken and yobbish behaviour on trains') was withdrawn after strong protests from the magistracy.

There are no juries in a magistrates' court, so the judgment is handed down from the 'bench'. Accused people can be defended in a magistrates' court, usually by a solicitor. However, it is entirely normal for the accused not to be represented by a lawyer. There is a high incidence of 'guilty' pleas in a magistrates' court. If you expect the clash of styles and approaches between defence and prosecution in a magistrates' court, familiar from many a hackneyed television or film dramas, you will be disappointed. Proceedings in the real world are often brisk, often low-key and undramatic, and most offences are dealt with **summarily**, that is, there and then without fuss. A developing area is to create a 'virtual' magistrates' court, where defendants will lose their right to have a courtroom hearing and physically to appear in court. Instead, video links between a police station and a magistrates' court are designed to speed up 'summary justice'. Young people, the mentally impaired, and any case involving more than one defendant, are currently excluded from the 'virtual hearing' process. A trial scheme was set up in 2009 and one case, involving a guilty plea to drink-driving, meant that the individual concerned was fined and banned from driving, merely hours after he was arrested. The process means that a person pleading guilty to an offence in future can be sentenced on the spot.

#### 2.9.2.2 'If it ain't broke ...'

Our view is that, although sometimes the magistracy creaks at the seams, and although the magistrates themselves (and certainly the lay ones) ought to be drawn from a wider cross-section of the community, and although their judgments may reflect society's current prejudices rather than some dispassionate concept of the law; the system works pretty well and it is difficult to think of anything as effective to replace it. We know of no system so obviously superior that it could substitute for or replace our magistracy or 'lower court', and we are likely to have something very like the present system and process for many years to come. That's not to say that it should be above reform, though.

### 2.9.3 **Referral to the Crown Court**

The magistrates' court plays other very important roles that we have not yet considered. All criminal cases, however serious, must come first to the magistrates' court for assessment of the weight of evidence (we discuss evidence at 5.2). This is often called the '**preliminary hearing**' or '**committal hearing**'. What this means in practice is that the magistrates ( stipendiary District Judge) will consider the evidence of the serious crime and listen to what the police or the Crown Prosecution Service (CPS) lawyers and any defence lawyers have to say about the charges and about bail for the accused. The accused may 'reserve defence' against the charge at this stage, and make no statement or admission to the court.

#### 2.9.3.1 **Bail**

The magistrate(s) will then refer, or 'commit', the case to be heard at the Crown Court, and make a determination about bail. The police will often oppose bail if they believe that the offender may offend again, or abscond (run away), or disappear. If their case is strong enough, the magistrates will remand the accused in custody. Alternatively, the magistrates may release the accused on bail or against a '**surety**' or bond of money. Occasionally this brings the amateur status of lay magistrates into sharp conflict with the police or CPS, where the former may be seen (in prosecution eyes) as too lenient or too trusting. Magistrates for their part sometimes regard the police or CPS as over-zealous about keeping people in prison while the case is prepared. You are unlikely to go to Crown Court as a PCSO; nonetheless you should know how the system works.

### 2.9.4 **Other roles for magistrates**

Some cases may take a year or more to come to trial; this can be a long time for a person to spend on remand in prison, given that the case against him or her has not been proved. Each case is considered on its own merits: for example, it is unlikely that a person accused and charged with a crime of great violence would be granted bail, but a person charged with a theft might be. The magistrates will determine which course to take, and often decide at committal, when the accused has to be returned to court for checks on the case's progress. Before we leave magistrates, there are a couple of minor but police-relevant duties that magistrates perform, of which you should at least be aware. These are the **attestation** of a police constable (the administering of the oath or affirmation which a constable makes in order to receive full warranted powers) and the signing of some arrest or search **warrants**. This makes the entry to property, or searches, legally permissible. Such warrants are usually for specific persons, specific buildings, or places and are valid for a specified time.

### 2.9.5 'Habeas corpus'

An arrested person, under the **Police and Criminal Evidence Act 1984** (PACE 84), must be charged and brought before a magistrate within 48 hours of his or her arrest (though the term may be varied by a senior police officer on short extension bases). This is the principle which you will often hear mentioned, called **habeas corpus**. This is Latin, meaning 'having or possessing the body'; in other words it is producing to be seen the person charged. It is a very old right of the accused, and goes back to mediaeval times. It was designed to prevent unlawful imprisonment, or stopping what we would now call 'detention without trial'. People who are not charged must be released (unless subject to the obscure terrorist-holding powers of the Home Secretary, which are in dispute anyway). You should equally be aware that human rights legislation (the right to a fair trial) is also in effect here: **it is a serious business to arrest and detain another person.** That person's welfare is important to the courts. Those with powers of arrest must exercise those powers responsibly and in a proportionate and justified way. And that means you, when you exercise your (admittedly more limited) powers to detain—so the safeguard of **habeas corpus** isn't academic.

## 2.10 **The Crown Court**

Sometimes referred to (wrongly) by the old name of 'County Court' and even sometimes as the much older '*Circuit Court*', the Crown Court is usually located on two or three sites throughout each county or shire. There will be at least one Crown Court in each major city. There is something inherently dramatic in the Crown Court setting, which is so much more majestic (deliberately so) than the magistrates' courts: the judge, robed and throned above the court; the prosecution and defence lawyers in gowns and wigs; the dark, formal dress of the court officials; the presence of uniformed escorts to the accused; the appearance, in 'not guilty' pleas, of a jury of twelve men and women; the wood panelling of the court and royal coat of arms on the wall behind the judge; the solemnity and ceremony; the often old-fashioned language (including Latin) and the confrontation between prosecution and defence; the sometimes brutal, always probing, questions to witnesses and victims; the questioning of the accused; the tensions whilst the jury considers its verdict; these are all elements of high drama. Some critics argue that the absurd melodrama of seventeenth-century costumes and wigs has no part in a modern criminal justice process. Indeed, in some cases such as those involving child witnesses, judges and barristers can and do remove their wigs. Nonetheless, the experience of appearing in a Crown Court is daunting for the average adult; it must be surreal to a child.

### 2.10.1 Functions of the Crown Courts

**The Crown Court tries criminal cases**. As noted above, such cases are always handled by a judge, who will have been appointed from within the legal profession (that is, usually having practised as a barrister or, more rarely, a solicitor). Judges begin as Recorders before progressing to 'Circuit' judges and then to High Court judges. Broadly, judges oversee proceedings in the Crown Court, usually giving considerable latitude to prosecution and defence lawyers, and direct the jury when law becomes complex or ambiguous. Judges sum up a criminal trial and, if a jury finds the defendant guilty, will pronounce sentence (how long the offender will be kept in prison). Judges are by no means unchallenged. Should the judge's summing up seem to have prejudiced the jury, the defence may appeal. The defence may also appeal against a sentence (though this can be fraught, because sentences can now be increased as well as decreased) or against some aspect of the trial which it perceives the judge to have mishandled. Appeals go formally to the Court of Appeal, and appeals from there go to the Supreme Court (opened in October 2009), where they are heard by the Law Lords. We have designed, at figure 2.3 a schematic of the various 'levels' of criminal justice in England and Wales (remember that Scotland and Northern Ireland are different).

### 2.10.2 The adversarial criminal justice system

The criminal justice system followed in the UK is usually called the 'adversarial' system. An 'adversary' is an opponent, and this reflects what happens, especially in criminal trials (but also in libel cases and in some defamation cases). The prosecution sets out to prove ('beyond reasonable doubt') that Person X committed the crime of which s/he stands accused. The prosecution case (determined as to viability not by the police but by the CPS) will use police and witness evidence to prove that the crime was committed, and that the person charged with the crime committed it. This will be opposed by Person X's defence team, if Person X has pleaded 'not guilty' to the charge. The defence team will do everything it can to show that Person X not only did not commit the crime, but could not have committed the crime. All this is part of the defence tactic to have the case dismissed, discredited, or made doubtful. The principle of 'beyond reasonable doubt' is precious in British law (though Scotland can return a jury verdict of 'not proven'), because the adversarial process is founded on the **presumption of innocence**. Indeed, critics of the adversarial system point to the deviousness of defence tactics in undermining a criminal prosecution. Sir David Phillips, a former Chief Constable of Kent and a past President of ACPO, is reported to have said: '*The purpose of a trial is to find out the truth. But we no longer have trials about who did it—the trial is always about whether somebody broke the rules in trying to find out who did it.*'

**Figure 2.3  Simplified diagram of the criminal justice processes in England and Wales**

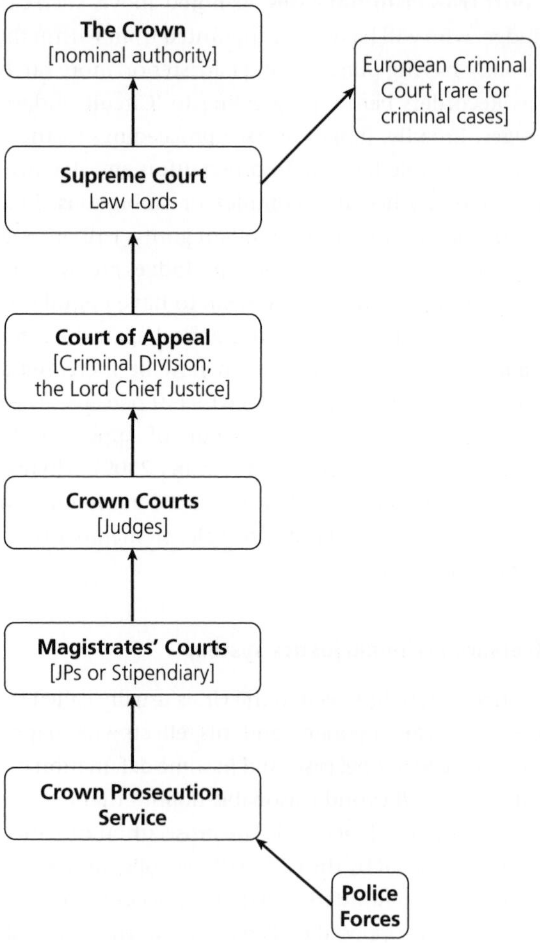

### 2.10.2.1 Court procedures and appearances

You will often hear people, particularly police officers, speaking bitterly about defence tactics and the 'artificial' tricks and ploys of a criminal justice system which is based on two sides slogging it out in court. You may even have to deal with witnesses who have been subject to such ploys. It's hard to remain impartial when you see people who have been confused, bewildered, bamboozled into contradicting themselves, or whose testimony is undermined by a resourceful (if unscrupulous) defence lawyer. However, you have to try to see this as business and nothing personal. This is not to say that the process is a game, far from it. It can be the most serious thing in the world to the family of an abused child, or to a woman accused of her partner's murder. However, since the CPS lawyers, criminal barristers, and defence counsel are doing this sort of thing all the time, they become so detached and objective that it can seem indeed a game to those who come for the first time, or who are emotionally traumatized by what has happened to them, watching the point-scoring or the unpleasantly deliberate attack on witness credibility or character. In practice, you are unlikely to go to a Crown Court as a PCSO, but you may have to deal with the confusion and frustration that witnesses or victims may feel about the experience. Study this section then, so that you can explain what goes on.

## 2.11 **Human Rights**

### 2.11.1 **The police role in supporting human rights**

The concept of human rights and the responsibilities of police officers in the preservation and maintenance of those rights runs throughout this book. Tuition in human rights should certainly have formed part of your initial training as a PCSO. At this stage, it is perhaps worth noting that the legislation concerning human rights marked a significant change towards an emphasis on rights ('you shall') rather than the usual focus of the law on prohibition ('you shall not'). By this we mean that most laws, until recently, **defined what constitutes wrongdoing** and how law enforcers and the criminal justice system should respond to this wrong-doing. Human rights legislation by contrast stresses an individual's entitlement to expect certain fundamental rights as part of the social contract between the person and the State and other forms of authority. **The Human Rights Act 1998** is the prime example. It falls to public authorities such as the police (and by extension, to a PCSO as a member of that police service), to maintain the fundamental rights of all individuals who come into contact with that authority.

### 2.11.2 **Origins of the concept of protecting human rights**

The roots of the Human Rights Act 1998 are to be found in a set of Articles containing rights, agreed by the **European Convention for the Protection of Human Rights and Fundamental Freedoms** (often referred to more briskly as 'the Convention' or in written form as the ECHR), which came into force in 1953 as part of the reconstruction of Europe after the Second World War, and was itself derived from the declaration of the United Nations of the principles of human freedom.

There are two main features of human rights legislation:

**First**, all new statute law must be compatible with the rights.

**Secondly**, an individual may take a public authority to a UK court if the authority has not acted in a manner compatible with the rights.

### 2.11.3 **What are the rights?**

These are normally described in terms of the 'Article number'.

| Article number | Article title |
|---|---|
| 2 | Right to life |
| 3 | Prohibition of torture |
| 4 | Prohibition of slavery and forced labour |
| 5 | Right to liberty and security |
| 6 | Right to a fair trial |
| 7 | No punishment without law |
| 8 | Right to respect for private and family life |
| 9 | Freedom of thought, conscience, and religion |
| 10 | Freedom of expression |
| 11 | Freedom of assembly and association |
| 12 | Right to marry |
| 14 | Prohibition of discrimination |
| 16 | Restriction on the political activities of aliens |
| 17 | Prohibition of the abuse of rights |
| 18 | Limitation on use of restrictions on rights |

(You may be wondering what has happened to Articles 1, 13, and 15. These refer merely to technical aspects of the adoption of the European Convention.)

### 2.11.4 **The three types of Convention rights within the Act**

There are three types of convention rights within the Human Rights Act 1998: absolute, limited, and qualified rights. We examine each in turn but this is only a summary.

#### 2.11.4.1 **Absolute rights**

Within these rights, the interests of the community as a whole cannot restrict the rights of the individual in any way. They are 'absolute'.

| Article number | Article title |
| --- | --- |
| 2 | Right to life |
| 3 | Prohibition of torture |
| 4 | Prohibition of slavery and forced labour |
| 7 | No punishment without law |

#### 2.11.4.2 **Limited rights**

These rights are not absolute because the articles are 'limited'.

| Article number | Article title |
| --- | --- |
| 5 | Right to liberty and security |
| 6 | Right to a fair trial |

An example of a limitation is in Article 5; the *right to liberty and security* does not apply if the detention is lawful as a result of six listed arrest situations and is carried out in the manner set down by law. One of these circumstances, for example, is when the arrest is made to ensure 'the detention of a minor by lawful order for the purpose of educational supervision or his lawful detention for the purpose of bringing him before the competent legal authority'.

Article 5 is of particular note for the PCSO. As we discuss in Chapter 3, you have powers to detain a person, using reasonable force if necessary, and for up to 30 minutes for one or more of a specified number of reasons.

#### 2.11.4.3 **Qualified rights**

These rights contain circumstances in which interference with them by the public authority is permissible if it is in the public interest and can be qualified; for example to prevent disorder or crime, for public safety, or for national security.

| Article number | Article title |
| --- | --- |
| 8 | Right to respect for private and family life |
| 9 | Freedom of thought, conscience, and religion |
| 10 | Freedom of expression |
| 11 | Freedom of assembly and association |

However, a public authority (such as the police) may only interfere with one of these qualified rights under one of three circumstances:

- The interference is lawful and must form part of existing common or statute law (see 3.2) such as the power to stop and search
- The interference is made for one of the specifically listed permissible acts in the interests of the public so as to prevent disorder or crime for public safety
- The interference is necessary in a democratic society because the wider interests of the community as a whole often have to be balanced against the rights of an individual, but it must be proportionate, not excessive, heavy-handed, or over the top.

### 2.11.4.4 Applying the Human Rights Act to community and neighbourhood policing

You may need to ask yourself the following questions in relation to any individual or group before you 'interfere' with their qualified rights:

- Are my actions **lawful**? Is there a common or statute law (such as the Police Reform Act 2002) to support my interference with a person's rights?
- Are my actions **permissible**? Am I permitted to interfere with a person's rights because it is in support of a duty such as the preventing of crime?
- Are my actions **necessary**? Do the needs of the many outweigh the needs of the few: in other words, must I take into account the interests of the community and balance one individual's rights against another's?
- Are my actions **proportionate**? Having considered everything, will my actions be excessive or could they be less intrusive and more in proportion to the outcome I need to achieve?

### 2.11.4.5 Human rights and the context of policing

A final point we might make about the importance of human rights in the context of policing, and specifically in the context of your work as a PCSO, is that you should always uphold such rights, never gratuitously infringe them. Occasionally you must interfere with an individual's rights where that person has adversely affected the needs of the many in our communities. No one has any 'right' to make the lives of others miserable, nor to impose his or her 'anti-social' behaviour upon others. You have a role to uphold the law, as do your police colleagues. You are often the last protection of the vulnerable or the last hope of the weak. The debate is yet to be properly aired in Britain of **whether the price of security is the erosion of liberty**. We look to human rights legislation to ensure that the balance is kept.

## Knowledge Check 8

1. What is the purpose of a coroner's court?

2. What are JPs?

3. What is a 'stipendiary magistrate' or District Judge?

4. What are 'petty offences'?

5. Which piece of legislation attempted to make uniform the sentencing of offenders?

6. What is 'committal'?

7. What does *habeas corpus* mean?

8. Who handles cases at the Crown Court?

9. Name and date the British legislation which incorporates The European Convention for the Protection of Human Rights and Fundamental Freedoms.

10. What is Article 6?

11. What are the three types of 'rights'?

# 3

# Knowledge and Skills

# 3.1 **Introduction**

This chapter looks in detail at the knowledge you will need to have in order to carry out the range of PCSO duties. No one will expect you to be able to do everything straight away. Indeed, it is more important at this stage that you understand 'why?' rather than understand 'how?'. 'How?' comes with practice and experience (see Chapter 4), 'why?' comes with knowledge and understanding. We concentrate most of our attention on a very substantial piece about your **General Duties and Powers,** covering each of the powers which may be conferred by your Chief Constable to PCSOs. You must remember that not all chief constables confer all powers, not all the designated powers available will come to you (it will depend on what you do), and that, although there is agreement on what a PCSO's 'standard 20 powers' should be, there is still some controversy and debate surrounding the Designation of other powers. We will task you to go and find out what PCSOs' designated powers are in your Force, and for the particular role you will be undertaking. Let's start with your legal status.

## 3.1.1 **Your legal status**

Your legal status derives from two sources: the first, as we have seen, is the Designation of powers from your Chief Constable (usually endorsed by your Police and Crime Commissioner, whose employee you are—as distinct from a police officer who is a 'Crown servant'), and the second derives, ultimately at least, from the Police Reform Act 2002 (which we abbreviate throughout as PRA02). We looked at Designation and what that entails in 2.6, so it is the second element, your status as derived from primary legislation, which we shall look at now.

### 3.1.1.1 **Police Reform Act provisions**

The Police Reform Act of 2002 was something of a 'catch-all' Act, which swept up a number of issues, ranging from the establishment of the Independent Police Complaints Commission (IPCC), the body which oversees and investigates complaints against the police in England and Wales, including the investigation of police shootings, through to clarification of the remit of the Ministry of Defence Police, notes on Mayor's Office for Policing and Crime housing, and the powers of the Secretary of State to make orders and regulations. Sandwiched in between all this is *Schedule 4*, dealing with Police Powers, of which a short part is to do with PCSOs (if you are really interested: principally Chapter 1 and sections 48–61 of Chapter 2). This can be a little confusing for people coming to PRA02 for the first time and expecting to find some sort of specific statement about the status, definition, and remit for PCSOs. Such language is not there.

### 3.1.1.2 **Designation**

Let's start by looking at the relevant parts of Schedule 4, Chapter 1 on police powers. Section 38, subsection (1), notes that '*the chief officer of police of any police force may designate any person who a) is employed by the Police and Crime Commissioner for that force and b) is under the direction and control of that chief officer, as an officer of one or more of the descriptions specified in subsection (2).'*

Section 38, subsection (2), goes on to specify that:

... the description of officers are [*sic*] as follows—
a) community support officer
b) investigating officer
c) detention officer
d) escort officer.

---

**DISCUSSION POINT**

What seems to you to be significant about the power granted to the chief officer (Chief Constable or Commissioner) in subsection (1) of section 38?

---

Whilst these two sections enable a chief officer to designate you and your colleagues, they actually give that chief officer a great deal more latitude than simply investing you with the powers that we are going to examine in detail in 3.2.

### 3.1.1.3 The importance of the PCC

We noted briefly above that an important phrase in the Act is *'employed by the Police and Crime Commissioner (PCC)'*, because all **police staff** are employed by the PCC. The PCC role was first defined by the Conservative Party in 2005, drawing on similar roles in the USA. The first elections to the posts, one for each force in England and Wales outside London, were held in November 2012. The role of the PCC is to oversee the efficient, effective, and economical work of the individual police force and, as far as is possible, to reflect the wishes and priorities of the communities which the force serves. That said, PCCs have no formal powers over operational police decisions, deployments, or what is or is not investigated, nor can the PCC set more than the most general and strategic priorities for chief officers. But it would be a bold (or foolish) chief constable who ignored the express wishes of his or her PCC particularly since the PCC has the power to 'hire and fire' the chief constable.

### 3.1.1.4 Doing your duty

That said, the second part of subsection (1) contains an important statement about where authority lies and refers to 'any person who b) is under the direction and control of that chief officer'. What *'under the direction and control'* means in effect is that you are expected to perform to the expected professional standards for a PCSO. You will be expected to adhere to Force ethical norms and standards (see 1.5), to carry out your duties diligently and with proper expertise and skill, and to conform to Force priorities and operational orders (rather than going off and doing what you feel like). You are expected to behave as one entrusted with a public office should behave: honourably, fairly, without discrimination (without prejudice), always demonstrating high levels of skill and knowledge. Also it means that once you are Designated as a PCSO within your Force, the Designations have legal status, and therefore so do you, as long as you are in uniform and on duty. Subsection (4) of section 38 of PRA02 specifies that:

> ...'a chief officer of police...shall not [D]esignate a person
> ...unless [s/he] is satisfied that the person—
> (a) is a suitable person to carry out the function
> (b) is capable of effectively carrying out those functions and
> (c) has received adequate training in the carrying out of those functions and in the exercise and performance of the powers and duties to be conferred on [him or her] by virtue of the [D]esignation.

You may like to refer to 2.6, which looked at Designation in more detail.

### 3.1.1.5 Definitions concerning the capability of a PCSO

We interpret this to mean that a chief officer need not Designate someone of whom s/he is not confident. '*Suitable*' means that someone who is a PCSO is expected to be a responsible citizen, to have a law-abiding profile, and not to have criminals of any kind as friends (instances have been known). '*Capable*' refers to having the required physical fitness and mental resilience to do the job properly. Default on either of these could lead in extreme cases to dismissal or, in less severe cases, to redeployment or withdrawal of designated powers. The important thing is that you have been adequately trained to do what is required of you. The training you receive has an implicit two-way contract. This requires the Force to make sure that you know what to do in most eventualities, and that you have the skills and knowledge to respond adequately in the few instances which cannot be foreseen or planned for. It is implicit that you will approach the training and acquisition of knowledge responsibly and with an eagerness to learn. It also means, of course, that you are trained in the primary role of being a PCSO, not a detention officer, or an investigating officer, or an escort officer, each of which roles requires separate and different skills training, even if some parts overlap with yours.

### 3.1.1.6 Derivation of your legal status as a PCSO

**We believe that it is really important for you to know from where you derive your legal status,** how your powers are vested in statute, and to whom you are responsible. People may ask you where your powers in law come from (and we look at this in 3.2) so it would be well if you were conversant with the Act which gave birth to your role and which specified the powers which your Chief Constable or (London) Commissioner has designated for it.

### 3.1.2 **Criminal law in brief**

Before you read (and learn) the next section (3.2 on PCSO powers), you should be aware of the 'headline' components of criminal law. In the summary table which follows, we introduce you to the basics.

| The Law in England and Wales | PCSOs have **street and life skills, knowledge**, and the **powers** vested in them by Parliament to give PCSOs the legal status to carry out their duties. |
|---|---|
| • **Statute law** (modern)<br>• **Common law** (ancient) | The law in England and Wales is split into two main areas, ancient and modern, or common law and statute law. **Statute law** includes Acts of Parliament that you may be familiar with, such as the Police Reform Act 2002 under which PCSOs were first introduced and given legal standing. **Common law** was not written down but was agreed by our ancestors as the expected behaviour of a civilized society, such as laws against theft or murder. Nearly all countries in Europe have 'common law', established by practice and custom, still in force. |
| • **Statute law** (primary and secondary legislation) | **Statute law** is legislation that is written down and provides the basis upon which the modern day legal system in England and Wales is founded. It consists of the creation of Parliamentary Acts (primary) and *subordinate* (secondary) legislation such as orders or regulations, for example in road signs and the offences committed if they are contravened. |
| **Acts of Parliament** (primary), eg<br>• *Police Reform Act 2002*: which introduced PCSOs<br>• *Road Traffic Act 1988*: most motoring offences | Government ministers take advice from professional public bodies such as the police and judges, as well as from surveys of public attitudes, as a result of which ministry officials are commissioned to begin the process of creating an Act of Parliament by drafting a *Bill* (an Act apart from its formal approval). The Bill is then put before both Houses of Parliament (Commons and Lords) for debate, modification, and acceptance (or defeat). |
| | If accepted ('passed'), it is placed before the monarch to receive Royal Assent, at which stage it becomes an **Act of Parliament.** Examples include: the Police Reform Act 2002, under which the role of PCSO was created and the Road Traffic Act 1984, under which a PCSO has the power to stop a vehicle on a road. |
| • **Subordinate** (secondary) legislation, eg Statutory Instruments | This is secondary legislation but has no less importance than its parental Act of Parliament in terms of meeting a perceived need in society. **Subordinate legislation** allows changes to be made to existing legislation by government ministers without having to go through the full parliamentary procedure. An example of this kind of legislation is called a **Statutory Instrument.** |

| | |
|---|---|
| • **Statutory Instruments** (SI) | Legislation that regularly requires updating, such as codes of practice, penalties, and alterations, can be made in the form of Orders, Regulations and Rules. Examples include The Removal and Disposal of Vehicles Regulations 2002 SI (**Statutory Instrument**) No 746, in which the Secretary of State, in exercise of the powers conferred upon him/her by sections 3 and 4 of the Refuse Disposal (Amenity) Act 1978, provided for the removal and disposal of vehicles. This power in turn is used by the PCSO to act within the neighbourhood to arrange for abandoned or burnt-out vehicles to be taken away. |
| • **Local byelaws** | Within towns and cities, local authorities are empowered to make **byelaws** in their areas to deal with local problems such as restrictions on parking, and the use of recreational areas and other public places. Byelaws are enforceable in the areas designated for their use and do not extend to surrounding borough areas unless stated. |
| • **Common law** (ancient) | Before Parliament began to make enactments, the law in England and Wales was common to everyone. No new **common law** is made these days but the laws remain in being, dealing with offences such as: <br> • Murder <br> • Manslaughter <br> • Perverting the course of justice. |
| **Case law:** <br> • Precedents set by decisions in court | Although common law is no longer made, 'precedents' are set through decisions by members of the judicial system such as judges. These are the result of legal arguments in court by the prosecution or defence counsel, or by appeals to higher judgement, and are written down as guidance to future court cases. These decisions are referred to as **case law.** |

## KEY POINT—CASE LAW

One such case law decision has a bearing on the evidence of identification of a suspect, for which you must learn the mnemonic ADVOKATE, as a result of the case of *R v Turnbull* [1976] 3 All ER 549. To decipher this legal 'coding', it is necessary to know that these abbreviations tell you where to find commentary on the case. It means that this case can be found in *Volume 3* of the *1976 All England Law Reports on page 549*. 'R' is an abbreviation for 'Regina' (the Crown as prosecutor, or 'Rex' when the monarch is a King), 'v' for 'versus' (against), and *Turnbull* is the name of the defendant.

## KEY POINT—ADVOKATE

**ADVOKATE** Stands for :

**A**  Amount of time under observation

**D**  Distance between witness and suspect

**V**  Visibility at the time

**O**  Obstructions to view

**K**  Known or seen before by the witness

**A**  Any reason to remember suspect (if only seen occasionally and not well known)

**T**  Time lapse between observation and subsequent identification to the police or to the PCSO

**E**  Error or material discrepancy between the description given to the police or to a PCSO and the actual appearance of the accused

---

**The classification of offences:**
- Summary
- Indictable offences:
  - Either Way
  - Indictable Only

Offences are classified according to their severity and impact on the community. Offences with less relative impact, such as those associated with minor aspects of road safety and public disorder, can only be dealt with at a magistrates' court and are referred to as **Summary offences.**

Another group of offences with a bigger impact can be tried either at a magistrates' court or a Crown Court, and are called **Either Way** offences, like theft. The third category of most serious offences can only be tried at a Crown Court and are referred to as **Indictable only** offences, as they are heard before a judge and jury. However, apart from classifications according to the location where offences are tried, there is another group heading required for a number of powers of investigation, such as arrest by a person other than a constable. This group includes *Either Way and Indictable only* offences and together they are called **Indictable offences.**

---

**Criminal liability:**
- **Criminal act (actus reus)**
- **Guilty mind (mens rea)**

To be found guilty of a criminal offence a suspect must not only carry out a criminal act (actus reus) but it must be also proved that the person did so with a guilty mind (mens rea). Evidence accumulated by an investigating officer will therefore include what the suspect was seen or heard to do by a witness in order to prove that the suspect committed an offence. In addition the suspect will be given an opportunity to explain his/her actions and what s/he was thinking at the time. The investigating officer, a police officer, or a PCSO will question the suspect on points to prove the offence.

---

**The Police and Criminal Evidence Act 1984:**
- **Codes of Practice (protection of individuals' rights)**

The judicial guidelines governing the treatment of suspects by an investigative authority (such as police officers or PCSOs) are contained in the Police and Criminal Evidence Act 1984, Codes of Practice. The Codes themselves are not binding and therefore it is not a criminal offence if the Codes are breached. However, the consequences of not applying them may lead a court to decide that the evidence placed before it is inadmissible. There are eight main sections ranging from Code A, the exercise of statutory powers of Stop and Search, to Code H, the detention of terrorism suspects. The most important code for PCSOs is Code C which involves the detention, treatment, and questioning of persons, for which strict guidelines must be followed.

| | |
|---|---|
| **Methods of disposal for a suspect:**<br>• **Punishment or education?**<br>• **Court hearing or no court hearing?** | Many people would argue that the only way to stop a person committing another offence is to punish that person; others see a need to educate the offender, so that the offence is not repeated. Either of these alternatives should lead to a change (reform) in the person and that is why both the courts and the investigative agencies of England and Wales have the power to apply penalties to people who break the law for minor offences. The aim is also to speed up the court processes. This may include a debate around discretion: the decision to charge or not to charge, to report or not report, exercised by a police officer or a PCSO, in the execution of their duty. There are some areas, of course, where discretion cannot be exercised, such as in serious or violent crime. |
| **Non-court appearance:**<br>• **Fixed penalty notices**<br>• **Penalty notices for disorder**<br>• **Police cautions**<br>• **Conditional cautions** | The fixed penalty notice system allows people who commit less severe offences, such as traffic-related crimes, the opportunity to pay a fixed fine instead of going to court. The 'penalty notices for disorder' scheme is similar and provides the opportunity to deal with people who have committed low-level public nuisance offences. Both schemes are designed to relieve the burden on administration and the courts, and both forms of notice may be issued under designated powers by a PCSO. A police caution is a formal warning given by a senior police officer to an adult who has admitted his/her guilt. A conditional caution may be given to an adult if the suspect agrees to comply with the conditions attached to it. Failure to comply with the conditions attached to any of the schemes will render the suspect liable to prosecution in court. |
| **Non-court appearance (juveniles):**<br>• **Reprimand**<br>• **Final warning** | A person under the age of 17 is referred to in law as a juvenile. A reprimand is a formal warning given to a juvenile by a police officer on admission of guilt of a first offence that is of a minor nature. A final warning is also a formal warning but in addition sets up a referral of the juvenile to the Youth Offending Team which can monitor the young person's future actions. |
| **Court appearance:**<br>• **Written charge and requisition**<br>• **Charge**<br>• **Arrest warrant** | If a decision is made to prosecute a suspect at court, criminal proceedings will be instituted by the issuing of a document called a written charge. At the same time a requisition will be issued which requires the person to appear before a magistrates' court to answer the written charge. These documents will then be served upon the person. For more serious offences, a suspect can be charged with an offence, which is a formal written accusation informing the suspect that s/he is to face a court appearance. A warrant is a written authority issued by a magistrate or a judge authorizing the persons named on the warrant to carry out the arrest of a person in order to place him/her before a court. |

| **Prosecution of offenders:** | In order to promote fairness and impartiality and to relieve the |
|---|---|
| • **The Crown Prosecution Service** | burden of responsibility on police authorities, the prosecution of suspects in courts is dealt with on behalf of the Crown (the State) by a government legal agency called the Crown Prosecution Service or CPS. Its responsibility is to take a case once it has been investigated by one of the investigative authorities (which include PCSOs) and present the case to a court (magistrates' court or Crown Court) for a decision on whether or not a suspect is guilty. CPS lawyers are professionally qualified in the law, like their defence team counterparts, but cannot command such high fees. The normal description of a CPS lawyer is one who acts 'pro bono publico'—'for the public good' rather than private gain. Much the same may be said of many defence lawyers who appear under the legal aid scheme. Recent reductions in the fees payable in criminal cases have caused controversy among defence and CPS lawyers alike. The Justice Ministry seems determined to reduce the cost of the legal aid bill (which of course is paid by the taxpayer). |

### 3.1.3 Summary

Although the law in England and Wales appears complicated and segmented, with a number of organizations holding different responsibilities, it is regarded throughout the world as one of the foremost examples of a criminal justice system. We may think sometimes that it creaks at the seams, that it is boringly nit-picking, and that it is both slow and ponderous, but the fairness and impartiality which should characterize any Criminal Justice System are perhaps more important than speed of resolution. The only alternative to the rule of law is anarchy, hence the strategic importance of the law as a hedge between society and tyranny, or order and chaos.

Time for a Knowledge Check on everything that you have looked at so far in this chapter:

### Knowledge Check 9

1. Where do your powers as a PCSO come from?

2. Who can 'hire and fire' a chief constable?

3. Your duties define you as 'any person who [...] is under the direction and control of that chief officer'. What does 'under the direction and control' mean?

4. In the context of your employment as a PCSO, what two things does 'capable' mean?

5. What is the difference between statute law and common law?

6. What is the distinction between primary and secondary legislation?

7. Where would a 'Summary Indictment' be heard?

8. Where could 'Either Way' be heard?

9. What is only heard at a Crown Court?

10. What two things must be proved for criminal guilt?

11. Which of the 'Codes' in the *Police and Criminal Evidence Act* 1984 (PACE) applies most directly to PCSOs?

12. What is a police caution?

13. Who, in law, is a 'juvenile'?

14. How are criminal proceedings instituted against a person once a decision to prosecute is made?

15. What does 'pro bono publico' mean?

## 3.2 **Powers and Duties of a PCSO**

This section is long and very thorough, and it shows you all the implications behind using each of the powers which your Chief Constable may have designated you to have. You may not have some powers; but as we do not know which they are and how your own particular Force parcels them out, and since your role and related powers may change, it's best to include all which you *could* have. We have omitted, however, those specialist powers that relate to an entirely separate function, such as that of being a traffic warden. We relate the exercise of your powers to practical examples, where possible. That is why it is important that you check carefully with your own Force to ascertain which of the 53 possible powers and (incorporated with them) the 20 'standard' powers you have been designated to have. You may be interested that the Home Secretary appears to be actively considering whether to extend PCSOs' powers in a bid 'to bolster neighbourhood policing'. At the time of writing, this was a consultation exercise with chief constables and police and crime commissioners and no formal announcements had been made about any augmentation of the basic powers 'suite' which PCSOs have. But it is entirely possible that through 'fast-track' legislation, your powers might change during the lifetime of this book.

We shall continue to offer short Knowledge Checks throughout the section, to help you 'fix' what you have read.

### 3.2.1 **Powers and duties in one section**

We're sorry that this is so long; we think that you are unlikely to read it through in one go, but rather dip in when you want to check your references and your understanding of a particular power. It is best to have all the Powers and Duties here in one section, to avoid you spending ages thumbing through to find a particular power.

### 3.2.1.1 'Standard powers': attempts to bring order to the variations

Before we discuss the powers themselves, we need to set the scene and illustrate some of the factors involved in PCSOs' powers. In 2005, the Home Office published a consultation paper entitled *Standard Powers for Community Support Officers and a Framework for the Future Development of Powers*; its purpose was to address inconsistencies in the Designation of PCSO powers as set out in Schedule 4 to the Police Reform Act 2002. As the Home Office succinctly put it, 'CSOs in different [police] forces can be designated with some of the available powers, all of the powers or occasionally none of the powers.'

### 3.2.1.2 ACPO's response

One of the more articulate responses came from the then-ACPO leader on PCSOs and Neighbourhood Policing Teams, Peter Davies, who noted that there must continue to be a distinction between what a PCSO does and what a police officer does, and that therefore the standard powers should reflect this. He went on to support the notion of a national set of minimum powers, but sounded a warning note that there was a danger of 'mission creep' if PCSOs were being asked more and more to take on roles traditionally ascribed to, or empowered through, police constables. ACPO itself deprecated this 'mission creep' (as did the Police Federation) because, they argued, PCSOs do not have the training to be able to do things that a warranted officer can do. Sensibly, Peter Davies made ACPO's position clear, when he said: 'The national set of powers **must not include powers that are coercive** or otherwise lead to a higher than normal risk of confrontation, of harm to persons, or of infringement of human rights.'

Extensions of a PCSO's powers can be counter-productive

ACPO and the Police Federation have shared a concern since the inception of PCSOs, that gradual (even surreptitious) extensions of PCSOs' powers would impinge on the proper role of a **warranted police officer** (that is, a police officer who has a constable's powers as granted under warrant). Not only would such extensions be subversive of a police officer's role, and indeed provide the 'policing on the cheap' gibe with some substance, but they would also run the risk of exposing the individual PCSO to a situation, especially a confrontational one, which s/he could not control and for which s/he was not trained (see Chapter 2). There seemed to be real and present dangers in confusing the two roles.

### 3.2.2 Powers for PCSOs

The following table sets out what the standard PCSO powers are and the legislation from which the powers derive.

| Power | Legislation |
|---|---|
| **Environmental Powers** | |
| Issue fixed penalty notices (FPNs) for dog fouling | Para 1(2)(c) of Schedule (Sch) 4 to *Police Reform Act 2002* (PRA02) |
| FPN for littering | Para 1(2)(d) of Sch 4 to PRA02 |
| FPN for graffiti/fly-posting | Para 1(2)(ca) of Sch 4 to PRA02, inserted by section 46 of the *Anti-Social Behaviour Act 2003* (ASBA03) |
| Remove abandoned vehicles | Para 10 of Sch 4 to PRA02, and under regulations made in section 99 of *Traffic Regulation Act 1984* |
| Transport powers | |
| FPN for cycling on a pavement | Para 1(2)(b) of Sch 4 to PRA02 |
| To stop cycles | Para 11A of Sch 4 to PRA02, inserted by section 89(3) of ASBA03 |
| Stop vehicles for testing, escort abnormal loads, and carry out road checks | Paras 11, 12, and 13 of Sch 4 to PRA02 |
| Require name and address for road traffic offences | Para 3A of Sch 4 to PRA02, inserted by para 6 of Sch 8 to *Serious and Organised Crime and Police Act 2005* (SOCAP05) |
| Direct traffic and place traffic signs | Para 11B of Sch 4 to PRA02, inserted by para 10 of Sch 8 to SOCAP05, and para 13A of Sch 4 to PRA02, inserted by para 11 of Sch 8 to SOCAP05 |
| Issue public notice for disorder (PND) for throwing fireworks, and trespassing and throwing stones on a railway | Section 80 of *Explosives Act 1875* and sections 55 and 56 of *British Transport Commission Act 1949* |
| Seize vehicles used to cause alarm | Para 9 of Sch 4 to PRA02 |
| Alcohol and tobacco powers | |
| Limited power to enter licensed premises | Para 8A of Sch 4 to PRA02, inserted by para 9 of Sch 8 to SOCAP05 |
| Enforce certain licensing offences (including sale of alcohol to person who is drunk, sale to children, etc) | Para 2(6A) of Sch 4 to PRA02, inserted by paras 3(3) and 3(8) of Sch 8 to SOCAP05 |
| Require persons drinking in designated area to surrender alcohol | Para 5 of Sch 4 to PRA02 |
| Require persons aged under 18 to surrender alcohol | Para 6 of Sch 4 to PRA02 |
| Search for alcohol and tobacco (using 'reasonable belief') | Para 7A of Sch 4 to PRA02, inserted by para 8 of Sch 8 to SOCAP05 |

### Alcohol and tobacco powers

| | |
|---|---|
| To seize tobacco from a person aged under 16 (and dispose of it) | Para 7 of Sch 4 to PRA02 |
| Seize drugs and require name and address for possession of drugs | Paras 7B and 7C of Sch 4 to PRA02, inserted by para 8 of Sch 8 to SOCAP05 |
| PNDs for sale of alcohol and consumption etc, all relating to persons under 18 | Sections 146(1), 150(1) and (2), and 151 all of *Licensing Act 2003* and section 12 of *Criminal Justice and Police Act 2001* |
| Issue PND for drunk and disorderly behaviour and drunk in highway | Section 91 of *Criminal Justice Act 1967* and section 12 of *Licensing Act 1872* |

### Powers to tackle anti-social behaviour

| | |
|---|---|
| Require name and address for anti-social behaviour | Para 3 of Sch 4 to PRA02, inserted by para 3(10) of Sch 8 to SOCAP05 |
| Deal with begging | Para 2(6)(ac) and 2(3B) of Sch 4 to PRA02 (see also paras 3(4), 3(5), 3(6), and 3(7) of Sch 8 to SOCAP05) |
| Disperse groups and remove persons under 16 to their place of residence | Para 4A of Sch 4 to PRA02, inserted by section 33 of ASBA03 |
| Issue PND for breach of fireworks curfew, possession of cat 4 firework, possession of excessively loud firework, etc | Fireworks Regulations 2004 under section 11 of *Fireworks Act* 2003 |

### Enforcement powers

| | |
|---|---|
| Require name and address for relevant offences | Para 1A of Sch 4 to PRA02, inserted by para 2 of Sch 8 to SOCAP05 |
| Issue FPN for truancy | Para 1(2)(aa) of Sch 4 to PRA02, inserted by section 23 of ASBA03 |
| Detain (up to 30 minutes for person believed to have committed a relevant offence) | Para 2 of Sch 4 to PRA02, inserted by para 3(2) of Sch 8 to SOCAP05 |
| Enforce byelaws | Paras 1A(3), 2(3A), 2(6)(ad), 2(6B), 2(6C), 2(6D), 2(6E), and 2(6F) of Sch 4 to PRA02; see paras 2, 3(4), 3(7), and 3(8) of Sch 8 to SOCAP05 |
| Photograph persons away from a police station | Para 15ZA of Sch 4 to PRA02, inserted by para 12 of Sch 8 to SOCAP05 |
| Search detained persons for dangerous items or items to assist escape | Para 2A of Sch 4 to PRA02, inserted by para 4 of Sch 8 to SOCAP05 |
| Use reasonable force to prevent a detained person making off | Para 4 of Sch 4 to PRA02 |

| Enforcement powers | |
| --- | --- |
| Use reasonable force to transfer control of detained persons | Paras 2(4A), 2(4B), 4(ZA), and 4(ZB) of Sch 4 to PRA02 (see paras 2, 3, and 4 of Sch 9 to SOCAP05) |
| Remove children in contravention of curfew notices to their place of residence | Para 4B of Sch 4 to PRA02, inserted by section 33 of ASBA03 |
| [Prevent or stop persons] destroying or damaging property, causing alarm, harassment or distress | Section 1(1) of *Criminal Damage Act 1971* and section 5 of *Public Order Act 1986* |
| [Issue a] PND for wasting police time, giving false report, false alarm, etc | Section 5 *Criminal Law Act 1967*, section 127(2) *Communications Act 2003*, and section 49 *Fire and Rescue Act 2004* |
| Use reasonable force | Section 38 of PRA02, but PCSO only has this power if a PC would have power to use reasonable force in same situation |

| Security powers | |
| --- | --- |
| Enter and search any premises for purposes of 'saving life and limb' or preventing damage to property. | Para 8 of Sch 4 to PRA02 |
| Stop and search in authorized areas (powers under *Terrorism Act 2000*) | Para 15 of Sch 4 to PRA02 |
| Enforce cordoned areas (again under section 36 of *Terrorism Act 2000*) | Para 14 of Sch 4 to PRA02 |

Let's briefly refresh what you have just studied:

## Knowledge Check 10

1. What sanction can you use against someone cycling on a pavement?

2. Give an example of when you might issue a Penalty Notice for Disorder (PND).

3. What power enables you to seize alcohol?

4. What do paras 7B and 7C of Schedule 4 of the Police Reform Act 2002 entitle you to do?

5. Which Act enables you to issue a penalty notice for disorder for 'drunk and disorderly behaviour'?

### 3.2.2.1 A formidable list of powers

Although it does not compare with a police officer's powers, or with the even greater powers of a customs officer, **you have up to 38 powers to detain, require,** enter, seize, demand, dispose of, and enforce a lot of things. It is one thing to have a range of powers, it is another to know when to use them and when to use your discretion, to know when to intervene and when to wait and watch. In the sections which follow, our principal aim is to help you in precisely these areas:

**What does the power mean? When do you use it? Why do you use it?**

### 3.2.2.2 Powers' layout

Your powers have been split into the following categories according to Home Office circular 033/2007: *those which are standard and those that are designated at the discretion of chief officers*, including the powers to issue penalty notices for disorder. Each of the powers is laid out in the same way. We give the power a **context** (when you might use it) and then **analyse the power, the circumstances** in which it can be used, **and the offence**(s) to which it relates. We hope that by presenting each power in tabulated form like this, it will be easier to look up and easier to absorb. However, you will still have to commit large parts of this to memory.

### 3.2.3 Standard powers

#### 3.2.3.1 Power to stop cycles, power to issue fixed penalty notices for cycling on a footpath

Context

If a designated PCSO has reason to believe that a cyclist has committed an offence of riding a cycle on a footpath, the PCSO has the power to require the cyclist to stop the cycle, to require his or her name and address, and to give a person a fixed penalty notice for riding on a footway as an alternative to conviction.

---

**Offence—Riding on a footway: s 72 Highway Act 1835**

---

Mode of trial and penalty: Summary—level 2 fine.

*Points to consider to prove the offence*

1. That the person on the cycle is riding purposefully, for example in and out of pedestrians, or taking a short cut, or avoiding riding on the road or pushing the cycle.
2. That the area in which the cycle is being ridden is identifiable as a footpath.
3. The name and classification of the road that the footpath borders.
4. That you made a note of the description of the suspect.
5. That you used ADVOKATE [see Key point] to evidence identification of the person.

---

## Power to stop cycles: s 163(2) Road Traffic Act 1988.*

[*To avoid lengthy repetition, we shall refer to the Road Traffic Act 1988 from this point forward as **RTA88**.]

*Circumstances under which the power can be used*

1. The cycle is being ridden on a road (includes a footpath).
2. You are in uniform and clearly make a request for the cyclist to stop.

### *Offence*—Failing to stop a cycle: s 163(2) RTA88

Mode of trial and penalty—Summary—level 3 fine.

*Points to consider to prove the offence*

1. All of the above.
2. That you were in uniform and clearly made a request for the cyclist to stop.
3. That you had reason to believe the cyclist was committing an offence of riding on a footpath.
4. That you made a note of the description of the cycle, rider, and direction of travel.
5. That you used ADVOKATE to evidence identification of the rider.

### *Offence*—Failing to give name and address when required: para 1A(5) of S4PRA02

Mode of trial and penalty—Summary—level 3 fine.

*Points to consider to prove the offence*

See **3.2.3.4: Failing to give name and address when required by a PCSO**, where the Points to Prove are itemized in respect of failing to give name and address when required.

### 3.2.3.2 Power to issue fixed penalty notices for littering

Context

If a designated PCSO has reason to believe that a person has committed an offence of littering, the PCSO has the power to require his or her name and address and issue him or her with a fixed penalty notice as an alternative to conviction.

---

**Offence—Littering: s 87 Environmental Protection Act 1990**

---

*Method of disposal:* Local authority fixed penalty notice.

*Mode of trial and penalty:* Summary—a fine not exceeding level 4.

**NB: Although this is an offence for which a lower tier penalty notice for disorder can be issued, a PCSO cannot issue a PND for this offence.**

*Points to consider to prove the offence*

1. That the littering took place anywhere in the area of a principal litter authority (eg a local authority).
2. That the littering took place in an area which is open to the air (eg the entrance to a large shopping complex but not a telephone box with a gap at the bottom of the door).
3. That the littering took place in an area to which the public have access with or without payment (not privately owned).
4. That the person threw down, dropped, or deposited any litter on land or in water and left it.
5. That the littering took place without being authorized by law and without the consent of the owner.

---

**Offence—Failing to give name and address when required: para 1A(5) of S4PRA02.**

---

*Mode of trial and penalty:* Summary—level 3 fine.

*Points to consider to prove the offence:*

See **3.2.3.4: Failing to give name and address when required by a PCSO**, where the Points to Prove are itemized in respect of failing to give name and address when required.

---

### 3.2.3.3 Power to issue fixed penalty notices in respect of offences under dog control orders

Context

If a designated PCSO has reason to believe that a person has committed a dog offence on any land for which a 'control of dogs' order has been made by a local authority, the PCSO has the power to require his or her name and address and issue him or her with a fixed penalty notice as an alternative to conviction.

---

**Offence—Fouling of land by dogs and the removal of dog faeces: provision of a dog control order s 55 of the Clean Neighbourhoods and Environment Act 2005.\***

---

[\*To avoid lengthy repetition, we shall refer to Clean Neighbourhoods and Environment Act 2005 from this point forward as **CNE05**.]

Refer to local authorities for local control order references.

*Points to consider to prove the offence:*

1. That the defecation took place on land subject to a control order which is open to the air on at least one side *'and to which the public are entitled or permitted to have access (with or without payment)'*.
2. Evidence of defecation by the dog, eg through observation by you or a witness using ADVOKATE to support evidence of identification.
3. Failure of the person in charge of the dog to remove the faeces from the land. Mitigating circumstances:
   - The person in charge of the dog has a reasonable excuse.
   - The person is registered as blind.
   - The owner, occupier, or authority of the land consents.
   - The person subsequently places the faeces in a suitable receptacle nearby.

---

**Offence—The keeping of dogs on leads: provision of a dog control order s 55 CNE05.**

---

Refer to local authorities for local control order references.

*Points to consider to prove the offence*

1. That the dog was not on a lead on land subject to a control order which is open to the air on at least one side *'and to which the public are entitled or permitted to have access (with or without payment)'*.
2. Evidence of the dog not wearing a lead, eg through observation by you or a witness using ADVOKATE to support evidence of identification.

---

**Offence—The exclusion of dogs from land: provision of a dog control order s 55 CNE05.**

---

Refer to local authorities for local control order references.

---

**The number of dogs which a person may take on to any land: provision of a dog control order s 55 CNE05.**

---

Refer to local authorities for local control order references.

*Points to consider to prove the offence*

1. That the dog was excluded from land subject to a control order which is open to the air on at least one side *'and to which the public [is] entitled or permitted to have access (with or without payment)'*.
2. Evidence that the dog was on the land, eg through observation by you or a witness using ADVOKATE to support evidence of identification.

---

**Offence—Failing to give name and address when required: para 1A(5) of S4PRA02.**

*Mode of trial and penalty:* Summary—level 3 fine.

*Points to consider to prove the offence:*

See 3.2.3.4: **Failing to give name and address when required by a PCSO,** where the Points to Prove are itemized in respect of failing to give name and address when required.

---

See also **Power to issue fixed penalty notices for dog fouling on designated land.**

## Knowledge Check 11

1. What can a PCSO do when someone commits the offence of cycling on a footpath?

2. What is the penalty level for failing to stop?

3. Which section of which Act of 1990 deals with the offence of littering?

4. What 'points to prove' include a requirement that the area of the offence 'is open to air' and is one 'to which the public have access'?

5. What can't a PCSO do about this offence?

6. What is the alternative to a conviction for failing to remove dog faeces from designated land?

7. Name two mitigations to the requirement to remove dog faeces from designated land.

8. What failure to cooperate with you might incur a level 3 fine?

9. How would you evidence identification of an offender?

### 3.2.3.4 Power to require name and address from a person who has committed a 'relevant offence', a 'relevant licensing offence', or who has offended against a 'relevant byelaw'

Context

A PCSO who is designated under para 1A of S4PRA02 has the power to require the name and address of a person who has committed a 'relevant offence', a 'relevant licensing offence', or has offended against a 'relevant byelaw'. Such a Designation can specify any number of 'relevant offences', 'relevant licensing offences', or 'relevant byelaws' and does not have to specify them all.

If the suspect fails to comply with the requirement, or gives a name and address which the PCSO reasonably suspects to be false or inaccurate, the suspect commits an offence.

If the PCSO is further designated under para 2, he/she may then detain the person and await the arrival of a police officer or request the suspect to accompany the PCSO to the police station (see 3.2.4.4).

If the PCSO is designated under para 4, he/she may use reasonable force during the detention of the suspect (see 3.2.4.4).

## Power to require name and address: para 1A of S4PRA02

*Circumstances under which the power can be used*

1. That you are designated under para 1A of S4PRA02.
2. That you had reason to believe that the person had committed a 'relevant offence', a 'relevant licensing offence', or offended against a 'relevant byelaw'.
3. That you required the person to give you his or her name and address.
4. That the place in which you made the requirement in relation to a 'relevant offence', a 'relevant licensing offence', or 'relevant byelaw' was one to which the offence or byelaw related.

## Definition of 'relevant offence': para 2(6) of S4PRA02

Any offence which is:

1. An offence for which a fixed penalty notice can be issued and includes:
   - Penalty notices for disorder, eg drunk and disorderly behaviour (see 3.2.5.1),
   - Fixed penalty notices for truancy (see 3.2.4.1),
   - Fixed penalty notices for riding a cycle on a footpath (see 3.2.3.1),
   - Fixed penalty notices for dog fouling (see 3.2.4.3),
   - Fixed penalty notices for graffiti or fly-posting (see 3.2.5.2),
   - Fixed penalty notices for litter (see 3.3.2),
   - Fixed penalty notices for offences under dog control orders (see 3.2.3.3).
2. An offence of knowingly contravening a direction given to disperse groups and remove persons under 16 to their place of residence (see 3.2.4.9).
3. An offence committed in a specified park (see 3.2.3.18).
4. An offence relating to begging (see 3.2.4.6).
5. An offence which is a 'relevant byelaw' (see 3.2.4.5).
6. An offence which appears to you to have caused:
   - 'injury alarm or distress to any other person, or
   - the loss of, or any damage to, any other person's property'.

### Definition of 'relevant licensing offence': para 2(6A) of S4PRA02.

Any of the following offences under the Licensing Act 2003, which are:

1. Selling or attempting to sell alcohol to a person who is drunk (PND), **s 141**.
2. Obtaining alcohol for a person who is drunk (not PND), **s 142**.
3. Selling alcohol to a person under 18 years (PND), **s 146(1)**.
4. Purchasing alcohol by a child (not PND), **s 149(1)(a)**.
5. Purchasing alcohol on behalf of a child (not PND), **s 149(3)(a)**.
6. Purchasing alcohol on behalf of a child for consumption on relevant premises (not PND), **s 149(4)(a)**.
7. Consuming alcohol by a person under 18 years (PND), **s 150(1)**.
8. Allowing a child under 18 years to consume alcohol (PND), **s 150(2)**.
9. Sending a child to obtain alcohol (not PND), **s 152(1)**.

(see 3.2.4.7 and 3.2.5.1 for details of the above offences).

### Definition of a 'relevant byelaw': para 2(6B)–(6F) of S4PRA02.

1. A byelaw included in a list of byelaws which have been made by a relevant body such as:
   - a county council,
   - a district council,
   - a parish council,
   - a London Borough Council, and
   - the chief constable of the police force for the area has agreed its inclusion in the list.
2. The list of 'relevant byelaws' must be published for the benefit of the general public.
3. The list may be amended by agreement with the chief constable and the relevant body, but the alterations must be published.
4. The agreement can also be made between the Secretary of State and the local chief constable (see 3.2.4.5 regarding your powers to enforce 'relevant byelaws').

### Offence—Failing to give name and address when required by a PCSO: para 1A(5) of S4PRA02.

*Mode of trial and penalty:* Summary—level 3 fine.

See 3.2.4.4 for details of your power to detain under PRA02.

*Points to consider to prove the offence*

1. That you were designated under para 1A of S4PRA02.
2. That you had reason to believe that the person had committed one of the offences for which you can require the suspect to give his/her name and address.
3. That you were in uniform and clearly made a request for the person's name and address because you had reason to believe s/he had committed one of the offences for which you can require the suspect to give his/her name and address.
4. That you made a note of the description of the suspect.
5. That you used ADVOKATE to evidence identification of the person.

### 3.2.3.5  Power to require name and address for anti-social behaviour

Context

A designated PCSO under para 3 of S4PRA02 has the same power as a police officer under s 50 PRA02 to require any person s/he believes to have been acting in an anti-social way to give his or her name and address.

If the suspect fails to comply with the requirement or gives a name and address which the PCSO reasonably suspects to be false or inaccurate, the suspect commits an offence.

If the PCSO is designated under para 2, s/he may then detain the person and await the arrival of a police officer or request the suspect to accompany the PCSO to the police station (see 3.2.4.4).

If the PCSO is designated under para 4, s/he may use reasonable force during the detention of the suspect (see 3.2.4.4).

### Power to require name and address for anti-social behaviour: para 3(1) of S4PRA02.

*Circumstances under which the power can be used*

1. That you are designated under para 3.
2. That you are in uniform.
3. That you have reason to believe that the person:
   - was acting previously, or
   - is acting at the time

   in an anti-social manner (causing or 'likely to cause harassment, alarm or distress to one or more persons not of the same household as [him/herself]'.
4. That you required the person to give you his/her name and address.

> **Offence—Failing to give name and address when required by a PCSO: para 1A(5) of S4PRA02.**

*Mode of trial and penalty:* Summary—level 3 fine.

See 3.2.4.4 for details of your power to detain under PRA02.

Points to consider to prove the offence:

- See 3.2.3.4: **Failing to give name and address when required by a PCSO**, where the Points to Prove are itemized in respect of failing to give name and address when required.
- If you are designated under para 4, you may use reasonable force during the detention of the suspect (see 3.2.4.4).

### 3.2.3.6 Power to require name and address for road traffic offences

Context

If designated, a PCSO has the power to regulate traffic and pedestrians in a road for the purposes of escorting a vehicle or trailer carrying a load of exceptional dimensions either to or from the relevant police area. If a driver or pedestrian fails to comply with the directions, a designated PCSO has the power to require them to give their name and address. If the suspect fails to comply with the requirement or gives a name and address which the PCSO reasonably suspects to be false or inaccurate, the suspect commits an offence.

If the PCSO is further designated under para 2, s/he may then detain the person and await the arrival of a police officer or request the suspect to accompany him/her to a police station (see 3.2.4.4).

If the PCSO is designated under para 4, s/he may use reasonable force during the detention of the suspect (see 3.2.4.4).

> **Power to require the name and address of a *driver* who refuses to comply with a traffic direction from a PCSO who is for the time being directing traffic and pedestrians for the purposes of escorting abnormal loads: s 165(1) RTA88.**

*Circumstances under which the power can be used*

1. That all of the criteria in 3.2.4.1 were satisfied.
2. That you are designated under para 3A of S4PRA02.
3. That you informed the suspect you had reasonable cause to believe they had neglected or refused to comply with traffic directions.
4. That you requested the name and address from the suspect.

> *Offence*—**Failing to give name and address when required by a PCSO: para 3A(2) of S4PRA02.**

*Mode of trial and penalty:* Summary—level 3 fine.

See 3.2.4.4 for details of your power to detain under PRA02.

*Points to consider to prove the offence*

See 3.2.3.4: **Failing to give name and address when required by a PCSO,** where the Points to Prove are itemized in respect of failing to give name and address when required.

---

**Power to require the name and address of a pedestrian who refuses to comply with a traffic direction from a PCSO, who is for the time being directing traffic and pedestrians, for the purposes of escorting abnormal loads: s 165(1) RTA88.**

*Circumstances under which the power can be used*

1. That all of the above criteria in 3.2.4.1 in relation to a pedestrian failing to comply with traffic directions were satisfied.
2. That you are designated under para 3A of S4PRA02.
3. That you informed the suspect you had reasonable cause to believe they had neglected or refused to comply with traffic directions.
4. That you requested the name and address from the suspect.

---

> *Offence*—**Failing to give name and address when required by a PCSO: para 3A(2) of S4PRA02.**

*Mode of trial and penalty:* Summary—level 3 fine.

See 3.2.4.4 for details of your power to detain under PRA02.

*Points to consider to prove the offence*

See 3.2.3.4: **Failing to give name and address when required by a PCSO,** where the Points to Prove are itemized in respect of failing to give name and address when required.

---

### 3.2.3.7 Power to require a person who is consuming alcohol in a designated place to stop drinking and to surrender the alcohol and its containers to a PCSO

Context

A designated PCSO has the power to require a person whom s/he believes is or has been consuming, or intends to consume alcohol in a designated public place, not to consume that alcohol and to surrender any alcohol or container for alcohol. If the person fails to comply with either of the requirements placed upon them, s/he commits an offence (see 3.2.5.1). The PCSO also has the power to dispose of the alcohol surrendered.

If the PCSO is further designated under para 7A(2) and the suspect fails to surrender his/her alcohol and/or container, the PCSO has the power to search the suspect. If the person fails to consent to being searched without reasonable excuse, s/he commits an offence and the PCSO may make a requirement for the suspect's name and address. If the suspect fails to comply with the requirement or gives a name and address which the PCSO reasonably suspects to be false or inaccurate, the suspect commits an offence. If the PCSO is further designated under para 2, s/he may then detain the person and await the arrival of a police officer or request the suspect to accompany the PCSO to the police station (see 3.2.4.4). If the PCSO is designated under para 4, s/he may use reasonable force during the detention of the suspect (see 3.2.4.4).

---

**Power to require a person consuming alcohol in a designated public place to stop drinking and to surrender the alcohol: s 12 CJP01.**

*Points to consider before using your powers*

1. That the area is designated.
2. That you believe the person:
   - is, or
   - has been consuming, or
   - intends to consume
   alcohol in the designated place.

*Your powers*

1. To require the person not to consume anything which is, or which you reasonably believe to be, alcohol.
2. To require the surrender of anything in the person's possession which is, or which you reasonably believe to be, alcohol or a container for alcohol (sealed or unsealed).
3. To dispose of anything surrendered to you in such manner as you consider appropriate (see your local policy for details).

---

**Power to search for alcohol/containers: para 7A(2) of S4PRA02.**

*Circumstances under which you can search*

1. That all the circumstances surrounding your power to seize alcohol from a person were satisfied.

2. That the person from whom you wanted to seize the alcohol/container had failed to surrender it to you.
3. That you reasonably believed s/he had alcohol/containers in his/her possession.

*Circumstances surrounding the search*

1. That you only search to the extent that is reasonably required to find the alcohol/containers.
2. That you cannot require a person to remove any of his or her clothing in public other than an outer coat, jacket, or gloves.
3. That, when you find what you are looking for, you can seize and dispose of it (see your local policy for disposal).

---

**Offence—A person who without reasonable excuse fails to consent to being searched is guilty of an offence: para 7A(5) of S4PRA02.**

*Penalty and mode of trial:* Summary—fine not exceeding level 3.

*Points to consider to prove the offence*

That, before you carried out the search, you informed the person that, without reasonable excuse, failing to consent to being searched is an offence.

---

**Offence—Requirement to give name and address: para 7A(7) of S4PRA02**

See 3.2.4.4 for details of your power to detain under PRA02.

*Requirement to give name and address*

That you may require the person's name and address if s/he fails to consent to being searched.

---

**Offence—Failing to give name and address when required by a PCSO: para 1A(5) of S4PRA02.**

*Mode of trial and penalty:* Summary—level 3 fine.

See 3.2.4.4 for details of your power to detain under PRA02.

*Points to consider to prove the offence*

See 3.2.3.4: **Failing to give name and address when required by a PCSO**, where the Points to Prove are itemized in respect of failing to give name and address when required.

---

### 3.2.3.8 Power to require a person who is under 18 (and/or a person who supplies alcohol to a person under 18) to surrender the alcohol and its containers to a PCSO

Context

A designated PCSO has the power to require a person who s/he reasonably suspects to be under 18, or to be a person who is or has been supplying alcohol to another person under 18, to surrender any alcohol in his/her possession and to give his/her name and address.

The PCSO also has the power to require such a person to surrender sealed containers of alcohol if the PCSO has reason to believe that the person is or has been consuming, or intends to consume, alcohol. The power continues with the authority to dispose of the alcohol that is surrendered.

If the PCSO is further designated under para 7A(2) and the suspect fails to surrender his/her alcohol and/or container, the PCSO has the power to search the suspect.

If the suspect refuses to be searched, the PCSO may make a request for the suspect's name and address.

If the suspect fails to comply with the request, or gives a name and address which the PCSO reasonably suspects to be false or inaccurate, the suspect commits an offence.

If the PCSO is further designated under para 2, he/she may then detain the person and await the arrival of a police officer or request the suspect to accompany the PCSO to the police station (see 3.2.4.4).

If the PCSO is designated under para 4, he/she may use reasonable force during the detention of the suspect (see 3.2.4.4).

---

**Power to require a person who is under 18 (and/or a person who supplies alcohol to a person under 18) to surrender the alcohol and its containers to a PCSO: para 1 of S4PRA02 and s 1 Confiscation of Alcohol (Young Persons) Act 1997.\***

[\*To avoid lengthy repetition, we shall refer to the Confiscation of Alcohol (Young Persons) Act 1997 from this point forward as **CAYP97**.]

*Points to consider before using your powers*

1. That the person is in a relevant place, eg:
   - any public place (accessible on payment or otherwise),
   - not on licensed premises,
   - any place which is not a public place to which the person has unlawfully gained access, such as gate-crashing at a private party.
2. That you reasonably suspect the person is in possession of alcohol and that either:
   - s/he is under 18, or
   - s/he intends the alcohol to be consumed by a person under 18 in a relevant place, eg an adult supplying an under-18 with alcohol, or

- s/he is or has been recently in the company of a person under 18 who has consumed alcohol in a relevant place, eg an adult who has recently accompanied an under-18-year-old who has alcohol.

*Your powers*

1. To require the surrender of **anything** in the person's possession (the under-18-year-old and/or the person accompanying/supplying the under-18-year-old) which is, or which you reasonably believe to be:
   - alcohol, or
   - a container for alcohol (sealed or unsealed).
2. To require the person under 18 or the person accompanying/supplying the person under 18 to state their name and address.
3. To dispose of anything surrendered to you in such manner as you consider appropriate (see your local policy for details).

---

## Power to search for alcohol/containers: para 7A(2) of S4PRA02.

*Circumstances under which you can search*

1. That all the circumstances surrounding your power to seize alcohol from a person were satisfied.
2. That the person from whom you wanted to seize the alcohol/container had failed to surrender it to you.
3. That you reasonably believed s/he had alcohol/container in his/her possession.

*Circumstances surrounding the search*

1. That you only search to the extent that is reasonably required to find the alcohol/containers.
2. That you cannot require a person to remove any of his or her clothing in public other than an outer coat, jacket, or gloves.
3. That, when you find what you are looking for, you can seize and dispose of it (see your local policy for disposal).

---

*Offence*—**A person who without reasonable excuse fails to consent to being searched is guilty of an offence: para 7A(5) of S4PRA02.**

*Penalty and mode of trial:* Summary—fine not exceeding level 3.

*Points to consider to prove the offence*

That, before you carried out the search, you informed the person that failing without reasonable excuse to consent to being searched is an offence.

---

---

**Requirement to give name and address: para 7A(7) of S4PRA02.**

---

See 3.2.4.4 for details of your power to detain under PRA02.

*Requirement to give name and address*

That you may require the person's name and address if s/he fails to consent to being searched.

---

---

*Offence*—**Failing to comply with a requirement to surrender alcohol or state name and address: s 1(3) CAYP97.**

---

*Mode of trial and penalty:* Summary—a fine not exceeding level 2.

*Points to consider to prove the offence*

1. That, at the time you made the requirement, you informed the person concerned of your suspicion and that failing without reasonable excuse to comply with your requirement was an offence.
2. That the person failed to surrender anything in his/her possession which you reasonably believed to be alcohol or a container for alcohol.
3. That the person failed to state his/her name and address.
4. That the person did not have a reasonable excuse for not complying with your requirements.
5. That you have evidence of sight, hearing, or smell to support your belief of the possession of alcohol.
6. That you made a note of the description of the suspect.
7. That you used ADVOKATE to evidence identification of the person.

---

### 3.2.3.9 Power to search and seize tobacco from a person aged under 16 years

Context

A designated PCSO has the power to seize tobacco in the possession of a person apparently under 16 years and dispose of it.

If the PCSO is further designated under para 7A(2) and if the suspect fails to surrender his or her tobacco, and the PCSO reasonably believes that the suspect has it in his/her possession, the PCSO has the power to search the suspect.

If the person fails to consent to being searched without reasonable excuse, s/he commits an offence and the PCSO may make a request for the suspect's name and address.

If the suspect fails to comply with the request, or gives a name and address which the PCSO reasonably suspects to be false or inaccurate, the suspect commits an offence.

If the PCSO is further designated under para 2, s/he may then detain the person and await the arrival of a police officer or request the suspect to accompany them to the police station (see 3.2.4.4).

If the PCSO is designated under para 4, s/he may use reasonable force during the detention of the suspect (see 3.2.4.4).

## Power to seize tobacco from a person aged under 16 years: s 7(3) Children and Young Persons Act 1933.

*Points to consider before using your power*

1. That you were in uniform.
2. That the objective was to seize tobacco or cigarette papers.
3. That the person was apparently under the age of 16.
4. That the person was smoking.
5. That the person was in a street or public place.

*Your powers*

1. To seize tobacco or cigarette papers.
2. To dispose of the tobacco or cigarette papers in a manner prescribed by the Police and Crime Commissioner (PCC) (refer to your Force's policy).

## Power to search for tobacco: para 7A(3) of S4PRA02.

*Circumstances under which you can search*

1. That all the circumstances surrounding your power to seize tobacco from a person under 16 years were satisfied.
2. That the person from whom you wanted to seize the tobacco had failed to surrender it to you.
3. That you reasonably believed s/he had the tobacco in his/her possession.

*Circumstances surrounding the search*

4. That you only search to the extent that is reasonably required to find the tobacco.
5. That you cannot require a person to remove any of his or her clothing in public other than an outer coat, jacket, or gloves.
6. That, when you find what you are looking for, you can seize and dispose of it (see your local Force policy for disposal).

---

**Requirement to give name and address: para 7A(7) of S4PRA02.**

See 3.2.4.4 for details of your power to detain under PRA02.

*Requirement to give name and address*

That you may require the person's name and address if s/he fails to consent to being searched.

---

*Offence* **A person who without reasonable excuse fails to consent to being searched is guilty of an offence: para 7A(5) of S4PRA02.**

*Penalty and mode of trial* Summary—fine not exceeding level 3.

*Points to consider to prove the offence*

1. That, before you carried out the search, you informed the person that failing without reasonable excuse to consent to being searched is an offence.
2. That you made a note of the description of the suspect.
3. That you used ADVOKATE to evidence identification of the person.

---

### KEY POINT

Remember: You need to make a dynamic risk assessment (5.7) on whether any seizure (alcohol, cigarettes, drugs) will exacerbate a situation—by provoking hostility or resistance, for example.

---

This is something we cannot emphasize enough: the importance of using your discretion as a PCSO: knowing when to be hard (invoking the law and your powers) and when to be more tolerant. You will find that understanding the use of discretion will come with experience and practice, but you should be aware at the outset—on your very first patrol—that you do not always need to exercise your powers even though you have been granted them. Your inter-personal and communication skills are crucial weapons in your armoury as a PCSO. Sometimes verbal persuasion can be just as effective as robotically rattling off your powers, and more often than not acting as a human being yourself will yield better results than dogmatically insisting on compliance because you can enforce it.

Dog fouling is an excellent example of this; you are more likely to 'encourage' someone to pick up dog mess by politely asking them and explaining that a lot of children play in the area, than by invoking The Dogs (Fouling) Act 1996. Acting with discretion is often referred to as **'ways and means'** in the policing sphere. The Army thinks of gaining the trust of local populations as **'winning hearts and** minds' and such an approach is excellently demonstrated in the PCSO role. It is better to get people on board than to have them resistant to you.

Before we go to the Knowledge Check, consider this task:

---

**Task**

**List 5 disadvantages to using your powers** (so that you are aware of the responsibilities involved)

---

**Knowledge Check 12**

1. Give two examples of what might constitute a 'relevant licensing offence'.

2. Give an example of a 'relevant body' that can make or enforce 'relevant byelaws'.

3. What power do you share with a police officer under the Police Reform Act 2002 (para 3 of Schedule 4 in your case, section 50 in the police officer's case)?

4. What can you require someone to do if you are empowered to detain?

5. What could you do if a vehicle driver ignores your instructions whilst you are managing the movement of an 'abnormal load'?

6. What can you do about someone who is drinking alcohol in a 'designated place'?

7. What can you do with the alcohol?

8. What might form 'reasonable suspicion' in your mind when seeing adult people with younger people and carrying alcohol?

9. If you intend to search for alcohol containers, what can you require a person to do preparatory to a search?

10. What factor might lead you to seize tobacco from someone in the street?

### 3.2.3.10 Power to enter and search any premises to save life and limb or prevent serious damage to property

Context

A designated PSCO has the same power as a police officer to enter and search any premises in the relevant police area for the purpose of saving life or limb or preventing serious damage to life and property **(but remember Dynamic Risk Assessment (5.7), and do not yourself become a casualty through misplaced enthusiasm in an attempt to be heroic).**

You may find helpful the acronym **RIFLE**, which is used widely in PCSO and police training, as a reminder of action when using this power.

> **R – Risk assess** the environment you are presented with and judge whether forced entry is necessary
>
> **I – Inform** Force Control and your supervisor that you are entering a building (most forces prefer you to get authorization from a sergeant over the radio before entering)
>
> **F – Find** the most appropriate access point that will result in the least damage
>
> **L – Look/ Listen** for any potential hazards, eg an aggressive dog or mechanical alarm
>
> **E – Explain** loudly who you are and that you work for the police when entering

---

### Power to enter and search any premises to save life and limb or prevent serious damage to property: s 17(1)(e) PACE84.

*Circumstances under which the power can be used*

1. That you are designated under para 8 of S4PRA02.
2. That you entered and searched any premises in the relevant police area for the sole purpose of saving life or limb or preventing serious damage to life and property.
3. That the premises were any place including any:
   - vehicle,
   - vessel,
   - aircraft,
   - tent, or
   - moveable structure.
4. That you only searched to the extent that is reasonably required for the purpose of saving life and limb or preventing serious damage and no further.

---

### 3.2.3.11  Power to seize vehicles used to cause alarm

Context

A designated PCSO has the power to stop and seize a vehicle which s/he has reason to believe is being used in a manner which contravenes s 3 or s 34 of the Road Traffic Act 1988 (careless and inconsiderate driving and prohibition of off-road driving/riding) under s 59 of the Police Reform Act 2002.

---

### Power to stop and seize a vehicle: s 59 PRA02.

*Points to consider before using the power*

1. That the motor vehicle is being or has been used on any occasion in a manner which:
   - contravenes s 3 or s 34 of the Road Traffic Act 1988 (careless and inconsiderate driving and prohibition of off-road driving, see below); and

2. That the motor vehicle is being used or has been used in a manner which is causing, or is likely to cause or has caused:
   • alarm, distress, or annoyance to members of the public;
3. That you warn the person driving that you will seize the vehicle if its use is continued or repeated; and
4. it appears to you the use of the vehicle has been continued or repeated.

*Circumstances under which a warning is not required*

1. It is impracticable to give a warning;
2. You have already given a warning in respect of any use of that motor vehicle or of another motor vehicle by that person or any other person on the same occasion; or
3. You have reasonable grounds to believe the driver has been given a previous warning in the past 12 months.

*Your powers*

1. To order the person driving it to stop the vehicle if it is moving.
2. To seize and remove the motor vehicle.
3. In order to exercise the powers above, to enter any premises (not a dwelling) on which you have reasonable grounds for believing the motor vehicle to be, only when in the company, and under the supervision of, a constable.

---

### *Offence*—Careless and inconsiderate driving: s 3 RTA88.

*Points to consider to prove the offence*

1. That a person is driving a mechanically propelled vehicle (any vehicle powered by mechanical means).
2. The vehicle is being driven on a road or other public place.
3. The vehicle is being driven:
   • without due care and attention, or
   • without reasonable consideration for other persons using the road or public place.

---

### *Offence*—Prohibition of off-road driving/riding: s 34 RTA88.

*Points to consider to prove the offence*

1. That a person is driving a mechanically propelled vehicle (MPV) without lawful authority:
   • on to or upon any common land, moorland, or land of any other description, not being land forming part of a road, or
   • on any road being a footpath, bridleway, or restricted byway (unless previously it was shown on a map as a road or for obtaining access to land using an MPV).

**131**

2. That the MPV was not driven on land for the purposes of parking within 15 yards of a road.
3. That the MPV was not driven on land for the purposes of dealing with an emergency.

---

### Offence—Failing to stop the vehicle at the request of a PCSO: s 59(6) PRA02.

**NB:** s 59(6) of the PRA02 is not listed as an offence for which you can require name and address (viz: under para 3A of S4PRA02).

*Points to consider to prove the offence*

1. That you had reasonable grounds for believing that a motor vehicle has been driven carelessly or without consideration or in prohibition of off-road driving/riding on any occasion.
2. That you gave an obvious direction to a mechanically propelled vehicle to stop which was evident to the driver/rider.
3. That the driver refused to comply with your directions.
4. That you made a note of the description of the suspect and vehicle.
5. That you used ADVOKATE to evidence identification of the person.

---

### 3.2.3.12 Power to remove vehicles which are illegally parked, causing an obstruction or danger, or broken down on a road

Context

A designated PCSO may remove from a road vehicles which are illegally, obstructively, or dangerously parked, or broken down. The purpose of the power is to enable the PCSO to deal with obstructions which are a matter of **urgency** that would affect people using a road currently or in the future, thereby preventing situations such as large traffic jams. Situations under which removal can take place are as follows:

---

#### 1. Broken down: reg 3(1)(a) RDVR86.

*Points to consider*

That the vehicle **broke down** on a road, for example a vehicle with a seized engine which cannot be moved under its own power.

---

#### 2. Causing an obstruction: reg 3(1)(a) RDVR86.

*Points to consider*

That the vehicle was permitted to remain at rest on a road in such a position, condition, or circumstance as to cause **obstruction** to persons using the road, such as a vehicle left unattended outside the exit to a building housing or utilizing emergency services vehicles.

---

## 3. Causing a danger: reg 3(1)(a) RDVR86.

*Points to consider*

That the vehicle was permitted to remain at rest on a road in such a position, condition, or circumstance as to cause **danger** to persons using the road, such as a vehicle or part of a vehicle left unattended at the side of a road without wheels or left with the chassis standing on piles of bricks.

## 4. Illegally parked as a result of a prohibition: reg 3(1)(b) RDVR86.

*Points to consider*

That the vehicle was permitted to remain at rest on a road in contravention of a **prohibition**, for example at rest in the area of a junction controlled by a stop sign.

## 5. Illegally parked as a result of a restriction: reg 3(1)(b) RDVR86.

*Points to consider*

That the vehicle was permitted to remain at rest on a road in contravention of a **restriction**, for example at rest in the area of white line hatchings near a traffic island or junction.

## 6. Broken down and illegally parked as a result of a restriction: reg 3(1)(b) RDVR86.

*Points to consider*

That the vehicle **broke down** and remained at rest on a road in contravention of a **prohibition**, such as having broken down on a route designated for use by buses and pedal cycles only.

## 7. Power to remove vehicle: reg 4A RDVR86.

A designated PCSO may:

1. remove any vehicle in any of the circumstances described above or
2. 'arrange for its removal from that road
   * to a place which is not on that or any other road, or
   * may move it or arrange for its removal to another position on that or another road'.

### 3.2.3.13 Power to control traffic for purposes other than escorting a load of exceptional dimensions

Context

If designated, a PCSO has the power to regulate traffic in a road and give directions to a person driving or propelling a vehicle, and to do so for the purposes of a traffic survey. Similarly, a PCSO has the power to regulate vehicular traffic in a road and give directions to a pedestrian. If a driver or pedestrian fails to comply with the directions, the PCSO has the power to require their name and address.

If the suspect fails to comply with the requirement, or gives a name and address which the PCSO reasonably suspects to be false or inaccurate, the suspect commits an offence.

If the PCSO is further designated under para 2, s/he may then detain the person and await the arrival of a police officer or request the suspect to accompany him/her to a police station (see 3.2.4.4).

If the PCSO is designated under para 4, s/he may use reasonable force during the detention of the suspect (see 3.2.4.4).

---

**Power to direct traffic in a road and for the purposes of a traffic survey: para 11B(1)(1) of S4PRA02.**

*Purpose and circumstances under which the PCSO has the power to direct traffic*

1. During the regulation of traffic in a road.
2. *To direct a vehicle to stop*, eg stopping traffic at a junction in the interest of promoting road safety.
3. *To make a vehicle proceed in, or keep to, a particular line of traffic*, eg by directing vehicles to use particular parts of a road to avoid obstructions perhaps.
4. To direct traffic in the above ways while a traffic survey of any description is being carried out on or in the vicinity of a road.

---

**Power to direct a person on foot in a road: para 11B(1), (2) of S4PRA02.**

*Purpose and circumstances under which the PCSO has the power to direct pedestrians*

1. During the regulation of vehicular traffic in a road.
2. To direct pedestrians to stop proceeding along or across a carriageway, eg by requesting pedestrians to wait at the kerbside of a road in the interests of promoting road safety while vehicular traffic is beckoned on.

---

---

*Offence*—Whilst *driving* a motor vehicle, neglects or refuses to comply with traffic directions given by a PCSO: s 35(1) or (2) RTA88.

---

*Mode of trial and penalty:* Summary—a fine not exceeding level 3, discretionary disqualification, and obligatory endorsement with three penalty points, if committed in respect of a motor vehicle.

*Points to consider to prove the offence*

1. That you were acting in the lawful execution of your duty.
2. That you were directing traffic in a road for the purposes of the regulation of traffic in the relevant police area.
3. That you were engaged in the regulation of traffic in a road and gave an obvious direction to a vehicle to stop which was evident to the driver.
4. That you were engaged in the regulation of traffic in a road and gave an obvious direction to a vehicle to proceed in, or keep to, a particular line of traffic, which was evident to the driver.
5. That the driver refused to comply with your directions.
6. That you made a note of the description of the suspect.
7. That you used ADVOKATE to evidence identification of the person.

---

**Power to require the name and address of a *driver* who refuses to comply with a traffic direction from a PCSO who is for the time being directing traffic: s 165(1) RTA88.**

*Circumstances under which the power can be used*

1. That all of the above were satisfied.
2. That you are designated under para 3A of S4PRA02.
3. That you informed the suspect you had reasonable cause to believe they had neglected or refused to comply with traffic directions.
4. That you requested the name and address from the suspect.

---

*Offence*—Failing to give name and address when required by a PCSO: para 3A(2) of S4PRA02.

---

*Mode of trial and penalty:* Summary—level 3 fine.

See 3.2.4.4 for details of your power to detain under PRA02.

*Points to consider to prove the offence*

See 3.2.3.4: **Failing to give name and address when required by a PCSO**, where the Points to Prove are itemized in respect of failing to give name and address when required.

---

---

*Offence*—**Whilst a pedestrian on foot, refuses to comply with traffic directions given by a PCSO: s 37 RTA88.**

---

*Points to consider to prove the offence*

1. That you were acting in the lawful execution of your duty.
2. That you were directing vehicular traffic in a road in the relevant police area.
3. That you gave an obvious direction to a pedestrian to stop proceeding along or across the carriageway which was evident to the person.
4. That the person did not stop and refused to comply with your directions.
5. That you made a note of the description of the suspect.
6. That you used ADVOKATE to evidence identification of the person.

---

**Power to require the name and address of a *pedestrian* who refuses to comply with a traffic direction from a PCSO who is for the time being directing traffic and pedestrians: s 165(1) RTA88.**

*Circumstances under which the power can be used*

1. That all of the above in relation to a pedestrian failing to comply with traffic directions were satisfied.
2. That you are designated under para 3A of S4PRA02.
3. That you informed the suspect you had reasonable cause to believe they had neglected or refused to comply with your traffic directions.
4. That you request the name and address from the suspect.

---

**Offence—Failing to give name and address when required by a PCSO: para 3A(2) of S4PRA02.**

---

*Mode of trial and penalty:* Summary—level 3 fine.

See 3.2.4.4 for details of your power to detain under PRA02.

*Points to consider to prove the offence*

See 3.2.3.4: **Failing to give name and address when required by a PCSO**, where the Points to Prove are itemized in respect of failing to give name and address when required.

---

### 3.2.3.14 Power to carry out a road check under section 4 of the Police and Criminal Evidence Act 1984

Context

If designated, a PCSO has the power in the relevant police area to carry out a road check under s 4 of the Police and Criminal Evidence Act 1984 which has been authorized by a senior police officer to locate a witness or suspect in connection with an indictable offence, or a person unlawfully at large. For the purposes of carrying out such a road check, the PCSO also has the power to stop vehicles on a road.

---

**Power to carry out a road check: s 4 PACE84.**

*Points to consider when using the power*

1. That the s 4 Police and Criminal Evidence Act 1984 road check has been authorized by a police officer of the rank of superintendent or above except in an urgent case.
2. That the vehicles are stopped for the purposes of ascertaining if they are carrying:
   (a) a person who has committed an indictable offence other than a road traffic offence or a vehicle excise offence;
   (b) a person who is a witness to such an offence;
   (c) a person intending to commit such an offence; OR
   (d) a person who is unlawfully at large, such as an escaped prisoner from HMP.

---

**Power to stop a mechanically propelled vehicle: s 163(1) RTA88.**

*Points to consider to prove the offence*

1. That you are in uniform.
2. That you are carrying out a s 4 Police and Criminal Evidence Act 1984 road check.
3. That you gave an obvious direction to a mechanically propelled vehicle to stop which was evident to the driver.
4. That the mechanically propelled vehicle was being driven on a road.

---

**Offence—Failing to stop a mechanically propelled vehicle on being required to do so: s 163(3) RTA88.**

*Mode of trial and penalty:* Summary—a fine not exceeding level 3.

*Points to consider to prove the offence*

1. All of the above.
2. That the driver refused to comply with your directions.
3. That you made a note of the description of the suspect and vehicle.
4. That you used ADVOKATE to evidence identification of the person.

---

**137**

### 3.2.3.15 **Power to place traffic signs**

Context

If designated, a PCSO has the power to place temporary traffic signs on a road during emergency incidents such as the scene of a road traffic crash or other abnormal road policing incident. If a driver fails to comply with a traffic sign placed by a PCSO, s/he commits an offence.

---

*Offence*—Placing on a road or any structure, a traffic sign: s 67(1) RTR84. Meaning of traffic sign which can be placed: s 64(1) RTR84.

---

*Circumstances under which the power to place temporary traffic signs on a road can be used*

1. Signs which can be placed are those which include 'object or device (whether fixed or portable) for conveying to traffic on roads or any specified class of traffic, warnings, information, requirements, restrictions or prohibitions of any description'.
2. Signs to be placed on a road or any structure on a road.
3. Signs to be placed in consequence of extraordinary circumstances.
4. Purpose of placing signs to include indications of prohibitions, restrictions, or requirements relating to vehicular traffic.
5. Placing of signs must be necessary or useful to prevent or alleviate congestion or obstruction of traffic, or danger to or from traffic.
6. Includes directions given by signs at the site of a traffic survey.
7. Signs to be placed for a maximum of seven days.

---

---

*Offence*—Failing to comply with traffic signs placed by a PCSO: s 36 RTA88.

---

*Mode of trial and penalty:* Summary—a fine not exceeding level 3, discretionary disqualification, and obligatory endorsement with 3 penalty points.

**NB:** S 36 RTA88 is not listed as an offence for which you can require name and address under para 3A of S4PRA02.

*Points to consider to prove the offence*

1. That the traffic sign was of the prescribed size, colour, and type.
2. That you were on duty, in uniform, the sign was lawfully placed on or near a road, and you made a note in your PNB of the time and location of the sign placing.
3. That a person driving or propelling a vehicle failed to comply with the indication of the sign.
4. That a note was made of the description of the driver and details obtained of the vehicle.
5. That ADVOKATE was used to evidence identification of the driver.

---

## Knowledge Check 13

1. What might make your entry and search of premises legal?

2. What is the origin of this power?

3. What constitutes 'premises' in this law?

4. If you see someone driving carelessly or inconsiderately, what can you do about it?

5. You can remove from a road, vehicles 'illegally, obstructively or dangerously parked or broken down'. What law grants you this power? (Hint: it has been amended by Statutory Instrument.)

6. What *specifically* can you do when exercising your power (11B(1)(1) of section 4 of the PRA2002) to direct traffic on a road?

7. What sanction can you apply to a pedestrian who ignores or 'refuses to comply' with a traffic direction from a PCSO?

8. Who can authorize you to carry out a road check under section 4 of PACE84, and why?

9. What defines a 'traffic sign'?

### 3.2.3.16 Power to stop and search persons and vehicles to prevent terrorism and the power to maintain a cordon area during a terrorist investigation

**Figure 3.1 Police cordon**

Context

A designated PCSO in an authorized area has the power to stop and search persons and vehicles to prevent terrorism activity but only whilst in the company and under the supervision of a police officer.

A designated PCSO has the power to maintain the cordoned area under terrorist investigation (figure 3.1).

## Power to stop and search persons and vehicles to prevent terrorism activity: s 44 of the Terrorism Act 2000.*

[*To avoid lengthy repetition, we shall refer to the Terrorism Act 2000 from this point forward as **T00**.]

*Circumstances under which the power to stop and search can be used*

1. That you are designated under para 15 of S4PRA02.
2. That an authorization under s 44 of the T00 exists.
3. That you are in the company and under the supervision of a police officer.
4. That the only purpose of the search is to find articles of a kind which could be used in connection with terrorism.
5. That the search can be carried out whether or not you have grounds for suspecting the presence of articles of that kind.
6. That you stop and search vehicles including anything
   - **in** the vehicle,
   - **on** the vehicle,
   - **carried** by the driver,
   - **carried** by any passenger of the vehicle.
7. That you search anything carried by a pedestrian.
8. That you seize and retain anything discovered in the course of your search or the search made by a police officer.
9. That your powers **do not** extend to searching drivers of the vehicles or their passengers, pedestrians, or people in general.

---

### Offence—Failing to stop a vehicle or wilfully obstructing a PCSO in the exercise of powers to stop and search under s 44(1) and (2) T00: s 47 T00.

**NB:** The consent of the Director of Public Prosecutions (DPP) is required before proceedings for an offence against this section are instituted.

*Mode of trial and penalty:* Summary—3 months' imprisonment and/or a fine not exceeding level 5.

*Points to consider to prove the offence*

1. That you are designated under para 15 of S4PRA02.
2. That an authorization under s 44 of T00 exists.
3. That you are in the company and under the supervision of a police officer.
4. That the suspect failed to stop a vehicle when you requested him or her to do so; or
5. that the suspect wilfully obstructed you whilst you searched anything:
   - **in** the vehicle,
   - **on** the vehicle,

- **carried** by the driver,
- **carried** by the passenger of the vehicle,
- carried by a pedestrian.

6. That you made a note of the description of the suspect.
7. That you used ADVOKATE to evidence identification of the person.

---

### Power to maintain a cordon area during a terrorist investigation: s 36 T00.

*Circumstances under which the power to maintain a cordon can be used*

1. That you are designated under para 14 of S4PRA02.
2. That the cordon area has been designated for the purposes of a terrorist investigation.
3. That you may:
   '(a)  order a person in a cordoned area to leave it immediately;
   (b)  order a person immediately to leave premises which are wholly or partly in or adjacent to a cordoned area;
   (c)  order the driver or person in charge of a vehicle in a cordoned area to move it from the area immediately;
   (d)  arrange for the removal of a vehicle from a cordoned area;
   (e)  arrange for the movement of a vehicle within a cordoned area;
   (f)  prohibit or restrict access to a cordoned area by pedestrians or vehicles'.

---

### Offence—Failing to comply with an order, prohibition or restriction imposed by a CSO in the area of cordon: s 36(2) T00.

**NB:** This is not a 'relevant offence' for the purposes of para 1 of S4PRA02 when using your powers to require a suspect's name and address.

*Mode of trial and penalty*: Summary—3 months' imprisonment and/or a fine not exceeding level 4.

*Points to consider to prove the offence*

1. That you are designated under para 14 of S4PRA02.
2. That the cordon area has been designated for the purposes of a terrorist investigation.
3. That a person had failed to comply with one of your requirements above.
4. That the person did not have a reasonable excuse for failing to comply with your requirements.
5. That you made a note of the description of the suspect.
6. That you used ADVOKATE to evidence identification of the person.

---

### 3.2.3.17 Power to photograph persons away from a police station

Context

A designated PCSO has the power to photograph a person away from a police station who has been:

* arrested,
* required to wait by a PCSO for the arrival of a police officer,
* issued with a PND or FPN for a 'relevant offence', and

to require the removal of any item or substance from the face of the person being photographed, or, on refusal, to remove the item or substance him/herself.

---

**Power to photograph persons away from a police station: s 64A(1A) PACE84.**

*Circumstances under which the power can be used:*

1. That the photography takes place elsewhere than at a police station.
2. That the person taking the photograph is a police officer or designated person, such as a PCSO.
3. That the photography takes place with the person's consent; or
4. That the photography takes place without consent which was withheld or impracticable to obtain.
5. That the person being photographed has been:
   * arrested by a police officer or designated person,
   * arrested by a person other than a police officer and then taken into custody by a police officer or designated person,
   * required to wait by a PCSO for the arrival of a police officer,
   * issued with a PND or a FPN for a road traffic offence by a constable,
   * issued with a penalty notice by a PCSO (see sections in this chapter for relevant offences),
   * issued with a penalty notice by an accredited person (a person outside the police 'family', such as a Trading Standards Officer).

*Circumstances surrounding the requirement to remove coverings*

1. That the person proposing to take the photograph may require the person to be photographed to remove:
   * any item or any substance,
   * worn on or over,
   * the whole or any part of,
   * the face or head, and
2. That, if the requirement is not complied with, the person proposing to take the photograph may remove the item or substance him/herself.

*Purpose for which the photograph is taken*

The use by, or disclosure for any purpose related to:

- 'the prevention or detection of crime,
- the investigation of an offence,
- the conduct of the prosecution,
- the enforcement of a sentence'.

The photograph, once taken, can be retained but cannot be used or disclosed except for a related purpose.

---

### 3.2.3.18 Power to enforce park trading offences

Context
A designated PCSO has the power to seize non-perishable items suspected to have been used in the commission of a park trading offence.

---

**Power to seize non-perishable items suspected to have been used in the commission of a park trading offence: s 4 of the Royal Parks (Trading) Act 2000.**

*Circumstances under which the power can be used*

1. That you are designated under para 7 of S4PRA02.
2. That you are a Metropolitan Police Service PCSO.
3. That you suspect a person was either carrying on a trade or business, offering, hiring, or exposing anything for sale, or had anything in his/her possession for the purpose of sale or hire, in a Royal Park.

*What can be seized*

Anything of a non-perishable nature which a person has in his/her possession or under his/her control which you reasonably believe to have been used in the commission of an offence under s 6 of the Royal Parks and Other Open Spaces Regulations 1997.

---

### 3.2.4 Discretionary powers

### 3.2.4.1 Power to issue fixed penalty notices for truancy

Context
A designated PCSO has the power to issue an FPN to the parent of a child of compulsory school age who is registered and fails to attend school on a regular basis; this is a 'relevant offence'. The parent escapes conviction if the penalty is paid in accordance with the notice.

A PCSO who is designated under para 1A of S4PRA02 has the power to require the name and address of a person who has committed a 'relevant offence'. If the suspect fails to comply with the requirement, or gives a name and address which the PCSO reasonably suspects to be false or inaccurate, the suspect commits an offence.

If the PCSO is further designated under para 2, s/he may then detain the person and await the arrival of a police officer or request the suspect to accompany the PCSO to the police station (see 3.2.4.4).

If the PCSO is designated under para 4, s/he may use reasonable force during the detention of the suspect (see 3.2.4.4).

### *Offence*—Failure to attend school regularly: s 444A E96.

*Method of disposal*

Penalty notice—under The Education (Penalty Notices) (England) Regulations 2004

*Mode of trial and penalty:* Summary—a fine not exceeding level 3.

*Points to consider to prove the offence*

1. The offence took place in England.
2. The child was of compulsory school age, 5–16 years.
3. The child was a registered pupil at a school.
4. The child failed to attend on a regular basis, or
5. The child was a boarder at a school and was absent in any part of the school terms except when sick or because of an unavoidable cause.

*Circumstances under which the child will not be taken to have failed to attend school on a regular basis:*

1. *Where the child is not a boarder:*
   - S/he was on leave.
   - S/he was sick.
   - S/he was observing a religious event.
2. *When the parent can prove (not applicable if the child has no fixed abode):*
   - the school is not in walking distance (for under 8 years: 2 miles, for over 8 years: 3 miles),
   - no suitable transport arrangements have been made, or
   - no boarding accommodation has been arranged, or
   - no other place at a school was made available by the local authority.
3. *When the parent can prove (applicable if the child has no fixed abode):*
   - his or her employment requires him or her to travel from place to place,
   - the child has attended school as regularly as the work allowed,
   - the child is 6 or over and has attended on at least 200 occasions in the last 12 months.

> *Offence*—**Failing to give name and address when required by a PCSO: para 1A(5) of S4PRA02.**

*Mode of trial and penalty:* Summary—level 3 fine.

See 3.2.4.4 for details of your power to detain under PRA02.

*Points to consider to prove the offence*

See 3.2.3.4: **Failing to give name and address when required by a PCSO**, where the Points to Prove are itemized in respect of failing to give name and address when required.

---

### 3.2.4.2 Power to remove truants and excluded pupils

Context

A designated PCSO has the power to take pupils of compulsory school age back to their school or to other premises selected by the local authority if the pupils are found in a public place and believed to be truanting. The power also extends to children and young persons of compulsory school age who have been excluded, have not been admitted to another school, and cannot justify being in a public place.

---

**Power to remove truants and excluded pupils and return them to school or designated premises: s 16 of the Crime and Disorder Act 1998**

*Circumstances under which the power can be used*

1. That you are designated under para 4C of S4PRA02.
2. That the local authority has, for the purposes of removing children and young persons of compulsory school age, designated premises to which they can be removed, and
3. That the local authority has notified the chief officer of police for that area of that designation.
4. That the power can only be used:
   (a) in an area specified in a direction given by a police officer of or above the rank of superintendent, and
   (b) during a specified time period.
5. That you find in a public place, in a specified area and time, a child or young person who you have reasonable cause to believe:
   (a) is of compulsory school age, and
   (b) is absent from school without lawful authority.

**If all the above are satisfied, you can remove the child or young person to designated premises, or to the school from which s/he is absent.**

6. That you find in a public place, in a specified area and time during school hours, a child or young person who you have reasonable cause to believe:

**145**

(a) is of compulsory school age,

(b) has been excluded from a relevant school on disciplinary grounds, either permanently or for a specific time,

(c) has not been admitted to another school, and

(d) cannot reasonably justify being in a public place.

**If all the above are satisfied, you can remove the child or young person to designated premises.**

---

**Useful terms:**

**Designated premises** are not defined by the Crime and Disorder Act but will include premises selected by your local authority.

**Lawful authority** means sickness, unavoidable cause, permitted leave, or a day set apart for religious observance.

**Relevant school** means an institution providing primary, secondary, or combined education, but does not include the further or higher education sector.

**School hours** means any time during a school session or a break between school sessions.

## Knowledge Check 14

1. A designated PCSO in an authorized area can stop and search persons and vehicles to prevent terrorist activity; subject to what condition?

2. What is the source of this power?

3. Under what circumstances can a PCSO photograph a person away from a police station?

4. What can you require the person to do before photographing him or her?

5. Why would you take a photograph?

6. What can you seize from a person suspected of 'carrying on a trade or business, offering, hiring or exposing anything for sale, or [having] anything in his/her possession for the purpose of sale or hire, in a Royal Park'?

7. What is truancy?

8. What is 'compulsory school age'?

9. A PCSO can take children of 'compulsory school age' back to school or somewhere else designated by a local authority. Where does this power come from?

### 3.2.4.3 Power to issue fixed penalty notices for dog fouling on designated land

Context

If a designated PCSO has reason to believe that a person in charge of a dog has committed an offence of failing to remove any faeces as a result of the dog defecating on designated land, the PCSO has the power to require his or her name and address and issue a fixed penalty notice as an alternative to conviction.

---

*Offence*—Dogs fouling on designated land: s 3 Dogs (Fouling of Land) Act 1996.

---

*Mode of trial and penalty:* Summary—fine not exceeding a level 3 fine.

**NB:** Due to a repeal of legislation in 2005, no further land can be designated under this Act, but the offence can still be enforced on land previously designated.

*Points to consider to prove the offence*

1. That the defecation took place on land that has been designated for the purposes of this Act by a local authority.
2. Evidence of defecation by the dog, obtained through observation by you or a witness, in which case the use of ADVOKATE will support evidence of identification.
3. Failure of the person in charge of the dog to remove the faeces from the land. Exceptions:
   (a) The person in charge of the dog has a reasonable excuse.
   (b) The person is registered as blind.
   (c) The owner, occupier, or authority of the land consents.
4. The person subsequently places the faeces in a suitable receptacle nearby.

---

---

*Offence*—Failing to give name and address when required: para 1A(5) of S4PRA02.

---

*Mode of trial and penalty:* Summary—level 3 fine.

*Points to consider to prove the offence*

See 3.2.3.4: **Failing to give name and address when required by a PCSO**, where the Points to Prove are itemized in respect of failing to give name and address when required.

---

See also **Power to issue fixed penalty notices in respect of offences under dog control orders.**

### 3.2.4.4 Power to detain and use reasonable force to prevent a person making off or to transfer control of a detained person

Context

A PCSO who is designated under para 2 of Sch 4 to the Police Reform Act 2002 has the power to detain a suspect who fails to furnish his or her name and address, or gives incorrect details, under the following circumstances:

1. When a PCSO is designated under para 1 and requests the name or address of a person who is suspected of committing a 'relevant offence' (see 3.2.3.4), except some 'relevant licensing offences' (see 3.2.4.7).
2. When a PCSO is designated under para 3 and requests the name or address of a person who is believed to be acting, or to have been acting, in an anti-social manner (see 3.2.3.5).
3. When a PCSO is designated under para 3A and requests the name or address of a person who is believed to have committed a listed road traffic offence (see 3.2.3.6 and 3.2.3.13).
4. When a PCSO is designated under para 7 and the suspect does not consent to being searched for alcohol or tobacco (see 3.2.3.9).
5. When a PCSO is designated under para 7 and the PCSO reasonably believes the person to be in possession of a controlled drug (see 3.2.4.11).

A PCSO who is designated under para 2 of Sch 4 to the Police Reform Act 2002 also has the power to detain a suspect in the following circumstance:

- When a PCSO is designated under para 1, s/he believes a suspect is committing an offence relating to begging and the suspect fails to stop the activity on request (see 3.2.4.6).

Under the above circumstances, the PSCO has the power to detain the suspect for up to 30 minutes whilst awaiting the arrival of a police officer, or to request the suspect to accompany him/her to a police station if the suspect elects to do so. If during either period the suspect makes off, s/he will have committed a further offence. In relation to byelaws you have any power a police officer has under a 'relevant byelaw' to remove a person from a place to which that 'relevant byelaw' refers (see 3.2.4.5).

## Power to use reasonable force

A PCSO who is designated under para 4 has the power to use reasonable force under the following circumstances:

1. To prevent the suspect under detention from making off from him/her whilst waiting for the **arrival of a police officer.**
2. To prevent the suspect under detention from making off from him/her until s/he has **transferred control** of the suspect to a police officer.
3. To prevent the suspect under detention from making off from him/her whilst s/he **accompanies the suspect to a police station.**
4. To prevent the suspect under detention from making off from him/her while s/he accompanies the suspect to a police station until s/he has **transferred control of the suspect to a custody officer.**
5. To prevent the suspect from making off (or escaping) and to keep control in relation to using his/her powers to:

- disperse groups and remove persons under 16 to their place of residence (see 3.2.3.3);
- remove children in contravention of curfew notices to their place of residence (see 3.2.3.4).

### Power to detain: para 2(3) of S4PRA02.

*Circumstances under which the power can be used*

1. That you are designated under the relevant para of Sch 4 to the Reform Act 2002 to apply the power or investigate the offence (see applicable sections).
2. That you are designated under para 2 of Sch 4 to the Reform Act 2002 to detain.
3. That you had reason to believe that the suspect had committed an offence.
4. That you required the suspect to give you his/her name and address.
5. That the place in which you made the requirement in relation to a 'relevant byelaw' was one to which the byelaw related (see 3.2.4.5).
6. That the suspect failed to comply with your requirement; or
7. That you had reasonable grounds for suspecting that the suspect had given you a false or inaccurate name and address.
8. That the 'relevant licensing offence' was not one of the following committed on licensed premises:
   - **selling or attempting to sell alcohol to a person who is drunk**
   - **selling alcohol to a person under 18 years**
   - **allowing a child under 18 years to consume alcohol (3.2.5.1).**

*Circumstances surrounding the requirement to remain with you until the arrival of a police officer*

1. That all of the above have been satisfied.
2. That you request the suspect to wait with you for a period not exceeding 30 minutes for the arrival of a police officer or to accompany you to a police station.

### Power to use reasonable force to prevent a detained person making off while waiting for a police officer: para 4 of S4PRA02.

*Circumstances under which you can use reasonable force*

1. That you are designated under para 4 of Sch 4 to the Reform Act 2002.
2. That you had required the suspect to wait with you for a period not exceeding 30 minutes for the arrival of a police officer.
3. That the person did not comply with your requirement.

### Responsibility to remain with the suspect under detention while waiting to transfer control to a police officer: para 2(4A) of S4PRA02.

*Your responsibilities to remain with the suspect and to transfer control*

That, having made the request for the suspect to remain with you for 30 minutes to await the arrival of a police officer, you are under a duty to remain with the suspect until you have transferred control of the suspect to the police officer.

### Power to use reasonable force to carry out your responsibilities to remain with the suspect and transfer control to a police officer: para 4ZB of S4PRA02.

*Circumstances under which you can use reasonable force*

1. That you are designated under para 4ZB of Sch 4 to the Reform Act 2002.
2. That, having made the request for the suspect to remain with you for 30 minutes to await the arrival of a police officer, you are under a duty to remain with the suspect until you have transferred control of the suspect to the police officer.
3. That the suspect did not comply with your requirements to remain with you until you could transfer control.

### Request to the suspect under detention to accompany you to the police station: para 2(4) of S4PRA02.

*Circumstances surrounding the request to accompany you to the police station and the election of the suspect to do so*

1. That the circumstances under which to use the power to detain were satisfied.
2. That you requested the suspect to accompany you to a police station in the relevant area.
3. That the suspect elected to do so.

### Power to use reasonable force to prevent a detained person making off while accompanying you to the police station: para 4 of S4PRA02.

*Circumstances under which you can use reasonable force*

1. That you are designated under para 4 of Sch 4 to the Reform Act 2002.
2. That you requested the suspect to accompany you to a police station in the relevant area.
3. That the suspect elected to do so.
4. That the suspect did not comply with your requirements to remain with you.

## Your responsibilities to remain with the suspect under detention whilst accompanying you to the police station to transfer control: para 2(4B) of S4PRA02.

*Your responsibilities to remain with the suspect and transfer control*

1. That, while you were taking the suspect to a police station (or waiting to transfer control within a police station), you:
   - remained with the suspect until control was transferred to the custody officer,
   - treated the suspect as being in your lawful custody until your control was transferred,
   - were under a duty to prevent the suspect from escaping and to assist in keeping him/her under control all the while you were at or in the vicinity of a police station whilst transferring or having transferred control to the custody officer.

## Power to use reasonable force to carry out your responsibilities to remain with the suspect and transfer control to the custody officer: para 4ZB of S4PRA02.

*Circumstances under which you can use reasonable force*

1. That you are designated under para 4ZB of Sch 4 to the Reform Act 2002.
2. That you took the suspect to a police station.
3. That you were carrying out your duties until lawful control was transferred.
4. That the suspect did not comply with your requirements.

### *Offence*—Making off having been detained by a PCSO: para 2(5) of S4PRA02.

*Mode of trial and penalty:* Summary—a fine not exceeding level 3.

*Points to consider to prove the offence*

1. That your reasons for detention were lawful.
2. That the suspect made off whilst subject to a requirement of waiting with you for 30 minutes, or
3. That the suspect made off while accompanying you to a police station, or
4. That the suspect failed to comply with your responsibilities to transfer control to a police officer, or
5. That the suspect failed to comply with your responsibilities to transfer control to a custody officer.
6. That you made a note of the description of the suspect.
7. That you used ADVOKATE to evidence identification of the person.

NB: For the power to detain in relation to offences connected with begging and use of reasonable force, see 3.2.4.6.

For the power to use reasonable force in relation to dispersing groups and removing young persons, see 3.2.4.9.

### 3.2.4.5 Power to enforce byelaws

Context

A designated PCSO has the power to investigate offences committed under relevant byelaws. From a list of byelaws, a 'relevant byelaw' is one that has been agreed between a chief constable and a relevant byelaw-making body.

Such byelaws are 'relevant offences' for the purposes of a PCSO requiring the name and address of a suspect during the investigation and for asking the suspect to remain until a police officer arrives (see sections on Power to require name and address and Power to detain).

Failure to provide a name and address, having been required to do so, is an offence.

If designated under para 2, a PCSO can also enforce a byelaw by removing a person from a place if a constable would also have the power to enforce a byelaw in that way.

---

### Power to require name and address: para 1A(3), of S4PRA02.

*Circumstances under which the power can be used*

1. That you are designated under para 1A of S4PRA02.
2. That you had reason to believe that the person had committed an offence against a 'relevant byelaw'.
3. That you requested the person to give you his or her name and address.
4. That the place in which you made the request in relation to a 'relevant byelaw' was one to which the byelaw related.

---

### *Offence*—Failing to give name and address when required by a PCSO: para 1A(5) of S4PRA02.

*Mode of trial and penalty:* Summary—level 3 fine.

See 3.2.4.4 for details of your power to detain under PRA02.

*Points to consider to prove the offence*

- See 3.2.3.4: **Failing to give name and address when required by a PCSO**, where the Points to Prove are itemized in respect of failing to give name and address when required.

---

### Power to remove a person from a place: para 2(3A) S4PRA02.

*Circumstances under which the power can be used*

1. That you are designated under para 2 of S4PRA02, and
2. That you are designated under para 1A of S4PRA02 (power to require name and address).
3. That, in the first instance, a constable has the power under the relevant byelaw to remove a person from a place.

### Legislation that defines a 'relevant byelaw' as a 'relevant offence': para 2(6)(ad) of S4PRA02.

*Definition of a 'relevant byelaw' as a 'relevant offence'*

In para 2 S4PRA02 a 'relevant offence' means any offence which is an offence under a 'relevant byelaw'.

### Legislation that defines a 'relevant byelaw': para 2(6B)–(6F) of S4PRA02.

*Definition of a 'relevant byelaw'*

1. A byelaw included in a list of byelaws which have been made by a relevant body such as:
   - a county council,
   - a district council,
   - a parish council,
   - a London Borough Council, and
   - the chief constable of the police force for the area has agreed its inclusion in the list.
2. The list of 'relevant byelaws' must be published for the benefit of the general public.
3. The list may be amended by agreement with the chief constable and the relevant body, but the alterations must be published.
4. The agreement can also be made between the Secretary of State and the local chief constable.

### 3.2.4.6 Powers and legislation to deal with begging and associated offences

Context

A designated PCSO under para 1 has the power to deal with any person who is begging or asking for charitable donations and then require his or her name and address.

In addition, a PCSO who is designated under para 2 has the power to detain a person who is committing an offence associated with begging and, after requesting the suspect to stop, which is then refused, can detain the person to await the arrival of a police officer.

If the PCSO is designated under para 4ZA, s/he has the further power to use reasonable force to impose a requirement on the suspect to remain with him/her whilst awaiting the arrival of a police officer and to keep control of him/her until the custody of the suspect is transferred.

See also 3.2.4.4, Power to detain and use reasonable force to prevent a person making off or to transfer control of a detained person.

See also 3.2.4.8, Power to search detained persons for dangerous items or items that could be used to assist escape.

---

**Offence—Begging or asking for charitable donations: s 3 Vagrancy Act 1824.**

*Mode of trial and penalty:* Summary—a fine not exceeding level 3.

*Points to consider to prove the offence*

1. That you found the suspect begging for charitable donations in any of the below named places; or
2. That you found the suspect procuring or encouraging any child or children to beg for charitable donations in any:
   - public place,
   - street,
   - highway,
   - court, or passage.

---

**Offence—Obtaining donations under false or fraudulent pretences: s 4 Vagrancy Act 1824.**

*Mode of trial and penalty:* Summary—a fine not exceeding level 3.

*Points to consider to prove the offence*

1. That the suspect showed a wound or deformity in order to obtain donations; or
2. That the suspect endeavoured 'to obtain donations of any kind under any false or fraudulent pretences'.

## Power to detain when dealing with begging (if designated): para 2(3B) PRA02.

*Circumstances under which the power can be used*

1. That you are designated under para 2.
2. That you reasonably suspected a person to be committing an offence relating to begging.
3. That you required the suspect to stop whatever s/he was doing and to wait with you for a period not exceeding 30 minutes for the arrival of a police officer.

## Power to search detained persons for dangerous items (if designated): para 2A PRA02.

See 3.2.4.8: **Power to search detained persons for dangerous items or items that could be used to assist escape.**

## Power to use reasonable force to prevent a detained person making off (if designated): para 4 of S4PRA02.

See 3.2.4.4: **Power to detain and use reasonable force to prevent a person making off or to transfer control of a detained person.**

*Offence*—Making off having been detained by a PCSO: para 2(5) of S4PRA02.

See 3.2.4.4: **Power to detain and use reasonable force to prevent a person making off or to transfer control of a detained person.**

*Offence*—Failing to give name and address when required by a PCSO: para 1A(5) of S4PRA02.

*Mode of trial and penalty:* Summary—level 3 fine.

*Points to consider to prove the offence*

See 3.2.3.4: **Failing to give name and address when required by a PCSO**, where the Points to Prove are itemized in respect of failing to give name and address when required.

### 3.2.4.7 **Power to enforce 'relevant licensing offences' and similar offences**

Context

A designated PCSO has the power to enforce 'relevant licensing offences'. Where these offences apply to members' clubs, such as working men's clubs which are licensed, they cease to be 'relevant licensing offences'.

Useful definitions for this section

'Relevant premises' means:

1. licensed premises (pubs, off-licences);
2. premises in respect of which there is a club premises' certificate (members' clubs); and
3. premises which may be used for a permitted temporary activity (occasions such as wedding receptions on non-licensed premises).

**NB:** For information on issuing a PND in relation to these offences, please refer to 3.2.5.1.

---

*Offence*—**Obtaining alcohol for a person who is drunk (not PND): s 142(1) LO3.**

---

*Mode of trial and penalty:* Summary—a fine not exceeding level 3.

*Points to consider to prove the offence*

1. That the offence took place on 'relevant premises' (see above).
2. That the suspect (any person) knowingly:
   - obtained, or
   - attempted to obtain alcohol.
3. That the alcohol was for consumption on those premises.
4. That the person for whom the alcohol was intended was drunk.

---

*Offence*—**Purchasing alcohol on behalf of a child for consumption on certain premises (not PND): s 149(4)(a) LO3.**

---

*Mode of trial and penalty:* Summary—a fine not exceeding level 5.

*Points to consider to prove the offence*

1. That the suspect:
   - bought, or
   - attempted to buy alcohol.
2. That the alcohol was bought or attempted to be bought on 'relevant premises' (see above).
3. That the alcohol was bought for consumption by a person aged under 18.

---

---

*Offence*—**Sending a child to obtain alcohol (not PND): s 152(1) LO3.**

---

*Mode of trial and penalty:* Summary—a fine not exceeding level 5.

*Points to consider to prove the offence*

1. That the suspect knowingly sent a person under 18 to obtain alcohol.
2. That the alcohol was sold or to be sold on 'relevant premises' (see above).
3. That the alcohol was to be consumed off the premises.
4. That the alcohol, if not obtained from 'relevant premises', was obtained from any other premises from which it was delivered in the course of sale or supply.
5. That the person under 18 does not work at the 'relevant premises' delivering alcohol.
6. That the person under 18 was not sent by a police officer or weights and measures inspector.

---

*Offence*—**Purchasing alcohol by a child (not PND): s 149(1)(a) LO3.**

---

*Mode of trial and penalty:* Summary—a fine not exceeding level 3.

*Points to consider to prove the offence*

1. That the suspect is under 18 years.
2. That the suspect buys or attempts to buy alcohol.
3. That the suspect did not buy or attempt to buy at the request of a police officer or weights and measures inspector.

---

*Offence*—**Failing to give name and address when required by a PCSO: para 1A(5) of S4PRA02.**

---

*Mode of trial and penalty:* Summary—level 3 fine.

See 3.2.4.4 for details of your power to detain under PRA02.

*Points to consider to prove the offence*

See 3.2.3.4: **Failing to give name and address when required by a PCSO**, where the Points to Prove are itemized in respect of failing to give name and address when required.

---

### 3.2.4.8 Power to search detained persons for dangerous items or items that could be used to assist escape

Context

A designated PCSO has the same power as a police officer in relation to a person who has been detained at a place other than a police station, to search that person for any item which may present a danger to him/herself or others or assist his/her escape from lawful custody. Having found any such item, the PCSO may seize and retain the item.

### Power to search detained persons for dangerous items or items that could be used to assist escape: para 2A of S4PRA02.

*Circumstances under which you can search*

1. That you are designated under para 2 of S4PRA02.
2. That the person had committed a 'relevant offence' or an offence connected with begging.
3. That you had required the person's name and address and s/he had not complied or given false details or had failed to stop his or her activity in relation to begging.
4. That you had required the person to wait with you for 30 minutes for the arrival of a police officer.
5. That you had detained the person at a place other than a police station.
6. That you had reasonable grounds for believing the detained person might present a danger to him/herself or others.
7. That you had reasonable grounds for believing the detained person had anything which he/she might use to assist him/her to escape from lawful custody.

*Circumstances surrounding the power to seize*

1. That you had reasonable grounds for believing that the person being searched might use the item(s) you found to cause injury to him/herself or any other person.
2. That you had reasonable grounds for believing that the person being searched might use the item(s) you found to escape from lawful custody.
3. That you seized and retained anything you found on exercising your power other than an item subject to legal privilege, for example, a letter from the person to his/her legal representative.

*Responsibilities after the search*

1. That, having seized or retained anything, you:
   - tell the person from whom the items were seized where s/he can make enquiries about the recovery of the objects,
   - request the assistance of a police officer and comply with the instructions from the constable as to the method of disposal for the seized item.

---

### KEY POINT

Again, as we warned with your powers to effect seizures of alcohol, tobacco, and drugs, you should make a dynamic risk assessment (see 5.7) before searching under this power, since your action, or intended action, *could* provoke violent resistance.

**Knowledge Check 15**

1. What alternative is there to conviction of a person in charge of a dog who has committed an offence of failing to remove any faeces [...] from designated land?

2. What exceptions apply?

3. How long may a PCSO detain someone pending the arrival of a police officer?

4. What is the alternative course of action?

5. Why do you have the power to use 'reasonable force'?

6. What constitutes a 'relevant byelaw'?

7. What sort or organizations or bodies make byelaws?

8. What do you need to consider to prove the offence of begging?

9. What might be 'false or fraudulent pretences' in begging?

10. What is the penalty for obtaining alcohol for a person who is drunk?

11. What power do you have to search someone for 'dangerous items'?

12. What exception applies to your power to seize and retain an item during a search?

### 3.2.4.9 Power to disperse groups and remove persons under 16 to their places of residence

Context

A PCSO's power to disperse groups and remove persons under 16 to their places of residence cannot be used without two designations: first, a written authorization made by a senior police officer, with the consent of the local authority, to designate an area in which the power can be used and, secondly, the PCSO must be designated under para 4A.

Where the PCSO is further designated under para 4ZB, s/he may use reasonable force to prevent members of the dispersed groups and 'removed persons' from making off, and to keep them under control.

---

**Power to disperse groups: s 30(1) ASB03.**

*Circumstances under which the power to disperse groups can be used*

1. That a written authorization designating an area has been made by an officer of at least the rank of superintendent.
2. That you are designated under para 4A of S4PRA02.
3. That you are in uniform.

4. That there was a group of two or more persons in any public place in the designated area.
5. That you had reasonable grounds for believing that the presence or behaviour of that group:
   - has resulted, or
   - is likely to result in any members of the public being:
   - intimidated,
   - harassed,
   - alarmed, or
   - distressed,

in which case you can then give one or more of the following directions to the members of the group:

(a) To disperse either immediately or by such time as you specify and in a way you specify.
(b) To leave the designated area or any part of it, either immediately or by such time as you specify and in such way as you specify (**only applies to members of the group whose place of residence is not within the designated area**).
(c) To prohibit their return to the designated area or any part of it for a period you specify (not exceeding 24 hours) from when the direction was given (**only applies to members of the group whose place of residence is not within the designated area**).

Your power to disperse does NOT extend to any members of any groups who are taking part in a lawful trade dispute or a lawful procession.

---

---

**Power to remove persons under 16 to their place of residence:** s 30(6) ASB03.

*Circumstances under which the power to remove persons under 16 to their places of residence can be used*

1. That a written authorization designating an area has been made by an officer of at least the rank of superintendent.
2. That you are designated under para 4A of S4PRA02.
3. That you are in uniform.
4. That the time is between 2100 hrs and 0600 hrs.
5. That you find a person in any public place in the designated area who you have reasonable grounds for believing:
   - is under the age of 16, and
   - is not under the effective control of a parent or a responsible person aged 18 or over.

6. That you **do not** have reasonable grounds for believing that the person would be likely to suffer significant harm if removed to his or her place of residence.

**Only if all of the above are satisfied can you remove the person to his/her place of residence.**

---

### Power to use reasonable force to disperse groups and remove persons under 16 to their places of residence: para 4ZB of S4PRA02.

Refer to 3.2.4.4 for further details regarding reasonable force.

*Circumstances under which you can use reasonable force*

- That you are designated under para 4ZB of S4PRA02.
- That all of the above circumstances relating to the power to use reasonable force to disperse groups and removal of persons under 16 to their places of residence were satisfied.
- That the member of the group or person under 16 made off from you or you were unable to keep him/her under control.

---

### 3.2.4.10 Power to remove children in contravention of child curfew notices to their places of residence

Context

A designated PCSO has the power under para 4B to remove children in contravention of child curfew notices to their places of residence. The purpose of the curfew notices made by a chief officer of police or a local authority is to prevent children under 16 from being in areas without a responsible adult. The areas, hours, and ages of the children to whom the curfew relates will be dictated by the curfew notice.

Where the PCSO is further designated under para 4ZB, s/he may use reasonable force to prevent the removed persons from making off and to keep them under control.

---

### Power to remove children in contravention of child curfew notices to their places of residence: s 15(1) Crime and Disorder Act 1998.

*Circumstances under which the power to remove children can be used*

1. That a local authority or a chief officer of police has made a local child curfew scheme which has been confirmed by the Secretary of State and suitably advertised.
2. That the notice specifies the curfew hours, the ages of the children to be banned, and the relevant public place.
3. That you are designated under para 4B of S4PRA02.

4. That you have reasonable cause to believe the child is in contravention of a ban imposed by a curfew notice by way of age, time, and locality.
5. That you **do not** have reasonable cause to believe that the person would be likely to suffer significant harm, if removed to his or her place of residence.

**Only if all of the above are satisfied can you remove the child to its place of residence.**

---

---

### Power to use reasonable force to disperse groups and remove persons under 16 to their place of residence: para 4ZB of S4PRA02.

Refer to 3.2.4.4 for further details regarding reasonable force.

*Circumstances under which you can use reasonable force*

1. That you are designated under para 4ZB of S4PRA02.
2. That all of the above circumstances relating to the power to remove children in contravention of child curfew notices to their places of residence were satisfied.
3. That the child you were removing made off from you or you were unable to keep him/her under control.

---

### 3.2.4.11 Power to seize drugs and require name and address for possession of drugs

Context

A designated PCSO has the power to seize obviously-placed drugs or concealed drugs found when searching for alcohol, tobacco, or dangerous items. Until a constable instructs him/her what to do with the drugs, the PCSO must retain them. If the PCSO finds drugs in a person's possession or has reason to believe that a person is in possession of drugs, then the PCSO may require that person's name and address. An appropriately designated PCSO may detain a person on failure to comply with the requirement.

---

### Power to seize drugs: para 7B(1) and (2) S4PRA02.

*Circumstances under which you may seize and retain the drugs*

1. That you are designated under para 7B and 7C of S4PRA02.
2. That you find a controlled drug in a person's possession.
3. That the drugs were found whether or not you were using your powers to search for alcohol, tobacco, or dangerous items.
4. That you reasonably believe the person is in unlawful possession of the drugs.

---

## Requirement for name and address to be given on request: para 7B(3) S4PRA02.

*Circumstances under which the requirement to furnish name and address can be made*

1. That you find controlled drugs on the person; or
2. That you reasonably believe the person in is possession of a controlled drug.
3. That you reasonably believe it is unlawful for the person to be in possession of the drugs.

---

### Offence—Failing to comply with a requirement for name and address: para 7B(5) S4PRA02.

*Mode of trial and penalty:* Summary—A fine not exceeding level 3.

See 3.2.4.4 for details of your power to detain under PRA02.

*Points to consider to prove the offence*

1. That you found a controlled drug in a person's possession.
2. The circumstances under which the drugs were found, whether or not you were using your powers to search for alcohol, tobacco, or dangerous items; or
3. That you reasonably believed the person was in possession of a controlled drug.
4. That you reasonably believed the person was in unlawful possession of the drugs.
5. That you requested the person's name and address.
6. That the person refused to give you their name and address.
7. That you made a note of the description of the suspect.
8. That you used ADVOKATE to evidence identification of the person.

---

## Responsibilities of the PCSO once drugs have been found: para 7B(4) of S4PRA02.

*Responsibilities*

1. Inform the person from whom the drugs were seized where enquiries about the recovery of the drugs can be made if the person maintains s/he was in lawful possession of them.
2. Request the assistance of a police officer and comply with the instructions from the constable as to the method of disposal for the drugs.

---

### 3.2.4.12 Limited power to enter and search premises to investigate licensing offences

Context

If designated, a PCSO has a limited power to enter and search licensed premises for the purposes of investigating relevant licensing offences. PCSOs may not

**163**

enter clubs (members-only clubs, NOT nightclubs) and must enter all premises with a constable unless the premises are licensed for the sale of alcohol off the premises.

---

### Power to enter and search premises to investigate licensing offences: s 180 Licensing Act 2003*

[*To avoid lengthy repetition, we shall refer to the Licensing Act 2003 from this point forward as **L03**.]

*Circumstances under which the power can be used*

1. Premises that are entered and searched include 'any place and includes a vehicle, vessel or moveable structure'.
2. That one or more of the following licensing offences are being committed on those premises:
   - sale of alcohol to a person who is drunk,
   - obtaining alcohol for a person who is drunk,
   - sale of alcohol to a child,
   - purchase of alcohol by or on behalf of a child,
   - consumption or allowing consumption of alcohol by a child,
   - delivering alcohol to a child (see later sections on these offences).
3. That the premises are not 'club' premises (members-only clubs, NOT nightclubs).
4. That you are in the company of a police constable UNLESS you reasonably believe the premises holds an off-licence only, in which case you can enter by yourself.
5. That you use reasonable force only in exercising this power (See 3.2.4.4 on reasonable force).

---

### 3.2.4.13 Power to stop vehicles for testing

Context

If designated, a PCSO in uniform has the power to require a motor vehicle to stop on a road for the purposes of being tested by an authorized examiner.

This power is necessary because although authorized vehicle examiners such as employees of the Department of Transport have powers to test and inspect motor vehicles, they do not have powers to stop the vehicles on the road in the first place.

NB: Do not confuse this kind of 'road check' with a s 4 PACE 1984 'road check' for which you have additional powers to stop vehicles relating to indictable offences and escaped prisoners.

## Power to stop vehicles for testing: s 163(2) RTA88

*Points to consider when using the power*

1. That you are in full uniform.
2. That the road is a highway or any other road to which the public has access.
3. That the vehicles you stop are motor vehicles, defined as mechanically-propelled vehicles intended or adapted for use on a road, such as a car or articulated lorry.
4. That the person on whose behalf you stopped the vehicle is an authorized examiner, such as *bona fide* employees of the Department of Transport.

### 3.2.4.14  Power to direct traffic and pedestrians for the purposes of escorting abnormal loads

Context

If designated, a PCSO in uniform has the power to direct traffic and pedestrians for the purposes of escorting a vehicle or trailer carrying a load of exceptional dimensions either to or from the relevant police area.

### Power to direct traffic and pedestrians for the purposes of escorting abnormal loads: s 12(1) of S4PRA02

- *To direct a vehicle to stop* whilst engaged in the regulation of traffic in a road, eg stopping other traffic at a junction to allow the abnormal load to continue its journey in the safest way.
- *To make a vehicle proceed in, or keep to, a particular line of traffic,* eg by directing vehicles to use the outside lane of a dual carriageway only in order to pass the abnormal load in the interests of road safety.
- *To direct pedestrians to stop,* eg by requesting pedestrians to wait at the kerbside of a road to allow the abnormal load to pass in the interests of road safety.

*Offence*—**Whilst driving a motor vehicle, neglects or refuses to comply with traffic directions given by a PCSO: s 35(1) RTA88**

*Mode of trial and penalty:* Summary—A fine not exceeding level 3, discretionary disqualification, and obligatory endorsement with three penalty points, if committed in respect of a motor vehicle.

*Points to consider to prove the offence*

1. That you were acting in the lawful execution of your duty.
2. That you were directing traffic for the purposes of escorting a vehicle or trailer carrying a load of exceptional dimensions either to or from the relevant police area.
3. That you were engaged in the regulation of traffic in a road and gave an obvious direction to a vehicle to stop which was evident to the driver.

4. That you were engaged in the regulation of traffic in a road and gave an obvious direction to a vehicle to proceed in, or keep to, a particular line of traffic, which was evident to the driver.
5. That you made a note of the description of the suspect.
6. That you used ADVOKATE to evidence identification of the person.

---

**Offence—Whilst a *pedestrian* on foot refuses to comply with traffic directions given by a PCSO: s 37 RTA88**

*Points to consider to prove the offence*

1. That you were acting in the lawful execution of your duty.
2. That you were directing traffic for the purposes of escorting a vehicle or trailer carrying a load of exceptional dimensions either to or from the relevant police area.
3. That you were engaged in the regulation of traffic in a road and gave an obvious direction to a pedestrian to stop which was evident to the person.

---

### 3.2.5 Powers to issue Penalty Notices for Disorder that can be designated by chief officers

#### 3.2.5.1 Licensing and alcohol related offences

Context

A designated PCSO can issue a PND to a person who has committed 'relevant fixed penalty offences' which are alcohol-related. A designated PCSO may require the name and address from a suspect, but even a designated PCSO under para 2 of Sch 4 to the Police Reform Act 2002 may not detain for those 'relevant licensing offences' which are most likely to be committed by licensees. Remember that you need to caution the person to whom you are issuing a PND. Can you remember the Caution?

> You do not have to say anything, but it may harm your defence if you do not mention when questioned/now*, something that you later rely on in court. Anything you do say may be given in evidence.
>
> (*depending on the circumstances of the caution)

---

**Offence—Selling or attempting to sell alcohol to a person who is drunk (PND): s 141(1) LO3**

**NB:** If designated under para 2 of S4PRA02 a PCSO cannot detain a person who has committed this offence on licensed premises if his or her name and address cannot be obtained.

*Mode of trial and penalty:* Summary—a fine not exceeding level 3.

*Points to consider to prove the offence*

1. That the offence took place on
   - licensed premises, such as pubs, off-licences, or
   - premises which may be used for a permitted temporary activity (occasions such as wedding receptions on non-licensed premises).
2. That the suspect was:
   - any person who works at the premises, or
   - the holder of the licence or a designated premises supervisor on licensed premises, or
   - the premises user of a permitted temporary activity.
3. That the suspect sold or attempted to sell alcohol to a person who was drunk; or
4. That the suspect allowed alcohol to be sold to such a person.

---

**Offence—Selling alcohol to a person under 18 years (PND): s 146(1) LO3.**

**NB:** If designated under para 2 of S4PRA02, a PCSO cannot detain a person who has committed this offence on licensed premises if his/her name and address cannot be obtained.

*Mode of trial and penalty:* Summary—a fine not exceeding level 5.

*Points to consider to prove the offence*

That the suspect (any person) sold alcohol to an individual under 18 anywhere.

*Defences*

1. The suspect believed the individual was 18 or over.
2. The suspect took all reasonable steps by asking for evidence of age and the evidence would have convinced a reasonable person.
3. Nobody could have reasonably suspected as a result of the individual's appearance that s/he was under 18.
4. The suspect exercised all due diligence to avoid committing the offence.

---

**Offence—Purchasing alcohol on behalf of a child (PND): s 149(3)(a) LO3.**

*Mode of trial and penalty:* Summary—a fine not exceeding level 5.

*Points to consider to prove the offence*

1. That the suspect:
   - bought, or
   - attempted to buy alcohol.
2. That the alcohol was bought or attempted to be bought on behalf of an individual under 18.

---

---

**Offence—Consuming alcohol by a person under 18 years (PND): s 150(1) LO3.**

---

*Mode of trial and penalty:* Summary—a fine not exceeding level 3.

*Points to consider to prove the offence*

1. That the suspect was under 18.
2. That the suspect consumed alcohol.
3. That the alcohol was consumed on 'relevant premises' (see 3.2.4.7).

---

**Offence—Allowing a child under 18 years to consume alcohol (PND): s 150(2) LO3.**

---

**NB:** If designated under para 2 of S4PRA02, a PCSO cannot detain a person who has committed this offence on licensed premises if his or her name and address cannot be obtained.

*Mode of trial and penalty:* Summary—a fine not exceeding level 5.

*Points to consider to prove the offence*

1. That the suspect worked at the premises in a position that can authorize the prevention of such consumption.
2. That the suspect allowed the consumption of alcohol on 'relevant premises' (see 3.2.4.7).
3. That a person under 18 consumed the alcohol.
4. That the person consuming the alcohol was not 16 or 17 and drinking beer, wine, or cider at a table meal and in company with a person aged 18 or over.

---

**Offence—Delivering alcohol to a person under 18 years or allowing such delivery (PND): s 151 LO3.**

---

*Mode of trial and penalty:* Summary—a fine not exceeding level 5.

*Points to consider to prove the offence*

1. That the suspect worked on 'relevant premises' (see 3.2.4.7), paid or unpaid.
2. That the suspect knowingly delivered alcohol sold on the premises.
3. That the suspect delivered to a person under 18; or
4. That the suspect worked in a position on 'relevant premises' that could prevent such a delivery but still allowed somebody else to make the delivery.
5. That the delivery was not meant for an adult who had lawfully purchased the alcohol.
6. That the person under 18 did not work at the 'relevant premises' involving the delivery of alcohol.
7. That the alcohol is not sold or supplied for consumption on the 'relevant premises'.

---

*Offence*—**Drunk and disorderly behaviour (PND): s 91 Criminal Justice Act 1967.**

---

*Mode of trial and penalty:* Summary—a fine not exceeding level 3.

*Points to consider to prove the offence*

1. That the suspect was drunk.
2. That the suspect behaved in a disorderly manner.
3. That the place where the person was drunk, was a public place.

---

*Offence*—**Drunk in the highway (PND): s 12 Licensing Act 1872.**

---

*Mode of trial and penalty*

For points to consider 1 and 2:

Summary—Fine not exceeding level 1.

For points to consider 3 and 4:

Summary—one month's imprisonment or a fine not exceeding level 1.

*Points to consider to prove the offence*

1. That the suspect was found drunk.
2. That the suspect was on:
   - 'any highway, or
   - other public place,
   - whether a building or not, or
   - on any licensed premises'; or
3. That the suspect was 'drunk while in charge on any highway or other public place, of any
   - carriage,
   - horse,
   - cattle, or
   - steam engine'; or
4. That the suspect was 'drunk when in possession of any loaded firearms'.

---

*Offence*—**Failing to comply with a requirement to stop drinking or surrender alcohol: s 12(4) CJP01.**

---

(See 3.2.5.1 on issuing PNDs and using the Caution for PNDs.) *Mode of trial and penalty:* Summary—a fine not exceeding level 2.

*Points to consider to prove the offence*

1. That you are designated under para 5 of S4PRA02.
2. That, at the time you made the requirement, you informed the person concerned that, without reasonable excuse, failing to comply with your requirement was an offence.

3. That the person continued to drink what you believed to be alcohol after you required him or her to stop; and/or

4. That the person failed to surrender anything in his/her possession which you reasonably believed to be alcohol or a container for alcohol.

5. That the person did not have a reasonable excuse for not complying with your requirements.

6. That you have evidence of sight, hearing, or smell to support your belief of the consumption or possession of alcohol.

7. That you made a note of the description of the suspect.

8. That you used ADVOKATE to evidence identification of the person.

---

### 3.2.5.2 Power to issue fixed penalty notices for graffiti and fly-posting

Context

If a designated PCSO has reason to believe that a person has committed an offence in connection with acts of graffiti (figure 3.2) and/or fly-posting, the PCSO has the power to require his or her name and address and to give a person a fixed penalty notice as an alternative to conviction (remembering the Caution, see 3.2.5.1).

**KEY POINT**

There are no specific offences of producing graffiti or fly-posting and therefore they are investigated and prosecuted using the following legislation.

**Figure 3.2 Graffiti on a wooden fence**

---

### *Offence*—Damaging property: s 1(1) Criminal Damage Act 1971.

---

*Method of disposal*

Penalty notice for disorder (upper tier)—under Criminal Justice and Police

Act 2001. (See 3.2.5.1 on issuing PNDs and using the Caution for PNDs.)

[*To avoid lengthy repetition, we shall refer to the Criminal Justice and Police Act 2001 from this point forward as **CJP01**.]

*Mode of trial and penalty*

- If the value of the damage is **below** £5,000:
  Summary—three months' imprisonment and/or a level 4 fine.
- If the value of the damage **exceeds** £5,000 then it becomes an EITHER WAY offence:
  Summary—six months' imprisonment and/or a fine.
  Indictment—ten years' imprisonment.

*Points to consider to prove the offence*

1. That the suspect did not have any lawful excuse to cause the damage, such as s/he had no reason to believe s/he had the owner's consent.
2. That the property was damaged, for example a wall was defaced by paint from a spray can, or
3. That the property was destroyed or damaged beyond repair.
4. That the property belonged to someone other than the suspect (it can be jointly owned).
5. That the suspect intended to damage or destroy the property and s/he meant to do it, or
6. That the suspect was reckless as to whether or not the property was damaged or destroyed; s/he took a risk in his or her actions.

---

### *Offence*—Pulls down or obliterates a traffic sign: s 131(2) of the Highways Act 1980.

---

*Method of disposal*

Local authority fixed penalty s 43( 1) ASB03

*Mode of trial and penalty:* Summary—level 3 fine.

*Points to consider to prove the offence*

1. That the suspect did not have lawful authority or reasonable excuse.
2. That the suspect pulled down a traffic sign, milestone, or direction post, or
3. That the suspect obliterated a traffic sign, milestone, or direction post.
4. That the traffic sign, milestone, or direction post was placed on or over a highway.
5. That the traffic sign, milestone, or direction post was placed lawfully.

---

---

### Offence—Painting or affixing things on structures on the highway etc: s 132(1) Highways Act 1980.

---

*Method of disposal*

Local authority fixed penalty s 43(1) of the Anti-Social Behaviour Act 2003.*

[*To avoid lengthy repetition, we shall refer to s 43(1) of the Anti-Social Behaviour Act 2003 from this point forward as **S43ASB03**.]

*Mode of trial and penalty:* Summary—level 4 fine.

*Points to consider to prove the offence*

1. That the suspect did not have the consent of the highway authority, or any authorization or reasonable excuse.
2. That the suspect painted, inscribed, or affixed any letter, sign, or other mark.
3. That the letter, sign, or other mark was left on the surface of any highway, tree, structure, or words on or in a highway. (See figure 3.3.)

---

### Offence—Affixing posters: para 10 of s 54 of the Metropolitan Police Act 1839.

---

*Method of disposal*

Local authority fixed penalty S43ASB03.

*Mode of trial:* Summary.

*Points to consider to prove the offence*

1. That the suspect did not have lawful authority or reasonable excuse.
2. That the suspect personally affixed or placed the poster if it was an advertisement.
3. That the posters were affixed within the Metropolitan Police Area.
4. That the posters were affixed without the consent of the owner or occupier.

---

### Offence—Defacement of streets with slogans etc: s 20(1) London County Council (General Powers) Act 1954.

---

*Method of disposal*

Local authority fixed penalty.

*Mode of trial:* Summary.

*Points to consider to prove the offence*

1. That the suspect did not have lawful authority or reasonable excuse.
2. That the suspect painted or inscribed slogans.
3. That the streets in London were defaced as a result of the suspect's actions.

---

---

**Offence—Displaying advertisement in contravention of regulations: s 224(3) Town and Country Planning Act 1990.**

---

*Method of disposal*

Local authority fixed penalty S43ASB03.

*Mode of trial and penalty:* Summary—level 3 fine.

*Points to consider to prove the offence*

1. That the suspect did not have lawful authority or reasonable excuse.
2. That the suspect displayed an advertisement in contravention of planning regulations.
3. That the suspect did not have authority from the local planning authority.
4. That the suspect personally affixed or placed the advertisement.

---

**Offence—Failing to give name and address when required by a PCSO: para 1A(5) of S4PRA02.**

---

*Mode of trial and penalty:* Summary—level 3 fine.

**NB:** Once designated under para 2 of S4PRA02, you have the power to detain a person for 30 minutes to await the arrival of a police officer, if the suspect fails to give his or her name and address or s/he gives a false one.

See 3.2.3.4: **Failing to give name and address when required by a PCSO**, where the Points to Prove are itemized in respect of failing to give name and address when required.

---

### 3.2.5.3 Powers and legislation to deal with the unlawful supply, possession, and misuse of fireworks

- **Throwing fireworks in a public place**
- **Unlawful possession of a category 4 firework**
- **Unlawful possession by a person under 18 of an adult firework**
- **Breach of a fireworks curfew (night hours)**
- **Supplying excessively loud fireworks**

Context

A designated PCSO has the power to issue a PND to a person who has committed an offence of:

- Throwing fireworks.
- Unlawful possession of a category 4 firework.
- Unlawful possession by a person under 18 of an adult firework.
- Breach of a fireworks curfew.
- Supplying excessively loud fireworks.

Such a PCSO can then request a name and address from the suspect, who commits a further offence if he/she fails to comply with the request or gives false or inaccurate details.

A PCSO who is designated under para 2 of Sch 4 to the Police Reform Act 2002 also has the power to detain a suspect who failed to comply with your request for his/her name and address.

A PCSO who is designated under para 4 has the power to use reasonable force on the suspect to remain with him/her whilst awaiting the arrival of a police officer and to keep control until the custody of the suspect is transferred.

See also 3.2.4.4, Power to detain and use reasonable force to prevent a person making off or to transfer control of a detained person.

See also 3.2.4.4, Power to search detained persons for dangerous items or items that could be used to assist escape.

---

### Offence—Throwing fireworks in a public place: s 80 of the Explosives Act 1875.

See 3.2.5.1 on issuing PNDs and using the Caution for PNDs.

*Mode of trial and penalty:* Summary—a fine not exceeding level 5.

*Points to consider to prove the offence*

1. That you are designated under para 1 of Sch 4 to the Police Reform Act 2002 to issue PNDs.
2. That the person:
   - threw,
   - cast,
   - fired

     **any firework**
   - in, or
   - onto

     **any**
   - highway,
   - street,
   - thoroughfare, or
   - public place.

---

### Offence—Possession of a category 4 firework (reg 5, Fireworks Regulations 2004*)): s 11 Fireworks Act 2003.*

[*To avoid lengthy repetition, we shall refer to the Fireworks **Act** 2003 from this point forward as **F03**, and to the Fireworks **Regulations** 2004 from this point forward as **FR04**.]

See 3.2.5.1 on issuing PNDs and using the Caution for PNDs.

*Mode of trial and penalty:* Summary—6 months' imprisonment and/or a fine not exceeding level 5.

*Points to consider to prove the offence*

1. That the person had possession of a category 4 firework.
2. That the person was not a person who is employed by, or in business as:
   - a professional organizer of firework displays,
   - operator of firework displays,
   - firework manufacturer,
   - firework supplier,
   - local authority organizer of firework displays,
   - entertainments' special effects organizer,
   - Government organizer of firework displays,
   - Armed Services organizer of firework displays or pyrotechnics (such as for military tattoos) and who possesses the firework in question for the purposes of his/her employment or business.

---

### Offence—Possession by a person under 18 of an adult firework (reg 4 FR04): s 11 F03.

*Method of disposal*

Penalty notice for disorder (upper tier)—under CJP01.

See 3.2.5.1 on issuing PNDs and using the Caution for PNDs.

*Mode of trial and penalty:* Summary—6 months' imprisonment and/or a fine not exceeding level 5.

*Points to consider to prove the offence*

1. That the person was under 18.
2. That the person possessed an adult firework.
3. That the person was in a public place.

---

### Offence—Breach of a fireworks curfew (reg 7 FR04): s 11 F03.

See 3.2.5.1 on issuing PNDs and using the Caution for PNDs.

*Mode of trial and penalty:* Summary—6 months' imprisonment and/or a fine not exceeding level 5.

*Points to consider to prove the offence*

1. That the person used an adult firework during 'night hours' (see below for definition).
2. That the period was not a 'permitted firework night' (see definition below).
3. That the person was not a local authority employee putting on a local authority or commemorative firework display.

---

---

**Offence—Supplying excessively loud fireworks (reg 8 FR04): s 11 F03.**

See 3.2.5.1 on issuing PNDs and using the Caution for PNDs.

*Mode of trial and penalty:* Summary—6 months' imprisonment and/or a fine not exceeding level 5.

*Points to consider to prove the offence*

That the person:

- supplied,
- offered, or
- agreed to supply

any category 3 firework exceeding 120 decibels.

---

### Useful terms

'**Firework**': Fireworks (Safety) Regulations 1997.
'Any device intended for use as a form of entertainment which contains, or otherwise incorporates, explosive and/or pyrotechnic composition, which burns and/or explodes to produce a visual and/or audible effect.'

'**Category 3 firework**': FR04
A display firework that can be used by the general public but only at larger displays where the audience gets no closer than 25 metres and the debris is not scattered beyond 20 metres.

'**Category 4 firework**': FR04
A professional firework that cannot possibly be sold to the general public because of its size and potential power and requires a specialist to be in possession of it.

'**Adult firework**': FR04
Any firework that does not comply with part 2 of British Standard 7114 (tested for safety, explosive strengths, etc) 'except for a cap, cracker snap, novelty match, party popper, serpent, sparkler or throwdown'.

'**Public place**': FR04
'…includes any place to which at the material time the public have or are permitted access, whether on payment or otherwise'.

'**Night hours**': FR04
Starts at 2300 hrs and ends at 0700 hrs the next day.

'**Permitted fireworks night**': FR04

'(a)  beginning at 11 pm on the first day of the **Chinese New Year** and ending at 1 am the following day;

(b)  beginning at 11 pm on **5th November** and ending at 12 am the following day;

(c)  beginning at 11 pm on the day of **Diwali** and ending at 1 am the following day; or

(d)  beginning at 11 pm on **31st December** and ending at 1 am the following day.'

---

*Offence*—**Failing to give name and address when required by a PCSO: para 1A(5) of S4PRA02.**

*Mode of trial and penalty:* Summary—level 3 fine.

See 3.2.4.4 for details of your power to detain under PRA02.

See also 3.2.4.4: **Power to detain and use reasonable force to prevent a person making off or to transfer control of a detained person.**

See also 3.2.4.4: **Power to search detained persons for dangerous items or items that could be used to assist escape.**

*Points to consider to prove the offence*

See 3.2.3.4: **Failing to give name and address when required by a PCSO**, where the Points to Prove are itemized in respect of failing to give name and address when required.

---

### 3.2.5.4  Offences connected to malicious, false, and diversionary activities

- **Wasting police time or giving a false report**
- **Sending annoying or offensive messages via a network**
- **Making false fire alarms**

Context

A designated PCSO has the power to issue penalty notices for disorder (and using the Caution (3.2.5.1)

Three of the offences for which a PND can be issued are:

1.  Causing wasteful employment of the police.
2.  Sending annoying or offensive messages via a network.
3.  Making false fire alarms.

Having been designated under para 1 of S4PRA02 to issue PNDs, the PCSO has the power also to require the name and address of the suspect. Failure to comply is a separate offence.

**Figure 3.3 Damaging property: vandalized telephone box**

If the PCSO is further designated under para 1 of Sch 4, s/he can detain the person if s/he does not prove his or her name and address, or it is incorrect (see 3.2.4.4).

If the PCSO is further designated under para 2, s/he may then detain the person and await the arrival of a police officer or request the suspect to accompany the PCSO to the police station (see 3.2.4.4). If the PCSO is designated under para 4, s/he may use reasonable force during the detention of the suspect (see 3.2.4.4).

---

*Offence*—**Causing wasteful employment of the police: s 5(2) Criminal Law Act 1967.**

---

*Method of disposal*

See 3.2.5.1 on issuing PNDs and using the Caution for PNDs.

*Mode of trial and penalty:* Summary—6 months' imprisonment and/or a fine not exceeding level 4.

*Points to consider to prove the offence*

1. That the suspect caused any wasteful employment of the police.
2. That the suspect knowingly made a false report tending to show that an offence had been committed; or

3. That the suspect knowingly made a false report to give rise to apprehension for the safety of any persons or property; or
4. That the suspect knowingly made a false report tending to show that s/he had information material to any police enquiry.

---

**Offence—Sending annoying or offensive messages via a network: s 127 Communications Act 2003.**

*Method of disposal*

See 3.2.5.1 on issuing PNDs and using the Caution for PNDs.

*Mode of trial and penalty:* Summary—6 months' imprisonment and/or a fine not exceeding level 5.

*Points to consider to prove the offence*

1. That the suspect sent or caused a message or other matter to be sent by means of public electronic communications which was:
   - grossly offensive, or
   - indecent, or
   - obscene, or
   - of a menacing character, or
2. that the suspect for the purpose of causing annoyance, inconvenience, or needless anxiety to another:
   - sent a false message via a public electronic communications network, or
   - caused such a message to be sent, or
   - persistently made use of a public electronic communications network, and
   - that it was not done in the course of providing a television service under the Broadcasting Act 1990.

---

**Offence—Making false alarms: s 49 Fire and Rescue Services Act 2004 (England only); s 31 Fire Services Act 1947 (Wales only).**

*Method of disposal*

See 3.2.5.1 on issuing PNDs and using the Caution for PNDs.

*Mode of trial and penalty:* Summary—3 months' imprisonment and/or a fine not exceeding level 4.

*Points to consider to prove the offence*

1. That the suspect knowingly:
   - gives, or
   - causes to be given

a false alarm of fire to a person acting on behalf of a fire and rescue authority.

---

---

*Offence*—**Failing to give name and address when required by a PCSO: para 1A(5) of S4PRA02.**

---

*Mode of trial and penalty:* Summary—level 3 fine.

See 3.2.4.4 for details of your power to detain under PRA02.

*Points to consider to prove the offence*

See 3.2.3.4: **Failing to give name and address when required by a PCSO**, where the Points to Prove are itemized in respect of failing to give name and address when required.

---

## Knowledge Check 16

1. What two factors or 'designations' must be in operation before you can disperse groups and/or remove persons under 16 to their places of residence?

2. What 'reasonable grounds' must you have to disperse groups?

3. What time factor governs your power to remove someone to his or her place of residence?

4. What is the purpose of a 'curfew notice'?

5. If you find drugs when you are searching, what should you do?

6. Which premises can a PCSO NOT enter to investigate 'relevant licensing offences'?

7. Why are PCSOs used in support of authorized examiners of road vehicles?

8. What are the *points to prove* for the offence of being 'drunk and disorderly'?

9. No specific offences exist for producing graffiti or for fly-posting; so what legislation can you use?

10. Who may lawfully possess a category 4 firework?

11. What defines a firework?

12. What are three of the offences for which a PND can be issued?

---

### 3.2.5.5 Powers and legislation to deal with threatening or abusive behaviour likely to cause harassment, alarm, or distress

Context

A designated PCSO has the power to issue a PND to a person who has committed an offence of using threatening or abusive behaviour likely to cause harassment, alarm, or distress. Such a PCSO can then require a name and address from the suspect who commits a further offence if s/he fails to comply with the requirements or gives false or inaccurate details.

A PCSO who is designated under para 2 of Sch 4 to the Police Reform Act 2002 also has the power to detain a suspect who fails to comply with the PCSO's request for his/her name and address.

A PCSO who is designated under para 4 has the power to use reasonable force on the suspect, to remain with him/her whilst awaiting the arrival of a police officer, and to keep control until the custody of the suspect is transferred.

See also 3.2.4.4: **Power to detain and use reasonable force to prevent a person making off or to transfer control of a detained person.**

See also 3.2.4.4: **Power to search detained persons for dangerous items or items that could be used to assist escape.**

---

*Offence*—**Using threatening or abusive behaviour likely to cause harassment, alarm or distress: s 5 Public Order Act 1986.**

---

*Method of disposal*

See 3.2.5.1 on issuing PNDs and using the Caution for PNDs.

*Mode of trial and penalty:* Summary—a fine not exceeding level 3.

*Points to consider to prove the offence*

1. That you are designated under para 1 of S4PRA02 to issue PNDs.
2. That the person used any of the following conduct:
   - threatening, or
   - abusive,
   - words or behaviour, or
   - disorderly behaviour.
3. That the person displayed any of the following conduct:
   - threatening, or
   - abusive,
   - writing, signs, or other visual representation.
4. That the person took part in any of the above conduct in the hearing or sight of a person who was likely to be caused:
   - harassment,
   - alarm, or
   - distress.
5. That the conduct could be seen or heard in public (even if the conduct took place in private).
6. That the suspect intended his/her conduct to be:
   - threatening, or
   - abusive, or
   - disorderly.

7. That the suspect is aware that his/her conduct is:
   - threatening, or
   - abusive, or
   - disorderly.

---

**Offence—Failing to give name and address when required by a PCSO: para 1A(5) of S4PRA02.**

*Mode of trial and penalty:* Summary—level 3 fine.

See 3.2.4.4 for details of your power to detain under PRA02.

*Points to consider to prove the offence*

See 3.2.3.4: **Failing to give name and address when required by a PCSO**, where the Points to Prove are itemized in respect of failing to give name and address when required.

---

### 3.2.5.6 Trespassing on railway property

Context

If designated, a PCSO has the power to issue a penalty notice for disorder to any person who trespasses on railway property as long as s/he fulfils the criteria for issuing a PND (see 5.2.8 for issuing criteria).

---

**Offence—Trespassing on railway property: s 55(1) British Transport Commission Act 1949.**

*Method of disposal*

See 3.2.5.1 on issuing PNDs and using the Caution for PNDs.

*Mode of trial and penalty:* Summary—a fine not exceeding level 3.

*Points to consider to prove the offence*

1. That the person was trespassing on any:
   - railway lines,
   - sidings, tunnels,
   - embankment cutting or similar work connected to a Railway Board, or any other Railway Board lands in dangerous proximity to
   - railway lines,
   - any other works, or
   - electrical equipment connected to the working of the railway.
2. That a public warning to persons not to trespass on the railway existed in the form of a clearly exhibited notice or sign sited at the railway station closest to the incident.
3. That you made a note of the description of the suspect.
4. That you used ADVOKATE to evidence identification of the person.

---

---

*Offence*—Failing to give name and address when required by a PCSO: para 1A(5) of S4PRA02

---

*Mode of trial and penalty:* Summary—level 3 fine.

See 3.2.4.4 for details of your power to detain under PRA02.

*Points to consider to prove the offence*

See 3.2.3.4: **Failing to give name and address when required by a PCSO**, where the Points to Prove are itemized in respect of failing to give name and address when required.

---

### 3.2.5.7 Throwing stones or objects at railway equipment

Context

If designated, a PCSO has the power to issue a penalty notice for disorder to any person who throws stones or objects at railway property as long as the offence (and offender) fulfils the criteria for issuing a PND.

---

*Offence*—Throwing stones or objects at railway equipment: s 56(1) British Transport Commission Act 1949.

---

*Method of disposal*

See 3.2.5.1 on issuing PNDs and using the Caution for PNDs.

*Mode of trial and penalty:* Summary—a fine not exceeding level 3.

*Points to consider to prove the offence*

1. That the person unlawfully:
   - threw,
   - caused to fall,
   - caused to strike at, against, into or upon, any
   - engine,
   - tender,
   - motor carriage, or
   - truck

   used upon or any works or equipment upon any railway or siding connected to a Railway Board.
2. That the projectile was a stone or other object.
3. That the object was likely to cause damage or injury to persons or property.
4. That you made a note of the description of the suspect.
5. That you used ADVOKATE to evidence identification of the person.

---

---

*Offence*—**Failing to give name and address when required by a PCSO: para 1A(5) of S4PRA02.**

---

*Mode of trial and penalty:* Summary—level 3 fine.

See 3.2.4.4 for details of your power to detain under PRA02.

*Points to consider to prove the offence*

See 3.2.3.4: **Failing to give name and address when required by a PCSO**, where the Points to Prove are itemized in respect of failing to give name and address when required.

---

### 3.2.6 Power of arrest (for persons other than a constable) under section 24A of the Police and Criminal Evidence Act 1984

Whether or not you are designated to detain a person under para 2 of the Police Reform Act 2002, you—and any other citizen in England and Wales—have a power to **arrest** any person who is committing or has committed an **indictable offence** (see 3.1.2). The power of 'the citizen's arrest' is based on a number of conditions being met, none greater than the necessity for the offence for which the arrest is being made, being an indictable offence. It is worth noting that there is an earlier piece of legislation that supplements s 24A of PACE: it is s 3 of the Criminal Law Act 1967 which (in summary) states that reasonable force may be used in self-defence (including a pre-emptive strike) and can also be used to assist with the arrest of a wanted person unlawfully at large.

#### 3.2.6.1 Powers of arrest

To help you understand the power of arrest, there follows a description of the component parts in paragraphs. The power is available to every citizen other than a police constable. It is, for example, the power to arrest that store detectives use to detain a person they suspect of shoplifting. This power of arrest, therefore, includes you. It does not mean you have to use it. This book recognizes the sometimes ambiguous framework under which you work and your association with the community which you support, but the power to arrest is there should you require it. The term 'arrest without warrant' still exists in modern day legislation to differentiate between warrants of arrest issued by courts and powers of arrest for which no warrant is required:

1. The power can be used to arrest a person who is in the act of committing an **indictable offence.** This means that the person making the arrest can see the suspect carrying out the crime there and then.

2. Another opportunity to use the power is when somebody other than a constable has reasonable grounds for suspecting a person to be committing an **indictable offence.** We have already discussed in other sections that 'reasonable grounds' are subjective. Let's say you had been given a description by a witness of a person spraying a shop front and you went inside and saw a person of the same description standing with a spray can in his/her hand next to a wall with fresh paint on it. As the suspect was not in the process of spraying right at that moment but may have been about to start spraying again, you would have 'reasonable' grounds for suspecting the person to be committing the offence.

3. An indictable offence is an offence that can be tried **either way,** either in a magistrates' court or in a Crown Court, such as theft. An offence that can be tried on indictment only in a Crown Court and nowhere else, is a serious or major crime, such as manslaughter or murder. These classifications of offences are together known as 'indictable offences'. You will know the classification of an offence by looking at each of the offences you have the power to deal with. Here the mode of trial and penalty will be listed. Obviously, those offences listed as summary can only be tried in a magistrates' court and are therefore not indictable offences.

### Indictable offences 'in the past'

(4) In the first two situations above, in which you would be entitled to use the power of arrest, the suspect was committing an indictable offence and the situations referred to something happening at the present time. The power can also be used when an indictable offence has been committed in the past. An example of this would be if you were given a description by a witness of a person spraying a shop front and you went inside and saw a person of the same description walking away from a wall with fresh paint on it. The suspect would no longer be **committing** the offence, but the offence would have been **committed.**

### 'Completion of the offence'

(5) A suspect in England and Wales is innocent until proven guilty. Some legislation makes reference to a person being 'guilty' of committing an offence. This way of writing is simply trying to say 'a person who has just arrived at the end of completing the offence'. This power of arrest is one of those pieces of legislation. An example would be if you had received a description from the witness, and then you had gone inside the 'Precinct' and seen the suspect standing next to the paint on the wall, having just completed the damage and throwing the can into the rubbish bin; you would arrest 'at the end of completing the offence'.

### Grounds for suspicion of guilt

(6) In the past, when an indictable offence had been committed, there was a fourth situation in which the power of arrest could be used. This was when the person making the arrest has reasonable grounds for **suspecting** another to be guilty of the offence. (This is the most tenuous of the four situations under which the power of arrest can be used.) Using the 'Precinct' example again, having received the description given by the witness, you go inside, see the graffiti on the wall of the shop and see a person walking away from it who fitted the description given by the witness. The witness's description, if sufficiently distinctive, gives you grounds for 'suspecting' the offender.

### 'Reasonable grounds' and 'believing an arrest is necessary'

(7) Having considered the situations under which the power can be used, we are now going to consider the **conditions which have to be met as far as circumstances are concerned.** (Therefore, without either of the following two circumstances ((8) and (9)) being present, the power cannot be used.)

(8) The person making the arrest must have *reasonable grounds for believing that the arrest is necessary*. The reasons that make the arrest necessary are listed in points (11) to (14) below. If the arrest is not necessary for one of these reasons, along with the circumstances dictating that it is not reasonably practicable for a constable to make it, the power of arrest cannot be used.

(9) In addition to meeting the requirements of having reasonable grounds for *believing that the arrest is necessary*, it must appear to the person making the arrest that *it is not reasonably practicable for a police constable to make it instead*. The person making the arrest must therefore not only believe it is necessary for one or more of the reasons listed below, but, for example, because of the length of time it might take a police officer to arrive, the person must make the arrest there and then.

### Necessity

(10) To meet the *necessity* criterion, the person making the arrest must believe the suspect is going to carry out one or more of **four** activities which must be prevented. If the person making the arrest does not have reasonable grounds for believing that the arrest is necessary to prevent the suspect from carrying out one or more of these four activities, then the arrest cannot take place.

### Prevention of injury to self or others

(11) The *first* of the four reasons is to prevent the suspect from causing physical injury to himself/herself or any other person. An example of this would be if the suspect was in possession of an article which s/he could use upon him/herself or on any other person, including the person making the arrest.

Preventing the suspect from suffering injury

(12) The *second* of the reasons is to prevent the suspect from suffering physical injury. An example of this would be if the suspect was surrounded by a group of people who were intent upon causing the suspect harm owing to the crime s/he had allegedly committed (a common instance when people find out where a convicted paedophile is living).

Preventing loss or damage

(13) The *third* of the reasons is to prevent the suspect from causing loss of or damage to property. An example of this would be if the suspect was in possession of proceeds from the crime s/he had committed and was about to throw them away into a place from which they could not be recovered.

Preventing the suspect from 'making off'

(14) The *fourth* and final reason is to prevent the suspect making off before a constable can assume responsibility for him/her. An example of this would be if the suspect was not complying with the request to remain until a police officer arrived or s/he appeared to be about to make off.

We will look now at requirements placed upon you by the Police and Criminal Evidence Act 1984 Codes of Practice and your own designated powers.

### 3.2.7  Recording of encounters with the public not governed by statutory powers

The Police and Criminal Evidence (PACE) Act 1984 Codes of Practice Code A, para 4.12 states that there is no national requirement to make any record, or give any person any receipt as a result of any encounter in which a PCSO requests a person in a public place to account for themselves, ie their actions, behaviour, presence in an area, or possession of anything. However, forces have discretion to direct PCSOs to record the self-defined ethnicity of persons if there are concerns which make it necessary to monitor any local disproportionality. Local policy may also dictate that in the event of a person challenging a request to account for themselves, they should be provided with information about how they can report their dissatisfaction.

## 3.3  Checking Your Own Designated Powers

### 3.3.1  The law

Under the Police and Justice Bill 2006, signed into law as the **Police and Justice Act 2006** in November 2006 and enacted from April 2007, PCSOs have standard powers, which we looked at in 3.2.3. Having now taken you through the powers and duties of a PCSO, there is an ongoing task for you to ascertain with what specific powers you have been designated by your Chief Constable.

### 3.3.1.1 The reassurance of possessing the powers

It has been argued that just as a police officer has a range of powers which s/he doesn't always need to use, so a PCSO needs the reassurance of possession of the powers, even though not be called upon to use them in the normal run of duty. The powers are there in case they are needed.

---

**DISCUSSION POINT**

Do you think that you need the standard powers, or would a set of specific powers tailored to the role you do be preferable?

---

We would like to make a closing comment which may seem contradictory after all the detail about what your powers are and how you use them, but it is none-theless an important thing to say. It is this: *you do not always need to use your powers to gain people's compliance. Legislative powers are the skeleton of your PCSO role, but knowing when to use them and when to reason on a personal level with people, is the true flesh of the job. Although your authority is vested in the law, you will be a more effective PCSO if you use your skills and charm to defuse a situation: powers should be a last, not a first, resort.*

Now, the final Knowledge Check for this chapter:

---

**Knowledge Check 17**

1. What actions may cause 'harassment, alarm or distress'?

2. What must be displayed at railway stations?

3. What are the *points to prove* in the offence of 'throwing stones or objects at railway equipment'?

4. When might you arrest someone?

5. What are the four activities that meet the 'necessary' criterion for arrest?

6. What must you do if you ask a member of the public to 'stop and account' for what they are doing?

7. What might be an exception to this requirement?

---

# The National Occupational Standards and Behavioural Competences

## 4.1 **Introduction**

This chapter looks in detail at what skills, standards, and competences you need when working as a PCSO, and indeed much of the material covered in this chapter will be relevant for those of you who have aspirations to join the regular police at some point. Most of you will undergo, or have already undergone, an in-Force structured training phase which will have provided the foundation for the specialist knowledge and understanding required in the role of a PCSO. The **National Occupational Standards** (NOS) draw heavily on this knowledge gained during initial training, and practical assessments and demonstration of competencies all form part of the journey to meet the NOS criteria. The NOS workbook that you commence during initial training (and any mentorship scheme provided by the individual force) is essentially a codified, auditable demonstration of your knowledge, attitude, skills, and overall capability to work as a PCSO. This may seem a bit sterile and academic, but as a PCSO you must always remember that you are a representative of the entire force, you are accountable as an individual for your actions, and you can be presented with a plethora of different scenarios and people; the NOS workbook therefore is ultimately a personal development tool to ensure you are as capable as possible to deal with whatever you are confronted with. As an individual you are expected to keep an evidence portfolio known as a **Student Officer Learning and Assessment Portfolio** (SOLAP) of your steady advancement towards competence, and attaining that competence, in each NOS, but this will also be supplemented, added to, and audited as appropriate by mentors, other PCSOs, police officers, trainers, and even members of the public.

### 4.1.1 **This chapter is a reference guide, not a 'crib'**

All this may sound a bit daunting and achievement may seem a very long way ahead, but this chapter will examine how the NOS workbook is formulated, the typical elements that are included, and furthermore how officers are assessed to attain successful completion. **However, we must sound one warning:** whilst we are very willing to guide and advise you through the NOS and the core behavioural competences, all the elements of which go into assessing you as competent and sufficiently skilled to perform your job well, what we cannot do is provide you with 'crib' answers. The reason for this is that the fundamental purpose of NOS is to promote self-reflection and personal development, identify any areas for improvement, whilst ensuring that you act according to legal regulations and Force policy. Simply providing you with 'crib' answers would essentially be a betrayal of this very important purpose. You must think, consider, assess, and record your own experiences in your SOLAP upon which your assessment will be based.

In other words, the assessment of *your* ability to reach this Standard is to be based on what *you* identify, *your* experiences in *your* beat or patrol or neighbourhood team, contributing to *your* Force objectives. Additionally, it will be assessed by *your* tutors, or police officer supervisors, or team supervisors, or sergeants, or whatever oversight system *your* Force uses.

One of the authors gives his personal experience of what it was like to learn and consolidate in the early phases of becoming a PCSO:

> Much of the knowledge and understanding required for each of the elements in the NOS' workbook was covered during the initial training phase. Many of the lectures, pre-reads and role plays were directed at developing us for the role of PCSO, whilst also having the secondary benefit of comprising much of the material required for the 'knowledge' and 'understanding' phases of the NOS workbook. However, a student officer cannot simply regurgitate this material, he or she has to analyse it and show an organic understanding of the learning to successfully complete this initial stage. Having undertaken the training stage at my Force headquarters, I then spent eight weeks under the mentorship of a highly experienced and knowledgeable PCSO. The practical development that I experienced during these eight weeks was remarkable as I was exposed to countless incidents and was required to respond in different ways (with the safety net of a seasoned officer to provide assistance where necessary). These experiences form the examples that demonstrated my behavioural competencies and built my confidence in the role. Ultimately the training phase and mentorship teaches you to walk confidently before you need to run. The experience generally will be the same for you, though of course the actual events will be different, as will your responses to them. Nonetheless, learning on the job with a PCSO tutor beside you is both immediate as an experience and profound as an insight into doing the job.

## 4.2  NOS and Associated Assessment Criteria

The National Occupational Standards are owned and developed by **Skills for Justice** (often rendered in the shorthand form of SfJ, though sometimes as S4J), which is the 'Sector Skills Council' for the 'Justice Sector'. This may not mean much to you, but you need to know that SfJ developed from National Training Organizations (NTOs) which used to exist as a kind of professional 'standards keeper' in many parts of the Service and Manufacturing industries. Successive surveys of 'skills at work' identified inconsistent attainment of necessary skills, patchy appraisal processes, unfair or subjective assessment of skills in some areas, and a general lack of rigour about the sorts of skills standards which people should be exhibiting in the performance of their roles.

### 4.2.1 NOS may change or reduce

**KEY POINT**

Readers should note that, at the time of writing (midsummer 2014) the NOS have been presented as they are currently for PCSOs. This does not mean they will not change, for policing is nothing if not cyclical and in constant flux, and it is your responsibility to ensure that **you are competent with the NOS required at the time of your training and first patrolling**. In other words, keep watching this NOS space. It is also important to emphasize that a PCSO's continued professional development is constantly monitored in his or her police force. Completing the NOS workbook is only the primary stage; you can expect to receive regular professional development reviews and will be expected to identify ongoing areas for development.

### 4.2.2 How the NOS developed

The NTOs emerged from this consensus on standards, but each NTO was aligned only to its particular 'niche' until combinations of 'skills sectors' began to coalesce in the late 1990s. By 2004, our own sector, Justice, had merged the Police Skills and Standards Organisation, the Custodial Care NTO, and the Community Justice NTO, each with their separate suites of occupational standards, into one: **Skills for Justice**. SfJ has produced, in consultation with expert practitioners, the National Occupational Standards for PCSOs, which are broadly based on the competences expected of a police patrol, or 'beat', officer but which have particular resonance for the PCSO role.

### 4.2.2.1 The NOS will change again

As we noted in the Key Point box above, we should not suppose that all NOS will remain fixed. In essence we will probably retain the core assessments but the NOS and associated assessment criteria are evolving and developing all the time, and they will 'mutate' to ensure that the developing needs of PCSOs, and the communities they serve, are met in the occupational standards. And this makes sense; until 2001, PCSOs did not exist. It would be odd indeed if the needs and standards of a newly-developing body within the extended police family did not change over time. It would be a bold prophet who attempts to predict what skills will be needed in technology in 20 years' time. The point of all this is to say that, whilst we can tell you what NOS are needed now, you should not assume that these are fixed and invariable. Things will change as being a PCSO will change, and the NOS need to keep in step. The ever-changing nature of the NOS workbook is perfectly exemplified by the reduction in elements required for successful completion of the NOS workbook; until recently there were 12 individual elements required for a PCSO, however these have now been halved to six elements which we will examine now.

#### 4.2.2.2 **What the NOS consist of**

Organizationally, the set-up as currently practised looks like this:

–   **Unit 001—Communicate effectively with people maintaining the security of information**
    Element 1—Understand how to communicate with people
    Element 2—Understand how to maintain the security of information in communications with people
    Element 3—Be able to communicate with people

–   **Unit 002—Provide initial support to victims and witnesses**
    Element 1—Know and understand the factors that affect victims and witnesses and impact on their need for support
    Element 2—Be able to communicate effectively with victims and witnesses
    Element 3—Be able to provide initial support to victims and witnesses
    Element 4—Be able to assess the needs and wishes of victims and witnesses for further support

–   **Unit 003—Gather and submit information to support law enforcement objectives**
    Element 1—Know and understand relevant legal and organizational requirements related to gathering and submitting information
    Element 2—Be able to gather and submit information that has the potential to support law enforcement objectives

–   **Unit 004—Provide an initial response to incidents—Crime/Non-Crime/ Traffic** (must be practically demonstrated on three occasions, minimum two different types required)
    Element 1—Know and understand relevant legal and organisational requirements for responding to an incident
    Element 2—Be able to gather information and plan a response to an incident
    Element 3—Be able to respond to incidents

–   **Unit 005—Prepare for, and participate in, planned enforcement operations**
    Element 1—Know, understand, and apply relevant legal and organizational requirements
    Element 2—Be able to prepare for, and participate in, planned law enforcement operations (Minimum: 2 different types of Operation)

–   **Unit 006—Manage conflict in a policing context**
    Element 1—Understand legislation and other relevant guidance related to managing conflict
    Element 2—Be able to apply conflict management skills and techniques
    Element 3—Use personal safety skills and any issued equipment

### 4.2.2.3  Plotting your progress: the NOS workbook software

As you progress through each element and subcategory of the NOS electronic workbook identified above, your journey as a student officer will be indicated by a percentage bar graphic. This informs you of your progress through the workbook and highlights any outstanding elements yet to be completed, the idea being that your time is managed appropriately for the required work load. Training staff will intermittently examine your portfolio and validate the quality of the material to confirm it is to the required standard. They will also comment where necessary if progress is too slow.

The NOS workbook is a standardized piece of software and as such will have an identical layout for every PCSO in every force; however, each officer's portfolio will be unique and contain different material. Your contact details, officer information, and Force number will all be viewable in one tab, whilst another tab is dedicated to a 'Daybook' facility. This is essentially a diary or log where you can record your daily activities, any praise you have received, any courses or computer packages you have completed and allows you to comment on your progress as a student officer.

### 4.2.3  What do NOS do?

**National Occupational Standards describe competent performance in terms of an individual's work; defining what needs to be achieved rather than what needs to be done.** This means, simply, that you do not pass or fail NOS, you either achieve the competence or you are not yet competent. This makes the NOS very flexible in terms of what you have to demonstrate or evidence about competence to your assessor. Further, the NOS can help you as an individual, and your Force as an organization, to face current challenges by ensuring that you (and the organization) have the necessary knowledge, understanding, and skills. What is more, a PCSO in West Midlands Police will be judged on the same independent and objective criteria through NOS as will a PCSO (*SCCH*) in Dyfed–Powys Police (*Heddlu*). This gives a common performance benchmark across all forces in England and Wales.

### 4.2.3.1  How are NOS organized?

The whole set of NOS for the PCSO 'occupational group' is called a '**workbook**' which is divided into individual **units** which group together the outcomes required to demonstrate competence. The whole **unit** then becomes a statement of that **competence**. It sounds complex but is not; indeed when you look at the sample NOS we work through later on (4.3), simplicity is actually key to understanding what is required. Each unit contains:

A **unit summary**: This is not part of the standard, but it does give you a context and suggests how the unit is applied in your daily work, specifying some of the activities involved.

**194**

An example might be **Unit 005:** *Prepare for, and participate in, planned policing operations*, where part of the **unit summary** is:

> This unit is about contributing to planned policing operations. The unit applies to all types of pre-planned policing operations such as crowd control, football matches and galas and the use of ANPR (automatic number plate readers)...
>
> **Elements** Units are divided into separate **elements**. Typically there are about four in each unit, but they can vary from a single element to five. Each **element** contains both '**performance criteria**' and '**range**'.

An example is

– **Unit 003—Gather and submit information to support law enforcement objectives**

where there are two elements:

> Element 1—Know and understand relevant legal and organizational requirements related to gathering and submitting information
> Element 2—Be able to gather and submit information that has the potential to support law enforcement objectives.

As we have already identified, each element within a unit will consist of a 'Knowledge and Understanding' section (usually **Element 1**), and then a practical demonstration of the skill (usually **Element 2**) to exemplify a holistic, rounded competency and foundational understanding. This is exemplified above in the two elements relating to information within the police service.

In this example the first element would look at how information gained by the officer can be submitted within the constabulary. There would be particular emphasis on regulations, force policy and legislation relating to the gathering and submitting of information such as Management of Police Information and the *Data Protection Act*, whilst also asking the officer to show an understanding of the importance of submitting information to support the 'policing purpose'. The **second element** will be a practical demonstration of this understanding: for example the officer may submit a '5x5x5 intelligence report', provide feedback on a particular tasking, or—a key responsibility of the PCSO role—submit a 'ward return' detailing the dynamics of the community and its current issues that require action from the police.

**Performance Criteria** These describe what you need to demonstrate your competence. Please note that these are not merely lists of tasks to do, nor are the criteria simple chronologies of how to achieve competence.

**Knowledge and Understanding** You will remember these as the first two parts of KUSAB. In Chapter 3 we talked about the 'why?' of your powers as the vital bit about understanding. We said then that the 'how?' (skills) part would come later. Both 'how?' and 'why?' combine now in this part of each NOS to give assessors the opportunity to assess that **you know how to do something and you know why you should do it**. This includes the requirement that you know and understand relevant facts, opinions, theories, and principles in the particular Standard.

**Evidence Requirements** This describes what you need to prove, or demonstrate that you have achieved, the required competence in this particular unit or range.

This is the whole point of the Unit, because if you can produce the proof (evidence) that you are competent, you can then move on to another aspect of learning.

**Assembling your evidence of competence** This gives an indication of the way in which evidence should be assembled, and you will note the parameters that have been set on how evidence is to be presented. You will see a further example of this later on. You will need to approach the business of demonstrating your competence in a logical, structured, and deliberate manner. Your portfolio of written and attested evidence must reflect this organized approach; practise now getting your evidence requirements together in a clear presentation.

### 4.2.3.2 The wider application of competences

Individual units may serve to specify the performance standard needed to complete a particular task or they may be grouped together to define competent performance in a role. Your BCU Commander has a suite of Units to define his or her competences just as you do. They may be different in outcomes and levels of competence, but the essence is the same in both cases. Indeed, nearly all roles in the police service, including many of those for police staff, are now defined by NOS and core behavioural competences (which we deal with later). They are used to assess for recruitment, selection, and promotion, and are used too as the basis of a **Personal Development Review** (PDR; what used to be called an 'appraisal') to ascertain development needs. The important point about all of this is that NOS now underpin everything we do in terms of objectively assessing whether or not we can do a particular job or role in policing, and, by extrapolation, to help others decide whether an individual may have the potential to perform competently.

---

**DISCUSSION POINT**

In our judgement, your competence, assessed across a range of standards, is more important than your powers, though not all will agree with us. Do you?

---

### 4.2.3.3 Assessment

You will be assessed, not just during your training, or during your probation, but throughout your career with the police. Why? Well, skills abrade, or wear away. Your recall of what to do may get a bit rusty if you are not performing the task on a daily basis. A line manager (supervisor or direct manager) will assess your performance against a range of tasks which will be underpinned by NOS, and the core behavioural competences, and may decide in discussion with you that you need a refresher, or an opportunity to demonstrate competence in areas where you are not currently tested but which are parts of your role. This isn't something done *to* you passively, but *with* your agreement and (we hope) enthusiastic participation. The technical name for this—which you will come across often, and which we have talked about in the previous sections—is **continuous professional development** or 'CPD'. It can also be described as keeping all your competences sharp.

### 4.2.3.4  How is assessment made?

So, how are you assessed? There are several ways in which assessment may be made, and it is always helpful to discuss with your assessor which you prefer and which you are most comfortable with. That said, your assessor will want to see the full range of assessments used. The following are the standard assessment methodologies which you can expect to experience.

### 4.2.3.5  Observation of your work activity

This relates to the assessor observing you as you carry out your usual duties and assessing your competence against one or more of the relevant units that make up the PCSO NOS Workbook. You will record the fact that you were observed for a particular task or performance criterion, and an officer or mentor will write up a brief statement about what they observed, usually in a 'Word document' format and how it signed off one of your competencies.

### 4.2.3.6  Observation of 'products'

This method entails the assessor looking at the end product of an activity or task. Most of the time, an assessor will not need to observe you doing the work which led to the end product; it is enough that you have achieved the end product, and the assessor will be able to judge whether or not you are competent. An example might be in drawing up an action plan for agreement with members of the community about graffiti. The assessor need not sit through the consultation period with community members (though that might be productive in assessing your other competences), nor observe you through the period when you were hunched over your keyboard or staring into space hoping for inspiration. The action plan itself may be enough to demonstrate that the end product entailed all the consultation and thinking time. Or it may not: the assessor may send you back to try again if the action plan does not show you to be competent in this task. You may have missed some important aspects of planning (such as identifying the perpetrators) which puts your competence in doubt. This is where self-reflection is crucial as it will assist in your understanding of why something has failed, why an incident escalated as it did, and how you could have acted differently to produce a different outcome. Note too that the assessor may ask you questions to confirm your understanding and to ensure that you did the task without help. These are called 'ADQs' (Assessor-Directed Questions) and may be used to evidence your competence or your need for further development. Many of the criteria in many of the units will entail ADQs as a matter of routine.

### 4.2.3.7 Testimony

Just as a witness statement in a court of law carries a certain weight, so in your SOLAP portfolio of evidence of your competence, a witness testimony is important. **The testimony is a written statement confirming that you have carried out a particular task or activity competently.** It must be completed by someone who knows the subject thoroughly. Testimony is a useful source of evidence of your competence, since your assessor cannot be expected to observe everything you do.

### 4.2.3.8 Content of the testimony

We cannot prescribe what a witness should say about you in evidence but you should be aware that assessors will be looking for **balance** in the testimony, **accuracy, evidence** that the witness knew what s/he was talking about, **honesty** (you can't be expected to get everything right, and an assessor would be suspicious of someone who did), and **relevance.** Practical examples will help the evidential process and the testimony should be collected at or around the time of the action or task. It may not always be possible to get a contemporaneous (*at the time*) account as testimony, but going back six months later is unlikely to persuade your assessor of the testimony's timeliness.

### 4.2.3.9 Student officer's explanation of a process

You might be asked by your assessor to describe how you carried out a particular action or task, or you may be invited to describe what you would do in a given set of circumstances. This method is often used to assess your knowledge (for example of the police Caution or about one of your powers) or those parts of the range that might be difficult to evidence at the time. For example, your assessor might ask you to explain what procedures are involved in reporting a 'suspicious' or sudden death. It isn't always possible to produce a body on demand, so the assessor may resort to your explanation of what you would do in the circumstances. The evidence of your competence may be recorded on an ADQ form or as a separate entry. Either way, the evidence needs to be referenced carefully.

### 4.2.3.10 Written questions

The assessor may give you some questions in written form and invite you to write your answers; either there and then, or at your leisure. Be warned that the assessor will follow up the written questions with verbal questions when you submit the evidence: this is to ensure that you understood what you were doing and that the written answers were your own, unaided, work. The method could be used on any of the performance criteria, but it is likely that the assessor will use the written question to test your knowledge of a process. As before, the evidence of your reply should be filed as evidence in your assessment portfolio (SOLAP), and it would help if the assessor signs the answer to show that s/he has seen and read what you have said. Unlike the ADQs, when it is the assessor's responsibility to write up the question and answer, *written answers are your responsibility.* Don't separate the answer from the question: this will look inefficient in your portfolio and may lead to such confusion that the written answer is disregarded and you will have to do the whole thing all over again.

### 4.2.3.11 Projects

These are helpful, practical ways in which a range of competences can be evidenced. The important points are that you agree the scope of the project with your assessor, its length, and when it needs to be assessed. Do not embark on an ambitious project to hit as many competences as you can or you may find yourself bogged down in detail, casting about frantically for additional range material, and running out of time to get testimony or assessor evidence. **Make sure instead that the project is small, self-contained, short in duration, and able to be done by one person:** you.

#### An example of a project: creating a skateboard park

A sample project that meets these requirements might be to scope the cost, siting, and contents of a skateboard park on common land near a problem estate. You would need to talk to members of the community (witness testimony); ascertain what land is available (councils, borough departments, agencies, partnerships); ascertain costs of the land (Land Registry, estate agencies); identify sources of finance (local businesses, local charities, local youth groups, fund-raising activities); and purchase of equipment (local youth who will use it, other such projects, suppliers). If you undertook to do all this, you would hit a number of competences simultaneously and your performance criteria would be well evidenced. If you could get your assessor to observe you doing some of it as well, you'd end up with a useful range of evidence in your portfolio and you would have been doing your job properly too.

### 4.2.3.12 Simulation and role play

SfJ is rightly sceptical of too much role play or simulation: you do not get to be an effective PCSO by living only in a classroom or acting out scenes away from the real world. Correspondingly, there are few occasions when simulation or enactment will suffice for the NOS evidence. As you work through the NOS you will see which criteria permit simulation or enactment (role play) and which do not.

**199**

### 4.2.3.13 What happens once your competence has been assessed?

If you are assessed as competent, the assessor signs off the relevant evidence and helps you plan for your next assessment, or any outstanding work still to be completed. In some forces, NOS are linked with a National Vocational Qualification (NVQ) so that you can receive certified recognition of your completion of the course.

What to do if you are assessed as 'not yet competent'

If you are assessed as **'not yet competent'**, your assessor may ask you questions to cover gaps, or plan another opportunity for you to collect sufficient evidence, or set a date to review what you need to complete the evidence. You will be given reasonable time to amass what is needed, and it is important that you see the assessor as an objective support to you, and you should make sure that you tap into his or her expertise and experience in assessing PCSOs.

## 4.3 NOS—An Exemplar

In order to illustrate the practical utilization of the NOS, we are now going to provide an example of how one particular National Occupational Standard can be completed. However, this comes with an ethical warning—this example is an illustrative one designed to aid learning within this book. It is not intended to be a 'cut and paste' for your own portfolio and there will be variations in the NOS competencies examined by individual constabularies. The NOS workbook is a role specific assessment of your competency to operate as a PCSO; failure to treat it with sufficient respect or dedication will produce a poor performance in this early stage of your career and may mean you are not signed off as an independent officer.

We will not labour this point but it has been made at the outset and repeated here. Don't forget that your highly intelligent and expert trainers also read this book....

### 4.3.1 Completing NOS Unit 2

In order to provide an illustrative example we are going to use *NOS Unit 2— Provide Initial Support to Victims and Witnesses*. This is a typical competency that will be examined in a NOS workbook as it is a fundamental responsibility of a PCSO, and it therefore serves as an ideal example for us to explore in detail. This example has **four elements**, each divided into sub-sections, detailed below.

> *Element 1—Know and Understand the factors that affect victims and witnesses and impact on their need for support.*
>
> 1. *Describe how crime impacts on victims and witnesses*
> 2. *Explain the reasons why it is important to recognise and address the needs of victims and witnesses*

3. *Identify the range of needs that victims and witnesses (including those who are particularly vulnerable) may have, and the ways in which they can be addressed*
4. *Explain why it is important to involve those with parental responsibility when working with children affected by crime or anti-social behaviour*
5. *Describe how to use legislation, guidelines of good practice, charters and service standards to benefit and protect victims and witnesses*
6. *Identify appropriate sources of advice and support to assist meeting an individual's need for support.*

The initial words of each of these sub-sections provide an immediate clue as to the evidence needed to complete this section—Describe, Explain, Identify, Explain, Describe, and Identify. This element of Unit 2 requires **your** understanding and it would not be inconceivable to expect a PCSO to complete this unit whilst in the induction training phase. After all, many of the presentations, pre-reads, and educational material you receive will be geared towards these precise topics.

A good understanding of your NOS portfolio at the training stage will help you to complete those sub-sections where your *knowledge* is being asked for. It will also have the further benefit of cementing this new knowledge before applying it practically on the streets. We encourage you to complete the theory element of your NOS **as you receive the educational inputs**, since one of the fundamental requirements of you in the police is management of your workload and this is your first opportunity to prove this capability as an officer.

### 4.3.1.1 Remaining elements

The remaining three elements with their sub-sections are as follows:

*Element 2—Be able to communicate effectively with victims and witnesses*

1. *Communicate with individuals appropriately taking account of:*
   - *PACE (Police & Criminal Evidence Act 1984)*
   - *their level of understanding*
   - *their preferred form of communication*
2. *Encourage individuals to express their own views about their immediate needs by creating an appropriate environment, actively listening and using appropriate:*
   - *Body language*
   - *Position*
   - *Tone of voice*
3. *Explain when in contact with individuals, the force's policy in respect of:*
   - *Confidentiality*
   - *Who will have access to the information they provide*
   - *How the information will be recorded and stored*
4. *Maintain contact with individuals as necessary*
5. *When communicating with victims and witnesses ensure your actions:*
   - *Apply principles of equality, diversity and non-discrimination*
   - *Manage risks to health and safety*

**Element 3—Be able to provide initial support to victims and witnesses**

1. *Give initial support that is appropriate to the individual's needs*
2. *Explain clearly to individuals the range of services available from the force, providing details of how to access these services and those of other relevant organisations*
3. *Make clear and accurate records of:*
   - *The individual's immediate needs*
   - *The initial support provided*
4. *When providing initial support to victims and witnesses ensure your actions:*
   - *Value the person as an individual*
   - *Show awareness of diversity*

**Element 4—Be able to assess the needs and wishes of victims and witnesses for further support**

1. *Discuss with individuals the nature and extent of their needs helping them to identify their priorities and how they could be addressed*
2. *Explain clearly to individuals the range of support and other services available from the force and other organisations*
3. *Make clear and accurate records of:*
   - *The individual's needs and wishes*
   - *The agreement reached*
   - *The resulting actions taken*
4. *When assessing the needs of victims and witnesses ensure actions:*
   - *Apply principles of equality, diversity and anti-discrimination*
   - *Manage risk to health and safety*

### 4.3.1.2 Evidencing competence

It is clear from the language employed in Unit 2—Elements 2–4 that evidence cannot be supplied from the classroom or any theory-based learning. This is where a 'real' example is needed, bearing in mind that the aim of the entire exercise is to evidence competency.

---

**Task**

Consider what type of incident, event or occurrence would provide evidence to complete this Unit within the NOS. Please bear in mind that this needs to be PCSO-related evidence.

---

There is no definitive answer to this question nor is there any definitive way to submit evidence so please use the guidance you receive from your police force (especially from trainers, tutors, and experienced colleagues).

### 4.3.2 Example of evidence

That said, we would like to supply an example that can be used to evidence this NOS unit. There are some liberties taken with this example and for that you have to excuse us, but within the confines of this book, we are endeavouring to be illustrative not exhaustive.

It is also useful to be reminded at this point that whilst we are discussing Unit 2, there could be other NOS elements that could be evidenced using this example—the competent PCSO will be confident enough to be 'lateral' in working out what evidence applies to what competency. Your actions at one incident may provide material for a number of different competences.

### 4.3.2.1 A Seaside Incident

You are a PCSO on patrol in a small coastal resort. It is summer, the schools are on holiday, and there are lots of tourists visiting your picturesque town. There is even sunshine. You have spent the morning directing lost tourists, engaging with local business owners, and undertaking a visible patrol of known day-time hot-spots for anti-social behaviour. You are making your way back to the police station via the High Street for a well-deserved cup of tea.

Just before you reach the Police Station you hear behind you a dull crunching sound and the noise of a car accelerating away. You turn round to see that a parked car has a large dent in the car on the passenger side and that there is a shaken elderly lady sitting there. There are two people—a woman and a teenage boy, pointing up the road and speaking to you excitedly in a language you do not understand.

---

**Task**

List what actions you would take at this point.

**NB** again there is no definitive answer but clearly there are some things you should do and probably in a prescribed or logical order.

---

You speak to the elderly woman who explains that she is not injured but from her speech and general demeanour, you can see that she is in shock. She keeps asking you to contact her husband who has gone into a nearby shop to buy a newspaper.

The foreign woman cannot speak English but her teenage son, who speaks some rather fractured English, explains that they are Portuguese tourists on a day trip to the town and that he saw a large black car hit the lady's car—he thinks it might have been a 4x4. He points in the direction which the car took after it had sped away.

You call for paramedics to attend to the elderly lady whom you ask to remain in the car. The reason for this is that you want medical support to assess her condition and to confirm that she is uninjured. You keep talking to her to comfort her and assure her you will speak to the husband.

You radio for assistance to deal with the incident and ask the Portuguese boy if he will take his mother to the front counter of the police station down the road from the incident, so you can ask some more questions which you do not want to do in the street.

An ambulance with a paramedic team and police assistance arrive quickly (this is an example after all!) and you have been able to speak to the victim's husband who has returned from buying a paper. He is very agitated at the situation and is understandably concerned for his wife. You explain to the man what has occurred and you take his details. A colleague takes over and you return to the police station.

In an interview room adjacent to the front counter, you ask the teenage boy to translate your questions to his mother and he agrees. In this way you are able to obtain necessary witness details and a basic account of what happened. You also explain that a more formal interview with an interpreter may be required to provide a statement and try to 'de-jargonize' this so that the two visitors understand. Ensure that you explain that their importance is as witnesses: they have done nothing wrong.

This example could go on through many more phases of course, but is only an illustrative example.

### 4.3.2.2 What has this to do with the PCSO National Occupational Standards?

The short answer is **everything**; after all, in providing evidence of your competency to perform the role, you would use such examples to demonstrate what you did and why.

It can be a common mistake with some PCSOs to want to use 'major' incidents to evidence their professional competency. However, we have shown you that the role of the PCSO is as wide as it is long, and therefore your NOS portfolio should encompass a spectrum of roles, actions, and incidents (some of them 'everyday' or commonplace, like our example) to be a true reflection of what you can do. A minor incident can be just as illustrative of your competencies as a critical incident involving many other people. Indeed, a small incident often shows how well you personally have grasped a situation and done something positive to resolve any problems.

---

**Task**

Using the example of 4.3.2.1 explain how you could evidence Elements 2–4 of Unit 2 of the PCSO NOS.

---

### 4.3.2.3 Actions as evidence

The following is a table that highlights how, in the example we provided, the actions of the PCSO can be used to evidence the completion of Unit 2. Once again it is illustrative only.

### 4.3.2.4 Summarizing comment

There is room for interpretation within this example and no doubt you will have additional views about other things in the incident that could be used for

| Unit, Element, Sub-section | Evidence |
|---|---|
| *2.2.1—Communicate appropriately* | Use of the Portuguese son to provide immediate explanation but use of an interpreter for subsequent detailed statements from both witnesses |
| *2.2.2— Encourage cooperation* | Transferring the Portuguese visitors to the police station for initial interview ensured that questioning was done in a more appropriate situation, away from the incident |
| *2.2.3—Organizational policies* | This would be explained to the witnesses at the time of the statement |
| *2.2.4—Maintain contact* | PCSO ensured that the contact with the victim was constant until medical support arrived |
| *2.2.5—Ensure communications are cognizant of diversity* | The use of the Portuguese son was appropriate to the need for early information and by transferring to the station it was appropriate for the health and safety of the witnesses |
| *2.3.1—Initial Support* | The initial support provided to the elderly victim was both appropriate and supportive of the situation |
| *2.3.2—Access to services* | Victim Support services would be explained to the victim and her husband at an appropriate stage |
| *2.3.3—Clear and accurate records* | All evidence would be supported by clear and concise PNB entries as well as statements |
| *2.3.4—Value and diversity awareness* | The support in this example to both victims and witnesses exemplified this NOS and would be evidenced appropriately |
| *2.4.1—Prioritize individuals' needs* | The needs of the victim centred on medical attention and then dealing with her request for her husband |
| *2.4.2—Explain clearly* | The victims and the witnesses would be supplied with appropriate support for their situation; for example medical assistance for the victim as a priority and then an interpreter for the witnesses' statements |
| *2.4.3—Clear and accurate records* | All evidence would be supported by clear and concise PNB entries as well as statements |
| *2.4.4—Ensure actions comply with diversity and H&S* | The needs of the victim would be considered a priority and therefore your actions are consonant with her needs, as were the needs of the witnesses. The operational priority to get immediate information was achieved via the son, but formal statements would be obtained later using an interpreter |

completion of the NOS. You may also have noticed that we have simply signposted the evidence requirements; we have not provided a statement for each, because it is important that these entries are completed in your own words.

### Knowledge Check 18

1. What does NOS mean?

2. Where do you show evidence of your competence?

3. How many NOS for PCSOs were there up to 2013 and how many are there now?

4. How is your progress registered in the NOS workbook?

5. Why is there no 'Pass/Fail' in the NOS?

6. Into what are Units subdivided?

7. Where would you find Knowledge and Understanding?

8. What keeps 'all your competences sharp'?

9. Name three ways in which you might be assessed for NOS

10. Who or what are 'nominals'?

## 4.4 Linking PCSO Duties with Intelligence Reporting

The **NOS** require you to make sure that you know the correct intelligence reporting procedures for your Force. It will become evident to you within a couple of weeks of working in your community, what varied forms of community intelligence you will be party to. That is why we say that evidencing this unit should not be difficult for you.

### 4.4.1 Contributing to the intelligence or knowledge 'picture'

The key point to remember with intelligence is that you might think you are submitting a trivial piece of information, but to the intelligence analyst working on the bigger picture, it may be the final piece needed to make sense of a situation. You will soon receive feedback as to the usefulness or otherwise of the intelligence you submit. You should note that one of the primary functions of a PCSO is to develop an insightful, localized knowledge that will be of benefit to the police force in understanding the dynamics of a community, its *nominals* (people known to the police) and the crime/anti-social behaviour in the area. As such, intelligence forms a crucial part of the daily duties of a PCSO in any constabulary.

## 4.5  The National Intelligence Model (NIM): Intelligence-gathering and Intelligence-led Policing

**What is intelligence and what has it to do with policing?** This section steps away from the National Occupational Standards for a moment, to discuss what is meant by **intelligence**, the **NIM**, and **intelligence-led policing.** We feel that it is important to include this explanation and commentary, because you will come across many references to the subject, both written and verbal, in the course of your work; and you may well be tasked to obtain local intelligence with an assumption that you know what is wanted and how you should obtain it.

### 4.5.1  Is your police force intelligence-led?

A word of warning first, perhaps. You may well be a member of a police force which has never fully embraced intelligence-led policing. Equally, you may have joined a Force in which intelligence-led policing is alive and well. Again, you may be in a police force which is struggling to accommodate a number of policing models, from intelligence-led policing through problem-orientated policing to neighbourhood reassurance or community-focused policing. These models are not necessarily incompatible, but may have different emphases, depending sometimes on the 'mission' articulated by your Chief Constable, sometimes through the priorities established by the Police and Crime Commissioner, or, sometimes, as a result of the kinds of crime which dominate your BCU or Force. In this section, our focus is exclusively on the role and function of intelligence about crime and criminals. Some commentators on intelligence in policing can obscure rather than clarify the issues, giving rise to comments like this: '*Intelligence-led policing has been defined as **the gathering of information designed for action**'* (Grieve in Harfield *et al*, 2008: 4). Yes, quite. But so is a train timetable. Resounding clichés of this kind do not take us very far forward, and instead we might construct for ourselves some idea of what 'criminal intelligence' is about.

### 4.5.2  Defining intelligence and knowledge

Let us begin by trying to build a straightforward definition: *what distinguishes ordinary information from intelligence, when it is about crime?*

### 4.5.2.1  The nature of information

You will be used to accessing all sorts of sources of information, from reference books to Google or 'Ask Jeeves' searches on the internet. You rightly expect most information to be freely available; you would expect to be able to find out a fair bit about the police force you have joined or are contemplating joining, for example, and to be able to find out what is involved in becoming a police officer.

However, information about crimes and criminals is not normally easy to obtain in advance of the commission of a crime. Those criminals who do signal their crimes in advance may do it vaguely, getting tanked up on 'alcopops' in advance of a fist fight on a Saturday night, for example; or indirectly, like the loner who has no 'previous' for sex offences; or privately, such as a muttered threat of violence in a pub or club.

### 4.5.3 Need to know

Criminals actually spend a lot of time preventing information about their activities from leaking out. They often apply the principle of *'need to know'* far more rigorously than most police forces, in our experience, by not confiding any details of planned criminal activity to anyone not directly implicated in the planned crime (we touch on this briefly below). This often extends even to immediate family members and long-established friends.

#### 4.5.3.1 Careless talk can get you nicked

Criminals know that loose talk, or wagging tongues, will eventually find an appreciative audience at the local police station, and unpleasant surprises in the form of arrests *in flagrante* (at the scene of the crime in commission of the criminal act) await those who do not keep their plans to themselves.

#### 4.5.3.2 Intelligence about crimes and criminals

This may suggest to you that **criminal intelligence** (*information about what is planned or intended in terms of crime*) is hard to come by. It is. But that doesn't mean that it is impossible to obtain or that it is hopeless trying to penetrate the intentions of known 'lifestyle' criminals. The information may not be complete, in fact it seldom is, but indications here and suggestions there, linked with some definite facts somewhere else (such as may be obtained from covert surveillance), might add up to a positive indication that a crime is planned. So this may help us to build the first part of a definition when we say that:

> *Criminal intelligence* is information obtained about criminal intentions, which criminals do not want known.

Key questions in criminal intelligence
In other words, criminal intelligence can be *'secret'* in the sense that a criminal does not want to let it be known. The key questions will be: What is going to happen? When will it happen? Where will it happen? Who will be involved? What will they do? Who or what is the victim or target? How do the criminals expect to get away with the crime? How long has this been in the planning? What is the expectation of profit? (If the crime has already happened, valuable

intelligence can be indicators or information about who did it and why—this is particularly important with 'stranger violence', such as rape, murder, or assault.)

### 4.5.4  Crime types

You can see that we are mostly assuming that the crime in prospect is **acquisitive**, that is, a crime which makes money, such as theft, robbery, embezzlement, defrauding, deceiving, illegal importing, drugs smuggling, sex or people trafficking; the commission of the offence or the provision of illegal services are intended to make a profit for the criminals. This is not always the case, of course. Some criminal intelligence can be about **violence**, the activities of gangs to eliminate rivals, pithily described by the police as '*bad on bad*'; about the **discouragement of others**, rife among rival brothel-keepers and pimps in the sex trade, for example; or about **maintenance of position**, where no one is allowed to come in on an established criminal's 'patch', for instance. We can therefore add a little more to our developing definition:

> **Operations to disrupt criminal actions, or mounting an operation after a crime has been committed to expose the offenders, using covert methods and based on intelligence, is called intelligence-led policing.**

We mean by this that, because the criminal will not willingly give up the secret information about what he or she plans, or has already done, in the commission of a crime, police forces have to devise ways in which the information—partial or incomplete, as we have said—is to be obtained. It is worth noting that 'intelligence-led policing' as a concept is slowly giving way to a more general term: **knowledge-based policing**, which makes use of *all* sources of information about crime and criminals, including that which is openly and publicly available. However, we are here concerned with obtaining special criminal information which is held secretly by others. We will look briefly at some of the methods of obtaining this information later. In the interim, there is another important principle about intelligence which we need to discuss.

### 4.5.5  Assessing intelligence

Weighing and evaluating the intelligence, giving it a context, linking it with other known intelligence, adding in facts such as the replacement of items, the previous history of known offences and offenders (the '*modus operandi*' or characteristic, 'signature', activity, of the criminal), together with analysis of things like 'hot spots' and 'hot victims', where similar crimes are geographically or socially concentrated, leads to **assessed intelligence**. Intelligence which is not assessed is often of limited value, or is bitty and fragmented, or is simply misleading. This is why the intelligence assessment activity is sometimes compared to completing a jigsaw: the fitting together of apparently unrelated pieces of information is a skilled activity undertaken by a trained analytical researcher.

As a PCSO, the two questions in the forefront of your mind when receiving any intelligence from a secondary source (such as a member of the public) is firstly *how* do they know this information, and secondly *who* else knows it (whether it is exclusive or widely known)?

### 4.5.5.1 Completing our definition of criminal intelligence

So, when we talked about you submitting an intelligence report on something you learned, it is important to distinguish that piece of the jigsaw from the larger picture. The final part of our definition might now look like this:

> **Intelligence which is assessed and evaluated has value; it is the basis for police operations.**

**KEY POINT**

Intelligence must also be distinguished from evidence which could be admitted in a court of law; the standard of proof for such evidence is infinitely beyond that for establishing, in a police force, the probability of intelligence being true or not. Intelligence, both in its gathering and in its interpretation, is an art not a science, and it is as prone to error and inaccuracy as any other human endeavour. Remember 'weapons of mass destruction' in Iraq?

In other words, all the contexts, additions, other snippets, and analysed facts are brought together and an assessment is made. This is where your bit of reporting finds its context. What we can now offer, in effect, is a working description of the practical use to which intelligence is put in a policing context (edited for style and content):

> **Criminal intelligence is secret information obtained covertly about crimes and criminals, which is sanitized, assessed, and evaluated in order to mount police operations to disrupt, frustrate, or bring to justice, those involved.**

This isn't the official, police approved, intelligence-led definition; it is our own description, but it shows you the difference between 'ordinary' information and intelligence. It describes what is involved in building an intelligence picture about crime and criminality, and it shows you the value of intelligence in how '*the battle is the pay-off*' when a police operation is mounted successfully. You may not have the complete picture as a PCSO (indeed, you may only have a very small part) but at least you can see how the operation in which you were involved was conceived and developed.

### 4.5.6 Examining the National Intelligence Model (NIM)

We now need to look at the model which lies behind most intelligence-led policing. It is the **National Intelligence Model** (NIM), of which figure 4.1 is an example:

**Figure 4.1 Simplified diagram of the National Intelligence Model**

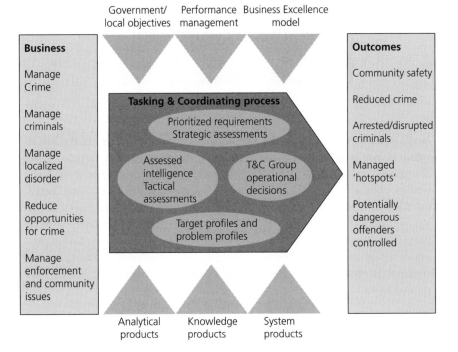

It is important to note that most police forces use the NIM (all officially have the model) but sometimes the way in which it is used varies from force to force. So, what we are going to describe may not be exactly what happens in your Force, please note that we are discussing the **typical use of the NIM** rather than force-specific use.

### 4.5.6.1 Interpreting the NIM

You 'read' the model from left to right. Note that the primary determinants (the **business**) are **managing crime, criminals, and disorder** of all kinds, together with crime reduction and community issues (which includes enforcement, such as curfew orders and summonses). The *outcomes* are controls on these things: **reduced crime, controlled criminality** (including through arrest and disruption) **and disorder, controlled offenders** (particularly the potentially dangerous), and **managed hotspots**.

**Figure 4.2 Theft from vehicles and damage to them is symptomatic of volume crime (see Example below)**

## Tasking and coordinating

In the middle is the engine of the *Tasking and Coordinating Process*, the T&CP, which in turn is affected by government and local **objectives** and targets—as we discussed earlier—management of police **performance**, and the use of the business excellence model. The T&C Group uses **analytical products** (your '5x5x5 intelligence report', assessed and evaluated and put with other pieces of the jigsaw); **knowledge products** which include what we know about the type of crime, the place where it happens, the victims of the crime, and the MO of prolific or repeat offenders; and **system products**, which include Force and national criminal databases and intelligence 'traces', criminal records, past crimes, hotspots, and so on.

## Strategic and tactical intelligence, plus profiles

These lead to **strategic assessments**—determining what is important in the longer term, and **tactical assessments**—determining what we are going to do about the problem now. Finally, the *Tasking and Coordinating Process*, bringing together all the **intelligence and knowledge resources** within the context of the assessments, produces **profiles of the targets** for operations together with **profiles of the problems** faced by the BCU.

### 4.5.6.2 Practical example of the use of the NIM

This may all seem a bit abstract and theoretical, so let us populate and describe the whole process using a real-life example.

**EXAMPLE**

Your town has been plagued by volume crime (**Government objective**) involving thefts from vehicles, mostly private cars (as shown in figure 4.2), but also thefts of tools from vans and some quite brazen thefts from lorries and larger vans outside transport cafes ('**hotspots**') or when parked on the dual carriageway lay-bys (**crime, criminals and disorder**). Local opinion is fuelled by criticism in the district newspapers and by a vociferous campaign led by highly-vocal local councillors. They have pressured the BCU Commander, who in turn has asked the T&C Group to come up with solutions (**local objectives**). You were told by a local resident that at least three local youths had been seen to be suddenly 'in the money', wearing expensive clothes, flashing banknotes, and living well beyond their normal job-seeker's benefit. Another person, a parent concerned that the three youths were exercising a bad influence on her daughter, suggested to you that the youths were stealing from cars and passing the stolen items to Billy Parker, a dealer and would-be antiques trader who organizes weekly boot-fairs in the summer months at the back of the market near the river (**knowledge and analytical products**).

You pass this information to your BCU Intelligence Unit as a 5x5x5 report (remembering to put a sanitized copy in your portfolio…) and think no more about it. Meanwhile, your snippet, with the names of the suspects, joins other intelligence (**assessed intelligence**) to form an intelligence package, which is then presented to the T&C Group at its weekly meeting (**prioritized requirements**). The requirement then is made of BCU source handlers to get more information, and you are also tasked to go and get more detail from the original sources of information. You do this and submit another 5x5x5, but you are still unaware of the general interest which this has generated. The **assessed intelligence** is added to what the BCU knows about volume crime thefts from motor vehicles and a number of names are added to the list of possible suspects (**knowledge products**). Billy Parker, who has a criminal record for theft and minor drugs-dealing (**system products**), is placed under surveillance. The T&C Group, chaired this time by the BCU Commander, authorizes a covert operation to monitor Parker closely (**T&C Group operational decision**). He is caught in possession of stolen goods, arrested, and charged. Some of those on the list of suspects are arrested and questioned. (One agrees to become an informant and is dealt with later.) The focus of the police operation is against Parker and the route for the stolen items to be turned into cash (**managed hotspots**).

From this, the police learn about Henry Wood, an apparently respectable property dealer who lives in a large detached house in the smart residential area of town, and who seems to act as a conduit for Parker's 'fencing' of the stolen items, but Wood is selective: only the best quality items are accepted by him for sale elsewhere. Intelligence suggests that he is commissioning some thefts 'to order', which means that Wood lets it be known what he wants to be stolen and then waits for it to materialize. This intelligence is added to other traces and a new operation is ordered, this time with Wood as the focus (**business excellence model, disrupted criminals**).

The outcome a few weeks later is that Parker pleads guilty, is sentenced to 18 months, and the youths are given community orders of varying lengths (**outcomes:**

**potentially dangerous offenders controlled, reduced crime, controlled criminality, community safety**). Press and media coverage is generally complimentary and the BCU Commander looks happier than for some time (**performance management**), though it won't last. Eventually, the plaudits find their way to you too, and you remember to thank your original sources of information.

#### 4.5.6.3 The use of intelligence to disrupt crime is open-ended

This example has shown you the NIM process from start to finish, but we have made it deliberately open-ended. We wanted to suggest to you that linkages such as those between Parker and Wood often occur in criminal investigations, and a man like Wood, outwardly conventional and law-abiding, might never have come to notice had it not been for the spate of vehicle-related thefts bringing pressure to bear on local priorities in crime fighting. He was the end of one part of the investigation, and the beginning of another. Your information also played its part, so we hope that you're feeling pleased with yourself.

#### 4.5.6.4 Criticisms of the NIM

You should not suppose that we accept the NIM as some sort of Holy Grail of criminal intelligence. It is not. Indeed, some commentators have drawn attention to potential pitfalls, such as this from Clive Harfield: '*The greatest vulnerability of the NIM is its exposure to the possibility that the processes could be followed and the various tick-boxes achieved without intelligence-led policing actually happening*' (Harfield *et al*, 2008: 2). This describes a mechanistic approach to criminal intelligence which defeats the whole purpose and point of painstakingly acquiring usable information in a criminal context. It has actually happened in police forces across England and Wales, and in some has tainted the notion of intelligence-led policing. Be aware then that some of your colleagues may be sceptical of the NIM's efficacy, if it has not been properly utilized in the past.

#### 4.5.7 Other aspects of intelligence and crime: criminals, informants, and source handlers

We have some more parts of the intelligence scene to cover, but you may well be asking at this point why we are spending time and space on one aspect of policing, rather than covering, say, community-focused policing in exhaustive detail. Our answer to this is in two parts: first, the thrust of this entire book is about community policing and your role, as a PCSO, in the neighbourhood police team concept, so a few pages on intelligence-led policing are not disproportionate; secondly, we have commented throughout the NOS discussions on your role as local 'eyes and ears'.

Giving you the proper context for intelligence, and its undoubted contribution, among other things, to a reduction in crime, seems to us a sensible course of action. It gives a rationale for you to pass on what you learn locally and shows you how operations (in which you may play an active part) are conceived, developed, and mounted in your BCU. Reasons enough, we suggest, to turn now to look at **informants** and **source handlers**. One caveat: these are hugely complex areas of modern policing and we can only skim the surface. Look for more detail in the box following figure 4.3 (4.5.7.5) and look at the Reference List at the end of the book; but better yet, go to your local Intelligence Unit and talk to the people there about what they do.

### 4.5.7.1 Informants

The police and other law-enforcement agencies usually call an informant a **CHIS**, which stands for Covert Human Intelligence Source. Criminals give informants less neutral names such as 'nark', 'snout', and 'grass'. Because informants, or CHIS, give information about crimes and criminals, it follows that they are themselves usually involved in, or party to, criminal activities. Most of the time, ordinary people don't come across criminal information of high and immediate value; the police rely instead on 'participating informants' (sources of information who are themselves involved in crime) to give intelligence of operational use. This is not to downplay the value of intelligence from the community, because this can often be very useful in building a picture of criminal activity and the prevalence of crimes.

### 4.5.7.2 RIPA 2000 (the Regulation of Investigatory Powers Act)—governing the use of informants

The real distinction is that criminals will know more about crimes in prospect than will members of the public; it is therefore the former upon whom the police must concentrate. The police use of informants is governed by the **Regulation of Investigatory Powers Act 2000**, known colloquially as '**RIPA**', which lays down procedural rules for recruitment of CHIS, their 'handling' and use, and their reward. There are especially stringent rules for the use of juvenile informants (for obvious reasons; the opportunity to exploit a young person unfairly is high). When the police identify a suitable informant or have one volunteer his or her services to the police, there has to be **authorization** from the Force, usually through a designated superintendent, before an approach or recruitment is made. Such authorization normally lasts a year and may be inspected by a nationally appointed **surveillance commissioner** who will determine whether the case is properly justified and run. Some forces have their own internal scrutiny of CHIS and CHIS handling through an Operational Security Officer (**OPSY**).

### 4.5.7.3 RIPA governs covert relationships

This may seem a bit rarefied to you, since as a PCSO you will not be employed in the handling of CHIS. However, you need to know that RIPA governs covert relationships to obtain criminal intelligence and that you cannot cultivate anyone as a CHIS on your patch without authority. This does not mean that people can't tell you things, of course. It means that you can't recruit a criminal informant to work for you for money without going through the proper procedures. You are far more likely to find that you receive 'lifestyle' intelligence about criminals living on your patch, or snippets about who is up to what and when. All this is worth reporting, but it is only subject to RIPA procedures if you cultivate someone deliberately to provide you with criminal intelligence. Such people do exist, of course, and it is just about feasible that you might get a volunteer. If you do, don't be tempted to run the CHIS yourself. You don't have the extensive training involved in being a professional source handler and you would be falling foul of RIPA in any case. Make sure that you report any approach, and you could then be instrumental in setting up a first contact between volunteer and potential police handler. Don't get too excited though; there is often a considerable gap between the first tentative shufflings of contact and the engagement of a paid informant.

### 4.5.7.4 You may contribute intelligence but you don't need to know the bigger picture

Another point to make is that, even if a contact made by you is developed into a CHIS, you are not likely to know much about it. You don't have any **need to know**, do you? Unless something really drastic happens (such as the urgent need for exfiltration of a CHIS because of a life-threatening situation), you will be kept out of the developing intelligence picture and the relationship will be handled exclusively within the intelligence unit in your BCU, or rarely, for sources with especially good or very sensitive access, from a central team at Headquarters.

#### 'Sanitizing' intelligence

The intelligence obtained from a CHIS is passed to the BCU's Research and Development Unit, which combines the report with other pieces of intelligence (like a snippet which you have provided) and the report will be **sanitized**. This means that any feature which might identify the source(s) of the intelligence is removed. The essence of the intelligence is not changed or modified; only its context or circumstances are disguised. The resultant report will also be assessed. As we saw earlier, this means that the intelligence will be given meaning, and the access, reliability, and provenance of the source will be designated (through the 5x5x5 system of evaluation).

### 4.5.7.5 The intelligence 'package'

The resultant combination of the sanitized intelligence, analysis, assessment, and evaluation makes up an **intelligence package** which, as we have seen, is presented to a T&C Group. Thus, we have essentially come full circle: secret criminal intelligence is gathered, reported, assessed, analysed, sanitized, combined with other information, given a context and an evaluation, is presented to an operational planning group, and helps to determine policing operations against crime and criminality. We could express the intelligence 'cycle' in a '*virtuous circle*' diagram as shown in figure 4.3.

**Figure 4.3 The 'virtuous circle' of intelligence, from tasking to operation**

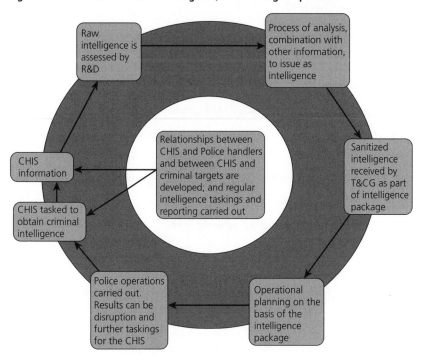

**Further Reading**

For those of you who are interested in exploring this murky subject a little further, good texts include:

Phillips, D. Sir, Caless, B, and Bryant, R, 'Intelligence and its application to operational policing' (2008) 1(4) *Policing: A Journal of Policy and Practice* 438–446.

Kleiven, M, 'Where's the intelligence in the NIM?' (2007) 9(3) *International Journal of Police Science and Management* 257–73.

Hanvey, P, *Identifying, Recruiting and Handling Informants* Home Office Police Research Group, Special Interest Paper Series 5 (1985).

John, T and Maguire, M, 'Rolling out the National Intelligence Model: Key Challenges' in K Bullock and N Tilley (eds), *Crime Reduction and Problem-Oriented Policing* (Willan, 2003).

A good general text is Tim Newburn's *Handbook of Policing* (Willan, 2003), in which Nick Tilley's essay 'Community Policing, problem-oriented policing and intelligence-led policing' is outstanding.

There is also the quirky *Handbook of Intelligent Policing; Consilience, Crime Control and Community Safety,* edited by Harfield, C, MacVean, A, Grieve, J, and Phillips, Sir D (Oxford University Press, 2008).

**Knowledge Check 19**

1. What does NIM mean?

2. How does Harfield describe 'intelligence-led policing'?

3. How do we describe criminal intelligence?

4. What do we call crime that is about making money illegally?

5. What two things should be in your mind when you receive intelligence or information about criminals?

6. Give our working definition of the practical use of intelligence.

7. What is the T&C Process?

8. How do you pass on intelligence within the Force?

9. What threatens NIM's usefulness?

10. What is an 'informant'?

11. What is a CHIS?

12. What does RIPA stand for?

13. Who might inspect authorization to run an informant?

14. What is 'sanitizing'?

# 4.6 The 'Golden Hour' of Scene Preservation and the 'Continuity of Evidence'

**KEY POINT**

The term 'golden hour' is in frequent use among police officers and you will often hear it applied to the immediate aftermath of a crime scene or to the first report of an incident. **It means that the time immediately after first police arrival at a crime scene or incident is of vital importance for the preservation of evidence.**

Traces of physical evidence may still be very fresh (footprints and fingerprints, for example) and people's recall of events may be clear and focused. Sometimes, poor management of a crime scene can mean that evidence is lost or obliterated (for example by rain washing away bloodstains), that material can be carelessly imported into a crime scene from outside, and that slight traces (such as when the offender leaned against a parked car nearby) may be lost for ever, because they were never properly noted in the first place.

### 4.6.1 **First officer attending**

You are often going to be the first officer attending (FOA) a crime scene, because you are the one on patrol to whom members of the public will come to say that something somewhere is not quite right. It may be that no one has seen the occupants of No 42 for a week, or it may be that a neighbour reports hearing screams, or someone may report a broken window or forced door. There is an expectation of, and an obligation on, you that you will get right the police response and any subsequent investigation, because you did the correct things in the correct sequence at the outset. That makes this section of enormous value to your credibility, so learn it well.

Let us look at a case study of how <u>not</u> to manage a crime scene.

### 4.6.2 **First on the scene**

Consider the following: you are on routine patrol when an agitated postal worker tells you that there is something wrong at a house around the corner. You accompany this person to the premises, a semi-detached house with a longish drive which has shrubs on either side. The postal worker shows you that when she attempted to put letters through the box, she met an obstruction. When she stooped and looked through the letter box, she could see someone slumped on the floor in the hall and what looked like blood on the stair carpet behind. What do you do?

---

#### **Case Study**

You are a solidly built person, and so you shoulder-charge the door which, at the third attempt, gives way and splinters around the lock and hinges. The entire door crashes inwards, dislodging whoever was behind it. You are just in time to catch an expiration from the slumped body, which is now, of course, a corpse. In the hallway it looks as though there is blood everywhere, because some of it is sticking to your shoes, but, pausing only to check for signs of life on the body behind (now actually under) the front door, you rush upstairs to check if there is anyone else in the house. There is no one in any of the bedrooms but someone has evidently been sick in the bathroom. Feeling slightly green, you use the shower head to flush away the debris from the side of the bath before resuming your search. Coming downstairs at speed, you slip and cannon into the postal worker who had come nervously over the threshold and was standing at the foot of the stairs, and the pair of you end up in a welter of arms and legs in the front room, where you notice that there is glass all over the floor. You ask the postal worker to sweep it up (mindful of the health and safety of others) while you search the remaining rooms downstairs. Pausing only to use the downstairs loo (well, it has been quite a day in one way or another), you open the back door and check the back patio. Only a few muddy footprints there, probably from the children

---

playing outside, but you walk over the mud to make sure no one is hiding. Back in the kitchen and cross about your muddy boots, you notice that there is a knife missing from the large wooden rack and you walk back to the front door to look at the body. Sure enough, there is the missing knife sticking out of the dead person's chest. You pull it out to check that it is in fact the one, before shoving it back in. (It's OK, you were wearing gloves.)

Now is the time to let Force Control know what is happening, so you phone in, using the phone conveniently located in the hall, to let them know, in some excitement, that you've come across your first suspicious death. 'Why is it suspicious?' you are asked. 'Because of the corpse and the blood', you reply. 'How do you know it's blood?' asks Control. 'It's red, still wet and sticky,' you reply drawing your thumb across a splash on the wall above your head. 'Someone will be with you in about twenty or thirty minutes,' says Control, 'meanwhile, get the place cordoned off.' Not having any tape, you use a ball of string from the kitchen to close off the front drive to the house and wait for reinforcements (pausing to let the postal worker out of the cordon; she walks away with a cheery wave). You fish out your PNB while you are waiting, and chat amiably with some of the neighbours.

### 4.6.2.1 Outcomes

You might be lucky enough only to be sent for retraining after this, but the greater likelihood is that you and the police will be parting company in short order. You have done nearly everything wrong that you could do, and you have not done what you should have done.

---

**Task**

Consider and list what you did wrong in the scenario, and explain what you should have done.

---

A model and comprehensive response

Our answer is long and complex, for reasons which will quickly become apparent. Although we have greatly exaggerated the combination of errors in this scenario, none of the individual actions which we itemize is particularly uncommon. Even experienced police officers can make a mess of a crime scene if they don't think before they act. In the list which follows, we have put the **identifiable error in the left-hand column** and the **proper course of action** (which you should have followed) **in the right-hand column**. We hope that you agree with our divisions, but by all means use any disputes as a discussion point with your colleagues.

| Errors | Remedies |
|---|---|
| *Breaking down the door*—the splintering and bits of door have now been added to the crime scene inside, contaminating it (and you). | Find another route in which will not wreck the crime scene within. |
| *'Expiration' from the (now) corpse*—perhaps literally the last gasp. Although you have an absolute duty to preserve life and limb, that does not include crashing through doors on top of people. Of course, saving life takes precedence over any other consideration, but that doesn't give you licence to wreck the place. | It is possible that the victim was alive when you arrived. Having found another route into the building which did not compromise the victim, you might have been in a position to render first aid in a life-saving measure. Unlikely, but possible. |
| *Blood in the hall sticking to your shoes* | You should not have entered the crime scene without some form of protection: in your rush to enter, you should not neglect to put on surgical gloves. You should have been aware of the possibility that the blood could be infected and you should have taken precautions for your own safety. You don't know at this stage whether all the blood is from the same source (it might be that of the victim and assailant mixed together). |
| *Body under the door*—irrevocably contaminating the crime scene (who knows what you have obliterated by causing the heavy front door to crash on the corpse, and who knows what you have imported from outside?). | Had you come by a different, non-invasive or non-contaminating route, you might have been able to check the victim for signs of life without treading blood everywhere. You might have spotted the knife earlier too. |
| *Rush upstairs*—actually better to check the ground floor first. | You don't rush anywhere at a crime scene, you proceed steadily and methodically. You should be thinking too about a common approach path (CAP) to avoid any cross-contamination. |
| *Flushing away the vomit*—(by the way, you are still spreading bloody footprints everywhere). | Body fluids can be a bit off-putting but you should **never** destroy potential evidence in this way. You don't know whose vomit it is (it might be the assailant's) and at this stage, you don't know if it will help the forensic investigation or not. Preserve it and note it, are the key actions for you. |
| *Coming downstairs at speed* | See above; don't rush anywhere on a crime scene. |

*(continued)*

| Errors | Remedies |
| --- | --- |
| *Crashing into the postal worker* | The postal worker should not have been there (an additional potential contaminant) especially since she is unlikely to have received crime training or be used to rather gory scenes of crime. You should prevent anyone else coming into the crime scene until colleagues arrive (the exceptions are paramedics to save life, or Fire and Rescue to extinguish a blaze or make safe). Had you not been rushing and had the postal worker not been present, there would have been no accident. |
| *Gross contamination of the crime scene—caused by falling on the postal worker and rolling over the glass in the front room.* | In addition to what we have said above, actually coming into contact with another (ungowned and unprotected) person on the scene will merely intensify the contamination of the scene. The glass in the front or sitting room might indicate a point of entry or the scene of a struggle. Either way, rolling in it doesn't help, and will, of course, smear or obliterate any forensic traces on the glass surfaces and wreck any 'pattern of fall' of the glass fragments. |
| *You ask the postal worker to sweep up the glass—thereby destroying any potential evidence completely.* | Leave things as they are. If broken glass is a health hazard, draw it to the attention of those who join you, but the scene must *not* be touched or altered in any way until a Crime Scene Investigator (CSI) has completed his or her work. |
| *Using the downstairs toilet* | How do you know that this is not a site for the recovery of evidence? You should not touch or *use* anything in a crime scene. |
| *Ignoring the muddy footprints outside* | How do you know that they belong to children? They might be relevant to the crime scene, and you should assume that they are and take steps to preserve them, such as covering them with a box or positioning a chair above them. If the weather is cold don't worry, but if it is wet you must do what you can to try to preserve the prints until a CSI can get a cast of them. Take care as you go outside: you'll need a CAP there too. Oh, and don't tread in the mud outside more than you have to. |
| *Walking about the ground floor* | You should stick to one CAP. The CSI will do the forensic examination of the rooms, not you. You should merely note the missing knife from the kitchen in your PNB and draw it to the attention of the CSI when s/he arrives, while minimizing your own contamination of the scene (mud, blood and all on your boots). |

| | |
|---|---|
| *Taking the knife out of the body* | **Never** touch anything which might be the murder weapon and especially do not remove it from where it was first found. The fact that you have gloves on is irrelevant: *you should not touch anything in a way which might damage potential evidence.* |
| *Letting Control know* | You should have done this before you entered the premises, and you should have been keeping them up to date throughout. |
| *Dialogue with Control … using the phone in the hall* | If the dialogue is as reported, then Control staff may gain redeployment along with you. More importantly, you should not use a telephone within the crime scene premises, for the same reasons of contamination which apply to not using other things on the premises. If you do not have a Force radio, you should have a 'job' mobile. If none of these things, get to a landline outside the crime scene or use someone else's mobile phone until someone with a radio arrives. |
| *Drawing your thumb across the blood* | The fact that you know the blood is still wet and sticky means that you have touched it. **Don't**. Never smear a blood stain in this way—especially as it is a high blood splash (above your head). Analysing 'blood spatter' is an important forensic technique because it gives an indication of the force used and the point of attack, among other things. |
| *Cordoning* | No harm in using string if you don't have cordon tape, but probably better not to use it—especially as you had to take it from the house. If you don't have cordon tape about your person, wait until it arrives in the kit carried in a police car. Meanwhile, closing external doors and preventing immediate access to the crime scene is more effective than trying to make a physical barrier (you'll only have to remove the string when the CSI and other officers come anyway). |
| *Letting the postal worker go* | You should be taking evidence statements and recording the personal particulars of any witnesses in your PNB. For all you know to the contrary at this stage, the postal worker might have done the deed, and at the very least she is a material witness who can describe—partially—the crime scene before you blundered into it. |

*(continued)*

| Errors | Remedies |
|---|---|
| *Chatting amiably with the neighbours* | Fine if you are on a conventional patrol to engage with the community in this friendly way, but you are at the scene of a murder, and you should be taking statements, questioning the neighbours about anything they may have seen or heard, and taking down their personal particulars in your PNB. *Being professional is what this is all about*, and you are utterly amateur in the left-hand column; properly competent in this column. |

### 4.6.2.2 Locard's 'principle of exchange'

A pioneer in forensic science, Edmond Locard (1877–1966), believed that material from a crime scene would be on the suspect, and material from the suspect would be at the crime scene. This is often rendered as **'every contact leaves a trace'**. It is a principle rather than a scientific law, but you need to know that in forensic investigation, *'transfer' is used as a demonstration of contact*; practically putting Locard's Principle in reverse. Such contacts include **'traces'** (paint, hairs, fibres, blood), **'impressions'** (fingerprints, footprints, tools, keyboards), and **'intangible data'** (such as that on computer hard drives, disk, or mobile phone data). This in turn raises the question of 'uniqueness'.

Things we use develop unique characteristics

We are familiar with the concept that each of us has individual fingerprints or that our DNA profiles are unique (except those of identical twins), but much other forensic investigation is based on a similar notion that things acquire uniqueness (or 'individualization') through use. The keyboard used to type these words will have different 'impressions' from those on your keyboard, because of the way that my fingers hit individual keys and because the keyboard is in my house and not in yours. The untested implication behind all this is that no two things can be identical (except at the particulate, molecular, or atomic level). That means that paint flakes from your car found against the shattered tree in someone's front garden raise the likelihood that your car hit the garden owner's tree (proving that you were driving the car at the time is more difficult, but you see the point).

'Leaps of faith' in forensic science

Scientists describe belief in the Locard principle of exchange and in the principle of the uniqueness of things as *'leaps of faith'* because they cannot be disproven scientifically, but that rarefied debate has not yet reached the criminal justice system, and is therefore unlikely to delay us in our assumption that forensic evidence is often compelling.

### 4.6.3 **The 'golden hour'**

We began by calling the period when a crime scene is discovered and support is summoned as the 'golden hour', noting its importance in the preservation of evidence. It is unlikely actually to be an hour unless the crime scene is in some remote place which is difficult to access, such as a mountainside or deep in a forest.

#### 4.6.3.1 **Locating resources and coordinating support**

Your early reporting of a possible crime to your Force Control is very important, because the allocation of resources calls for appropriate judgement and understanding of all the available facts. Otherwise, you might be supported by a dog team when what you really need is an armed response unit. So too, there might be need for coordination of other services and contributors (such as Transco for a gas leak, heavy building equipment from civil engineers for a collapsed road, commercial, RAF, or other police force helicopters for wide area searching, and so on). You can't do that, it has to be coordinated by the BCU Command or by Headquarters—especially in the invocation of *military aid to the civil power* (MACP), when anything from a unit of Royal Engineers with bridging equipment, to specialist Arctic-trained soldiers needed for a specific operation. The rule is therefore to **keep Control informed**.

#### 4.6.3.2 **Dos and don'ts at a crime scene**

So, what should you do, and what should you not do, at a crime scene when you are the FOA? You saw with our scenario that rushing in and blundering about is likely to be counter-productive. **Your first duty is to preserve life and limb**, so you have to enter the crime scene itself if there is the remotest possibility that you could intervene to save someone's life. Even if there is evidently a dead body at the scene, it is not for you to decide whether life is extinct or not. A CSI of our acquaintance once tried to argue that life was extinct because the 'body' was a skeleton, but even this was deemed rather to be the province of a 'suitably qualified medical person'. **Your second duty is to preserve evidence**. You should, in order, do the following:

- Ensure safety for you, anyone in the area, and anyone following you into the scene.
- Check the building or area for anyone vulnerable (remember that children can squeeze into very small spaces).
- Make a note of anything material which you see (possible murder or assault weapon, marks on a polished surface, broken windows, signs of forced entry).
- Make a sketch in your PNB of what is where, including the position of any body or victim, extensive bloodstains, and so on.
- Establish a **common approach path** (CAP) which does not impinge on any visible physical evidence (but be prepared for the CSI to change it if s/he thinks it necessary to do so).

- Talk to and record the particulars of any witnesses or people in the vicinity who might have information of use to an investigation.
- Secure the approach to the crime scene, with cordon tape to mark the 'exclusion zone' if you can, or by using your authority if not, perhaps by closing doors and gates leading to the scene. Remember not to attach cordon tape to any potential source of material evidence, nor to anything which may have to be moved (such as a car or gate).
- Recce for, and report, a suitable **RV** (meeting) point for the support which is on its way. That RV should be big enough to accommodate vehicles and enable them to turn around, and should be far enough from the crime scene to avoid contamination. In an urban setting, a pub car park or public car park may be suitable. If not, move the cordon outwards (it can always be tightened afterwards). In a rural setting, the nearest large area of hard-standing (such as a farmyard) may be suitable. Try to avoid fields unless absolutely necessary: in heavy rain such places rapidly become quagmires. Finally, where you can, try to make the CAP on firm ground, not grass or earth, as this will minimize the likelihood of cross-contamination.
- If you can, make further notes in your PNB about what you are doing and why—this will be relevant if matters come to court and for your duty statement, though we accept that you are likely to be pushed for time. Write up your notebook as soon as you can thereafter and certainly before you go off duty.
- On a related topic, you will need to note in your PNB to whom you handed control of the crime scene and when, in order to preserve the continuity of evidence, and so that the Force can ensure that there is an auditable trail from your arrival to the closure of the crime scene.

### Knowledge Check 20

1. What is the 'golden hour'?

2. What is 'FOA' and how might it affect you?

3. What is a CAP?

4. Why might 'blood spatter' be important to the forensic investigation of a crime scene?

5. Who formulated the 'Principle of Exchange'?

6. How is the Principle usually expressed?

7. Name two examples in each of (a) traces, (b) impressions, and (c) 'intangible data'.

8. Why is Locard's Principle called 'a leap of faith'?

9. What are your two duties at a crime scene?

# 4.7 **Dealing with Aggression and Abuse**

### 4.7.1 **NOS unit on 'Managing Conflict'**

During your training for the PCSO role, you would have been given advice about and practice in dealing with situations involving aggression and abuse. These form the backbone of your response to such circumstances and can be used within the NOS unit to demonstrate a successful completion of the criteria.

---

**Task**

What elements of your training could be utilized when dealing with a member of the public who is abusive or aggressive?

---

These are the tools and skills you would use to deal with hostility:

- **Officer Safety Training**—you will have been taught techniques to protect yourself from assault, as well as ways to disengage from dangerous situations. We hope you refresh these skills regularly.
- **Personal Protective Equipment**—such as your stab-proof vest.
- **Radio training**—how to call for assistance quickly and what information is crucial when making the call.
- **Patrol techniques**—knowing where you are at any time, knowledge of the area and some of the problems that could occur.
- **Communication techniques**—how to talk to people and, just as importantly, to listen to them. You could use '**Betari's Box**' as a reminder of how to communicate with people:

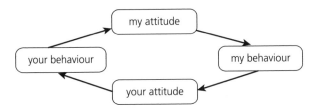

- **Disengagement**—it could be appropriate for you to remove yourself from that situation if you feel that your health and safety is being threatened.
- **Mediation techniques**—you may feel confident enough to attempt to resolve the issue by discovering the root causes of the aggression or abuse.

If there are any aspects of this answer that you are not conversant with, you should research them so that they can become part of your overall PCSO toolkit.

## 4.8 **Core Behaviours**

Now it is time to focus on what is needed from a PCSO in terms of behaviour.

| Behaviour Area | Behaviour | PCSO Role |
|---|---|---|
| **Working with others** | Respect for diversity | A |
| | Team working | C |
| | Community and customer focus | C |
| | Effective communication | B |
| **Achieving results** | Personal responsibility | B |
| | Resilience | B |

The PCSO Behavioural Standards: modified from Skills for Justice comparative data 2006.

You should remind yourself of the various references to behaviour, ethics, professional standards, and diversity throughout this book.

### 4.8.1 **How behaviours are measured and assessed**

Each behavioural area has a description of preferred behaviour and what your Force can expect from you. This description is followed by sets of **positive indicators** which show where the individual will attain competence in the behavioural standard. There is a corresponding set of **negative indicators** that demonstrate how an individual does not meet the required level of competence. Just as for the NOS, this is not a question of pass or fail: an individual officer is either competent or has yet to attain competence.

#### 4.8.1.1 Take the respect for diversity agenda seriously

In **respect for diversity** any demonstration of prejudiced or discriminatory behaviour (either towards colleagues or towards members of the public) is very likely to result in dismissal. The police service cannot afford to have its officers and staff at any grade showing intolerance for diversity, or not respecting the vulnerable in society whom we are pledged to protect. So be warned: the police service takes these matters very seriously indeed, and that means that you have to show that you accept and demonstrate the standards of required behaviour. It is not enough not to show discrimination—you should show that you will stand up for minority rights and champion those who are victims of disrespectful behaviour.

### 4.8.2 **Respect for race and diversity**

Your police force has a statutory duty in law. The Equality Act 2010 has extended the protection from the six equality strands to '*Nine Protected characteristics*', which are:

- age
- disability
- gender reassignment
- marriage and civil partnership
- pregnancy and maternity
- race
- religion and belief
- sex
- sexual orientation

Under this Act people are not allowed to discriminate, harass, or victimize another person because they have any of the protected characteristics. The Equality Act 2010 includes a *public sector Equality Duty* which states that public bodies must have due regard to the need to:

- Eliminate unlawful discrimination, harassment, and victimization
- Advance equality of opportunity
- Foster good relations between different groups

**That means you.** Under the 2010 Act, you are now obliged to act in promotion of the above as part of your statutory duties.

---

**Further Reading**

For more detail on the 2010 Equality Act and the nine protected characteristics, see <www.esfrs.org/equality/entryPages/equalityAct.shtml> accessed 29 May 2014.

---

### 4.8.3 **Team working**

Although you have independence, you often work alone, and you have a sturdy self-reliance, doing your job properly actually relies a great deal on team work and getting on well with others. This core behaviour, graded at a 'C', tends to emphasize the importance of team working with colleagues but, given the nature of your job as a PCSO, we think it should be extended to cover those partnerships and liaisons which you develop within the community and in which you are the catalyst or cement, either driving on or binding together the team effort (or both). The general description notes that you will:

> **Develop strong working relationships inside and outside the team to achieve common goals** [and that you will] **break down barriers between groups and involve others in discussions and decisions.** [In doing this you will] **work effectively as a team member and help to build relationships within the team, actively helping and supporting others to achieve team goals.**

> Adapted from Skills for Justice, *Core Behaviours* (2003);
> our additions are shown in square brackets.

### 4.8.3.1 You are part of a team

At the centre of this is a recognition by you that you cannot do the job effectively if you act on your own. You need others to help, each playing a different part.

### 4.8.4 Community and customer focus

This core behaviour, graded as a 'C', is fundamental to the work of a PCSO and covers what the customer (member of the community) wants, and how you can provide a high-quality service tailored to meet those, sometimes poorly-articulated, needs. It is about *being* the reassurance and living the message of support to the community which you serve.

### 4.8.5 Effective communication

Listening skills and being able to put ideas forward simply and effectively are keys to good communication and these are essential factors in your proper functioning as a PCSO. This core behaviour, graded at 'C', expects that you will be able to communicate ideas and information effectively.

### 4.8.6 Personal responsibility

This is about taking responsibility for making things happen and getting results, and will involve your motivation, commitment, and conscientiousness as a PCSO, as well as how much you can persist or persevere in the face of opposition.

### 4.8.7 Resilience

This final core behaviour, carrying a 'B' grading, deals with how you withstand frustrations, disappointments, and difficulties. It is about how you deal with negatives and how you stand up to things which would daunt a person of lesser self-belief. On the contrary, you show persistence, you are not cast down when things go wrong, you are dogged in your pursuit of goals, and you stay buoyant when others are preparing to pack it all in.

### 4.8.8 Thoughts about core behaviours and what they mean

A final word about core behaviours. Don't rush to evidence the positives in your behaviours; these will be observed in your actions by your assessors and supervisors throughout your appraisal period, and your competence will develop over time, building on the strengths which were identified in you when you were accepted at national selection and by your Force. The assessor or supervisor will speak to you directly if there is a problem, then and there, because there is no sense in waiting to do so at a formal appraisal period which may be weeks or months away. The idea is to get you to address the behavioural shortfall without delay. Don't be afraid of making mistakes. Your resilience will ensure that you can bear your failures with good humour, and thereby you will remain human and improvable, like the rest of us.

Finally, a knowledge check to end this chapter:

**Knowledge Check 21**

1. Name a Behaviour assessed at C.

2. How is a Behaviour measured?

3. Give three of the nine 'protected characteristics'.

4. Which Act governs this?

5. What is your public duty under the Act?

# 5

# Close Encounters

---

## 5.1 **Introduction—Setting the Scene**

In this chapter, we look at those elements involved in your day-to-day job of meeting and dealing with people. These encounters can require responses which develop from, or are complementary to, the Powers and the Competences which we examined in Chapters 3 and 4 respectively. We shall look at the nature of **evidence** and the importance of using your Pocket Note Book (PNB), and then look at areas of **negotiation** and **persuasion** in a PCSO's work (in other words, being effective and having an impact without resorting always to compulsion through the exercise of powers). We go on to look carefully at ways in which tense or angry situations can be **defused** and temperatures lowered. This is followed by an analysis of **aggression** and how you can deal with situations which become, or threaten to become, hostile and angry. We discuss your **safety awareness** training which is vital to your continued well-being and effectiveness as a PCSO. The chapter concludes with a detailed look at the process of making **dynamic risk assessments** and the part played by health and safety in your evolving role.

## 5.2 **Evidence**

### 5.2.1 **The Pocket Note Book (PNB)**

The importance of your PNB cannot be overemphasized. It is akin to your life support mechanism whilst on duty. Use it properly and the PNB will become a friend, an ally, and a necessity if you are to follow the policy guidelines of your Force. Ignore it and the PNB will rise like the Devil from wherever you keep it, accusing you of neglect and a lack of professionalism. The way you use your PNB will say a lot about you as an officer; others will think so too and will want to examine your recording standard from time to time. Note what it is for: **the primary function of the PNB is for evidence gathering during your investigation of offences and recording the duties you carry out.** To maintain your integrity and that of the living document, you must employ a number of processes:

- At the start of each duty, write the day, date, month, and year in block capitals and underline them

| | 01 |
|---|---:|
| MONDAY 14TH JANUARY 2008 | |

- Write down your call sign, your period of duty, and the name of the area you are patrolling as the very first entry at the start of each new day

| |
|---|
| Call sign—TT01, Duty—0800–1600, Patrol area—town centre. |

- Use the 24-hour clock to note down in the left-hand margin the times of your PNB entries

| 0745 | |
|---|---|

- Write down the location of the briefing you receive at the start of each day and/or the location from where you commenced your duty

| 0745 | On duty in Police Station. Received daily briefing from Sgt TAGGART. |
|---|---|

- Write down details of tasks you are given by supervisors and/or control rooms, and intelligence you receive from briefing and members of the public

| 0750 | Received taskings: Patrol the shopping areas—spray cans being used to paint graffiti on the walls and windows of the shops |
|---|---|

- Make your entries in a chronological sequence

| 0800 | Commenced foot patrol walking from police station to the shopping area. |
|---|---|

- For the purposes of demonstrating a logical sequence with no breaks, your entries should be timed and the location in which you make them noted (continuity of evidence)

| 0855 | North pavement 15 yards east of the south entrance to the shopping area—stopped by a member of the public. |
|---|---|

- Your objective should be to make entries at the same time as they happen, noting down what you see, hear, touch, taste, and smell (the physical senses produce *evidence*). If it is not possible do so (because you are administering first aid, for example), then make your entries as soon as practicable afterwards and give a reason in your PNB for the delay

| 0900 | Observe male spraying the wall of 'Buy One Get One Free' with a spray can on the western side of the walkway approx. 15 yards south of the exit to Daniell St. |
|---|---|

- When you ask a question of a person you are interviewing regarding an offence, or a witness about an incident, note down their replies *verbatim* (word for word) and in direct speech

| PCSO 0901 | "Excuse me, my name is PCSO Matthews and I have just seen you spraying this wall with a spray can". |
|---|---|
| Suspect | "What are you doing here? You lot never come round here. What if I am? It's my tag, nobody's ever——— stopped me before. I'm quite proud of it actually, do you like it? Do you want me to put me tag on your nice white shirt?...only joking!"——— |

- Make a note of the description of suspects that you investigate and, although it is your own PNB to make entries in as you see fit, make your writing legible so that, if necessary, other investigators and courts can read what you have written

| | Description of suspect: white male, 20 years, stocky build, a mass of dark bushy hair, round face,——— wearing glasses, clean shaven, approx. 5'8" tall with a scar over the left eye.——— |
|---|---|

- Write down the full names, addresses, and dates of birth of victims, suspects, and witnesses and write all surnames in block capitals

| PCSO | "Please tell me your full name, date of birth, and address."——— |
|---|---|
| Suspect | "Yeah, it's Toni Stalybridge, born 06/04/88, address 24, Morgan St, Tonchester, Tonford."——— |

- Make a note of the description and identifying features of property that forms part of your evidence

| | The graffiti were approx 33cm wide and 20cm tall. There were three symbols in total, all in the colour 'British Racing Green'. There were no other painting marks on what was otherwise a clean wall made of bricks and mortar measuring 2x1m below the front window of the shop. When I arrived the symbols were still wet to the touch and I could clearly smell the odour of cellulose paint.——— |
|---|---|

- Only write a single line of writing between each line on the page in your PNB and do not be tempted to make additional notes in any other part of the book. The only exception to this is when you make a drawing, in which case use the whole page

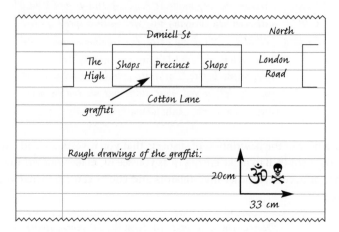

- Do **NOT** leave spaces in between words that could possibly be used to add words later. If you do leave spaces, then—draw—lines—in—between so that gaps cannot be filled. This is to ensure that your integrity is not called into question later on suspicion of adding evidence after the incident. Therefore, make sure you write on every line and page of the PNB

> The Precinct is a shopping area between ————
> Daniell St in the north east and Cotton Lane in the
> south, bordered east and west by The High and——
> London Road. ————————————

- If you accidentally turn over two pages at once, then draw a diagonal line across the blank pages and write 'omitted in error' across them

- Do not overwrite, erase, or obliterate errors. If you make a mistake, cross it out with a single line so that it can still be read, initial your error, and then continue with what you want to write immediately afterwards

> There were no other people around at the time, and
> none of the shops in the area was ~~closed~~ open JBM
> PCSO1 ————————————————

- Last few PNB tips:

| 1 | Always use black ink to make your entries so that the PNB can be copied successfully. |
| 2 | Do not write on scraps of paper as a substitute for your PNB whilst on duty, always use your PNB |
| 3 | The PNB remains the property of your Force and, as it contains vital evidence, you must look after it very well indeed. |

The rules surrounding the use of the pocket note books have been successfully summarized in police circles in the past by the mnemonic **NO ELBOWS(S)**, see Glossary. Statements must always be written in direct speech.

| | | 01 |
| --- | --- | --- |
| | NO ELBOWS | |
| E | Erasures. | |
| L | Leaves torn out or Lines missed. | |
| B | Blank spaces. | |
| O | Overwriting. | |
| W | Writing between the lines. | |
| S | Spare pages. | |

## 5.2.2 Record, retain, and reveal

A very important rule of evidence is that at all stages of an investigation all investigators of crimes (including PCSOs) have a responsibility to **record** and **retain** material which has some bearing on the offence under investigation (referred to as **relevant** material), even if it is not subsequently used by the prosecution. It is **relevant** whether it applies to the defence or to the prosecution case. As an investigator, you have the responsibility to **record** and **retain relevant** material relating to both sides.

### 5.2.2.1 The consequence of not recording

The consequence of *not* recording relevant material is that the Crown Prosecution Service (CPS) cannot share the material with the legal representatives of the suspect. This lack of **disclosure** could provide the defence with support for any argument made to the court that the accused has no case to answer or that the accused should be found not guilty, because the legal process was flawed.

### 5.2.2.2 Make records in a durable form

It is particularly important therefore, as far as witnesses or potential witnesses are concerned, that you make a record of their personal details in a durable form, in your case in your PNB, as soon as you make contact with them. Just as important is the need to record an outline of their evidence if you are not going to take statements from them straight away (see later in the chapter). If these steps are not taken, the prosecution case could be weakened. The importance of disclosure (even of things not done) arose from the case of *R v Heggart and Heggart* (November 2000 Court of Appeal). In this case, potential witnesses were located by police investigators but no statements of evidence were obtained from them.

### 5.2.2.3 Back to the example

Let's go back to what had happened with the graffitist. About ten minutes earlier, you were on patrol in the Precinct when you were stopped by a member of the public who gave you information about a man with a spray can. (Remember, even if the witness subsequently does not make a statement of evidence, you must record an outline of what s/he had to say in a durable form and your PNB will be the best place for that.)

| 0855 | North pavement 15 yards east of the south entrance to the shopping area—stopped by a member of the public. |
| Witness | "Excuse me, I have just walked through the area and I have seen a bloke spray painting the wall outside a shop called 'Buy One Get One Free' ". |
| PCSO | "Please give me a description of this person." |
| Witness | "Well, he's white, around 20 years old, stocky build, and his hair is a right mess 'cos it is a mass of dark bushy hair, round face, wearing glasses, clean shaven, approx. 5'8" tall, wearing a black top with a hood and some of those baggy jeans and dirty white trainers." |
| PCSO | "What exactly did you see him do?" |
| Witness | "As I walked past, he was spraying a symbol on the wall outside the shop, it looked foreign to me. He was using a spray can, must have got it from the car superstore because it's the same colour as my old car, 'British Racing Green'. It's even metallic. The spray can he was using ran out and he threw it in a rubbish bin nearby. Here it is, you take it." |
| PCSO | "Please may I have your name and address as I may want to take a statement from you at a later stage?" |
| Witness | "Pat OLDFIELD, born 09/09/70, 221B, Baker St, Tonchester, Tonford; telephone 37510. I can't stop, I'm late for work, but I do think I've seen the guy before somewhere." |

#### 5.2.2.4 Recording the details of witnesses is vital

The necessity for you to record the details of witnesses and an outline of their evidence applies to all investigations. It is important to note therefore that these rules apply even if you find yourself in the middle of an incident for which you are not the 'officer in the case'. An example might be when police officers are dealing with an assault, a robbery, or any other crime which might attract a crowd. You walk around the corner on a routine patrol and there you see a number of potential witnesses. First of all, you should make a PNB entry of the time and location you find yourself in, and then, if witnesses come forward to you, make sure you record their details and an outline of their evidence.

##### Disclosure

Lastly, having obtained any **relevant** material, you must **reveal** the entries in your PNB to the CPS in the case above if the suspect is going to plead not guilty, and to the officer in the case for all other investigations. This can be done by submitting photocopies of your PNB.

### 5.2.3 Evidence of identification—*Turnbull* principles

You remember from Chapter 3 on the law in England and Wales what **case law** is and how it affects the investigative process. In Chapter 3 we referred to a major example of case law: *R v Turnbull* [1976] 3 All ER 549 which relates to the identification of suspects. As a result of this case, the evidence of any witness, including you, which involves observation of a suspect, must be gathered using the recommendations which were set as a precedent.

#### 5.2.3.1 Mnemonics to remember the importance of the case

'Turnbull', as it has come to be known, has a memory tool to help you remember its component parts. This is the mnemonic *ADVOKATE*. it is about *awareness of your observation and recording of identification details*.

#### 5.2.3.2 Think of *Turnbull* whenever you gather evidence

Every time you gather evidence about a person which results from your observation of them you must use every applicable aspect of *Turnbull* relevant to the incident/offence and make a note of it. Later, if you are required to make a statement of that evidence for a court case, you will be required to repeat the process and write down what you saw meeting the requirements of ADVOKATE. Be aware of the fact that you could lose sight of the suspect at any time and therefore take the earliest opportunity to write down a description.

### 5.2.3.3 *Turnbull* in our example

Let's return to our example of the graffiti artist inside the shopping area. At your first point of contact, you observed the suspect using the spray can on the wall. Now let's apply ADVOKATE to that incident. To help you meet the requirements of *Turnbull*, you may wish to write ADVOKATE in the margin of your PNB (a quick check on the meaning of the letters is in the Glossary).

### 5.2.4 Unsolicited comments by suspects (PACE Code C 11)

As a PCSO you will be required to investigate offences for which you have been designated (see 3.2, on powers). This section describes what you should do if the suspect you are investigating makes a comment before s/he has been cautioned or arrested, as what s/he says may contain information of evidential value. Comments which are made outside the framework of an interview are called '**unsolicited**' (voluntary) comments and the PACE Codes of Practice dictate a course of action to follow if such comments are to be documented. They are divided into two groups: **significant statements** and **relevant comments**.

### 5.2.4.1 Significant statements and relevant comments

Any comment made by the suspect at any time in your presence which contains significant information about the suspect's personal involvement in the offence and, in particular, an admission of guilt, is a **significant statement** (Code C 11.4A). Anything that the suspect says at any time which includes anything which might be relevant to the offence (Code C 11.13 and Note 11E) is a **relevant comment**.

### 5.2.4.2 Illustration from our extended example

As an example, think back to the previous section on Pocket Note Books when we introduced a suspect who was spraying graffiti on the wall of a shop in the shopping area. At the time you noted in your PNB the following conversation (see top of page 378):

| | |
|---|---|
| PCSO 0901 | "Excuse me, my name is PCSO Matthews, and I seen just seen you spraying this wall with a spray can." |
| Suspect | "What are you doing here? You lot never come round here. What if I am? It's my tag, nobody's ever stopped me before. I'm quite proud of it actually, do you like it? Do you want me to put me tag on your nice white shirt?...only joking!" |

Significant statement

These comments were made voluntarily by the suspect about his involvement in the offence; they were an admission of guilt and therefore this was a significant statement.

Relevant comment

If the suspect had said, 'If you had been five minutes earlier there would have been two of us, but you are too late', the comment would have been relevant to the offence and therefore a relevant comment.

### 5.2.4.3 Recording unsolicited comments (Code C Note 11E)

- Having written down any such comment into your PNB, note the time it was made and sign the entry using your usual signature:

| 0901 | The above statement was made in my presence and hearing by the suspect. Jo MATTHEWS PCSO——— |

- Show the PNB entry to the suspect when it is practicable and ask him or her to read it over and decide whether or not s/he agrees that it is a true record of what s/he said:

| PCSO | "Please read this entry. Do you agree it is a true record of what you said?" I handed my pocket book to the suspect to read.——— |
| Suspect | "Yes, I did say that."——— |

- If s/he **agrees**, ask him or her to sign your PNB at the end of the following statement (Code C Note 11E):

| PCSO | "Please sign the following statement, 'I agree that this is a correct record of what was said.'" Toni STALYBRIDGE ——— |

- If s/he **disagrees**, record in your PNB the extent of the disagreement:

| PCSO | "Please read this entry, do you agree it is a true record of what you said?" I handed my pocket book to the suspect to read.——— |
| Suspect | "No, I just said it was someone else."——— |

- Ask the suspect to read over the note you made on the content of the disagreement:

| PCSO | *"I have made a note of your disagreement. Please read it over and sign that I have done so correctly." I handed my pocket book to the suspect to read.* ——— |
|------|------|

- Ask him or her to sign that the disagreement has been recorded correctly:

| PCSO | *"Please sign the following statement, 'I agree that the above comment accurately reflects my*——— *disagreement about what I said earlier.' " Toni STALYBRIDGE* ——————— |
|------|------|

- Any refusal to sign should also be recorded and signed by anyone else who heard the comments (See Code C Note 11E):

| PCSO | *"I offered my PNB to the suspect to read and sign but he refused."*——————— |
|------|------|

### 5.2.4.4 Record anything which a suspect says at any time

By the very nature of your employment, you may well find yourself involved at the start of many types of investigations simply by being in the right place at the right time. **It is essential therefore that you record anything any suspect says at any time and follow the Code of Practice accordingly.**

### 5.2.5 Cautions

Proving the **guilty actions** (*actus reus*) and the **guilty mind** *(mens rea)* of the suspect at the time s/he carried out an offence (see 3.1.2) will require you to ask the suspect one or more questions. This constitutes an interview and is defined as the '*questioning of a person regarding* [his or her] *involvement in a criminal offence*' which must be carried out under caution (PACE Code C 11.1A). A suspect is given a caution forewarning him or her of the consequences of his or her actions should s/he decide to say anything, and the possible cost to his or her defence if s/he chooses not to say anything at this point, but later relies on things which s/he ought to have said at interview.

### 5.2.5.1 Landmarks in the investigation—triggers for the caution

The caution is given to a suspect at major landmarks throughout an investigation and it is at these locations that its wording differs depending on when the caution is administered.

- When a suspect is first suspected of committing an offence without being arrested, s/he is cautioned before being interviewed. Similarly, the caution will be administered just after the individual has been arrested and before s/he is interviewed at a police station. The words *'when questioned'* are said in this caution.
- When the investigation is completed and the suspect is charged, the suspect is cautioned to give him/her the last opportunity to say anything before the court appearance. The word *'now'* is said in this caution.

### 5.2.5.2 The three parts to a caution

The three parts to a caution are as follows:

1. *'You do not have to say anything*
2. *but it may harm your defence if you do not mention*
   (a) **'when questioned'**
   OR
   (b) **'now'**
   *something which you later rely on in court.*
3. *Anything you do say may be given in evidence.'*

### 5.2.6 Exhibits as evidence

To prove the existence of a material article seized in the course of an investigation, it is presented to a court as an exhibit. Examples of such items in the graffiti artist story would include the spray can of paint the suspect was using to spray the wall and, subsequently, any Closed Circuit Television (CCTV) recordings of the incident.

### 5.2.6.1 Reference tags

The first person who takes possession of the item after the commencement of the investigation (other than the suspect) is the person to whom the item is referenced; therefore the article receives a reference tag which is usually the person's initials and a sequential number. Everybody who later refers to that exhibit then uses the unique reference number derived from the person who first took possession of it, like this:

(1) A witness called **Pat OLDFIELD** sees a suspect using a spray can to paint graffiti on a wall. The suspect throws the spray can into a rubbish bin nearby and starts using a second spray can.
(2) The witness recovers the first spray can from the rubbish bin and gives it to **PCSO Jo MATTHEWS**. This spray can therefore has the reference number **PO/1** because it is the witness who first takes possession of it.

(3) **PCSO Jo MATTHEWS** then interviews the suspect and takes possession of the second spray can. This spray can receives the reference **JBM/1**.

(4) Both spray cans are taken to a shop owner to be identified. **PCSO Jo MATTHEWS** will refer to both exhibits as **PO/1** and **JBM/1** in his/her duty statement.

(5) The shop owner will refer to the identification of both spray cans and sign both labels of exhibits **PO/1** and **JBM/1**.

(6) In his/her statement the witness makes reference to handing the spray can that s/he found in the rubbish bin to **PCSO MATTHEWS**.

### 5.2.7 Closed Circuit Television evidence and the need to record, reveal, and retain

One of the products of modern technology in the fight against crime is town centre and retail CCTV camera and recording equipment. The recording of millions of images, including thousands of incidents up and down the country, has given courts the opportunity to prove or disprove accusations by both the prosecution and defence. Local knowledge of your area will help you to know which places are covered by CCTV and which areas are not.

#### 5.2.7.1 Relevant material

Previously we outlined what is **relevant** material and how it affects an investigation. If you think that CCTV may have captured an incident that you are investigating, then you must view the tape recording to find out if it contains **relevant** material in connection with:

- The offence being investigated.
- Any person under investigation.
- The circumstances in which the offence took place.

If you consider the contents of the tape contain nothing of relevance, you should make a summary of the content of the recording, note it in your PNB, and reveal to the CPS that you have viewed the tape. If in doubt, always seize the tape.

**Knowledge Check 22**

1. What is the primary function of the PNB?

2. What sequence should you use for entries in your PNB?

3. What do your physical senses produce?

4. What does 'verbatim' mean?

5. Explain what is meant by NO ELBOWS.

6. What responsibility do you have for evidence at all stages of an investigation?

7. What date was *R v Turnbull*?

8. What two kinds of comments might be made outside formal interviews?

9. What do you need to prove an offence?

10. Give all three parts to a Caution.

11. What is a 'reference tag'?

12. Why might you want to view CCTV in connection with an offence?

### 5.2.8 Penalty notices for disorder under sections 1 to 11 of the Criminal Justice and Police Act 2001: objectives of the system

The penalty notices for disorder (PND) scheme provides you with a speedy and efficient way of dealing with minor anti-social offences. It carries a crime prevention message and is a simpler way to administer justice. There are two tiers of penalty: an upper one attracting a fine of £80 and a lower one of £50 (see 3.2).

#### 5.2.8.1 Legislation

Community Support Officers are empowered under the PRA2002 to issue PNDs to persons aged 16 or over who have committed a penalty offence (see 3.2 for the list of offences). By accepting the notice and paying the penalty, the recipient is no longer obliged to go to court. However, having been issued with the notice, the recipient then has two choices. S/he can either pay the penalty or choose to go to court, but s/he must make this decision within 21 days of the issue of the notice, otherwise s/he may be fined one-and-a-half times the original penalty.

#### 5.2.8.2 Circumstances in which notices can be issued

To be in a position to issue a notice, you must have reason to believe that the person has committed an offence for which a PND can be issued and you must have gathered enough **evidence** to prove the offence (remember 3.2, 'Powers and duties of a PCSO', where we showed you the points to prove evidentially in applying the law). The incident itself must be of a simple kind and one that would benefit from being dealt with using the PND scheme. The suspect must be able to comprehend what is happening to him or her, such as having a reasonable understanding of English, or not being too drunk and incapable, and s/he must be amenable and cooperate fully. If the person is suspected of committing two or more related offences in addition to the one being considered, then a PND cannot be issued. The recipient must be aged 16 or over, and you must be satisfied with the validity of his/her age, identity, and address. Where a person aged 16 or over commits a penalty offence with a person under 16, a penalty notice cannot be issued to either person.

### 5.2.8.3 Contents of the penalty notice for disorder

There are two versions of the ticket. The English language version is a four-sheet document in six parts and the Welsh language version a five-sheet document in six parts; less the title sheet, these are:

| | | | |
|---|---|---|---|
| Part 1 Recipient copy ⎱ | | | (Welsh language |
| Part 2 Payment slip ⎰ | | | Sheet 2) |
| Part 2a Instructions | | | |
| Part 3 Hearing request slip | | | |
| Part 4 Central Ticket Office (CTO) copy | Sheet 2 | | (Welsh language Sheet 3) |
| Part 5 Hearing request (HR) copy | Sheet 3 | | (Welsh language Sheet 4) |
| Part 6a Details of recipient ⎱ Part 6b Statement of witness ⎰ | Sheet 4 | | (Welsh language Sheet 5) |

### 5.2.8.4 Process model for the issue of a PND

Figure 5.2 shows you the processes involved in the various stages of issuing a PND. Follow the 'flow' to see when you should issue a PND and when you should take other, alternative or lesser, actions.

### 5.2.9 Fixed penalty notices in respect of road policing

The fixed penalty notice (FPN) system for road policing offences was introduced in the 1980s and has therefore been established for much longer than the penalty notices for disorder (PND) scheme which we have just examined. The FPN scheme has similar objectives relating to time saving, speedier justice, and lessening the load on the courts. The scheme gives you the opportunity to issue a FPN (see figures 5.1 and 5.2) to any person whom you have reason to believe is committing or has committed a fixed penalty offence (see 3.2 for the lists of offences).

## Figure 5.1 Penalty Notice forms

**Penalty Notice: Parts 1–3**
Recipient copy, Payment slip, Instructions to Recipient, Court Hearing Request slip, and Court Hearing Request copy.

Good practice suggests that you should briefly explain the effect of the notice and the requirement it places on the recipient.

**METROPOLITAN POLICE SERVICE**
**PENALTY NOTICE**
**PENALTY AMOUNT £80**
IMPORTANT – READ THE NOTES ON THE BACK OF THIS FORM

**PART 1 RECIPIENT COPY** PN No. 0 1 /

TITLE SURNAME

FORENAMES

DATE OF BIRTH (ddmmyyyy) ADDRESS

POST CODE

OFFENCE TIME HRS. OFFENCE DATE

AT (LOCATION)

OFFENCE CODE DATE OF ISSUE

YOU (offence particulars) ……

CONTRARY TO (Act containing offence) ……

PLACE OF ISSUE: Street Custody

I acknowledge receipt of this Penalty Notice
Signature ……

ISSUED BY: Surname Signature

Warrant No. Division

Rank

**PART 2 COMPLETE ONE SIDE ONLY**
*Send **Part 2** and payment of **£80** to:*
**The Justices' Chief Executive, Central Accounting Office (Fixed Penalty), PO Box 31093, London, SW1P 3WT.**
**Telephone No. 0800 4000111**
I enclose the sum of **£80** as payment in respect of the offence mentioned in PART 1 of this notice.

**NAME** ……
(BLOCK LETTERS)
**ADDRESS** ……
(BLOCK LETTERS)
…… POST CODE

Or, you may phone the Tel. No. above or complete the following section and pay by credit/debit card.

I authorise the Justices' Chief Executive to debit my Mastercard, VISA, Switch or Solo account with the sum of £80.
Card Holder's Signature ……

Expiry Date Today's date

Credit/Debit Card No.

Issue No.

**PART 2a IMPORTANT**

**INFORMATION FOR THE IMMEDIATE ATTENTION OF THE PERSON IN RECEIPT OF THIS NOTICE**

You have been handed this notice because the police officer named in part 1 of this notice has reason to believe that you have committed the offence described in part 1. Within 21 days of the **date of issue** you **must either** pay the penalty **or** request that the matter be heard by a court. You may not do both.

If you fail to do either, a fine of 1 1/2 times the **penalty amount** shown in part 1 may be registered with a court as a **fine** against you or you may be charged with the offence for which this notice has been issued, as described in part 1. If you fail to pay the **fine** you may have to pay additional bailiff fees or you may be arrested. If you are charged and convicted you may have to pay court costs in addition to any fine imposed.

If you have been handed this notice for an offence under **section 5 of the Public Order Act 1986 only** (see part 1) you should be aware that there is a statutory defence to the offence under this section.

A record of this notice will be kept in the interest of justice for administration purposes. This information may be used to help decide whether or not to issue you with another disorder penalty notice in relation to any subsequent offences for which such notices may be issued.

**A. PAYING THE PENALTY**

If you or anyone else choose to pay the penalty amount specified in part 1 you must do so within 21 days of the date of issue, shown in part 1. If you choose to pay no further action will be taken in respect of the offence detailed in part 1: payment of the penalty involves **no admission of guilt** and will **not** result in a record of criminal conviction being made against you.

If you choose to pay the penalty shown in part 1 you may do so by either:

1. Phoning the telephone number in part 2 (the front half of the slip at the bottom of this notice) and quoting your credit/debit card details; or
2. Entering your credit/debit card details in part 2, detaching it and sending it to the address in part 2; or
3. Sending a cheque, money or postal order or cash for the full and exact amount shown in part 1 along with part 2 to the address shown in part 2.

If you wish to pay by credit/debit card you may do so using Mastercard, VISA, Switch or Solo only.
If you pay by method 2 or 3 (above) you **must** write the payer's/card holder's name and address in BLOCK LETTERS in the space provided in part 2.

Cheques, postal orders or money orders should be crossed and made payable to: *The Justices' Chief Executive.* If you choose to pay in cash this must be sent by registered post or an equivalent proof of posting must be obtained. If you require a receipt you must ask for one, and you must supply a stamped, self-addressed envelope. **WARNING: LATE OR PART PAYMENTS WILL NOT BE ACCEPTED. YOU WILL NOT BE SENT A REMINDER.**

**B. REQUESTING A COURT HEARING**

If you wish to contest the issue of this notice and have **your** case heard in a court of law you **must**:

1. Write your name and address in BLOCK LETTERS in the space provided in part 3 of this penalty notice (this side of the slip at the bottom of the notice).
2. Detach the slip along the perforation and send it to the address shown on the slip.

If you choose to request a court hearing you **must** do so by either returning part 3 of this penalty notice or by writing giving your details and an address at which a summons may be served on you. The summons will tell you when and where to attend court. Only the recipient of this Penalty Notice (the person named in part 1) may request a hearing.

**IF YOU HAVE ANY OTHER ENQUIRIES ABOUT THIS NOTICE PLEASE CONTACT THE OFFICE SHOWN AT PART 3**

**PART 3 METROPOLITAN POLICE SERVICE**

**PLEASE NOTE: YOU SHOULD COMPLETE ONE SIDE OF THIS SLIP ONLY. COMPLETE THIS SIDE (PART 3) IF YOU WISH TO REQUEST A COURT HEARING. ONCE COMPLETE SEND THIS SLIP TO THE ADDRESS SHOWN BELOW.**

**I wish to be dealt with by a court for the alleged offence described in part 1 of this notice: the Penalty Notice number is shown overleaf.**

NAME ……
(BLOCK LETTERS)
ADDRESS ……
(BLOCK LETTERS)
……

POST CODE

Signed …… Date

**Send to:** **The Officer in Charge, Traffic Criminal Justice OCU (Disorder Offences Section), PO Box 510, London, SW1V 2JP.**

This part must be given to the recipient.

These two dates will normally be the same, although they may, on occasion, be different, eg where an offender is arrested for drunkenness, allowed to sober up, and issued with a PND the following day.

For reference purposes this information will be detailed on the inside cover of the penalty notice booklet.

You should clearly indicate the offence for which the notice is being issued.

Suspects should be invited to sign for their penalty notice, although there is no compulsion. Signatures will provide useful evidence if a trial is requested.

**Figure 5.1** *Continued*

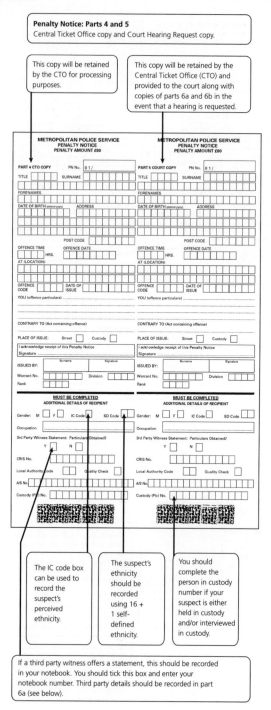

**Penalty Notice: Parts 4 and 5**
Central Ticket Office copy and Court Hearing Request copy.

This copy will be retained by the CTO for processing purposes.

This copy will be retained by the Central Ticket Office (CTO) and provided to the court along with copies of parts 6a and 6b in the event that a hearing is requested.

The IC code box can be used to record the suspect's perceived ethnicity.

The suspect's ethnicity should be recorded using 16 + 1 self-defined ethnicity.

You should complete the person in custody number if your suspect is either held in custody and/or interviewed in custody.

If a third party witness offers a statement, this should be recorded in your notebook. You should tick this box and enter your notebook number. Third party details should be recorded in part 6a (see below).

**Figure 5.1** *Continued*

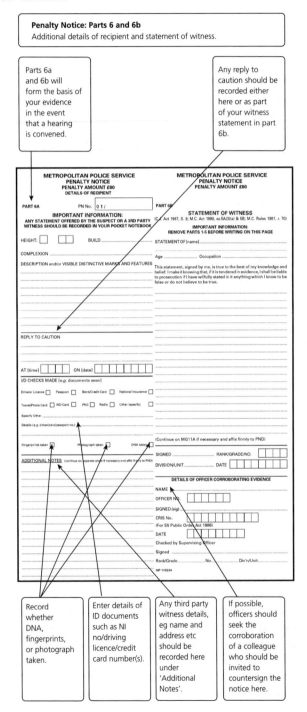

> **Penalty Notice: Parts 6 and 6b**
> Additional details of recipient and statement of witness.

Parts 6a and 6b will form the basis of your evidence in the event that a hearing is convened.

Any reply to caution should be recorded either here or as part of your witness statement in part 6b.

Record whether DNA, fingerprints, or photograph taken.

Enter details of ID documents such as NI no/driving licence/credit card number(s).

Any third party witness details, eg name and address etc should be recorded here under 'Additional Notes'.

If possible, officers should seek the corroboration of a colleague who should be invited to countersign the notice here.

Forms reproduced from the Criminal Justice and Police Act, ss 1–11; Penalty Notices for Disorder, Police Operational Guidance March 2005 available at <http://Police.homeoffice.gov.uk/news-and-publicationspublication/operation-policing/PenaltyNotices_March105.pdf?view=Binary>.

**Figure 5.2 Process model for the issuing of a PND by a PCSO**

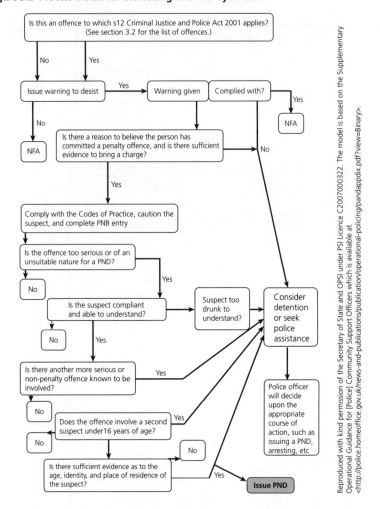

### 5.2.9.1 Types of fixed penalty notice you can issue

Non-endorsable (No penalty points can be added to a driving licence)
**1 Moving vehicle/cycle**—Offender seen: this FPN is issued to drivers/riders, including those aged 16 and 17, who are seen at the time of an alleged offence. The fixed penalty gives the named driver/rider 28 days in which to pay the fixed penalty or to request a court hearing. If no payment or hearing request is received within the specified period, a fine is registered automatically against the driver/rider. The fine will be registered at the offender's local magistrates' court and the fine amount is calculated as the fixed penalty amount (currently £30 for the majority of non-endorsable offences, see figure 5.3) + 50 per cent.

**Figure 5.3 Non-endorsable fixed penalty procedure—driver seen**

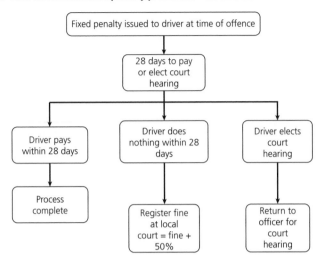

2 **Stationary vehicle**—Parking/Driver not seen: This is the standard 'parking ticket', whereby an FPN is attached to a vehicle suspected of involvement in an alleged offence. On his or her return to the vehicle, the driver is then given 28 days in which to pay the fixed penalty or to request a court hearing. If, within 28 days, no hearing request or penalty payment is received, a Notice to Owner (NTO) is sent to the registered owner/keeper of the vehicle involved in the offence from the Central Ticket Office. The owner/keeper of the vehicle is then liable for the offence and must pay the penalty or request a court hearing within a further period of 28 days.

### Action on receipt of the Notice To Owner (NTO)

On getting the NTO, the recipient also has the opportunity at that stage to state s/he was not the owner/keeper of the vehicle at the time of the offence, or that it was being driven by another person, or on hire (see figure 5.4). As an alternative, s/he can return a request for a court hearing from the person using the vehicle at the time, signed by the driver. If no response is received, a fine registration is issued against the recipient of the notice and registered at the offender's local magistrates' court. The fine registration is calculated as the fixed penalty amount (currently £30 for the majority of non-endorsable offences) + 50 per cent.

**Figure 5.4  Non-endorsable fixed penalty procedure—driver not seen**

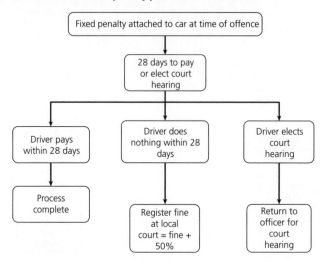

### PNB entries

Although there is no requirement to duplicate all the information noted on an FPN in a PNB, the following should be noted in the PNB every time:

- Time of issue
- Ticket reference number
- Vehicle registration number (if applicable)
- Offender's name.

### 5.2.9.2  Entries in the PNB when issuing an FPN

If there is not enough space on the FPN for a particular piece of evidence, then it should be noted down in the PNB. However, remember that the issuing of the FPN might not be the end of the process, nor necessarily an alternative to following the PACE Codes of Practice in relation to the treatment of a person under investigation. Therefore, always adhere to the Codes during the cautioning, interviewing, and reporting of the suspect.

### Spoiled tickets

If, for any reason, a ticket is spoiled, as a result of an accident or inclement weather, for example, then mark all three copies accordingly and forward them through a supervisor to the Central Ticket/Processing Office for cancellation.

### 5.2.9.3  Content of the non-endorsable fixed penalty ticket

Non-endorsable fixed penalty tickets are supplied in a booklet form, encased in a card cover. Each booklet (at the time of writing) contains ten notices. Printed on the front cover of the booklet is the notice type, the offences applicable to the type of notice, and codes and other information necessary for its completion.

Each ticket consists of three parts:

Part 1—Police copy
Part 2—Offender's copy
Part 3—Clerk's copy

### 5.2.9.4 Fixed penalty notice information

Most information that you will need for the completion of an FPN can be found on the cover of the booklet. However, should you want further information, the Police National Legal Database (PNLD) provides a database of fixed penalty law, offence wording, and coding. All police forces in England and Wales subscribe to this system and any further questions you have in relation to the scheme can be answered by accessing PNLD through *Blackstone's Police Operational Handbook 2014: Law & Practice and Procedure Pack*, edited by **Police National Legal Database (PNLD)** and **Clive Harfield, Ian Bridges,** and **Fraser Sampson**.

For further reading see Home Office (2014), *Road Traffic Offences: Guidance on Fixed Penalty Notices*, available at <http://www.cps.gov.uk/legal/p_to_r/road_traffic_offences_guidance_on_fixed_penalty_notices/>.

## Knowledge Check 23

1. Under what legislation are penalty notices for disorder (PNDs) issued?

2. How much is the current 'upper tier of penalty'?

3. What legislation empowers *you* to issue PNDs?

4. Name two factors that might make issuing a PND inappropriate.

5. Which came first: PND or FPN?

6. What two kinds of FPN are issued for traffic offences?

7. What is an NTO?

8. Who, respectively, gets a copy of the FPN?

### 5.2.10 The duty statement

For the purposes of presenting evidence before a court, any witness, including those in the police 'family', writes down his or her evidence in the form of a **statement**. This form is 11th in a series of approximately 20 forms contained in a prosecution document called the **Manual of Guidance**, used to build case files. It is therefore referred to as an 'MG11'. It is also referred to as a 'section nine statement' because under section 9 of the **Magistrates' Court Act 1980**, a person's evidence can be read out in court from such a statement if s/he has not been called as a witness.

### 5.2.10.1 The duty statement in detail

Based upon the incident with the graffiti artist, here is the duty statement applicable to that incident, assuming that the suspect had requested a court hearing or had pleaded not guilty. It has been designed in sections to help you understand the requirements for making a duty statement. (Some of what follows is adapted from an unpublished document *'A Guide to Form MG11, General Rules for Completion'* by Kent Police, reproduced by kind permission of the Chief Constable.)

The unique reference number (URN) at the top of the first page on the right will be generated by your own Criminal Justice Department or office.

- Always include your full name with your surname in capitals. If you usually write in capitals, then *underline* your surname.
- Always give your occupation as a Police Community Support Officer and add your collar/badge/PCSO number.

MG 11

**RESTRICTED (when complete)**

*WITNESS STATEMENT*
(CJ Act 1967, s.9; MC Act 1980, ss5A(3) (a) and 5B;
MC Rules 1981, r.70)

URN ☐☐☐☐

Statement of: *Jo Britton MATTHEWS*

Age if under 18: *Over 18* (if over 18 insert 'over 18')
Occupation: *Police Community Support Officer 001022*

- Always complete the 'number of pages' section on completion of the statement.
- Always sign the declaration and take very seriously the content of the warning each time you make a statement.
- Always date the statement. Retain each statement you make subsequently which relates to the same investigation and reveal them to the CPS. Never destroy previously completed statements.

This statement (consisting of  4  page(s) each signed by me) is true to the best of my knowledge and belief and I  make it knowing that, if it is tendered in evidence, I shall be liable to prosecution if I have wilfully stated anything in it, which I know to be false, or do not believe to be true.

Signature: *Jo Matthews PCSO1*          Date: *14th January 2008*

### Starting the statement

Always begin all statements with the **time, day, date, location, PCSO status** (foot patrol or mobile patrol), and details of any other **persons present** (normally other colleagues). Always use the 24-hour clock when making reference to timings to lessen confusion. Do not use the phrase '*At approximately...hours...*', it should be either '*At*' or '*Approximately*' but as a PCSO, you should be specific and use '*At...hours...*'.

If your evidence has been visually recorded, the box must be ticked accordingly. Do not start your statement with the words '*I am the above named person...*'. It is not necessary to include your name, title, number, or station at the start of the main body of text as this is clearly displayed in the first box. Always write statements in chronological order.

> Tick if witness evidence is visually recorded ☐
> *(supply witness details on rear)*
>
> At 0855 hours on Monday 14th January 2008 I was on foot patrol in uniform on the north pavement of Cotton Lane, 15 yards east of the south entrance to the Precinct, Tonchester. There I saw a member of the public who identified herself to me as Pat OLDFIELD

Always record relevant conversation in 'direct speech' (what the person actually said).

> Mrs OLDFIELD said to me "Excuse me, I have just walked through the Precinct and seen a bloke spray painting the wall outside a shop called 'Buy One Get One Free'." I said to Mrs OLDFIELD, "Please give me a description of this person." She replied "Well, he's white, around 20 years old, stocky build, and his hair is a right mess 'cos it is a mass of dark bushy hair, round face, wearing glasses, clean shaven, approx. 5'8"tall, wearing a black top with a hood and some of those baggy jeans and dirty white trainers." I asked, "What exactly did you see him do?" Mrs OLDFIELD replied, "As I walked past, he was spraying a symbol on the wall outside the shop, it looked foreign to me. He was using a spray can, must have got it from the car superstore 'cos it's the same colour as my old car, 'British Racing Green', it's even metallic. The spray can he was using ran out and he threw it in a rubbish bin nearby. Here it is, you take it." I then took possession of a "British Racing Green" spray can from Mrs OLDFIELD, exhibit labelled and marked PO/1.

### Precision in evidence

Use your senses to evidence what it is that you saw, smelled, touched, tasted, or heard. Be definite. Instead of saying 'I noticed', say 'I saw'. If you are unsure of a detail, then say so, as this will inform the reader that you have at least considered the point even if you are unable to give succinct details. Set the scene so that the reader can form a mental picture of the layout of the area.

> At 0900 hours the same day I entered the Precinct via the south entrance. The Precinct is a shopping area between Daniell Street in the north-east and Cotton Lane in the south, bordered east and west by The High and London Road. As I entered the Precinct, I saw a white male, 20 years, stocky build, a mass of dark bushy hair, round face, wearing glasses, clean shaven, approx. 5'8" tall spraying the wall of "Buy One Get One Free" with a spray can on the western side of the walkway approx. 15 yards south of the exit to Daniell Street.

Always include the identification points, highlighted by the case of *Turnbull*. Fully describe how it was you were able (or unable) to see the suspect so clearly.

> I had the suspect under observation for 30 seconds. It was this amount of time as I looked at my watch when I first saw the suspect and again when I made contact with him. The distance between me and the suspect was approx. 25 metres. I know this because when I started to walk towards the suspect I counted 25 steps. I could clearly see the suspect as the Precinct has a glass roof and the sun was shining through. There were no obstructions between me and the suspect; there were no shoppers at the time, as the shops were shut. I have not seen the suspect before nor did I know his identity. I remembered the suspect easily because he had a mass of dark bushy hair. There was no time lapse between me seeing the suspect and finally introducing myself, as I had him under constant observation for 30 seconds. I made the one and only recording of the description of the suspect as there was no break.

When setting out your statement, make use of paragraphs, but do not leave a blank line in between. You do not need to 'rule off' an incomplete line as you would do in your PNB.

> I walked up to the suspect and could clearly see that he had a scar over the left eye. I said to him, "Excuse me, my name is PCSO Jo MATTHEWS, and I have just seen you spraying this wall with a spray can." The suspect replied, "What are you doing here? You lot never come round here. What if I am? It's my tag, nobody's ever stopped me before. I'm quite proud of it actually, do you like it? Do you want to me to put me tag on your nice white shirt?...only joking!"

Always use proper grammar and sentence construction. Avoid abbreviations and the use of police jargon. Write in plain English, so that everyone can understand what you mean.

Surnames/family names should be written in CAPITALS. (If you habitually write entirely in capitals, then *underline* names.) This applies to all names written in a statement to avoid ambiguity and misunderstanding by the reader.

> The suspect identified himself to me as Toni STALYBRIDGE, born 06/04/88, address 24, Morgan Street, Tonchester. I could clearly see the graffiti which were 33cm wide and 20cm tall on the outside of the "Buy One Get One Free" shop. There were three symbols in total, all in "British Racing Green". There were no other painting marks on what was otherwise a clean wall made of bricks and mortar measuring 2 metres in length and 1 metre in height, below the front window of the shop. When I arrived, the sprayed symbols were still wet and I could clearly smell the odour of cellulose paint.

There is no requirement to record the caution in full. However, replies after caution should be recorded in direct speech.

> I said to STALYBRIDGE "It is an offence to damage the wall of this shop with paint from a spray can." I cautioned him and he replied, "Yeah go on, get it over and done with." At 0902 hours the same day, I had said to STALYBRIDGE, "Earlier, when I first walked up to you outside this shop, you said to me, 'What are you doing here? You lot never come round here. What if I am? It's my tag, nobody's ever stopped me before. I'm quite proud of it actually, do you like it? Do you want to me to put me tag on your nice white shirt?...Only joking!' STALYBRIDGE replied, "Yeah it's true, I did say all that."

Ensure that you correctly spell the names of places and people. Consider the effect on your credibility in court if important evidence, such as a location or a person's name, is spelled wrongly.

Take pride and care in the completion of your statement to avoid errors. Any errors you do make in the text should be corrected by striking through with one line. This should then be initialled in the margin. You **must never** overwrite a mistake or use correction fluid.

Always write in black ink.

Pages should be held together by use of a paper clip and not stapled.

> *I then said to STALYBRIDGE "I am reporting you and you may be prosecuted for the offence of causing criminal damage." I cautioned him and he replied, "Yeah, I understand, you've got a job to do." At 0910 hours the same day, the interview was terminated. STALYBRIDGE read the record of the interview and signed my pocket note book as correct. At 0915 hours the same day, I attended the security room at the Precinct. There I saw a person who identified herself to me as Gamme Ubelele NANATANGA. At that time I took possession of a CCTV video tape from Ms NANATANGA exhibit labelled and marked GUN/1.*

After the last word of the statement and at the bottom of the first and subsequent pages, sign your name (including your PCSO number).

There is no need for anybody to witness your signature (this is for witness statements only).

> Signature *Jo Matthews* PCSO1
> Signature witnessed by

At the top of each subsequent page print your name.

> Continuation of Statement of: *Jo Britton MATTHEWS*

In the top right hand corner of each page write the page number.

> Page No 2 of X

## Other details identifying you which you need to consider

Do not put your home address or home telephone number on the rear of an MG11 because of the potential consequences if a defendant obtained these details. Record your Force address in the **'Home address'** section in CAPITAL letters. Endorse the **'Home telephone number'** section as 'N/A'.

Include the telephone number of your police station in the **'Work telephone number'** section. The **'Preferred means of contact…'** section should be endorsed as 'N/A'. Delete **'Male/Female'** as appropriate. Include your 'Date and place of birth'. Complete the **'Former name'** section if you have one or endorse as 'N/A'. Your **'height'** must be included. The **'Identity Code'** section must be completed with your ethnic appearance code. The **'Dates of witness availability'** section does not have to be completed. Your statement should be accompanied by a completed MG10 which records your availability.

```
RESTRICTED - FOR POLICE AND PROSECUTION ONLY
                  (when complete)
```

**Witness contact details**
Home address: *c/o TONCHESTER CENTRAL POLICE STATION,*
*HIGH STREET, TONCHESTER, TONFORD*

Postcode: *TO1 9TF*

Home telephone No: *N/A*      Work telephone No: *01 1212999*

Mobile/Pager No: *N/A*        E-mail address: *PCSO01@999.co.uk*

Preferred means of contact: *N/A*

~~Male~~/Female (delete as applicable)

Date and place of birth: *25.04.1980*

Former name: *N/A*       Height: *5ft 8ins*   Ethnicity Code: *W1*

Dates of witness non-availability: *N/A*

The Victim Personal Statement does not apply to you (unless you are a victim) when you are making a duty statement. It applies to a witness.

The *'Statement taken by...'* section should be endorsed as 'N/A'. This is for you when you take a statement from a witness. The time and location of statement completion should be recorded in your PNB.

Signature *Jo Matthews PCSO1*

Signature witnessed by

All this may seem complicated, but with practice it will become a straightforward exercise. Don't let it become routine **and always take seriously the making of a duty statement**.

## Knowledge Check 24

1. What is an MG11?

2. What is it also called sometimes?

3. What information should you give in addition to your occupation as a PCSO?

4. What should all statements begin with?

5. What is 'direct speech'?

6. What should be written in capitals?

7. What should you use to hold the pages of your duty statement together?

8. What should you put as 'home address'?

## 5.3 The Upside—Winning through Negotiation and Persuasion

Having looked at the powers designated to the PCSO role at some length, and having recognized that not all of them will be in your arsenal, you could be forgiven for thinking about your role only in terms of how you may compel people to do things. However, as we have suggested earlier, the PCSO role is not merely the sum of all its power parts. We do not doubt that you need powers and the designation of them by your Chief Constable should be appropriate and proportionate (remember the PLAN principles?). However, the exercise of power, or requiring someone to do something because you have the power to require it, is not the whole story. It isn't even half of it.

### 5.3.1 What is your role?

It therefore follows that other skills must come into play and these skills are actually the bedrock of the PCSO role. Consider the title of the role itself. Which do you represent, the police or the community? Do you support the police in the community, or support (interpret) the community to the police? The truth is that both of these will exist at the same time. PCSOs can be the conduit between the police and the community, and convey the concerns of the community to the police, thus having a foot in both camps.

### 5.3.2 PCSO as a problem solver

If we take this problem/challenge further we can expand on the concept of winning through negotiation and persuasion and develop the idea of the **PCSO as a problem solver**. Michael Stevens, in his book *How to be a Better Problem Solver*, defines problem solving as 'transforming one set of circumstances into another, preferred state'.

You will know that 'problem solving' underpins many of the NOS and competences upon which a PCSO is judged, so this capability requires your full attention. In a very real sense, it will become something at which you become well-practised if your PCSO role sits within Neighbourhood Policing Teams, but you need to bring a critical, not to say sceptical, eye to bear upon what problem solving entails. If we look at the PCSO within the parameters of 'citizen-focused' policing, within the idea of actively engaging with the community, and within 'Neighbourhood Policing Teams', then perhaps the best judges of the preferred state are the people who live within that community. This may sound perfectly logical to you but in terms of traditional policing it is a radical departure from the prevailing and rather paternalistic idea that 'we are the police and therefore we know best'.

### 5.3.3 **The picture is complex and multilayered**

We appreciate that the examples we have talked about might be seen as oversimplified because any such consultation with the community has to take place over a period of time, and will ebb and flow in terms of enthusiasm, commitment, or scepticism from both the community and the police. You may find that different members of the community have different roles to play, you may equally find that some members of the community cordially detest other members of it, and you may have to act as referee on occasions. Indeed, your availability to concentrate on the specifics of the challenge is also a factor. You won't be dealing with one problem at a time and then moving on to the next only when the first is solved. You will be handling many tasks at the same time, some moving towards maturity, some only just being articulated.

> **EXAMPLE**
>
> Suppose that part of the neighbourhood includes families of asylum seekers, who feel alienated and unwelcome, and who have not been integrated with any community. You may want to start reaching out to them and engaging with them, but at the same time you may have to work with people in the neighbourhood, important opinion formers some of them, who may be unremittingly hostile to asylum families.

### 5.3.4 **Different options to consider**

Whilst there is no magic formula to success, there are certain aspects within this organic process of community consultation that could help you. These are wholly adaptable to local situations and may directly help you to engage with differing groups within your community. One of the key constraints in community policing is the fact that no community is homogeneous and therefore a 'one size fits all' approach is not likely to succeed and risks further alienating segments of the community. By utilizing a variety of consultative methods, you stand a better chance of reaching out to more members of the community. Always remember, though, that your job is to bring them together and to extract, if possible, some sort of working compromise. It isn't for you to do all on your own, so you will need to be tough-minded, able to delegate, and thick-skinned about making people do things.

#### 5.3.4.1 **Public meetings**

Public meetings are a traditional means of imparting knowledge or seeking approval but such meetings can also be used as discussion chambers designed to find out what the community wants from its police force. Consultation with the community needs to be seen as part of a process rather than an end in itself. It is not enough just to say 'well, we had a meeting' if nothing comes of it. Don't be tempted to hold meetings for meetings' sake—nothing is so likely to give the illusion of progress with no substance.

### 5.3.4.2 Surgeries

Rather than seeking a mass audience, a 'surgery' allows individuals to come forward with problems or concerns; surgeries can also elicit intelligence about the community. They can be held in a variety of locations, which allow for best face-to-face contact with the community. Good venues are libraries, health centres, leisure centres, school halls, and so on. The point is that, regularly, people can air their concerns to you on a private basis; sometimes simply talking to you is therapy enough for them. In the larger picture, though, you will want to do something in response to what you are told.

### 5.3.4.3 Questionnaires

Questionnaires can be used at either a macro or micro level and, importantly, can be used on one-issue subjects or in terms of a general 'forum'. They allow for people who cannot (or who will not) attend meetings or surgeries to have a voice, as well as providing for quantitative and qualitative evaluation of any schemes or initiatives undertaken. Be warned though; questionnaires have to be crystal-clear in what they are seeking. The questions must be unambiguous, thoughtfully designed, and not too long (or people will toss them away; not to mention the cost of reprographics). Get some advice from your Force corporate communications unit, which will ensure that your questions are properly framed and that you can quantify the results. Alternatively, you could go for a cheap and cheerful option of writing, say, five questions on an A4 sheet and pinning it up in a community centre or an appropriate notice board, inviting people to write to or e-mail you with their thoughts.

### 5.3.4.4 Mobile police stations

Many areas have mobile police stations or trailers that are used at fairs, fêtes, and gatherings to publicize such initiatives as community safety. These can also be used for community consultation and can be parked literally on the community's doorstep. Promotional material and free gifts, such as purse chains (to prevent them being snatched) or shed alarms (in an area where garden tools are frequently stolen), can be used to draw in an audience which can then also be consulted on more general community issues and concerns.

### Community engagement

Once again it is about the multi-tasking essence of community engagement, because even if the recipient of the purse chain or shed alarm does not want to be consulted by you about anything at all, then at the very least you may have prevented a purse snatch or the theft of a mower. Being seen as an approachable character, your unthreatening presence in a trailer devoted to security, may be all the invitation some people need to engage with you more deeply. The opportunity to talk to you is what is important.

### 5.3.5 **Permanence**

What is important to bear in mind is that once you have started the community engagement process, you have let loose a genie from the bottle. Community expectations will grow with each success or new initiative. Part of the (often voiced) public apprehension about the PCSO role is that people are anxious that it is merely the latest in a long line of much-heralded and then quickly-forgotten police or government initiatives (remember 'zero tolerance'?). There will be apprehension that, good as you are, you'll be gone tomorrow and that, even if the PCSO concept itself survives, there will be a new face every year or so. This unsettles people, particularly the elderly, who find that adjusting to change can be a source of acute worry.

#### 5.3.5.1 **Becoming a familiar face**

To be positive, as you walk your patrol beat, or engage with your particular remit in the community, you will begin to know people by name, begin to know who is in which family, who works where, which car belongs to which house, who goes to what school. Information like this is crucial to your role. You will also be the person people talk to about the problems that they perceive in the community. You will be quickly identified as 'the person in the know'. This allows you to publicize the initiatives you have started in your area but it also means that for every community there will be an infinite number of potential problems which individuals will expect you to solve. It therefore follows that consultation alone is not enough. What must occur in tandem with consultation is a process whereby the problems are ranked in terms of what needs to be done in what order. Once again who better to choose than the members of the community themselves, the very people who live day-to-day with these problems and their consequences? Once again, it is a signal departure from traditional policing, if you encourage the community to help you set your priorities rather than using a remote national policing plan or a slightly less remote Force policing plan.

### 5.3.6 **Choice is about managing expectation**

At this point it is important to note that the community does not have complete freedom to decide how it is policed. A community cannot decide that it is not bothered this month by street robberies and therefore has no interest in solutions and actions which might benefit others. It cannot ask the police to ignore criminal offences. Rather, what we are talking about is giving communities a say in how policing is achieved and this is where the PCSO needs to become a skilled diplomat, utilizing skills in negotiating and persuasion to assist the process and to ensure that it does not become unrealistic or unrepresentative. The National

Community Forum, in a report in 2006, discussed the importance and also the complexity of this:

> While choice can be empowering, unless it is handled carefully, it could exacerbate inequalities. Providing options is not sufficient to allow choice to empower people in deprived communities—there needs to be support to enable people to make use of the choices that are on offer.

### 5.3.6.1 Public meetings as benchmarks for action

A public meeting designed to find out community priorities can be taken as a benchmark for action. What is interesting is that this type of meeting tends to highlight what are thought of as low-level nuisances, rather than criminal problems. Numerous studies, collated in a 2005 Home Office Development and Practice Report, have shown that environmental factors will feature heavily in terms of community concerns:

> Community members tend to show the most concern over the physical and social fabric of their own neighbourhood. Therefore, they may be most readily motivated to participate in responses to these problems. Neighbourhood regeneration schemes can be very successful as a precursor to greater community confidence and participation.

### Regeneration issues

These regeneration issues often surround matters such as graffiti, rubbish, litter, dog mess, etc. They are not the most glamorous of problems to solve and some critics have argued that they are not ones for the police to be solving at all, yet if we ask the community for their concerns, we cannot then censor or ignore the outcomes of that consultation. **We need to be wary of the imposed solution from the 'we know best' patronage; it is based on hubris (pride) and territoriality, which does not bring with it a lasting answer to social decay.**

### 5.3.6.2 Plans determined by community consultation

Consulting the community and then negotiating a plan of what can be done together provides the PCSO with a strong local grounding for action. Whilst the end result could be a coercive use of powers on offenders, the path towards it has been aided by community engagement. The knowledge and skills developed by PCSOs in their locality will be vital to the success of any initiative. How could those residents afraid to leave their homes get greater reassurance? Better street lighting, targeted patrols, closure of alleyways? If the residents feel safer in walking around both in daylight and at night, then the initiative will be a success, but what has been achieved could be far greater than this one outcome. The process will have engendered a greater regard for the police and the partners they have worked with to get these results. Therefore, the expectations for action with the next problem and with the one after that, will be higher still and the process will begin anew. On all subsequent occasions, there is a platform to build upon.

The bad news about all this is that if you are good at winning through negotiation and persuasion, you'll be expected to do it again and again.

## 5.4 **Defusing Situations**

We have discussed at some length the 'upside' to the PCSO role and the skills needed to sustain the community engagement process, and we have highlighted some of the skills needed to start this particular ball rolling. However, you will also encounter situations where members of the community are not so amenable to this process and you will find occasions where you are required to defuse situations. The next section (5.5) will look specifically at dealing with aggression, whilst we will look now at non-aggressive situations which nonetheless need calming or defusing of tension. What is common to both situations is that the paramount factor is your own safety. **You are not a warranted Police Officer with the training, skills, or equipment to deal with open aggression.** Walking away and seeking suitable assistance is an entirely viable option and you should be conscious of the **Rules of Engagement** (see 2.2.5.2).

---

**DISCUSSION POINTS**

Where do the expectations for a PCSO to act to resolve a dispute come from?

What feelings might you have in walking away from a dispute?

---

### 5.4.1 **Dispute between neighbours—an extended example**

What difference could it make when you have to try to defuse a situation where the dispute is between individuals rather than between groups? Consider the following extended example involving two neighbours living in the residential part of town. You are in the area one sunny spring afternoon on a routine patrol when your attention is drawn by people shouting angrily. You turn the corner and come across two middle-aged men in their front gardens bellowing at one another. As you approach, you gather that most of the discussion involves *leylandii* hedges and car parking. Several other people have stopped to watch and the curtains are twitching in a few of the nearby houses.

---

**DISCUSSION POINTS**

At this stage, what are you thinking about?

Does this potential neighbour dispute have anything to do with you as a PCSO?

What differences might there be in resolving this angry quarrel as opposed to the shopping centre 'youth v. age' dispute which we discussed earlier?

---

### 5.4.1.1 **Sorting out disputes and spats**

We hope that you will be turning these matters over in your mind as you make your way towards the arguing neighbours. As a uniformed representative of the community, people will expect you to intervene and sort out this dispute, but these expectations do not mean that you have to become embroiled with every spontaneous argument you happen across. As you approach this neighbourly spat, you should be undertaking a dynamic risk assessment to see whether there are any factors that may preclude you from intervening. Has either party a weapon (actual or improvised) to hand? Are specific and violent threats being made? Is this dispute actually in serious danger of escalation? If you feel that things are getting out of hand, you would be right to radio for back-up so that trained police officers with their greater powers, more comprehensive training, and more sophisticated equipment can take control of any escalation in the quarrel, whilst you remain at a distance and observe/record the situation.

### 5.4.1.2 **Seek information to strengthen your working actions**

You are seeking to obtain information prior to problem solving so that you are working from a position of **informed strength**, which allows you to establish the independence which is crucial to seeking an effective and binding resolution. You must remain Solomon-like in your actions and judgements so that both parties feel that you are objective and fair. This is tricky to do because it is only natural that you might already have formed an opinion as to who is right and who is wrong.

### 5.4.1.3 **Detailed bickering**

Following your initial intervention in the neighbour dispute, you have obtained the following information: Mr Drake at number 43 believes that his neighbour Mr Peacock of number 45 has been deliberately parking his car across the driveway to number 43, which has prevented Drake from accessing his own driveway. Countering this, Peacock asserts that this has all arisen because he has complained about Drake's *cupressus leylandii* hedge at the rear of the property, which has drastically reduced the light to Peacock's rear garden. Both parties have been bickering for some time about these issues, but Peacock suggests that it has escalated recently because he threatened to go to a solicitor about Drake's hedge. Peacock also admits to deliberately winding up his neighbour by sometimes parking across Drake's driveway. You have also spoken to the neighbours on either side of the disputants who tell you that the tension between the two households has been palpable over the last couple of weeks and they fear that it could go further if nothing is done.

What strategies would you adopt in dealing with the issue?

Consider what other agencies could be involved in helping to solve this problem.

How would you characterize your role as a PCSO in settling this dispute?

### 5.4.1.4 Early and decisive intervention may defuse potential dangers

No one pretends that this is easy: you're dealing with imperfect, fault-ridden human beings, with all the variations in mood, tone, understanding, desire, and socialization that living in a community of similar beings will produce. You have to try your best to prevent things spiralling out of control, and your role is always going to be more effective if you intervene decisively and early, rather than waiting until one of the parties produces a shotgun (it has happened). *This is a key point for us to make* because the PCSO cannot simply move from dispute to dispute putting out each fire in isolation without making sure that the fires do not reignite at a later date (especially when you may not be nearby with an extinguisher).

> **Managing disputes and achieving solutions are key indicators of your role as a PCSO, and of your relevance to the community.**

Successful management of these problems will help to give you a meaningful role in the community and with each new situation/dispute you will gain more skills, understand what works and what doesn't, develop better and more practical strategies, and grow in confidence in your own abilities to take on the next problem you meet. Not only that, but as you resolve disputes successfully, word will get around and, in future, people may come to you directly and ask for your arbitration. That *would* be a useful community skill.

## 5.5 Dealing with Aggression

We have already glanced at the nature of aggression directed at you, the PCSO (4.7), but now we are going to look behind the manifestations of aggression and seek answers to the 'why?' and what you can do when confronted with outright hostility. Of course, we can encounter aggression from others towards us in almost every aspect of our daily lives, irrespective of whether we wear uniforms or not, or whether we are engaged in law enforcement and keeping the peace, or not. This is not to say that we live in a particularly violent society—certainly compared with other parts of the world, the USA for instance, parts of Africa, or the Far East, the UK is largely peaceable—nor are we more violent now than we have been in the past.

### 5.5.1 **The myth of the 'golden age'**

Though it has never been proven that the times we live in are more violent than those which have gone before, there is a widespread belief that there was a golden age, in the 1950s and early 1960s, when authority was respected, police officers admired, and you could leave your door open all day without being burgled (not that you had anything worth nicking...see Clarke (1999) and CRAVED items). Like any fantasy, this one is based in unreality and hedged about with wish fulfilment: police officers have hardly ever been loved (respected maybe, for a period in the 1860s–90s), there has *never* been a time when crime did not exist. The regret for the passing of 'respect' for age and seniority has much to do with a nostalgia for an unquestioning obedience to authority. That said, the chances are that as an ordinary citizen you will encounter at least one instance of verbal aggression in a year. As a PCSO on duty and in uniform, you will encounter five instances of verbal aggression and up to three instances of physical aggression, ranging from pushing and shoving to assault, in the course of a year.

#### 5.5.1.1 **Violence is endemic**

What this preamble suggests is that violence in our daily lives is nothing new and, despite the sensationalist parts of the media, not especially prevalent, at least at the serious end. The UK, Scotland and Northern Ireland included, has fewer murders in an average year (about 900 homicides) than South Africa (16,259 in 2012–2013, a 4.2 per cent increase on the previous year). What may be new, or at least characteristic of the age in which we live, is that multiple reporting of violence is much more likely to happen, and this may well skew our perceptions, making aggression seem more prevalent than it is. That can apply to the whole of crime and anti-social behaviour, where people feel less safe in their streets, towns, and communities, especially at night, than the level of recorded crime suggests that they should. Perception, then, is not the same as cold fact. Indeed, the perception of social disorder was one of the reasons for the introduction of the PCSO in the first place. This takes us back to our beginning: aggressive behaviour is all around us. We may even have learned to live with it as private citizens, and take it as a fact of modern life.

### 5.5.2 **What makes someone act aggressively?**

We can do no more in a book of this size than skim over the surface of human behaviour and psychology, but there are usually some recurrent triggers, or catalysts, which we can say with some certainty, provoke an aggressive response. Some of these are:

- **Frustration**
- **Inarticulacy**
- **Anger**

- **Defensiveness** or defence tactics
- **Desire to escape** the consequences of an action
- **Under the influence** of alcohol or drugs
- **Guilt; being caught out**
- **Fear (especially of some stereotype).**

### 5.5.2.1 **Responding emotionally**

You can see that most of these are emotions or feelings, and that is usually what aggression is: *an emotional response to a situation*, especially and particularly when an individual or group is backed into a corner from which there seems to be no way out except by fighting. We could define aggression in such a context as an **'attack on another, usually but not necessarily, as a response to opposition'.** Let's examine the various indicators noted above; always remembering that aggression does not have to entail physical assault.

## The nature of aggression

Aggression can be any demonstration of anger up to and including assault. It is likely, though, that physical assault may be preceded by posturing and aggressive language. Very few of us, other than quite rare **sociopaths** (*people who have no feeling for, or recognition of, social norms or behaviours*), will launch unprovoked attacks on another person without giving some indication that the attack is coming. Sometimes, the range of angry emotions can be linked, almost becoming a series. Suppose someone falls over on a slippery pavement and cracks his or her head and, on rising, finds some people laughing at his or her misfortune. (This laughter response is quite common. It has a long German descriptive name: *Schadenfreude*, meaning *gloating at someone else's hurt*.) The person may feel angry or embarrassed or plain silly for having fallen over. Of itself, the laughter is not likely to provoke aggression. But it might if accompanied with some sort of stereotyping, such as saying 'Stupid woman! Can't even stand up straight!', or 'Look at that; I always said Asians couldn't carry their booze...', 'That young idiot's pissed again... Typical!' These racist, 'ageist', or chauvinist comments may act like fuel on a fire, and provoke aggression out of sheer frustration or a feeling of being 'dissed' (not respected).

### 5.5.2.2 **Bottling up one's feelings**

Alternatively, the person might simmer in silence, because s/he can't think of a smart remark back, or cannot express how s/he is feeling. This inability to express oneself, or *inarticulacy*, is a common reason for frustration to turn to physical aggression (indeed, it can be part of the reason for domestic violence). Confronted sometimes with verbal aggression, such as shouted obscenities or homophobic chanting, individuals on the receiving end will respond with physical aggression—often the very response which the provoker wants, of course. Other instances of aggressive behaviour may arise because people are unable to put their anger into words, cannot express the turmoil of emotions within them, or do not find verbal aggression sufficient to expel the 'anger pressures' which they feel. It is a fact, of course, that those who are abused often go on to become abusers themselves; similarly, those who have learned aggressive behaviour at home or in school, may go on to use it themselves when adults.

### 5.5.2.3 'It's always someone else's fault'—defensive responses

Anger is a prevalent emotion; we meet it all the time but perhaps it is most common in responses to criticism. Some astute individuals, such as Anne Robinson or Simon Cowell, utilize their acid tongues and (often scripted) rudeness to others as a saleable product on television or other media. Most of us can identify with the sort of defensive emotions which criticism may evoke. We seek to excuse, deflect, or to put the blame on others for what are often our own shortcomings and inadequacies. Failure is not our fault; it's the teacher's, the doctor's, the police officer's, the probation officer's, the PCSO's; it's the fault of the system, of society's greed, it's the result of the class divide, it's any politician; **what it really, really isn't, is me.**

### 5.5.2.4 Aggressive responses when guilty

Scapegoats are always to hand if we want someone else to take the blame, and this defensiveness will often characterize responses to a PCSO intervening to enforce a law or regulation. You should be prepared for abuse and open hostility if you intervene to suggest to someone that he or she should pick up the litter s/he has just dropped. Guilt, and being caught out, can as easily provoke aggressive reactions as anger or frustration. None of us escapes such temptations to blame others, or, if there is no one else handy, to blame the law officer who has called us to account. All police officers have heard, at some time or other, the comment:

> Haven't you people got anything better to do than to pick on poor motorists/ drinkers/football fans/parents/young people/students/protesters/foxhunters/ party-goers...? Why aren't you out catching real criminals?

When desires are opposed...

You will certainly hear something similar if you intervene with young people whom you suspect of smoking or drinking under age. This takes us back to the original definition of aggression with which we began: aggression arises when wills or desires are **opposed**. Think of a toddler in a tantrum. Think how much scarier is an adult in a similar, thwarted, uncontrollable rage.

### 5.5.2.5 Alcohol-fuelled violence

People who have taken too much alcohol or illegal drugs can have personality changes of a marked kind. Alcohol can increase combativeness, anger, aggression, and it can heighten emotional responses, precisely because the normal social inhibitions have been loosened. The same artificial confidence which betrays us into thinking that we can drive brilliantly, or 'pull' someone to whom we are attracted, extends into other matters of one's prowess, such that intervention by others, especially the officially disapproving, may provoke sudden bursts of physical aggression. Fortunately, the signs are often there for you to see well in advance of any attack, and usually the alcohol makes it more difficult for the boozer to be pinpoint accurate in an assault. We dwelt on your options in these cases in 3.2, when examining specific powers. We noted then that **you must anticipate aggression if you stop people drinking (in a designated place) and take and dispose of their alcohol**. There is an ever-present need for you to assess risks dynamically in any situation where your actions might provoke an aggressive response.

### 5.5.2.6 **Drugs**

With drugs, the situation is similar, but reactions can be more aggressive. Drugs intensify perceptions (both of pleasure and of pain) for short periods—that is part of their dangerous seductiveness of course—but also, as the intensity subsides or begins to lose sharpness, so reaction sets in which often includes very powerful aggression. Add to this the fact that many drug takers are also criminals, who commit crimes to get money to feed the habit, and you may well find that a drug user may become very aggressive, not just to get away from you and the authority you represent, but also because he or she cannot bear the thought of being locked up and away from the next dosage or fix. You represent a tangible danger to the drug addict's habit, and as such, you are a legitimate target for attack. This is the convoluted reasoning which an addict may use to justify an attack on you or others. The effect is the same whatever the cause of the aggression: you are in uniform and in the firing line.

### 5.5.2.7 **The anger may turn on you because you're there**

The emotions of **guilt** (at being caught out at something) and **fear** are often similar in effect. Police officers will tell you that occasionally, kerb-crawlers seeking to set up a liaison with a prostitute can be very aggressive when challenged by someone in authority. There could be any number of reasons for this aggressive response, but principal among them are likely to be the fear of publicity, allied to guilt about what the kerb-crawler's partner might say if the whole episode came out. The same might apply to someone detected in homophobic or racist abuse (both crimes, of course). If people think that they can't get away with what they have done, and particularly if you have intervened and confronted them in the act, the guilt can be intense, and they can unload that guilt on you in short order: *you* are the killjoy, the Gestapo, the 'thought police', the fascist, the pig who has spoiled the fun; no harm was meant, some people can't take a joke, no lasting damage done, but you have to come along and interfere. This and much more is likely to be directed at you if you take action and provoke guilt in the offender. It is a form of defensiveness but it is more the fear of the consequence of being caught which provokes the aggression, not just the seeking of a way to escape.

### 5.5.3 What should you do if you become the target of aggression?

So far, we have talked about how and why people become aggressive and how your role within the community might well provoke aggression from those whom you detect doing wrong, breaking the law, being anti-social, or simply too drunk or drugged to care. Now it is time to consider what you should do when you become the target for aggression. The golden 'rule of *dis*engagement' for PCSOs is:

> **When in danger of assault, withdraw.**

#### 5.5.3.1 Modelling aggressive responses

There has to be a *context* in which the aggression has arisen (see figure 5.5; we noted earlier that only fairly rare sociopaths attack without warning) and we can express that context in a diagram like this:

**Figure 5.5 Aggression response spectrum**

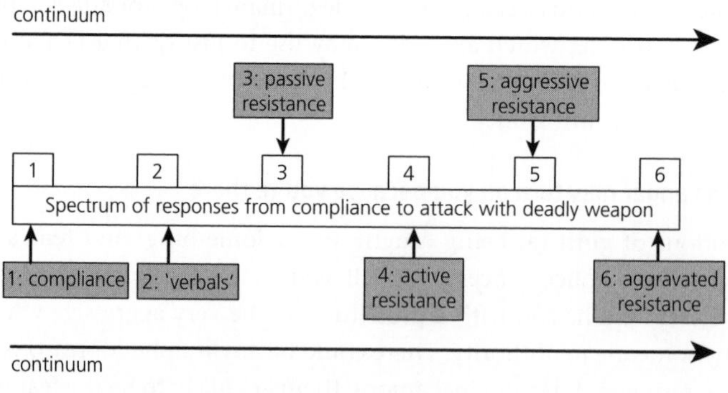

The intensification of aggressive responses

What this shows is that, in conventional aggression displays, there is a movement from compliant to really aggressive. That movement can be very swift and may not be linear (in other words, it won't necessarily pass through the stages shown, but jump across stages, depending on what is perceived as the level of provocation). What it *should* give you is time in which to respond and time to think.

### 5.5.3.2 **Response tactics**

You must look for *exit spots*, where you can get away from the aggressor, and visibly create space between you and the aggressor. The recommended distance is two metres (this is an approximation to two arms' lengths; the aggressor's and yours: you must keep the potential assailant 'at arm's length' if you can). Any attempt to shorten that distance must entail a step forward by the aggressor—which can then be matched by a step back by you, thus sustaining the distance. This should be accompanied by short commands, shouted by you, such as '**Back!**', '**Stay back!**', '**Step back!**' Keep your hands in sight, above your waist, and outstretched, palms towards the aggressor. This is not simply a pacific or 'calm down' stance; it is so that if the assailant suddenly produces a blade and slashes at you, your arms and wrists will take the impact rather than your face or vital organs.

### 5.5.3.3 **Think first, then react**

Of course, it's easy for us to write what you should do from the quiet of a study or workroom: it's quite another to react 'properly' and in textbook fashion, when you are alone in a tense situation, when it might be dark or raining, when you may be surrounded by menacing figures, and when your throat is dry and your heart pumping. We know; we've been there too. But if you can think about the *principles* of what we are describing, if you can give thought to how you might react and what the options are (even how not to get into the situation in the first place), and if you can rehearse with yourself (or better, with a trusted colleague) what you might be able to do, you stand a better chance of getting away unhurt than if you do not do these things.

### 5.5.3.4 **Advance the 'weak' leg**

Some other tips, garnered from years of 'front-line policing' and officer safety training. You have got a 'strong' leg or hand; in 85 to 90 per cent of people, this is the right leg and right arm. You may also see it referred to as the 'dominant' leg or hand. It is the hand you do most things with, and the leg which takes the brunt of leaning, standing, starting to walk, and so on. **Always stand at an angle to a potential aggressor, on your weak leg.** (Why? because if you are pushed, struck, or if you are rushed, your weight will go back on to your stronger leg and enable you to resist more effectively.)

### 5.5.3.5 **Look for escape routes**

Don't get yourself backed up to a wall, and never with your back to a shop window (you may end up going through it), because you are closing off escape or withdrawal routes. This is nothing to do with heroism or being powerful or tough; it has to do with your survival in a situation not of your seeking and, we hope, not of your making. You must constantly seek ways to back away from the confrontation, or defuse the emotions and aggression that are being displayed. Some of the aggression signs will be **posturing**. You've seen birds or animals in 'fighting display' in which every aggressive sign is flaunted, short of actual combat. Some people do the same in attempts to convince you that he (usually, but it can be female of course) is a dangerous and frightening adversary. It's your judgement whether you think the person is blustering or whether s/he really does intend you harm, but be sure before you respond. Remember how lame it will sound in court when you have to say that you *thought* you were going to be attacked and that is why you fractured the complainant's skull. Conversely, it will be no consolation to your family if you end up in hospital because you mis-judged your assailant's aggression signals.

### 5.5.3.6  Remember Betari's Box

You should also remember **Betari's Box**, (see figure 5.6) which we have already seen at 4.7, where your attitude and actions can impact on the actions and atti-tudes of another, sometimes adversely. In other words, aggression often provokes aggression. You should not fall into the trap of meeting like with like:

**Figure 5.6  Betari's Box**

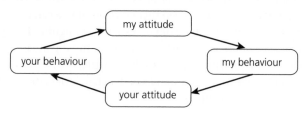

### 5.5.4  Flight, fight, or freeze: the chemical 'cocktail'

We have talked about options in this context, but the essential options are **flight, fight, or freeze**. This is the shorthand phrase for the action of a chemical 'cock-tail' in your body. Strong emotions, such as fear, anger, and extreme stress (such as you will experience in any potentially serious and aggressive confrontation) may trigger this chemical cocktail or combination:

- **Adrenaline** is the pre-eminent *fight or flight* chemical which increases your heart rate, increases the oxygen supply to your lungs, and pumps glucose into your blood for immediate energy.
- Another chemical is **dopamine**, which, with a similar substance called **nore-phrine**, gives you exhilaration, or the confidence to act, by speeding up nerve impulses in the brain; its effect is commonly described as 'clearing the mind'.
- **Nor-adrenaline** is a hormone which 'calls' blood from your hands, feet and face into the major organs, such as heart and lungs, to give you a burst of emer-gency energy.

- Another hormone chemical is **cortisol**, which may reduce the effect of shock, temporarily, so that a person is not necessarily incapacitated, although injured.
- Finally, there are **endorphins**, which are a kind of painkiller manufactured by your body at moments of extreme stress. (It's also the 'feel good' factor from strenuous exercise, and why we feel good after going to the gym.)

If you put all these chemicals together, you have a heady mixture which can act upon your body in a very short time frame—faster even than alcohol. There is a school of thought which says that, just as the body can feel deprived if normal exercise programmes are suspended for any reason, so someone habitually aggressive enjoys the 'high' of chemical responses which his or her aggression produces. We do not know whether this is the case or not, though it seems plausible; the idea of someone becoming habituated to violence and being turned on by it, is genuinely scary.

### 5.5.4.1 'Let down'

The effect of these chemicals is short-lived (enough merely to satisfy the flight or the fight) and you can be left feeling exhausted, drained, and a bit flabby, once the chemical balance is restored. Actors, who commonly experience this 'cocktail' of chemicals before a demanding performance, call the aftermath the 'let down' period, and there is no doubting how deflated you feel afterwards. The common 'freeze' response at the first sign of aggression is one which you will consciously have to overcome. Paralysis or inaction is not an option for you: 'flight or fight' are the horns of this particular dilemma.

### 5.5.4.2 Instinct is not always the best response

We have laboured the point a little, perhaps, that you need to be able to train yourself to think in stressful situations, but if you do not do so, you have to rely only on instinct to get you through, which isn't always enough. In fact, instinct can betray you into acting first and thinking afterwards, with horrendous consequences if you get it wrong. There are stories, for example, of people lashing out at a sudden noise only to find that the source of the noise is a frightened child or animal. You have to be **counter-intuitive**; this comes with practice and experience, and we discuss it further in the section on risk assessment (at 5.7). What we can do to help you in this thinking phase, is to fix a **conflict model** in your head. We have devised the 'hand-off' model, as in figure 5.7.

### 5.5.4.3 Explaining the hand-off conflict model

Let's start with your thumb, because the PLAN principles are those which ensure that you do not contravene a person's human rights. What you do has to be **proportionate** to the circumstances in which you find yourself. In the cold calm of a courtroom you might have to justify what you did in the heat of the stressful

**Figure 5.7 Hand-off conflict management model**

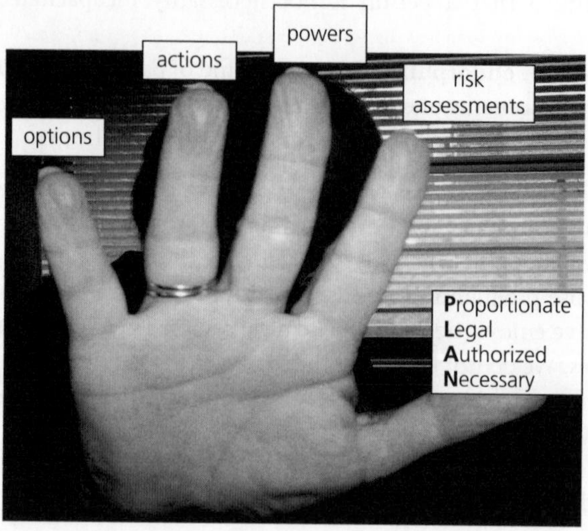

moment. Your actions must have been **legal** and **authorized**, so that you acted properly within your designated powers and authority. Again, a failure or short-fall here may result in some discomfort for you in court. Your actions must be **necessary**. The test will be whether there was any other option open to you short of meeting force with force. The law says that you can use 'reasonable force', as we saw in 3.2.24. But the law does not define 'reasonable'.

A case where 'reasonable force' was tested in court

There was a case in 1999 of Norfolk farmer, Anthony Edward Martin, firing a shotgun at night-time intruders into his farmhouse. As the result of the shotgun discharges, one of the intruders was killed and another injured. The farmer pleaded reasonable force in self-defence, but this was not accepted (there was also some doubt about the accuracy of his testimony). He was tried and sentenced to a prison term for murder, later reduced to five years for manslaughter, and he served three years before his release. The case occasioned some controversy and debate about self-protection and the protection of property. The fact remains that you might do what you think is reasonable, but the courts may take a very different view.

### 5.5.4.4 Actions, options, powers, and risk assessment

The fingers of our model hand tell you to think about your **actions**, which include what you *shouldn't* do as much as what you should. For example, you shouldn't make a bad situation worse by antagonizing an offender with moral-istic finger-wagging. Such actions are an invitation to retaliation. You must con-sider what **options** you have got in any potential conflict or confrontation: have you enough information to move away at this point and renew your enquiry or investigation under better circumstances later? Can you call in support from police officer colleagues? How long will it take them to get to you? Can you talk down this escalating situation with a bit of humour and self-deprecation? Consider your **powers**: do they cover this eventuality? Have you a tailor-made power to use in this case? Do you know your powers well enough to invoke the particular one you want to apply here? Is the use of power appropriate in this instance, or might a quiet word be more effective? Finally, you must **assess the risk** in a fluid, developing (or dynamic) way, as matters unfold:

- Is it worth pursuing this enquiry right now if it is going to cause this person to lose face in front of his friends? Wouldn't it be preferable to return to the topic later, when he is alone?
- Is there a physical risk to you if you follow those youths down this dark alleyway?
- Can you be serious in wanting to pursue someone on to a railway line?

Now time for a knowledge check. This one is slightly longer than usual to cover all the detail you have just studied.

## Knowledge Check 25

1. Define problem-solving.

2. Why is a 'one size fits all' approach unlikely to succeed?

3. Name three effective ways to consult within a community.

4. What concerns community members most?

5. What are 'regeneration issues'?

6. What is a 'dynamic risk assessment'?

7. What important principle should a PCSO keep in mind when dealing with a problem?

8. How many homicides are there in the UK (including Scotland and Northern Ireland) is an average year?

9. Name three 'triggers' for aggression.

10. What is the 'golden rule' for PCSOs when faced with the danger of physical assault?

11. What is number 4 on the 'aggression response spectrum'?

12. Why should you always advance your 'weak' leg?

13. What does adrenaline prepare you for?

14. Name another two of the components of the 'chemical cocktail' in your body.

15. What are the components of the 'hand off' model?

16. What does PLAN stand for?

## 5.6 Safety Training and Awareness

We have looked at ways in which you can try to take the sting out of a confrontation in 5.4 ('Defusing situations') and how you could respond when confronted with aggression in 5.5, but some of the difficulties or fraught situations which you will encounter during your time as a PCSO may have nothing to do with people behaving badly or unpleasantly. In the section which follows this one (5.7), we look at how an understanding of health and safety at work, as well as the ability to make risk assessments, will help you to perform properly in any crisis. Before that, in this short section, we look at your safety and that of others, your awareness of things going wrong around you, and the sorts of training which you might expect your Force to provide. We can't prescribe what your Force will give you in safety training, and this may vary according to how the individual Force assesses risks and problems. Please bear in mind, then, that what follows is based on what we think is 'typical' or 'average' in safety and awareness training, not what is mandatory.

### 5.6.1 An example of sudden crisis

Let's plunge you into a crisis at the outset of your foot patrol. In uniform, you are walking with due diligence and at the regulation pace, when you hear a tremendous crashing sound, a rumble, then what sounds like breaking glass, and you see what looks like a large cloud of dust or smoke rising up from an area to your right where building work has been going on. You sprint to the scene, calling Control as you go. When you arrive, you see that a network of scaffolding has apparently collapsed and part of the wall of a house has crashed down with it. *What are your action priorities?*

#### 5.6.1.1 Judge each emergency on its merits

No right or wrong answers here, because much of what is needed will be dictated by the situation. For example, are builders or scaffolders injured by the fall, or are they rising from the dust and rubble, perfectly all right except for a cloud of profanity? Is anyone else injured (perhaps house occupants, or those underneath at the time)? Your first and unchangeable priority will always be **'the preservation of life and limb'**, for which you can enter any building or site and render any necessary aid or help to ensure that lives are saved. We said earlier that this book is not a first aid manual, and we cannot contribute specifically to your learning of first aid, but we can say that your first duty would be to anyone injured. *What should you do?*

- Assess the injury
- Render appropriate first aid (including resuscitation)
- Call for help
- Prevent further danger.

### 5.6.1.2 Extending the example

By this time, others should have responded to what has happened: passers-by, other work people on the site, people living nearby, your colleagues, and other members of the emergency services. However, before they actually make it through the entrance to the site, you notice that there is an obstacle in the way: a large portable cement mixer has fallen on its side after being struck by a scaffolding pole and it will prevent vehicles such as ambulances from getting on to the site. You run to the spot and start tugging at the industrial-sized mixer. *What safety aspects should you be aware of?*

### 5.6.1.3 Risk assessment

The danger here is that you may hurt yourself taking on a 'manual lifting' task for which you are either:

- untrained, or
- physically not capable.

**When in doubt, don't.** Get some assistance, or better still, leave it to those on the site who are used to handling such equipment. For all you know, there is more wet cement inside the mixer, making it even heavier. Lifting things which are too heavy or bulky for you, or not knowing how to lift, could cause you severe injury, such as a back injury, hernia, or rupture. You would be more usefully employed in coordinating the efforts of those on site who are trained or experienced in moving heavy machinery. Indeed, such coordination could clear a larger area for the reception of emergency vehicles than you could manage on your own, as well as asserting your control of the situation.

### 5.6.2 Think about your and others' safety

As we commented above, we can't second-guess what training policies your Force will follow in terms of personal safety training and awareness, but they may include discussing or simulating scenarios of the kind outlined above, or they may consist of giving you the information and then testing your responses at real incidents. Either way, you need to give long and hard consideration to questions of safety, *yours and others'*, as we have noted in the preceding sections.

## 5.7 **Risk Assessment**

Unless you sit inside a sealed room, insulated against the world and impossibly padded against contact with anything or anyone from the outside, you will encounter risk. We meet risks all day and every day in our working lives, travel, relaxation, in our leisure, even in our sleep.

### 5.7.1 **Avoiding hazards**

Most of the time, our coping mechanisms are so automatic that we don't notice that we take avoiding action. We see an obstruction on the pavement and step into the gutter to walk around it. We register that there are icy steps on the way to the shopping centre and so step carefully and with smaller steps. We know that the cupboard in the bathroom is wonky and have evolved special techniques to balance things in it.

### 5.7.1.1 **Not trusting your instincts**

As a PCSO, you will have to be **counter-intuitive** about some risks. As we have noted before, this means that you should not always do what comes naturally; indeed you should deliberately avoid any kind of 'automatic' compensatory behaviour when you confront a risk. So, if you go past a house, smell burning, see smoke, and hear someone cry 'Help!' from an upper window, do you plunge straight in and rescue whoever it is? If you see that someone has slipped on an icy pavement, do you skid blithely to his or her rescue? Are you an inveterate plunger into flood waters to pull out drowning infants? Do you lift the car back bodily on to the hoist when it has dropped on someone? Do you stop runaway horses in your sleep?

### 5.7.1.2 **There are dangers in instinctive reactions**

Seriously, if you charge into a burning building, or try to lift something really heavy, or go into dangerous currents, you are not only unlikely to effect the rescue you hope for, but you are very likely yourself to be a casualty. Throwing a rope to someone in difficulties in water could be more effective than diving in to save them. Remember the case of Jordon Lyon who drowned in a lake in Wigan in 2007, which we looked at briefly at 2.8.3.4. Calling for expert help (from organizations like the Fire and Rescue Service) is probably better than going into a burning building on your own. It may not always be the case, and of course, these things are governed by their own circumstances, but the very least you can do, when facing a problem like this, is to make a **risk assessment**. What do we mean by a risk assessment? It means making sure, as far as you can do so, that no one will get hurt, or become ill, as a result of an action. Another way of looking at it is that:

$$\text{risk} = \text{hazard} \times \text{likelihood}$$

where **hazard** is the potential for harm, **likelihood** the chances of it happening, and **risk** the severity of the danger caused by the other two factors. (Incidentally, this is not a mathematical formula, just a model to explain the components.)

### 5.7.1.3 Life is about judgements of risk

To spend your life trying to avoid risks is impossible and a bit pointless. After all, if the pilot of the jet aircraft two miles up has a fit and falls unconscious, you're not going to be able to avoid the plane coming down on your head by thinking positively, or wearing a helmet (or even sheltering indoors). To act in this way, to try to protect yourself from all possible permutations of harm, is called being **risk-averse**. Inaction carries its own risks, since passivity may make circumstances worse than they need to be. But we are concerned with a positive approach to risk. The best PCSOs and police officers are those who ask '*what is the risk?*' and then '*what can we do about it?*'. At its simplest, answering those questions is making a risk assessment.

### 5.7.2 **Kinds of risk**

There are three kinds of risk assessment: **generic**, **specific**, and **dynamic**. Let's look briefly at the first two of these. A generic risk is one which exists in general terms for similar tasks. Think of the generic risks for stopping moving vehicles in a roadside check, or dealing with a drunken person. A **specific** risk is, as the name suggests, something which happens in a specific operation or activity. Here the generic assessment needs to be added to, or *augmented*, in order to include those specific and significant factors unique to the work activity. What you have to do here is to think in advance about what is proposed and decide what the hazards are, and how you will overcome them, or diminish them, in your planning. Usually the specific risk assessment is formally documented and may be included in your Force task briefing.

### 5.7.2.1 Dynamic risk assessment

**Dynamic** risk assessment is applicable to you in your everyday work (and it's not that different from the sorts of decisions you make each day in your leisure time). To assess risk, you make an individual judgement, based on your knowledge of the general or generic standard and past practical experience, so that you can act as safely as possible. As we saw earlier, in your professional life your desire to act quickly must sometimes be modified by counter-intuitive thinking. Dynamic risk assessments are made at the time, there and then. There is no time to write it down and discuss it, so the way you approach risk dynamically will say a lot about you as a person, especially when others look to you for a lead, as they will in any crisis. Suppose you come first on a scene where someone has fallen over and suffered deep cuts. Bystanders and the idly curious will expect you to render first aid and to know how to stop bleeding.

### 5.7.2.2 Again, think before you act

Before you rush in to mop up the blood, you must make a dynamic risk assessment of the hazards: do you have surgical gloves so that you can avoid blood-borne contaminants? If not—what alternatives are there? Are the cuts life-threatening? (For example, has the person slipped and been gashed by a broken bottle so that there is arterial bleeding?) Do you need to call an ambulance, because the person may also be in shock? What about the original hazard? Might other people slip and fall if that is not dealt with promptly? Can you see what caused the fall in the first place? Are there other injuries? Shouldn't you keep the crowd back so that you can properly render first aid? When it's all over, what should you do to prevent any ongoing contamination to yourself?

### 5.7.2.3 Always double-check injuries with health professionals

Incidentally, it is a good standard rule to suggest that any victim of an accident be taken, or go, to be checked by medical experts, either at a GP's surgery or at a Hospital A&E. No paramedic will ever mind being called to something apparently trivial, but there have been examples where there were hidden injuries not revealed on first examination. You may render *first* aid in such a situation (people will certainly expect you to) but remember that there may be a need for *second*, even *third* aid, each requiring progressively more medically expert treatment. The questions which you ask yourself in the paragraph above may appear to you to have slowed down the process of going to someone's aid. They have, but only very slightly. **As you grow in experience, you will find yourself making dynamic risk assessments as you approach any crisis, and by the time you arrive, you will have assessed and made all the necessary decisions.** That is why you will appear calm in such situations, and why you will make the right choices. Others may panic; with your dynamic risk assessment already made, you can take control.

### 5.7.2.4 Training in making risk assessments

Just as you should be trained in first aid, so you should be trained in making risk assessments; equally, just as first aid can be simplified to a few key principles, so can dynamic risk assessment. The standard way of presenting *what needs to be done* is through the mnemonic **SPRAIN**, thus:

| S | **Situation** | What am I dealing with? |
|---|---|---|
| | | What is going on? |
| P | **Plan** | What am I going to do? How will I do it? |
| R | **Risks** | What might get me or someone else injured or put in danger? |
| A | **Alternatives** | Are there other ways to do this? |
| I | | |
| N | **IN**crease safety | How do I reduce the risks and |
| | | yet do what I have to, making |
| | | it safer for all involved? |

This is a shorthand method of thinking things through, and can be applied to any situation where risk has to be assessed and catered for. Let's look at workplace situations, occasions when you will have to *make dynamic risk assessments on the job*. What sort of problems might you face? To make it easier to remember, we've devised another mnemonic, **BEWARE:**

| B | **B**iological (or chemical) dangers |
|---|---|
| E | **E**xposure to Fire |
| W | **W**eather conditions |
| A | **A**ssault or **A**sphyxiation |
| R | **R**adiological contamination |
| E | **E**ffort and physical exertion |

## Making it work

If you link **BEWARE** with **SPRAIN** you will be able to make effective dynamic risk assessments in the course of your daily work. We should emphasize that you will not encounter all these things at the same time or on the same shift...

### Knowledge Check 26

1. What is your 'first and unchangeable priority'?

2. What might be the result of trying to lift something very heavy on your own?

3. What are the dangers of instinctive reactions?

4. What is the risk-assessment 'formula'?

5. What are the three kinds of risk assessment?

6. What should you do after rendering first aid?

7. Explain SPRAIN.

8. What does the 'W' in BEWARE signify?

## 5.8 **Chapter Summary**

This chapter has been about the knowledge and skills which you need to help you become an effective and efficient PCSO. **What you know and what you do with what you know marks you out as a professional** and it is about understanding the 'why?' of what you do. We have shown you the great importance of evidence and how you use it, and how vital the proper maintenance of your pocket note book can be to justice outcomes.

The emphasis on enforcement (the exercise of powers) is actually only part of a **PCSO's** work, and often a small part. Far more time and effort is spent in finding solutions to community problems and we looked at your role in negotiating and persuading, to bring people together to solve such problems, and how you can be the ready catalyst for change and improvement. We noted that more effort should be expended in defusing difficult confrontations or conflicts than in trying to control people's aggression, but we acknowledged that, as an authority figure, you would inevitably encounter hostility. We gave you tactical advice and ideas, based on our experience, of how to deal with such situations as they develop. Safety training, responses to crises and accidents, counter-intuition, and risk assessment are all factors which you must consider, deliberately and consciously, in your efficient, professional approach to your daily duties.

A last thought: despite the fact that your PDP (SOLAP) will be checked for evidence that you have reached the requisite standards in knowledge and skills, and despite the natural emphasis within your Force on assessing your performance against some kind of template measure, it is in fact your performance in the community which really matters. Only if you can help to solve problems which bedevil or blight a community, if you can deal with people's concerns, if you can respond appropriately to anti-social behaviour, if you use your powers when you have to, and use a persuasive tongue when you don't, will any of these skills and this repository of knowledge be of the slightest practical use.

## 6.1 **Introduction**

In this chapter, we are going to examine your principal area of work; the community. It is here that you carry out your patrols, here that you respond to and speak with members of the community as well as with groups within that community, and here, when necessary, that you enforce orderly behaviour in the community.

### 6.1.1 **What is a community?**

We begin by trying to describe what a community is, or, more strictly, what communities are, because we all belong simultaneously to numbers of communities. They are not just the people who live where we do. Following this, we analyse the make-up of different communities and how we respond to them. Then we look at success and failure factors in communities.

#### 6.1.1.1 **Components of community**

We examine next some of the elements of community, such as how communities are socially organized, what constraints there are on behaviour, what the social taboos (curbs and conditions) are, and how behaviour is restricted. These are all aspects of community which you need to understand and respond to, in order to do your work effectively. This is followed by a complementary discussion about factors which encourage a sense of community and factors which inhibit that sense of community.

#### 6.1.1.2 **Community and the fear of crime**

This leads us to a parallel discussion of the fear of crime, as evidenced in successive annual British Crime Surveys, and what causes social unease, as well as looking at how communities deal with those fears. We discuss the concept of 'signal crimes' which enhance our understanding of the fear of crime.

#### 6.1.1.3 **Working with partners: relations with ethnic and diverse communities**

This takes us logically to a consideration of partnerships and the kinds of alliances, liaisons, and cooperative working which typify the PCSO's approach to problems within the community. We go on to look at the PCSO in relation to ethnic and diverse communities.

#### 6.1.1.4 **Policing models, consensual and compliant policing, citizen focus**

The chapter concludes with a brief survey of policing models and how the PCSO fits, or does not fit, into prevalent modelling. We then discuss the larger issues of the tensions between **consensual** and **compliant** policing (service or force?), before suggesting that a depiction of the future of neighbourhood policing might entail some citizen ownership. There are the usual notes, discussion points, tasks, and key points throughout.

## 6.2 **What a Community Can Be**

We often hear the word 'community' used as part of phrases such as 'the gay community', 'the academic community', and 'the business community'. Anecdotally at least, the use of the word 'community' seems to have grown in recent years, perhaps usurping the previous dominance of the elastic noun 'society'. This perhaps reflects, in turn, a perception that society/community is now more pluralistic (some would say, more fragmented) than before, although there is always the danger here of perpetuating the myth of the 'golden age' of a homogeneous, ideal society located somewhere in the 1950s. The widespread use of the word in many different contexts suggests that there is now a prevailing view that *rather than just a single community we have instead a series of interlocking and overlapping ones*. But as Myhill (2006: 6) notes:

> Community is a notoriously slippery concept, and many definitions exist in academic literature and elsewhere...

and we should perhaps be cautious in assuming a shared understanding of the meaning of the term. Andy Myhill directly echoes Nick Tilley's comment (2003: 315) that:

> the term 'community' itself is notoriously slippery. It often seems to imply shared norms, values and ways of life. Groups with these attributes need not be geographically defined, of course. In practice, the community of community policing most often does amount to 'neighbourhood'...

That said, we do try a description of our own on you a little later, precisely to achieve a '*shared understanding of the meaning of the term*' with you.

### 6.2.1 **Characteristics of a community**

Essentially, *communities are collections of individuals with something in common*, shown through forms of interaction and common ties between those individuals. Examples you might think about include communities that embrace a single ethnicity, or others that share roughly the same set of values. Note the characteristic that there needs to be evidence of some kind of interaction, and a feeling of 'belonging'. The strength of our 'sense of belonging' to our communities will vary, in part as a consequence of the perceptions of others. For example, members of visible ethnic minority communities may feel a common tie more than, say, the business community. In some cases we may wish *not* to belong to certain communities and may even deny that we do so. For example, some people who live on the borders of public housing estates may prefer not to be grouped alongside members of that community.

### 6.2.1.1 **There will be a range of views about PCSOs in any community**

It is probably the case that you will not find unanimity of opinion or shared values among all members of the same community. Views about PCSOs, for example, are likely to stretch across the full spectrum from approval to disapproval as much in one community as in another. However, this is not to say that there are not variations between different communities in, for example, their levels of anxiety concerning anti-social behaviour and crime (see Chapter 5) but these do not normally form defining factors.

### 6.2.1.2 Towards a descriptive 'definition'

Try this as a description of 'community', even if we cannot fully propose it, perhaps, as a dictionary definition:

> A community can be a number of people with some shared identity, including geographic, as a group of people who live or work in close proximity to each other. But community is more than this; it can encompass shared values, shared outlooks, shared concerns, shared origins or ethnicity, even shared beliefs. What makes a community is a sense of belonging to it—both being a contributor to the values of the community and in drawing strength from what the community gives back to you. In a real sense, it is about fundamental identity and meaning for many people.

The senses of **sharing** and **belonging** are profound emotions as well as strong concepts, which we need to look at in greater depth because they go to the heart of what you do as a PCSO. It is the sense of identity, of belonging somewhere, which gives a community its coherence and which also defines it. You need to know what it is if you are to encourage its development.

### 6.2.1.3 Is the 'community' real?

But how many of us would recognize these descriptions of a community? How many of us have a geographically distinct and defined sense of space outside where we live? How many of us, particularly in urban locations, have no sense of who our neighbours are? How else do we explain the neglect of elderly people who have died alone and whose bodies remain undiscovered for weeks? How else can we explain the systematic abuse of a child which goes unreported? How else should we account for the repeated cycle of domestic violence that never comes to the attention of the police? Why is there a tendency to wait for 'them' (usually the police or some other form of authority) to solve problems rather than 'us'? Isn't it true that many of us have better relationships with work colleagues than we do with the people who live three doors away?

---

**DISCUSSION POINT**

Think about the community in which you are physically located.

Could people die undiscovered in your street?

Could children or vulnerable people be abused and no one know?

Why?

Compare experiences with your colleagues and draw up a list of the factors which (a) make a community a positive shared experience and (b) a negative isolated experience.

---

### 6.2.1.4 **The community as 'home' or home as the location of the self**

The community in which we are physically located for the most part, which we usually designate as 'home', is the place where we feel most comfortable and most relaxed. But it can also paradoxically be where we can experience most fear or most vulnerability, because this 'home' is where our loved ones are located, where we enjoy our material possessions, where we keep the things which, if not intrinsically valuable, have most significance and 'value' for us. It is the place where we sleep, trusting in locks and other forms of physical security as well as the police, to keep us safe and unharmed.

#### Our own space is our security against encroachment

We invest such physical places with our personalities and dreams and we tend to think of them as inviolable (they *cannot be touched*). So, when these places are threatened, or seen to be at risk from prowlers, burglars, or vandals causing criminal damage, we may believe that our whole social fabric, our entire edifice of trust and security, is at risk. This directly contributes to personal anxiety and to the belief that, somehow, the 'community' (whatever it is) has let us down. Our trust in our surroundings has been violated. We begin to fear crime and criminals.

### 6.2.1.5 **This place has gone to the dogs**

This sense of the security of place, which is very deep-seated in the human psyche, may radiate outwards to embrace those who live alongside us, or it may not. Any PCSO who has spent time on a patrol beat will tell you that one recurrent and standard conversation which they have, usually but not exclusively with the elderly, concerns **the degeneration of the area, the fact that people don't know each other any more and that it has become a place where neighbours keep themselves to themselves.** This perception of the deterioration of social 'glue', which used to hold us together in a community, is very widespread.

#### It is not just the old and frail who fear crime and social decay

Worry about an apparent deterioration in social 'glue' is not confined to the very old, or to the housebound and frail, but may equally apply to the single parent, the mother with children under school age, people working from home, or the commuter who works many miles away for long periods during the week. All may seem to live *external* lives of fragile isolation. Many rely on family networks, or networks of friends, to supply the internal and emotional contact which living in a community normally provides. Others remain lonely and untouched by human interaction. Others take solace in the internet to create a 'virtual community'. Some people will tell you that they no longer intervene or remonstrate when they see anti-social behaviour because they are afraid of the torrent of abuse which this can unleash. Or they do not speak out when they hear a child cry or a woman sobbing because 'it is nothing to do with them'. Or they are too busy with their own lives to spend time interfering in other people's business. Or they have their friends and their family, thank you, and don't need anyone else, especially not those people down the road.

### 6.2.1.6 **Are we nostalgic for a mythical past?**

What has happened to society to produce this apparent fracture between what we assume to have been a warm, friendly community state where everyone cared about each other, and this anxious, cold, isolated, and uncommunicative modern reality? Is it true that we need to rediscover a sense of the group identity and a clear image of our place in the social structure in order to belong properly? Is the perception true that community has changed for the worse? Or is it variously a product of being old, poor, socially disadvantaged, or out of work? Was there ever a golden past in which most people could be trusted, where social roles and responsibilities were clearly defined, and where 'people knew their place'? Or is it, as some commentators claim (Hitchens, 2003), a world invented by film and television which never existed in reality? Is this lost, mourned, community as much a myth as the myth of the golden age of policing with PC George Dixon?

### 6.2.1.7 **Mobility inhibits us from belonging**

You may gather from the sheer number of questions above that we don't pretend to have the answers. The description of a community which we offered earlier suggested that belonging to or **identifying with a community was a reciprocal process; what you got out of it largely depended on what you put in.** The strength of the sense of identity may therefore stem from permanence, from long-term commitment, from continued residence and roots.

### 6.2.1.8 **Much of modern life is restless and impermanent**

Yet most of us do not live such settled, immobile lives unless we are sick, disabled, housebound, or very frail. Most of us move to where our work takes us, move to secure better prospects, move to a bigger house, or a better area, or a bigger garden, or an easier commute, move to get a better school for the children, move to care for an elderly relative, move to secure a different lifestyle, move because we don't like being in one place for too long, move because the grass is going to be greener somewhere else, or move because being 'nomadic' is part of contemporary life. Because of this mobility, we do not always know our present locality well, and the dilemma intensifies in an economic recession as we may have to move to find work but may find it hard to sell one house and buy another, or the threat of unemployment places house ownership or rental in jeopardy.

### 6.2.2 **Community described by demography and other factors**

A community may be described (rather than defined) in terms of its demography, location, and interests or combinations of these, as illustrated below.

| Aspect | [Examples] |
| --- | --- |
| Demography | Age (as in the community of 'elderly people') |
| | Gender ( a 'community of nuns') |
| | Ethnicity (a descriptor like 'the Afro-Caribbean community') |
| | Nationality ('the Turkish community in North London', 'the international community') |
| | Social class (eg 'the working class community') |
| Location | Place ('a council estate', a 'virtual community' on the internet, a 'gated community') |
| Interest | Interest or pressure groups (such as a faith association, the local branch of Animal Aid, a sports 'supporters' association) |

Your police force will have analysts who are able to produce maps, diagrams, tables, and charts describing the demographic and geographical nature of the communities that you support. Often these maps and diagrams are produced using a computer-based *Geographical Information System* (GIS). Try to access these to learn about different local 'communities' and how they overlap. Your local station might even have produced a 'Neighbourhood Profile' according to Force guidelines. This will include not only the demographic characteristics of a neighbourhood but also information about its infrastructure (both physical and human) and the fear of crime (see 6.4).

### 6.2.2.1 Finding out about your communities

Even if you are deployed as a PCSO to a particular location on a semi-permanent basis (for example to a town centre) you will still find yourself interacting with a number of communities, ranging from communities which share a common origin or ethnicity through to local communities of business people.

### 6.2.2.2 Researching your communities

You can undertake much research using the internet and libraries to discover more about the communities in your area. For example, which associations are active in your area? Is there a *Facebook* or *Twitter* devoted to the town? Where are the local schools? Which buses run where? What sporting/leisure facilities are there and where are the sports grounds? Who has been leading campaigns or voicing concerns about the community? In libraries or online, you will find back numbers of local newspapers. Read a selection, particularly of the letters pages, for the past year: this will give you a unique insight into what is preoccupying your community and may help you to identify those who are prominent opinion-formers or spokespersons for the community (look at 6.4, for example, under 'signal crimes'). Your Force or BCU media advisers may also alert you to local sensitivities, for example what happened the last time the BCU Commander attended a public meeting on your 'patch'. Don't forget that your Police Crime

**291**

Commissioner or member of the Commissioner's Police Crime Panel may be located in or near your communities and may have valuable insights into what concerns local people and what the various pressure groups in the neighbourhood might be. Equally, local people may be using district or borough councillors to represent them to the BCU Commander or higher.

### 6.2.2.3 Know who is where and when

You will obviously learn more, in certain respects, about the communities that you support through your direct day-to-day contact with them, for example through regular patrol of a town centre. However, bear in mind that research has shown (see Waddington *et al*, 2004, for example) that the **'available' population** (that is, the people you are likely to encounter on the streets) is not necessarily the same as the **resident population** (those who live in the area), and particularly so in terms of demography. This is because some will be at school, many will be at work, often some distance away, and some will not be on the streets unless transported by others, such as the sick, the immobile or housebound, and the very old or very young. To gain a genuine understanding of the 'mix' of your community, it will be necessary to encounter members from it at different times of day and different days of the week. A 'dormitory' suburb, for example, where many commute to work in a nearby city perhaps, may double its 'available population' after 1900 hrs, say, or on Saturdays and Sundays.

---

**Task**

1. Draw up a profile of the communities that you support, in terms of basic demography (age, gender, ethnicity)
2. Next, find the locations of:
   - Playgroups, pre-school groups, schools, colleges, and universities
   - Churches, mosques, gurdwaras, temples, chapels
   - Community centres, Citizens' Advice Bureaux, village halls
   - Sports Centres, exercise clubs, gyms, health clubs
   - Cinemas, clubs, night clubs, pubs, youth centres
   - Tourist attractions, museums, theatres, heritage sites
   - Libraries, cultural centres, and drinking clubs
   - GP surgeries, medical centres and practices, and NHS clinics
   - Council offices, Department for Work and Pensions (DWP) office, Social Services, and Environmental Department
   - Public and municipal housing, estates
   - Bridges, tunnels, underpasses, alleyways
   - Railway and underground stations, bus stations, taxi ranks
   - Parks and other green spaces
   - Sports grounds, fitness centres, and gymnasia
   - Cemeteries and crematoria

---

- Public amenities such as recycling centres
- Public toilets
- Relevant *Facebook* and *Twitter* internet sites

3. Find out who are the:
   - Local councillors and other elected representatives (**think:** your Police Crime Commissioner's staff and Crime Panel representatives might be able to help here)
   - Council officers and permanent staff
   - Community leaders, opinion formers, leaders of sporting organizations such as football or rugby or cricket teams, or the local fitness centre or swimming pool
   - Representatives of voluntary organizations such as Age Concern, the Scout Association, The Women's Institute, The British Legion, and so on
   - Local head teachers, principals, lecturers, and teachers
   - Managers of local supermarkets and other retail outlets

### 6.2.2.4 Where to look

There are numerous sources for this kind of information. We suggest that the National Census website <http://www.statistics.gov.uk/census/default.asp> is a good starting point. Indeed, the internet will provide you with much of the relevant information. Another good starting point for information about an area is <http://www.zoopla.co.uk/> which now incorporates UpMyStreet, but don't neglect estate agents either and some websites like <http://www.tripadvisor.co.uk/> which can tell you things about a community and location not on public information systems.

### Knowledge Check 27

1. Why is the term 'community' so hard to define?

2. How do the authors describe 'community'?

3. Give two examples of 'shared identity' in a community.

4. Why is 'home' important to us?

5. Who might worry that the social 'glue' isn't working?

6. What is *demography*?

7. What is GIS and what is it used for?

8. What is the difference between 'available population' and 'resident population'?

9. Give an example of where you might research your locality on line.

## 6.3  Factors which Encourage a Sense of Community

When we use the phrase 'sense of community' we are often referring to the extent, or otherwise, to which people identify with, and are concerned about, other people in their immediate vicinity. Note that our emphasis here is on **communities defined by location** rather than by *interest* or *demography* (see 6.2.2). This reflects the day-to-day reality of the work of the PCSO, concerned as it often is with particular areas of our villages, towns, and cities.

### 6.3.1  Historical examples of supposed 'community spirit'

There have been a number of occasions in the past where the sense of community ('community spirit') has apparently been so strong, and so widespread, as to enter public consciousness. Notable examples include Londoners' reaction to the Blitz during the Second World War and the actions of New Yorkers immediately following '9/11' (the terrorist attacks on the Twin Towers in New York and the Pentagon in Washington DC on 11 September 2001). However, these periods of heightened sense of community were relatively short-lived and some writers (particularly in the case of the Blitz) have questioned the existence of such a communal identity. Rather we are concerned here with the less tangible and more pervasive sense of place and community.

| Sense of community | [Examples] |
| --- | --- |
| Belonging | The community has a name ('the North Down Road community'), newsletters from local groups, decorations inside and outside houses during religious festivals |
| Ownership | Attention paid to maintenance of buildings and shared spaces, Neighbourhood Watch schemes, abandoned vehicles are quickly reported |
| Participation | Volunteering, taking active part in recycling schemes, allotments-uk.com, local community groups ('Mothers and Toddlers'), local *Facebook* groups, *Mumsnet* |
| Leadership | Individuals willing to accompany neighbours to make a case to the local council, 'spokespeople' appearing in the local media, visible and active local councillors |
| Mutuality | 'Time banking' (reciprocal support such as the giving of lifts, gardening, DIY jobs), mutual respect and tolerance between users of a local amenity |
| Rootedness | People living in a community for a significant length of time, often represented by a visible age distribution (the elderly, children, long-term house ownership) |
| Ties | Visible use of local tradespeople, neighbours lending tools, expertise |

### 6.3.1.1 **Sense of community**

What factors would seem to encourage a sense of community? We offer the following as possibilities:

### 6.3.1.2 **Exploiting community spirit**

What can you do, as a PCSO, to exploit or make use of the sense of community? We have commented throughout this book that you will have to urge, persuade, cajole, wheedle, coax, charm, humour, and otherwise pressure people to start thinking and acting like a community if they do not do so already, in order to achieve anything permanent or worthwhile in the community you serve. Part of that is knowing what a community is, but your overall strategy within your neighbourhood policing team will be to make use of those elements of 'community spirit' which you can identify and which welcome an approach from you.

### 6.3.1.3 **Analyse the community**

The first element, we would suggest, is to **analyse the groups** which we have categorized in the table above, and note which of them in your community you can approach or enlist immediately. Others may take longer and may require you to think through different inducements to help you or different ways in which you can persuade them to join in. Never underestimate the appeal of a 'bandwagon' because your activities to foster and encourage a sense of community identity and team spirit will develop a momentum of their own, and some organizations will come on board with you simply to be seen to do so.

### 6.3.1.4 **Allocate tasks**

The second element is in terms of the **allocation of work.** We suggest that you draw up a list of tasks in conjunction with the table of participants, or determinants of community spirit. That way you can ensure that, for every new recruit to your cause, whatever it may be (and we've looked at a number in the course of these pages) there is a real and defined task that they can take on. This will have the added benefit of ensuring that those who join you do so from a genuine sense of purpose. Those along just for the ride will look dismayed when you ask them to do something. Don't be afraid to nag.

## 6.4 **Fear of Crime—Fear Born of Social Unease?**

There is a general acceptance that the fear of crime has increased in the last decade or so, despite the fact that most forms of recorded crime have shown a decrease in the same period (although see Farrall and Gadd, 2004, for a critique). As Walker *et al* (2006: 34) note, 'despite the total number of crimes estimated by the BCS [British Crime Survey] falling over recent years, comparatively high proportions of people continue to believe crime has risen across the country as a whole and in their local area.'

It would also appear that members of particular communities are more likely to believe that both national and local crime has risen significantly when compared to others and also that they are likely to worry more about crime. The **British Crime Survey** suggests that the following demographic factors are significant in people's concerns:

- **Gender:** Women are more likely than men to feel that burglary and violent crime have risen.
- **Age:** Young people worry more about violence and car crime (although men and women in the 65 to 74 age group are most likely to perceive that there has been a significant increase in crime overall).
- **Ethnicity:** People from non-white ethnic groups are more likely to be concerned about crime than those from white groups.
- **Location:** Those living in urban areas are more likely to worry about crime than those who live in rural areas.
- **Accommodation:** Those living in the social rented sector are more likely to worry about crime than those who rent privately or own their own homes.
- **Newspapers:** Readers of the 'red top' (tabloid) newspapers are more likely to worry about crime than those who read the 'broadsheets' or 'quality press'.

[Source: Kershaw *et al* (2008) p 126 and Table 5/06.]

### 6.4.1 **Fear is not necessarily linked to being a victim**

It is important to note that those who feel most worried about crime or who perceive crime to be increasing, are not necessarily those who are actually the most likely to become victims of recorded crime. Having said this, it could be argued that the fear of crime alone is a form of harm to an individual. It is also the case that, for those in our communities who fear crime the most, the implications of crime can be profound. To put this another way, an elderly person's statistically 'irrational' fears about crime are in fact quite rational if the effect of crime on such a person is factored in. Think of this as some kind of calculation: **the risk may be low but the negative consequences are very high** (for example in terms of recovery from an injury) and so overall the outcome might be significant for the individual concerned.

### 6.4.1.1 **Fear is perception of the threat**

This has important implications for the PCSO. Part of the 'reassurance agenda' that gave rise to the creation of the PCSO in the first place is concerned with perceptions as much as reality. These perceptions may be affected by actions and forms of anti-social behaviour and minor disorder which are not of themselves criminal offences but which nonetheless influence an individual's sense of well-being and security. Perceptions may also be affected by the views of family and friends and media reports. Indeed, some people's persistent fear of crime may be influenced by the success or otherwise of local police interventions. You can consult the <http://www.police.uk/> website for detailed crime reporting by geographical district (in some areas, even down to an individual PCSO's 'beat'), to get a sense of whether or not the local crime statistics support people's feelings that they are at threat from crime. Those who have had a poor encounter with the police, particularly one in which their fears and worries were not seen to be taken seriously, are more likely to feel that the police are ineffective or incompetent. The fear of crime cannot be separated from other aspects of an individual's perception of the 'quality of life' of their communities such as the education their children receive, the housing stock in their area, and the cleanliness or otherwise of their neighbourhood, together with anxieties about continued employment, credit rating, and debt. The economic recession which began in 2008 has entailed a small rise in acquisitive crime. Home Office data published in October 2013 indicated a slight increase in the number of domestic burglaries since September 2012 and there has been a rise of 8 per cent in personal theft over the same period. Yet overall crime fell by 7 per cent (to 3.7 million recorded offences) in the period to June 2013 compared with the same period in 2012. This is the lowest overall crime level in the history of the Crime Statistics for England and Wales (CSEW), which began in 1981, and crime is now less than half its peak level in 1995. It seems though, that people's fears of knife crime, theft, burglary and robbery are not mollified by the overall decrease in recorded crime. [See data from the Office of National Statistics (ONS), available at <http://www.ons.gov.uk/ons/rel/crime-stats/crime-statistics/period-ending-june-2013/index.html> accessed 30 April 2014. The Crime Statistics for England and Wales (previously the British Crime Survey) are recorded annually and processed (interpreted) every six months or so. Your Force should keep you up to date with crime data for your county or metropolitan district.]

### 6.4.2 Fear of crime: the importance of 'signal crimes'

One of the features we have explored in relation to the role of the PCSO is that some of the problems brought to you by members of the public or delegated to you will not seem like policing issues (figure 6.1). We have touched upon these seemingly low-level, often environmentally focused, problems in previous chapters but it is important to understand why these particular issues are perceived by the public to be important in their communities. **It is directly relevant to the public's fear of crime and the way that this contributes to social unease.**

There is no right or wrong in this; each, in its time, has headed a list of priorities in a community. You may feel that some of these task items are not policing problems and therefore not applicable to a PCSO. Is the issue of broken street lighting a matter for police concern? What about litter? Is there really a policing element

**Figure 6.1  Graffiti on gates**

in the closure of the post office or the lack of a bus route into town? This is where the concept of **signal crimes** can prove useful to the PCSO and provides a good framework for the PCSO to start an exploration of his or her community's perceptions about crime.

---

**Task**

Consider this list of community-based problems. Put these problems in order of importance with 1 for the most important and 10 for the least important:
- Mini motorbikes on the pavements
- Post office closure
- Litter
- Graffiti
- Alcohol and drugs debris in the park
- Vandalism
- Abandoned cars
- Broken street lighting
- Unlit alleyways
- Lack of a bus route into town.

---

### 6.4.2.1  What is a signal crime?

The term was coined by Professor Martin Innes and a team at the University of Surrey, working closely with Surrey Police, in 2001–02, and subsequently it has proved influential in neighbourhood policing because it allows the police to view certain crimes or disorders from the perspective of the community, that is, to see them through the community's eyes:

The key idea of a Signal Crimes Perspective is that some crime and disorder incidents function as warning signals to people about the distribution of risks to their security in everyday life. Some crime and disorder behaviours matter more than others in shaping the public's collective perceptions of risk.

---

**DISCUSSION POINTS**

Think about the community in which you live. What events would cause you to reappraise risk perception in your own neighbourhood? (Discount any major crimes such as murder or rape and think instead about the so-called minor crimes or disorders.)

Would these affect your idea of safety?

Would your perception of how secure your neighbourhood is, be influenced by any of these issues?

---

## Crime signals lead to perceptions of other ills

Once spotted, these signals can lead to a heightened awareness and the perception that there are other examples in the neighbourhood, from littering to threats of anti-social behaviour. These perceptions may be affected by forms of minor disorder which are not of themselves criminal offences but none the less influence an individual's sense of well-being and security. Perceptions may also be affected by the views of family and friends and media reports.

### 6.4.2.2 Broken Windows theory

Linked with social disorganization arguments is the so-called **'Broken Windows'** theory made popular through the work of James Wilson and George Kelling in the USA. It could be argued that 'Broken Windows' theory has also been influential in the UK context, particularly in terms of past government thinking. We summarize the theory in the table below.

| Stage | [Examples] |
|---|---|
| Relatively minor evidence of perceived criminal or anti-social behaviour | A single broken window (perhaps accidental) in a building, left unrepaired |
| Greater feeling that a community is vulnerable and 'law and order is breaking down' | More windows are broken in the same building, deliberately |
| A breakdown in forms of social cohesion that normally militate against crime and disorder | People are less willing to frequent the area close to the buildings |
| More serious forms of crime 'move in' to occupy the vacuum | Drug dealers begin to operate, muggers move in, organized criminals exploit the opportunities now available |

---

**DISCUSSION POINTS**

How convinced are you by the 'Broken Windows' theory? If the theory is correct, what are the implications for the PCSO?

---

### 6.4.2.3 Criticism of the theory

There has been significant criticism of the 'Broken Windows' theory, largely because of the lack of supporting empirical evidence—that is, it has not been shown that the low-level problems identified by the theory by necessity lead to the more serious outcomes claimed; one element does not entail another. Despite this, 'Broken Windows' retains its attraction to some policy makers (particularly in the USA) and is often coupled with '*Zero Tolerance*' approaches to policing.

And if 'Broken Windows theory' is valid?

If the theory *is* valid then the implications for the PCSO are obviously to assist in facilitating the repair of the 'Broken Window' as soon as possible. For example, if the first stage is broken street lighting, then this will require coordination with the relevant county, borough, or district council highways department.

### 6.4.2.4 Signal crime and signal disorder

To look at this in more detail, we can identify three parts that make up a **signal crime/signal disorder**:

* The **expression**—the incident that makes a person concerned
* The **content**—how the person makes sense of the incident, particularly in the context of feeling at risk or being vulnerable
* The **effect**—what changes in the person because of the incident? For example, does it affect behaviour or how he or she feels?

We select as a fictional example an elderly resident in a town, Mrs Veronica Meldrew, who sees groups of disaffected youths congregating daily in the passage outside her house, engaging in rowdy behaviour and minor acts of vandalism. She might say, '*I see these kids outside my house every evening*' (the **expression**). '*They make me feel unsafe because they are always misbehaving*' (the **content**). '*I don't leave my house at night and keep my curtains closed*' (the **effect**).

### 6.4.2.5 Police responses likely to be low key—residents' fear will increase

Would the police respond to this sort of incident? Their resources are stretched and they have to prioritize depending on the seriousness of the situation. In this instance no criminal acts have been committed and therefore the police will concentrate on other incidents where a criminal offence *has* occurred. This reinforces the resident's perceptions about her safety, as well as reducing her confidence in the police. This perception Mrs Meldrew then shares with her family, friends, and acquaintances, in turn affecting *their* perceptions about the risk posed by the youths in the passageway. The unease that she feels, and her perceptions of her safety, spread out like ripples on a pond, causing concern and anxiety to a larger part of the community. This unease is what the Crime Survey of England and Wales records, and, as we commented earlier, the unease or anxiety can often be *despite* the reality of crime investigation and 'good' Force measurements.

### 6.4.2.6 Actions to tackle perceptions of risk

What is needed is action to tackle these perceptions of risk to increase public confidence and to improve relationships with the community. The problem may not strictly be a policing one but the fallout from inactivity from any agency will often end up at the police's door. Mrs Meldrew's perception is that the youths are engaging in anti-social behaviour and to her that is a police matter and therefore she expects a police response.

---

**DISCUSSION POINTS**

Consider the attitude of this particular resident—is she correct in expecting a police response?

Are there any other 'grey areas' where the police are often expected to deal with a problem that may not be strictly within their remit?

What should the police response be in such situations? What is your role as a PCSO in dealing with these tricky situations?

---

### 6.4.2.7 Control signals

The signal crime approach goes further in its analysis of the perception of risk within the community and asserts that, as well as an **expression**, a **content**, and an **effect**, there is also a **control signal** which can work towards reducing the fear factor. *The control signal is an authority response to the particular problem that seeks a solution.* This does not have to come solely from the police but could encompass things like the installation of CCTV, the erecting of fencing, an improvement in street lighting, and so on. Therefore the approach provides an opportunity to make things better for the community and accordingly it is not simply a negative proposition. This was identified some years ago in a national evaluation:

> The advantage of the signal crime approach is its focus on those factors that are disproportionately generative of insecurity. Once the causes of the problem are understood, one can begin to effectively act against them...Tactics and strategies can be designed and implemented at the local level...(and) can have a disproportionate impact on the causes of insecurity, increase public trust and confidence in the police and thereby provide greater reassurance to residents over their safety. Signal crime theory is a method for problem identification in which issues and problems that cause most concern to residents can be targeted...

### 6.4.2.8 The roles of the media

It is essential that the communication aspect of the signal crimes process be managed effectively, because the police response to them may be carried out in full view of the media. Newspapers could carry reports as may the other media outlets, TV, radio, internet blogs, and so on. The 'good news story' of a positive police response and a proactive intervention by the PCSO, as part of the neighbourhood team, is akin to the effect recognized in the evaluation we quoted earlier:

> Publicity and communication are recurrent themes...
>
> The strategy here is that 'good news stories' act as a confidence-building measure in the local area and communicate some of the positive gains made in reducing crime...The pre-emptive use of communication may assert more control over these perceptions, perhaps leaving less to the imagination of the recipients.

### 6.4.3 A media strategy

The PCSO needs to make sure that initiatives and successes are trumpeted and the wider community is aware of the steps being taken in neighbourhood policing. Each police station or BCU will have a media liaison officer who will be a handy contact for ensuring that good news stories are put into the public domain. Such stories can demonstrate reassurance policing or accentuate positive initiatives like youth clubs; but the positive spin ensures that the community hears some good news. Initiatives like these act as 'control signals' in the fight against the fear of crime. Episodes with visual impact could also be placed in the Force web pages, where the media may also pick them up.

### 6.4.3.1 Selling the 'good news' message

All media outlets should be exploited to send the 'good news' message and one of the things you can do in your own area is to explore the avenues you can use to communicate. It is also important to explore the demographics of your area to ensure that the media used are appropriate. Don't assume that everyone has access to the internet. Therefore use a variety of communication outlets to ensure you have targeted as wide a segment of the community as possible. Remember that pictures can help: don't forget positive images in this planning context.

### 6.4.3.2 Making an environmental visual audit

We will now explore how you can identify signal crimes/disorders within your community and how these can then be used to inform and shape your work within that neighbourhood. The key tool for this is the Environmental Visual Audit (EVA) or as it is sometimes known *a structured 'patch' walk*. The EVA is a way of looking at your designated community and identifying any signal crimes that exist within it. Essentially you walk around the neighbourhood and log all the problems that you can see.

> **Task**
>
> What signal crimes/disorders can you think of that may be seen in a neighbourhood? Have a look around your own neighbourhood to see if you can identify any.

Our model response

Our suggested answers might include the following (but the list is not exhaustive):

- Litter/rubbish strewn around
- Graffiti—racist/offensive?
- Vandalism
- Broken windows/fences
- Derelict houses
- Furniture in the garden
- Drugs paraphernalia, including abandoned needles
- Abandoned vehicles
- Prostitution—cards in the phone boxes, used condoms, 'cruising' cars
- Large groups of youths hanging about
- Dog mess
- Stray animals
- Broken street lighting—absence of lighting
- Alcohol debris.

The items listed are not necessarily indicative of a fear of crime within a community, but they do provide examples of things that give people a sense of unease. By identifying these in an EVA, you will provide a list of problems to solve in conjunction with other partnership agencies.

### DISCUSSION POINT

Looking at our suggested answers to the Task above, what agencies could you identify that would be useful in helping to solve these problems?

#### 6.4.3.3 **Partners in an EVA**

Partnership agencies could be invited on an EVA so that they can have an input, which would then build into a joint problem-solving approach. This works well where there is an agency that has a responsibility for a large part of the community, such as a local authority or housing association. It could also be useful to take a member of the community or a community representative on an EVA (day or night), so that they can identify problems you may not see or which you have missed. This therefore allows you to access the 'eyes and ears' of a community so that the signal crimes identified as being the ones that cause most unease, will be the ones dealt with first. This may build a sense of ownership within the community because people's views are seen as an integral part of the process. The EVA will provide a snapshot of the community, which can then be used to inform your work patterns. If the EVA is repeated at regular intervals then the progress made within that community in dealing with signal crimes and disorders could be easily charted, as well as allowing for new problems to be identified. In the course of time, this could become an excellent qualitative measure of the impact of PCSOs.

### 6.4.3.4 The wider value of an EVA

The EVA works particularly well with environmental signal crimes such as littering, fly tipping, abandoned vehicles, not clearing up dog mess, or graffiti, because these tend to be highly visible problems which can often be resolved quite quickly. The litter can be picked up, the abandoned cars removed and crushed, the walls cleaned, the graffitists and fly tippers prosecuted, and these actions will have a symbolic significance within the community. The fact that the police are acting, in conjunction with other agencies, to tackle neighbourhood issues, will demonstrate to the community that you are listening to their concerns and reversing the 'broken window' state of neighbourhood deterioration. The EVA will fit well into the community engagement process because it can be used at public meetings where the community is asked which of its problems it wants to be tackled first.

---

### Knowledge Check 28

1. Give two examples of what might encourage a sense of community.

2. What is 'the fear of crime'?

3. Give an example of demographic factors that may be significant in the 'fear of crime'.

4. Who is the source of the information about the demographic factors in Question 3?

5. In 2013, in what direction and by what percentage did theft from the person move?

6. When did the Crime Statistics for England and Wales (CSEW, formerly the British Crime Survey) begin?

7. What is a 'signal crime'?

8. What theory was proposed by James Wilson and George Kelling?

9. What are the three components of a signal crime or signal disorder?

10. What is a 'control signal'?

11. How might a media strategy help 'control signals'?

12. What is an EVA?

13. Give three examples of things you might see on an EVA.

---

# 6.5 **Partnerships**

In this and preceding chapters, we have explored many functions within the PCSO role and have looked at the community-based focus that is vital for the role to succeed. The idea of the PCSO as a **conduit** between the community and the police has also been touched upon:

Conduit—a means of transmission or communication.

This description suggests a genuine metaphor for the role of the PCSO. There is a transmission of ideas between the community and the police through the PCSO. The PCSO facilitates communication that works both ways and to the potential benefit of both sides: the police receive important community based intelligence; the community correspondingly has the ear of the police in dealing with its perceived problems (which may not be crimes and which may not normally attract police attention).

## 6.5.1 **Partnerships enter the mix**

This image of the PCSO as a channel between two distinct groups is not one-dimensional or monolithic. Equally important are the partnership agencies with which the PCSO works on a daily basis. The nature of police and community partnerships with other locally-based agencies and local government departments is important to the success of any civic enterprise which the PCSO, on behalf of the police, may seek to develop. The PCSO is firmly at the centre of this neighbourhood policing/community/agencies approach.

### 6.5.1.1 **How do partnerships work?**

To demonstrate the importance of the partnership approach to resolving community issues, consider the following:

> You are a PCSO working on an urban estate (mixed housing, both social and private) and at the heart of this community is a park that is the focal point for many of the problems brought to you at your regular community surgery. You receive complaints about matters such as litter, dog fouling, underage drinking, congregation of youths, criminal damage of the play park equipment, graffiti spraying, and so on. The residents complain to you that the park has become unsafe at night and that adults can feel intimidated by the youths who congregate there. Parents tell you that they have seen broken bottles on the children's play area, and there have been other reports of used hypodermic needles being found. The local children add that they cannot play football there because of the dog fouling and that there is only play equipment for younger children.

> **Task**
>
> Consider which agencies you would contact to deal with these issues.

Our model response

We don't think that there is a right or wrong response to this task, but we suggest that you ought to consider the following possibilities:

- **Park authorities**—is there a park keeper or green spaces warden who can help with this issue? Does the park authority have a retained gardening company who could help identify issues within the park? Who is responsible for the maintenance and who is responsible for the provision of the play equipment?
- **Local authority**—who can help with removing the graffiti? Is the same department responsible for the litter collections within the park? Is there an issue with the lighting that could make the park better lit at night?
- **Housing association**—if offenders can be identified and linked to a particular residence, can their anti-social behaviour be linked to their tenancy agreements? Is there a designated housing officer for this area? Do the residents have an association that could provide such information, as well as reassurance visits? What do residents want to see in the park? What would the community regard as success?
- **Education**—there are potential issues to do with alcohol and drugs and so schools visits to highlight the long-term issues of both problems may help.
- **Health**—as above, but to include comment or publicity or both about the dangers of used hypodermic needles.
- **Youth services**—are there outreach workers who could speak to the youths who congregate there to understand the issues? What do they want to see in the park: a skate park, a teen shelter, bike tracks?
- **Dog warden**—is the issue of fouling to do with irresponsible owners or stray dogs? How often does the dog warden patrol? Is the area known for strays? (Residents can help with information here.) Can the dogs be identified and then linked to owners? You, as the PCSO, would want to include the park on your patrol, and perhaps put up notices warning of the Fixed Penalty offences for dog-fouling. Is there a facility to dispose of bagged dog mess? Is it emptied frequently?
- **Charities**—is there funding available to help put some equipment into the park? Is there room for things like skateboard areas, or facilities for playing sport?
- **Local businesses**—can they help with funding/sponsoring some of the projects? Point out the advantages of 'virtuous' publicity and the inclusion of their logos on equipment or facilities.

- **Police**—enforcement is needed on the issues of drinking, drugs, anti-social behaviour, criminal damage, graffiti, etc.
- **Parents**—it is necessary to inform them about their children when the latter transgress, as well as providing access to support services to stop some of the low-level problems escalating further.
- **The community itself**—showing how the residents of the estate and the park users can help with these issues by setting up meetings, establishing surgeries, and collating information, as well as lobbying local councils, council officials, and media organizations. By doing these things the community has a voice on the issues and can strongly influence outcomes.

### 6.5.1.2 Joined-up and coordinated approaches to problems

This is by no means a guarantee of success. In any approach to resolving these issues, an agency on its own could only scratch away at one aspect of a pretty complex issue. A *joined-up partnership approach* is integral to dealing with problems in the round, particularly since the boundaries of organizational responsibility are so blurred. It would be easy to forget, in the complication of organizational accountability and negotiated responsibility, that **the real problem is encouraging the community to take ownership of its problems.** Part of your PCSO role will be to help to coordinate agency responses and to ensure that the needs of people living by the park, or wanting to use it as a recreation and leisure facility, are met. If you don't attempt a coordinated, joined-up partnership approach from the outset, it will be very hard to impose such a structure halfway through, and a project might drag on for far longer than it needed to.

### 6.5.1.3 Community Safety Partnerships

An organizational approach to solving issues within the community has been given formal structure through Community Safety Partnerships (CSPs), established in the **Crime and Disorder Act 1998**, and later amended by the **Police Reform Act 2002**. This provides a statutory framework for the 'joined-up partnership' approach and made the following authorities responsible for seeking a coordinated approach to community issues:

- **The police**
- **Local authorities**
- **Fire authorities**
- **Police authorities**
- **Primary care trusts** (England)
- **Local health boards** (Wales).

Colin Rogers, in his study of Crime Partnerships, provides a useful explanation of the rationale for cooperation:

Working together, these responsible authorities are required to carry out an audit to identify crime and disorder and problems of drugs misuse in their area, and to develop strategies that deal effectively with them. Partner organisations are required to work in cooperation with local education and probation authorities, and to invite the cooperation of a range of local private, voluntary, and other public and community groups, including the community itself.

---

**DISCUSSION POINT**

What do you think the advantages and disadvantages of this approach could be?

---

### 6.5.1.4 What Community Safety Partnerships should deliver

The Government has indicated what it expects CSPs to provide through partnerships or to develop through taking the lead in delivering a series of priorities:

- Make communities safer
- A key principle is that partnerships should have flexibility to tackle local priorities, including close links with neighbourhood policing to ensure a joined-up response to local concerns (including cooperation with the Police Crime Commissioner, see below); developing local partnerships, such as Safer Schools Partnerships, to deliver solutions in response to specific issues, as appropriate.
- Tackle the crime, disorder and anti-social behaviour issues of greatest importance in each locality, increasing public confidence in the local agencies involved in dealing with these issues.
- CSPs to hold at least one public meeting per year to engage the community in tackling crime and working closely with the police on the delivery of neighbourhood policing as a key mechanism for understanding the priorities of the community and for responding to local concerns.
- A major development in recent years has been the linking of the Police Crime Commissioner for each police force outside London with the CSP, so that regular meetings of the partnerships can be monitored by the PCC.

The government has noted that CSPs are made up of representatives from the 'responsible authorities', which are the:

- police
- local authorities
- fire and rescue authorities
- probation service
- health.

The responsible authorities work together to protect their local communities from crime and to help people feel safer. They work out how to deal with local issues like anti-social behaviour, drug or alcohol misuse and reoffending. They annually assess local crime priorities and consult partners and the local community about how to deal with them.

Working with Police and Crime Commissioners

Community safety partnerships and Police and Crime Commissioners (PCCs) work together by:

- CSPs sending their annual community safety plan and strategy to their local PCC
- One or more CSPs attending PCC meetings
- CSPs submitting any merger requests to their PCC (but the PCC cannot impose mergers)
- The PCC asking for reports from CSPs on specific issues
  [adapted and compressed from <https://www.gov.uk/government/policies/ reducing-and-preventing-crime--2/supporting-pages/community-safety-partnerships>, accessed 30 April 2014].

### 6.5.2 Research into community partnerships

In his work on *Community Engagement in Policing* (2012), Andy Myhill researched the literature around this topic and reached some interesting conclusions about some of the challenges relating to the partnership aspect of community engagement, which have profound implications for the work of the PCSO:

- Communities may not initially have the willingness to engage with the police, particularly in areas where there is a history of poor relations. This can be sometimes interpreted [...] as apathy. The police need to **foster trust and confidence** in these communities prior to attempting to secure community participation.
- Communities may not have the capacity to participate effectively in policing. Evidence suggests existing community networks are important to sustaining participation. The police will have to work with partner agencies to help **build capacity** in communities.
- Communities need to be **trained and educated** about their role in policing. If citizens are being encouraged to participate actively, the nature and scope of their role needs to be clearly defined.
- The police must **provide communities with good quality information** about crime in their local area on a real-time basis if they are to participate effectively in policing.
- The police must value the input and contribution of the public if partnerships are to be successful. Information flow must be two-way. The police need to **provide communities with feedback** on how their contribution is being used. If action is taken, this should be publicized. If action is not taken, the reasons for this should be explained.
- **Effective multi- and inter-agency working** is crucial for community engagement on wider community safety issues. This is particularly so in relation to environmental/quality of life issues.

---

**DISCUSSION POINT**

Looking at each of Myhill's points, how can the PCSO help in overcoming these challenges?

---

### 6.5.3 **Foster trust and confidence**

One of the key responsibilities of the PCSO role within this engagement approach is to gain the trust and confidence of the community in which PCSOs work. Part of this derives from the visibility of the PCSO within the community and this was one of the findings of the National Reassurance Policing Project. As communities become used to this presence in their midst, they are more likely to engage with the whole neighbourhood management process. However, visibility and walking around are not enough on their own, since trust and confidence do not emerge from an osmotic process based merely on presence. The need to be present in the community on a regular basis forms part of this but trust also relies on three key factors—**reliability, sincerity,** and **competence.**

### 6.5.4 **Building capacity**

One of the key objectives for any PCSO is to help provide opportunities for the community to participate in local problem-solving initiatives in an effort to move the community towards taking ownership of these problems. This requires more than just goodwill and the confidence of the residents involved. It involves utilizing the capacity within that community to band and bond together to tackle problems as well as involving the partnership agencies. One could argue, of course, that it is the job of the 'authorities' to provide help irrespective of whether the community itself is a cohesive force, but issues are better tackled when there is a will to **build capacity.** Building capacity may be difficult where there is a need to establish a shared identity first.

### 6.5.4.1 **Training and education**

Communities sometimes need to be encouraged to participate in local initiatives and the residents 'educated' about their potential role in helping to shape the partnership approach to policing. This needs to be done sensitively. The PCSO, having built up a degree of trust and confidence with community members, is ideally placed to help with this process in an empathetic and responsive manner. The PCSO should be in tune with the community's concerns and should have identified the leading players in the community who are in the best position to help with any initiative. By utilizing the structures that a PCSO has put into place, surgeries, public meetings, 'talking walls', and so on, the 'education' is better seen as part of a **continuous engagement** process which seeks to lead out from the community the abilities to solve problems, rather than impose solutions from outside. Ensuring that the community has basic skills, such as how to write a formal letter to a councillor, or how to set up a media campaign, involves skills training. Many people are eager to acquire skills (as opposed to knowledge) and it is probable that there will be some residents who want to know how to do things. The PCSO can act as a facilitator in such cases, putting people in touch and helping to secure the right community outcomes.

### 6.5.4.2 Provide information and feedback

One of the key initiatives used by Neighbourhood Management Teams across the UK is **PACT—Partners and Communities Together.** This is interpreted and implemented in many different ways by the police forces and agencies involved, so we can offer a description only of the generic process. The predominant approach is through the constructive use of 'surgeries' and public meetings. Used correctly, a PACT meeting can **foster trust and confidence**; it can help to **build capacity** within a community; it allows for the **training and education** of a community; and it can help with **effective multi-agency work.**

---

**DISCUSSION POINTS**

What PACT initiatives are there on your BCU? How can you get involved in its delivery?

---

### 6.5.4.3 Community meetings

The desire of a community to come together to discuss its problems can be facilitated by a PCSO to great effect by establishing community 'surgeries'. These could be held at schools, or in community centres, village halls, libraries, and so on—anywhere where there is a local authority-owned venue. This provides the residents with the opportunity to speak to their local PCSO, or other members of the extended policing family, about their concerns and issues. Surgeries often take the form of a 'drop-in', staffed at specific times for anyone in the community to visit. At the same time, surgeries or surgery venues can be used to provide information about crime reduction initiatives or other policing projects. 'Surgeries' can be taken physically to a community using a mobile police station so that the surgeries are not necessarily fixed in a geographical sense. This will enable the PCSO to reach out to different sections of the community, particularly in scattered 'beats'.

---

**DISCUSSION POINTS**

What problems could arise with community surgeries?

Where could you hold one on your 'patch'?

Do they have to be regular?

Are there costs involved?

Why might some people be reluctant to visit a mobile police station rather than, say, a local library?

---

### 6.5.4.4 **The value of public meetings**

Don't forget that public meetings provide an opportunity for you to introduce members of the community to the partners and partnership agencies to resolve the community's difficulties mutually. This gives each of the participants a chance to meet, engage, and understand each other, with you acting as facilitator. Don't forget that there may be a chance to invite the Police Crime Commissioner along and this will probably bring welcome publicity in its wake. Make sure though that you brief the PCC prior to the meeting: you will have things you want the PCC to emphasize and things you will not want mentioned. Be aware that such events could be hijacked by a PCC bent on re-election . . . Remember too that there are people who go to meetings and do nothing else. You mustn't let public meetings become a substitute for doing things and planning actions. You may have to be the catalyst to make other things happen.

**KEY POINT**

There are four key areas to consider when organizing a public meeting:

- The **venue**—what factors need to be considered in choosing a venue?
- The **rules**—what rules should be in place for a public meeting?
- The **agenda**—does a meeting need one?
- The **chairperson**—who should chair a public meeting and what qualities should they possess?

Our model response

Born of many years of engagement in public meetings, our suggestions in answer to the questions we have just posed are these:

- **Venue**—location, accessibility, adequate seating, neutral (does the building convey ownership of the issue to the community?), disabled facilities, refreshments available, cost, time of meeting, adequate parking, adequate lighting
- **Rules**—no heckling, adherence to the agenda and to timings, courtesy at all points, no shouting, one speaker at a time
- **Agenda**—provides the structure to a meeting, provides a written framework for the meeting, provides audience with the format
- **Chairperson**—disciplined, experienced, empathetic listener, moves the meeting on, adheres to agenda, well respected, community figure.

**KEY POINT**

For further information on organizing a public meeting, have a look at the following website: <http://www.resourcecentre.org.uk/information/organising-a-public-meeting/>, accessed 30 April 2014, which has really good guidelines about what can and can't be achieved by public meetings and what you need to organize in advance.

### 6.5.4.5 PACT at public meetings

The PACT process uses the meeting as a form of community dialogue and seeks to find the issues that are of concern in that community. The meeting often discusses these issues so that priorities can be put forward to the PACT Panel as objectives. It is on this basis that the **partners and communities** move forward together in solving the community's issues and concerns. The idea is that *by engaging everyone, partners, PCSO, and the community from the ground up*, the community priorities will emerge.

---

**Task**

A PACT Panel usually consists of leading community figures and partnership agencies—who do you think should compose such a panel?

---

Our model response

Our answers, again, are by no means prescriptive but we think that the following may be key players often found on a PACT Panel:

> Police representatives, housing officer, Neighbourhood Watch coordinator, faith leader(s), local business proprietors (or collective groups like the *Lions* or Chamber of Commerce), local councillors, parish councillors, residents' association members, representatives of local charities, school governors, head teachers, local authority officers, local citizens who have some prominent voice in the community.

You may be able to think of more. You should certainly be considering who, in your patch, should be approached to participate in a PACT panel: remember that it needn't be the same people each time. The composition of PACT panels should reflect the issues under consideration.

### 6.5.4.6 Effective multi-agency work

The final factor is that of effective multi-agency approaches and again the PCSO can be crucial to this activity at a community level. PCSOs can often deal with issues before they escalate into wider problems simply by having access to the agencies that can deal with that problem best; such as informing the local clean-up team from the council about fresh graffiti so that the team can remove the nuisance swiftly. This relies on the PCSO having a good knowledge of the partnership agencies available and making sure that this information is maintained in a readily available format. Direct numbers for key personnel (crucial to avoid the maze of bureaucracy that often surrounds getting hold of the right person) can be maintained on a **Key Individual Network** (KIN) or a contact list. This can then be made available to others to ensure a consistency of approach, as well as continuity should you move from your 'patch' or leave the job.

> **KEY POINT**
>
> Do you have a **KIN** (Key Individual Network)? If not, is your contact list available to others and kept up to date?

### 6.5.4.7 Proper partnerships are hard to achieve and need lots of work

The KIN approach is adequate for the daily PCSO routine of dealing with issues before they escalate but, at the strategic level, effective partnerships can be difficult to achieve. Gilling has identified the following factors as being crucial to establishing good partnership protocols:

- All partners having a **shared purpose**
- **Leadership** is needed to drive the process on
- An appropriate **structure** is required
- Appropriate **resources** are needed
- Appropriate **time** needs to be allocated to the process
- **Durability** is needed to provide the necessary consistency and continuity.

Even with this in place, being able to sustain an effective partnership can still require constant effort, tact, patience, and resilience:

> ...it is the very diverse make-up of many of the agencies that constitute partnerships [which] can be problematic. Attention is drawn to the inter-organisational conflict and differential power relationships that can occur. Partnerships, especially within the field of crime control and criminal justice, by their nature, draw together diverse organisations with very different cultures, ideologies, and traditions that pursue distinct aims through divergent structures, strategies and practices. Deep structural conflicts exist between the parties that sit down together in partnerships. Criminal justice agencies have very different priorities and interests, as do other public sector organisations, voluntary bodies, the commercial sector, and local community groups.

This is not intended to make you despair of ever finding an answer through the partnership approach, rather it is needed to show you how to ground the process in reality. By recognizing the limitations of such alliances and inter-departmental politics, PCSOs need be under no illusion about the magnitude of the task:

> The provision of Neighbourhood Policing and other related initiatives is most impactive, and has the most sustainable effects, when it finds ways to augment a community's informal social control resources. The police are not the ultimate guarantors of neighbourhood order and security. They are a standby institution

that can intervene when social order that is ordinarily maintained by the norms, rules and conventions of everyday interactions in neighbourhoods has been breached or threatened. Thus, formal social control needs to be construed as part of the solution, rather than the solution in and of itself.

---

### Knowledge Check 29

1. What is a 'conduit' in the PCSO context?

2. What sorts of organizations are involved in partnerships with the police?

3. What gives formal structure to problem-solving in communities?

4. What are the 'responsible authorities' in a CSP?

5. What might a PCSO seek as part of 'a continuous engagement process'?

6. What do the letters PACT stand for?

7. What are the four key considerations when organizing a public meeting?

8. Who should be on a PACT Panel?

9. What is a KIN?

---

## 6.6 Ethnic and Diverse Minority Communities

We have examined a number of aspects of community engagement in this chapter but we now turn to the issue of policing ethnic and diverse minority communities. This is a crucial area of policing as a whole but it has real resonance in the community sphere in which you work and for the role that you perform. One might be tempted to suppose that, after the **Macpherson Inquiry** (the 1999 report into the 1993 murder of Stephen Lawrence), the national picture in respect of race and diversity is slowly improving, but there is actually a long way still to go, both in the wider police family and in society as a whole, before we achieve genuine tolerance and respect for diverse minority communities. Controversies in the last decade have included gay marriage, the Catholic Church's adoption agency's refusal (subsequently moderated) to allow gay couples to adopt its orphans, and the Channel 4 television show *Big Brother* being riven with accusations of racism. Issues of race and diversity often exist under the surface of things, needing only an appropriate occasion for them to emerge.

### 6.6.1 'Hard to reach'

One phrase that you will often hear in relation to ethnic and diverse minority communities is 'hard to reach' groups (sometimes referred to as 'hard to hear' groups). These groups have assumed a symbolic significance in the pursuit of diverse policing. They are considered to be the groups that might require differing approaches or present a challenge in terms of attempting to involve these groups in the engagement process.

---

**Task**

What do you think is a 'hard to reach' group?
Write down a list of examples. Discuss with your colleagues what their experiences are of encounters with such groups.

---

Our model response

It is impossible to present a definitive list of 'hard to reach' groups because perceptions of what 'hard to reach' means will vary considerably (see Nicola Brackertz, 2007). There may be additional groups that provide purely local or regional examples, such as some 'Traveller' or 'New Age' communities. A 'sample' list of hard to reach groups was provided in a Home Office Development and Practice Report of 2005. Compare what you produced in answer to the task above with the following:

- Ethnic minority groups
- Gay and lesbian groups
- Children and young people, especially those at risk
- Disabled people
- Sex workers
- Victims of crime
- Homeless people
- Drug users
- The mentally disordered
- Rural/farming communities
- Older people
- Single mothers
- Poor and acutely economically-deprived people
- Illiterate people (about 13 per cent of the adult population, lest you think them invisible)
- Domestic violence victims
- Non-English speakers
- Those suspicious of the police
- Refugees
- Travellers
- Some faith communities
- Transient populations (for example the travelling community).

**DISCUSSION POINTS**

Were many of these groups on your list?

How many of these groups are represented where you work?

Did some of the groups mentioned surprise you?

### 6.6.1.1 'Hard to reach' may be stereotyping

One aspect of the debate on community engagement that is often overlooked but which needs to be considered by practitioners within the community policing environment, is the term 'hard to reach' itself. There is a possibility that people within communities that are designated with this term could find it patronizing or even offensive. It could be used as a term to stigmatize groups as being different, rather than one used to emphasize inclusion. By labelling, are we seeking to impose sanitized cultural norms onto a much more variable picture? Alternatively, it could be that using the phrase 'hard to reach' somehow implies that these minority groups are outside the norm and possibly reluctant to engage in processes with which the majority are happy to conform:

> The wide range of different meanings and applications of the term 'hard to reach' brings into question its utility as a term. It is clear that there are a number of population sub-groups that have traditionally been under-represented (or not represented at all) within formal consultation processes with the police and other official institutions. It is also clear that there exist [*sic*] a range of different groups that have traditionally had difficult relations with the police . . . However, few of these groups are hard to reach in any fundamental physical sense. It seems fair to say that there are a number of groups who have at least some elements in common in terms of their difficulties with the police. But in many cases 'hard to reach' actually means 'hard to engage with on a positive level'.
>
> [Jones and Newburn, 2001]

### 6.6.1.2 Beware of the stereotype

We might also note that treating these groups as having some sort of homogeneous identity fails to convey the complexity of the wide range or spectrum of individuals and preoccupations within any single group. There are black people who are happy to engage with the police, just as there are among representatives from any of the groups labelled as 'hard to reach'. Correspondingly, there are people in the larger population groups who will have nothing to do with the police at any price. Remember the dangers we emphasized earlier of '**ethnocentricity**'; the temptation to view everything unvaryingly from your own fixed individual cultural viewpoint, when in fact there are many, equally valid, viewpoints and positions. This is why it is called diversity, after all.

### 6.6.2 **The PCSO has a positive role to play in the community**

We have stated throughout this book our belief that the PCSO has a positive role to play in working with *all* diverse minority communities. This belief is not merely based on conjecture or unfounded theories; rather it is the natural result of the work the PCSO was intended to do. Your work is grounded in implementing 'managed neighbourhood policing', which entails sustained efforts to provide community engagement through genuine consultation. As part of what we have called a **conduit** to a partnership approach, your work with and for minority communities can also be included. The PCSO provides a highly visible presence to deter crime and anti-social behaviour, as well as supplying reassurance to the community.

---

**Task**

What other roles can you identify that PCSOs might bring to the communities in which they work?

---

#### 6.6.2.1 **Knowing the community…**

Other dimensions which the PCSO brings to the neighbourhood management equation are local knowledge and expertise, which will have been built up through hard work, positive interaction with members of all communities, and efforts to foster trust and confidence within the neighbourhood (all part of the engagement and partnership approach).

#### 6.6.2.2 **…and its background**

It is important to know some background to the minority communities you are working with, in the same way that research is crucial in any problem-solving approach. Do you consider that your knowledge of diverse communities is enough to answer these questions?

---

**Task**

Answer the following questions:

1. What is a Sikh temple called?
2. To the nearest million, how many people in the UK are defined as disabled under the Disability Discrimination Act?
3. What are Gammon, Shelta, and Cant?
4. What meat do Hindus abstain from eating?
5. What are the five basic duties for followers of Islam?
6. Where is Kosovo?
7. What is homophobia?
8. What are Ashkenazi and Sephardi(m)?

---

9. What is gender dysphoria?
10. Name any language spoken within the UK-based Chinese community.

Our model response

We suggest that these might be the answers which you may have researched (but did you *remember*?).

1. A *Gurdwara*
2. 10 million (figure from the Disability Rights Commission <http://www.direct.gov.uk/en/DisabledPeople/DG_10023362>
3. They are languages spoken by the gypsy-traveller community
4. Beef—the cow is considered to be sacred
5. **Shahadah**—declaration of one's faith; **Salah**—five compulsory daily prayers; **Zakah**—tithing of money to charity; **Sawm**—fasting during Ramadan; **Hajj**—the pilgrimage to Mecca (if you can afford it)
6. South-West Europe (think Adriatic Sea) bordered by Serbia, Montenegro, Albania, Macedonia, and Bulgaria
7. A fear, dislike, or prejudice directed towards lesbian, gay, or bisexual people, or a fear, dislike, or prejudice directed towards their perceived lifestyles, cultures, or characteristics
8. Ashkenazi—Jewish people originating from Central and Eastern Europe; Sephardi or Sephardim—Jewish people originating from Spain, North Africa, or Arabic (Middle East) regions
9. 'Gender dysphoria' is the accepted term for **transgender.** Remember this is about gender identity not sexuality
10. Mandarin, Cantonese, Hakka.

### 6.6.2.3 The immutability of the PCSO role from community to community

Putting this task in here was not to show off our knowledge or to highlight some possible gaps in your detailed understanding of diverse minority issues, rather it was to show that *it can be difficult for anyone to be aware of all issues across all minority communities.* You are not expected to be an expert on the communities that you work with, but you are expected to provide neighbourhood policing to all groups within your area of work and to ensure that they are part of the overall engagement process. **The role of the PCSO does not alter from community to community.** However, you should be aware of the particular issues within those communities which you specifically support, and ensure that you are being responsive to their diverse needs. Remember to ask if you don't know, and never to be too proud to seek help. Most communities will courteously explain themselves to you (if a trifle wearily sometimes). If you show a genuine interest, this will also galvanize the interest of those members of the groups who talk to you.

- **Diversity training**—this should have formed part of your PCSO Induction course and covered the main areas for your role. It will have involved discussion of the issues facing many communities in England and Wales, as well as wider issues relating to discrimination and equality.
- **Cultural awareness booklets**—some police forces produce for their staff cultural awareness booklets that identify key points in relation to diverse communities. These can be an invaluable source of information and have practical uses: for example there may be a section on the protocols of entering places of worship. Accessing this information could prevent you causing offence through ignorance.
- **Community Liaison Officers**—most police forces will have dedicated Community Liaison Officers, often part of the Neighbourhood Policing Team, whose job is to promote better community relations. They will be a good source of information about communities and can help you to identify key people within your neighbourhood with whom you should make contact.
- **Other agencies/support groups**—within your area there may be support groups dedicated to particular groups that offer help and advice to that community. Again, they can be accessed to provide information about a community: researching this mine of information would be a good first task on your arrival in a new BCU or 'beat'.
- **Police support groups**—within your Force there will be support groups available to police officers and police staff based on the diversity strands (race, sexual orientation, gender, disability, religion—maybe not age yet) and these can also offer support in making contact with community groups. Are you aware of the existence of these groups within your Force? Are there representatives in your BCU or your local police station?
- **Communities themselves**—as a PCSO, part of your role is to go and speak to people in the community, so you would be sensible to extend the same approach to the diverse communities represented in your neighbourhood, such as elderly groups (identified as one of the 'hard to reach' groups). Perhaps too, going to events organized for that community would be a good chance to get your face known and to speak to people about the issues facing them and to ask them what they want from neighbourhood policing. It also affords you the opportunity to ask about areas you are unsure of concerning that particular group. If invited into a mosque, you can ask what the culture and traditions demand if you are unsure. This in itself will demonstrate a willingness to learn and you will be respected for your politeness.
- **You**—you are a resource because you can gain the knowledge of a community, either through your own research, or by speaking to people within that community. We talked about the PCSO being a conduit for the partnership approach but also the PCSO can be a channel or route for improved community relations. You can achieve much in terms of raising people's diversity awareness through your own example.

---

**Task**

Looking at these sources of information/knowledge, how many have you utilized in your work so far?

Are there others, not on our list, that you can identify from your community?

---

### 6.6.3 **Not all groups will welcome you**

The PCSO has a proactive, outward-reaching role in seeking to involve diverse communities in the neighbourhood process which involves getting out there and making contact and dealing with the issues raised in the same way as with any other group. But it does come with a caveat. Not all groups will be responsive to approaches from the police and so your work will deal with local issues and problems rather than trying to eradicate entire social ills or change deep-seated discriminatory behaviour. Improved community relations will not happen overnight nor will relationships be established through one isolated contact, however well-meaning and informed:

> Although universal popular approval for the police can never be a realistic aim of police–community relations policies, improved dialogue with marginalised groups may provide the opportunities for addressing aspects of policing that exacerbate adversarial relationships. At a minimum, it should enhance the possibility of achieving some workable compromises.

This is not meant to put you off making the effort but rather to make sure that your expectations are realistic. Improvements can, and will occur, but **they take time.** Professor 'Tank' Waddington has discussed, in *Police Review*, research from the USA by Wesley Skogan, which concluded that **it didn't matter what the police did, they would receive little credit for it from the community.** If true (and the research is partial and US-focused), it is a depressing negative. In fact, of course, the public's attitudes to the police cannot be simplistically attributed to the PCSO without more convincing and local surveys.

---

**Knowledge Check 30**

1. When and what was the Macpherson Inquiry?

2. What are 'hard to reach' groups?

3. Give four examples of such groups.

4. What might be a problem with the term 'hard to reach'?

5. What is 'ethnocentricity'?

6. Give two examples of the resources available to a PCSO when engaging with diverse communities.

---

## 6.7 **Ethics and Standards of Conduct**

We need to say something about ethical behaviour and codes of conduct at this point, almost at the end of our book, because it is a subject that is gaining in importance. Indeed the College of Policing has launched a *Code of Ethics* for police officers and police staff, which of course includes you. The terms of the *Code* are not far removed from the ethical standards specified in Police Regulations, or those which underpin the Professional Standards Department in your Force. The 'new' 'Standards of Professional Behaviour' in the College's *Code* (published in July 2014) are predicated on the assumption that you and your colleagues will use the highest and most proportionate standards of

1. Honesty and integrity
2. Authority, respect, and courtesy
3. Equality and diversity
4. Use of force
5. Orders and instructions
6. Duties and responsibilities
7. Confidentiality
8. Fitness for work
9. Conduct
10. Challenging and reporting improper conduct.

These should be familiar, because they are derived in part from Police Regulations and are brought together for all members of the public 'police family' (see <http://www.college.police.uk/en/20972.htm>). And it isn't rocket science either: most of us, given time and the inclination, could come up with a similar set of principles of guidance by which conduct in public office is governed. An important addition is the 'use of force' to ensure compliance, which we discussed extensively in the PCSO context in Chapter 3 and again in Chapter 5. Make yourself familiar with the provisions in the *Code of Ethics* as soon as practicable, because they are now operative across England and Wales for all police and police staff. It is evident too, that the *Code* is seen by some as a step towards the 'professionalization' of police services. The College's CEO (CC Alex Marshall) comments in his Introduction:

> The Code of Ethics is one step towards obtaining full professional status for policing, similar to that seen in medicine and law.

We are not sure that policing is anywhere close to medicine or the law in terms of professionalization: making policing a graduate profession is surely a precursor as will be some form of 'doctrine' or 'knowledge repository' of police practice and wisdom on a par with the statute law and scientific medical knowledge. However, it is no bad thing to have such an aspiration. We're just not there yet.

A further provision is the clear statement of *'Policing Principles'*, which set out the 'spirit' of accountability that is behind the 'letter' of the *Code*:

**Accountability**
You are answerable for your decisions, actions and omissions.

**Fairness**
You treat people fairly.

**Honesty**
You are truthful and trustworthy.

**Integrity**
You always do the right thing.

**Leadership**
You lead by good example.

**Objectivity**
You make choices on evidence and your best professional judgement.

**Openness**
You are open and transparent in your actions and decisions.

**Respect**
You treat everyone with respect.

**Selflessness**
You act in the public interest.

To those of us who have been in public service for a couple of decades or more, this is redolent of Lord Nolan's 'Seven Principles of Conduct in a Public Office' (Nolan, 1995), and of course we would expect them to be, since such principles are immutable (they don't really change) and the probity that was required in a public or Crown servant 20 years ago is still required in 2015 and beyond.

### 6.7.1 **Professional Standards**

We discussed the nature of the standards expected of you as a PCSO at some length in Chapter 1. The reason for raising the subject again at this point is to look at a different aspect. Having joined the police, you have become a public servant. This is not a rehash of the discussion; it is more about what is expected of you in your role and the activities of the **Professional Standards Department** in your Force if things go wrong.

Another point to make is that the *Code* has the force of Statute, and there is no doubt that it will be invoked in any criminal proceedings against members of the police 'family' and will underpin any disciplinary processes. This is made clear in the opening paragraphs of the *Code*:

> As a code of practice, the legal status of the Code of Ethics [...] applies to the police forces maintained for the police areas of England and Wales as defined in section 1 of the Police Act 1996 (or as defined in any subsequent legislation).
>
> (Para 1.2.2)

That means that your Force's Professional Standards Department will use the provisions of the *Code of Ethics* in determining any action following a complaint about you or any investigation of your (of course, alleged) misconduct. Let's look at the process.

### 6.7.2 **Professional Standards Departments**

In every police force, there will be a **Professional Standards Department** (PSD) which used to be known as **Complaints and Discipline** (some old-style police officers will still call it that). This is a body composed largely of police officers, many of them detectives, who do specific jobs. What are these jobs?

As you might expect, details of the organization of PSDs vary from force to force, but most of them will be constituted like this:

| Complaints and discipline | Investigation |
| --- | --- |
| Police investigators | Police investigators (occasionally with police staff investigators) |
| Legal services | Security adviser(s) |
| Media advisers | Specialist surveillance staff |
| Administration and finance | Specialist technical staff |
| Freedom of Information responses, data protection issues, vetting for posts | Case preparation; liaison with **CPS** |
| Force standards, discipline, Police Regulations | |
| Application of the *Code of Ethics* (we think) | |

### 6.7.2.1 **Investigation of complaints and corruption**

As you can see, there is a dual role for PSDs: one side is to investigate **complaints** against members of the police force (which we think will now entail the *Code of Ethics*, but this has yet to be confirmed), and any serious infractions (breaking the rules) of **discipline;** the other is to **investigate** corruption or criminality among police officers and police staff. The complaints and discipline side can range from the trivial to the major, whilst the investigation side deals only with the major. There is no such thing as trivial corruption. Whilst we do not suppose for a moment that readers of this book would find themselves under investigation for corruption, you will excuse us for not going into detail. It is hard enough detecting corruption and criminality in the world at large. Doing it within a police force and investigating the actions of officers or police staff who may have detailed knowledge of techniques of surveillance and so on, is very hard indeed. So we will leave the investigation part of Professional Standards to one side and look instead at the part of PSD which we expect might concern you.

### 6.7.2.2 **Responses to you: complaints**

It is inevitable that, in your daily interactions with the public, there will be occasional friction. There may be times when, try as you might, someone cannot accept that s/he has done something wrong and that you are remonstrating, however gently, with him or her about behaviour. Equally, there may be times when you might get your responses spectacularly wrong, by being heavy handed, over-zealous, or too proscriptive of the behaviour of others. Parents will often refuse to accept that their children could possibly have done anything wrong or mischievous. 'Litterers' may not accept that they have dropped packages or food carelessly; they may even deny that the litter is theirs. There is often an aggressive response, as we noted earlier in Chapter 5, from those who have been caught out, whether cycling on a footpath or drinking under age. In addition, people may have exaggeratedly high expectations of what you can do (or what they think you can do), and may feel disappointed and let down when you cannot deliver; stereotypically for example, the unease elderly people feel when they see groups of young people 'hanging about'. You may not want to penalize the young people in the way the elderly might wish; even 'moving on' groups of people who have done nothing wrong may give rise to complaint. Some of this will be down to how well you manage expectations, but you cannot expect to please everyone.

### 6.7.2.3 **Formal complaints from the public**

This can translate itself into a complaint about your conduct. Such complaints are sometimes justified, especially if you have been unfair, a bit officious about enforcement, or you have not treated people with respect. At other times such complaints will be malicious, because the offender wants to get back at you for catching him or her out. Rarely, the complainant will be a 'serial litigant': the sort who complains about everything and who goes to law or to the discipline process on the slightest pretext. Your legal department will know who such people are and how best to deal with them. **It is the job of the Professional Standards Department to find out if the complaint is justified or not.** If it is justified, the outcome is sometimes financial compensation for the complainant, hence the need for the involvement of finance advisers and staff on the complaints side. If it is not justified, there is no further recourse other than an unblemished record for you and a note in PSD of the outcome. It is most unlikely that you will be able to counter-sue the complainant.

---

**KEY POINT**

There are further outcomes if the complaint against you is justified or upheld. What do you think these outcomes may be?

---

### 6.7.2.4 **Outcomes**

The additional outcomes, other than the payment of compensation to the aggrieved party, may range from the relatively minor, such as written 'advice' to you to mend your ways and behave differently in the future, to a major discipline enquiry leading to a hearing of your conduct in front of a chief officer. The worst outcomes of all might be that you are dismissed from the force and face criminal charges.

### 6.7.2.5 **An example of the disciplinary investigation process**

There is a spectrum of discipline, from treating the experience as a learning point right through to criminal trial, in which the complaint and discipline side of PSD is involved. In the case of police staff, this may involve expert human resources input as well as the investigation of your conduct by police officers. See the case study below.

---

### Case Study: Operation Worst-Case Scenario

You are on patrol in the town centre when you see a group of youngish boys drinking from lager cans in the entrance to the pedestrian mall. On your approach, two or three run away. The remainder, about seven or eight in number, eye your approach and decide to brazen it out. Some of them are evidently intoxicated. Having opened the conversation by telling the group that drinking in this area is not allowed, you are met with abuse. You tell the group that you think they are underage drinkers and that you are going to seize their containers of alcohol. Three or four of the group hand over their cans, more or less sullenly. You pour the contents down the gutter and turn back to the remainder of the group. One boy, bigger than the rest, and much bigger than you, jostles you and elbows you in the face when you try to take his can. You grasp his arm and push back. The boy slips, falls, and bangs his head hard on the edge of a bench. He lies still, eyes closed, bleeding from a scalp wound. The other boys scatter.

..............................................................................................................................................

You render first aid and summon support, including an ambulance. You ensure that the boy is looked after at the Accident and Emergency Department of the local hospital and identify the boy so that his parents can be informed. He recovers and is not badly hurt. You write up your account in your PNB and talk it through with your supervisor. Apparently, photographs were taken of the incident on a spectator's mobile phone and the police have asked for this as evidence. The next thing you know, you are suspended from duty and a person from PSD has come to see you to say that the boy and his parents have made complaints about you, alleging excessive force, assault, and harassment. An investigation has been ordered and in due course you will be interviewed under caution. You are referred to your local Unison branch office to obtain support and representation.

---

### 6.7.2.6 **Burdens of proof in the investigation**

We have called this a 'worst-case scenario' and in many ways it is; but it is actually all too common, and variations on the theme of 'excessive force' will be routinely investigated by PSD, whether into police officers or police staff. The process is different for police officers, who are served with a '*Regulation 15*' notice informing them of the PSD's investigation. This is often accompanied by physical movement from the police station where the officer is based to another place, or by suspension of the officer, pending the investigation.

PCSOs face 'civilian' investigation (not under Police Regulations)
In the case of police staff, the disciplines under Police Regulations do not apply. You are subject to a 'civilian' investigation code (which *may* entail transfer or suspension, depending on what you are alleged to have done). Before you think that the 'civilian investigation' is a better option, be warned. The burdens of proof in the investigation of wrongdoing or indiscipline by police staff are '*on the balance of probabilities*', not 'beyond reasonable doubt', which is the standard of proof at court. This may mean that the complainant will not have to prove the complaint beyond the fact that what is alleged 'probably happened', which is a much lower standard of proof. The investigative process is likely to entail enquiry into the allegation that you have breached the *Code of Ethics* (what used to be called 'misconduct in a public office').

### 6.7.2.7 **Investigation of alleged misconduct**

The other faintly scary aspect to all this is that you will be investigated, almost certainly, by police officers (rarely by police staff investigators) whom you do not know. The whole process may also take quite a long time: it is not unknown, for example, for an investigation into alleged misconduct to last nine months or a year. The person complained of (in this case you), may be the last to be interviewed. This might mean that you do not work with the community for a long time and will be interviewed only towards the end of that time. It is hard to sustain your morale all the while, especially since you will not necessarily be informed about the progress of the case against you. We hasten to add that this is only in the most extreme of cases, and you will have meetings with advisers in the interim (legal counsel may be provided by Unison, if you are a member, in very serious cases). One of the perennial complaints against PSDs is the length of time they take to investigate complaints, but, in their defence, the allegations have to be investigated meticulously and impartially, so that there can be no additional complaint of 'whitewash'. That said, PSDs can be overcautious and sluggish. You will only be suspended from duty if the allegation against you is very serious; otherwise you will be transferred or given a different role. Sometimes, you will be left *in situ*. Whatever the interim measures, the investigation into the complaint against you will be going on quietly in the background.

### 6.7.2.8 **The IPCC**

Sometimes really serious complaints (such as the lethal discharge of a weapon by a firearms officer, or a death in custody) may result in an investigation by the **Independent Police Complaints Commission** (IPCC), a statutory body which, as the name suggests, independently investigates allegations of wrongdoing by the police. In our case study, the IPCC is not invoked and the complaint from the parents and boy against you is handled internally.

---

**DISCUSSION POINT**

Your turn: what do you think that the outcome of the investigation into your actions will be?

---

How the case may turn out

It could go either way. The allegation against you is serious: you struck the boy, it is alleged, and occasioned actual bodily harm. The case outcome might depend on the recovery of the photographs or film on the bystander's mobile phone and also upon the testimony of witnesses—including the boys who saw it all happen.

Our model response

Our reading of this investigation (and we don't know what other complaints the PSD turned up about you) would be that you were innocent of assault, and that all you did was resist an attack launched by the drunken complainant. However, we would advise you that you blundered into the situation rather, and it might have been better in retrospect if you had called for back-up once it was evident that some of the drinkers were aggressively intoxicated. Remember the **Rules of Engagement** (see 2.2.5.2)? It's a fine judgement though, and you could well come out of the investigation without a single blemish.

### 6.7.3 **Complaints are part of the territory**

Experienced police officers will tell you that you are most unlikely to go through your police career without a complaint against you. Indeed, you would be unlikely to go for a year without complaint from someone that you were oppressive, heavy-handed, interfering, or incompetent, or that you exceeded your authority. Whenever you have some sort of confrontation with a member of the public, remember to note it in your PNB. If the Professional Standards Department (PSD) is called in to investigate a complaint against you, your meticulous PNB entries and records of what happened could make the difference between a *'balance of probability'* guilty charge and your exoneration from blame. It is important to add that the role of the questioner from PSD is professional, not personal. Whilst most of the Force may regard the PSD with some reserve, the officers in the department have a job to do. They are posted in and out as they are in any other part of the Force and they bring to the role the same professionalism, detachment, and 'imperturbable courtesy' which we hope you bring to yours.

---

**Task**

Get to know your Force PSD.

---

Some PSDs undertake close contacts with the rest of their Forces through open sessions, publicity about Force standards, and training inputs. Others remain professionally aloof, but that doesn't mean that staff in PSDs won't talk to you about what they do. Just don't expect detail about cases.

Above all, expect that, however ethically, straightforwardly, and honestly you behave in the course of your career as a PCSO, there will be complaints about you at some time. It comes with the territory.

**Knowledge Check 31**

1. Who has produced a policing Code of Ethics?

2. What is the PSD?

3. Give three of the 'professional standards'. Give two instances of expected 'right' behaviour.

4. What two roles are played by PSD?

5. When might there be friction in your job?

6. What is the 'civilian' burden of proof?

7. Who investigate really serious complaints?

## 6.8 General Summary

The last few years have seen the proposal and then the shelving of amalgamation of police forces. We have seen the rise of intelligence-led policing and its partial replacement by neighbourhood policing, which is now called community policing. We have witnessed the formation of SOCA and the NPIA and their dissolution; the disappearance of the National Crime Squad and the National Criminal Intelligence Service; the absorption of Centrex (police training) and PITO into NPIA; we have seen the National Crime Agency take over international and regional crime investigation in 2013, and we have seen the College of Policing take over police training, standards, ethics, and national guidance in the same year, whilst also taking over some parts of ACPO's self-appointed remit to speak for the Police Service; we have witnessed an increase in the accurate recovery of minute forensic evidence, including mitochondrial DNA; and we have seen the gradual erosion of the traditional role of the police officer in favour of a radical extension of the police family.

Police budgets have been cut heavily and financial support is reducing annually: there is not the money to do what the police used to do, and facilities, resources, staff, and equipment have all been reduced as a result of constraint. We have noted the abrupt and seismic change consequent on the arrival of the Police Crime Commissioner in late 2012; for the first time, the police are held to account by a democratically elected (if only by a very small absolute number) representative of the people. Power has moved, tangibly, from the police hierarchy to the PCC, to a general chorus of approval from all but the police ranks themselves. The Home Secretary has told the Police Federation to reform or be abolished (May 2014): the first ultimatum of its kind to the police 'staff association' and her message was received in stunned silence. Policing itself seems to be in a state of constant change, constant development, perpetual adjustment, and alignment. Nothing seems to stay the same. At the same time, we have encountered an unprecedented number of new laws and statutes introduced by successive governments, we have experienced political initiatives to deal with communities, from the 'Respect' agenda to the use of ASBOs, and we have all tried to come to terms with the meaning of the fear of crime in our communities.

### 6.8.1 Policing is mutable

You are a part of this broad change and flux. Though you probably cannot appreciate it amid the daily flurry of patrol, briefing, community contact, entries in your PNB, and dealing with a NTP remit, you too are a catalyst for change. After all, a dozen or so years ago your job did not exist and now you are very close to becoming a fixture in your neighbourhood. You need to pause a moment, and reflect on what that means.

### 6.8.1.1 Being a professional

Stopping to look at the scope and speed of change can leave one slightly breathless, and it is of little comfort to note that many of the initiatives that we have just mentioned have been false starts and some of the innovations, particularly those master-minded by politicians, lacked all contact with reality. To write about the future, then, is to invite ridicule if you get it wrong. The nature of being a professional in the police family is a central theme in this book, and we have tackled front-on what being a professional means in your everyday duties.

### 6.8.1.2 Continuing Debate

We have come to the end of our attempts to provide insights into the world of policing for the especial benefit of the PCSO, and to the conclusion of our debate and discussion about the sorts of things which PCSOs are being asked to do as they deploy with their police forces. We have emphasized throughout that merely referential concentration on PCSO Powers or the NOS and Behavioural Competences is not enough. **What PCSOs need is a context, a means whereby they can judge the value and the meaning of what they do.** If we have given you that context, we've done what we set out to achieve.

# Answers to Knowledge Checks

## Knowledge Check 1

1. Motivation is what drives or encourages you to do something. Many consider a role in the police service, nursing, teaching etc as a vocation/calling which requires exceptional levels of commitment and dedication. Applicants need to be aware that there are high expectations linked to the role, and only motivated individuals will prosper. Anyone with an attitude of 'that will do' will be found wanting very quickly and will most likely not get through the recruitment process.
2. 'Drive' is what motivates you, 'potential' is what you are capable of achieving.
3. They are looking for real-life examples that support the candidate's assertions.
4. Discretion is deciding what best to do in the circumstances. Taking actions proportionate to the problem is part of discretion.
5. Making someone an outcast because s/he is a member of a group we fear.
6. Strong personal emotions may get in the way of doing the job and may cloud a PCSO's judgement. Assessors at interview may reject those applicants who feel before they think.
7. What you are and what you do (discrimination has no place in policing).
8. Motives for doing things (conceits, desires, ambitions, hopes, and wish fulfilment).

## Knowledge Check 2

1. Resilience, Effective Communication, Respect for Race and Diversity, Personal Responsibility, and Teamworking.
2. Community and Customer Focus (not tested because you are unlikely to have experience of it as an applicant).
3. '*Understands other people's points of view and takes those views into account when responding to them; treating all people, irrespective of their appearance, or what they may have done, with dignity and respect all the time, whatever the situation or circumstance.*'
4. Continuous Professional Development (attaining and sustaining your behavioural competences are part of this process).
5. Positive and Negative.
6. An abbreviated word, or the initial letters of a number of words which make up a new 'word', like ACPO or MAPPA.
7. The 'protected characteristics' are what used to be called 'strands of diversity' or 'grounds of equality'. The nine characteristics are: age, disability, gender reassignment, marriage and civil partnership, pregnancy and maternity, race, religion or belief, sex, and sexual orientation.
8. Respect for Race and Diversity; failure in this competence means that you are unlikely to be accepted as a PCSO.

9. There are several. This is what we noted:

[…] *you actively support the team and individuals within it to achieve the objectives and that in doing so you are cooperative and friendly with others, whom you support. You are always willing to help others, but not afraid to ask for help yourself, and you develop mutual trust and confidence in those with whom you work. You willingly take on unpopular or routine tasks and you take pride in any of the teams of which you are a member.*

## Knowledge Check 3

1. Examples of how you meet some of the competences.
2. Applying to be considered; attending an assessment centre; passing medical, security, and reference tests.
3. Your National Insurance number, or, if you are not a British National, your passport number.
4. Convictions, cautions, 'spent' convictions, and any other offences (such as fixed penalty notices, speeding fines).
5. Your 'immediate or close family' is special to you but it might contain:

[…] *your mother, father, stepfather or stepmother, mother's or father's partner brother(s) and sister(s)—full, half or step, your spouse or partner, your spouse's or partner's parents or step-parents, your children (over 10 years), your partner's children (over 10 years), any grandchildren or step-grandchildren (over the age of 10), any other adults living at your address.*

6. Bankruptcy, county court judgments against you, and any large or unsecured debts (not mortgages).
7. Your current employment first and work backwards by date to your first employment.
8. Two: one 'character' referee and one employer or tutor referee.
9. Education broadly is about what you know and skills are broadly about what you can do (of course the line between them is blurred).
10. Because a substantial clash of values or a substantial difficulty in understanding another person and how you resolved the problem will tell assessors a lot about your suitability to be a PCSO.
11. Dealing with someone who was hearing impaired (deaf).
12. Questions to help you structure your replies.
13. Any four from :

*[G]o on highly visible uniformed foot patrols, support Community Beat Officers and Community Action Teams in solving local problems, make house visits to gather intelligence and offer public reassurance after minor crimes or anti-social behaviour, get involved with key people in the community, such as community, religious, and business leaders, work with Community Watch, Neighbourhood Watch, Business Watch, Pub Watch, Farm Watch, and Horse Watch schemes, protect crime scenes until police officers arrive, collect CCTV evidence, provide low-level crime prevention and personal safety advice, carry out low-level missing person enquiries, act as professional witnesses, attend court when needed, support crime prevention, engage with youths, interact with schools, support the Mobile Police Station, support Community Safety Partnerships.*

Note that this list is indicative, not definitive.

14. The Declaration.
15. Three and a half hours.
16. An interview, two competence tests, and two scenarios.
17. Little plays.
18. An actor, or someone pretending to be someone else.
19. '[I]n good health, of sound constitution and able both mentally and physically to perform the duties of a PCSO once appointed.'
20. Because your work will involve a great deal of physical activity, and the fitter you are, the better you will do it. Many police forces now routinely begin each training day with a run or some form of intensive aerobic exercise.

## Knowledge Check 4

1. 'Right behaviour' (including things like honesty, integrity, values, and standards).
2. *Police (Conduct) Regulations* 2012.
3. The ethical standards in *Police (Conduct) Regulations* 2012 include the following:

*Officers should respect confidentiality—they must not disclose confidential information unless authorized and they should not use confidential information for their personal benefit.*

*Police officers must act with fairness and impartiality in their dealings with the public and their colleagues.*

*Officers should avoid being 'improperly beholden' to any person or institution.*

*They should be open and truthful in their dealings.*

*They should discharge their duties with integrity.*

*They must obey all lawful orders.*

*Officers should oppose any improper behaviour, reporting it where appropriate.*

*Officers should treat members of the public and colleagues with courtesy and respect, avoiding abusive or derisive attitudes or behaviour. Think of the 'Nine Protected Characteristics' in this context, too (see Answer 8, also).*

*Officers must avoid favouritism of an individual or group; all forms of harassment, victimization, or unreasonable discrimination; and overbearing conduct to a colleague, particularly to one junior in rank or service.*

*Officers must never knowingly use more force than is reasonable, nor should they abuse their authority. Note that this is now embedded in the* Code of Ethics.

*Officers should be conscientious and diligent in the performance of their duties.*

*They should attend work promptly when rostered for duty.*

*Officers on duty must be sober.*

*Officers should always be well turned out, clean, and tidy.*

*Whether on or off duty, officers should not behave in a way which is likely to bring discredit upon the police service. But see also the College of Policing's* Code of Ethics, *published in July 2014, and discussed in Chapter 6. The* Code *replicates much of what is in Police Regulations but adds in what acceptable behaviours should be and what behaving ethically means.*

4. It is wrong to have an obligation to someone that gets in the way of your duty.
5. The National College of Policing.
6. IPCC and HMIC.
7. The same impartial respect.

8. The nine 'protected characteristics' are: age, disability, gender reassignment, marriage and civil partnership, pregnancy and maternity, race, religion or belief, sex, and sexual orientation. This is the second time we have asked you this question, so now you should be getting all nine perfectly!

9. A scale devised by an American psychologist, Gordon Allport, in 1953 which shows graphically how prejudicial treatment of minority groups can escalate and intensify.

10. 'Bad-mouthing' or prejudicial comment about members of a minority group.

## Knowledge Check 5

1. Community Support Officers in rural community support, not paid by the police.
2. Your appointment is made by a chief constable to a police force (section 38 of the *Police Reform Act* 2002).
3. Swyddog Cefnogi Cymuned yr Heddlu or SCCH.
4. Knowledge, Understanding, Skills, Attitudes, and Behaviours.
5. Any four from: police ranks, powers, crime scene investigation, gathering evidence, using a PNB, anti-social behaviour interventions, working with communities, engaging in partnerships, personal safety training, physical fitness, communications, first aid, human rights, race and diversity, or 'protected characteristics'.
6. A tendency to expand the PCSO job beyond its original remit and into areas traditionally the preserve of the police.

## Knowledge Check 6

1. Between three and eight weeks; there is no common route, though the Wider Police Family Initial Development Programme is intended to regularize what PCSOs are taught before patrolling with a tutor. Forces still differ in how much is formally taught at the start.
2. Your authority from your Chief Constable, usually specifying your powers.
3. Any three from: patrol, intelligence gathering, road safety, community 'surgery', interventions to deal with anti-social behaviour, dealing with littering, chairing and attending meetings, seizing alcohol or tobacco from juveniles, conducting a truancy sweep, manning police cordons, mediating in disputes, meeting local representatives of business and community, directing traffic, administering first aid, taking a statement from a victim, and many more.
4. Policing, reassurance, increasing orderliness, and accessibility.
5. Missing persons searches.

## Knowledge Check 7

1. Among the 'wider police family' are *'private policing' organizations, roads policing with the Department of Transport, 'immigration police' in the UK Border Agency, the Security Industries Authority, which licenses 'door stewards' among others, rural wardens, community support officers paid for from local authority funds, schools security officers, police staff, police and crime commissioners, and public/private investment schemes (PPIs).*
2. Unison.

3. In a 2006 Survey by the Home Office.
4. *Effectiveness* in reassurance, reducing anti-social behaviour, increasing confidence and *efficiency* (engaging in tasks that free up regular police officers).

## Knowledge Check 8

1. To determine how someone died.
2. Justices of the Peace (experienced lay magistrates).
3. A legally qualified person who is paid to hear and judge cases at the magistrates' court.
4. Those that attract fines or community service penalties rather than imprisonment.
5. The *Coroners and Justice Act* of 2009.
6. A hearing at magistrate level to refer a serious criminal case to the Crown Court.
7. 'Having the body': someone charged with a criminal offence must be produced in person in court.
8. A judge, sitting with a jury in 'not guilty' pleas.
9. The *Human Rights Act* of 1998.
10. The right to a fair trial.
11. Absolute rights, limited rights, and qualified rights.

## Knowledge Check 9

1. Primarily from the *Police Reform Act* of 2002, but also from your Designation by your Chief Constable.
2. A Police and Crime Commissioner, who also employs you.
3. We don't expect you to get all of the explanation, but essentially it is about your professional standards:

   *you are expected to perform to the expected professional standards for a PCSO (or indeed, to the professional standards of any member of the police staff). You will be expected to adhere to Force ethical norms and standards, to carry out your duties diligently and with proper expertise and skill, and to conform to Force priorities and operational orders (rather than going off and doing what you feel like). You are expected to behave as one entrusted with a public office should behave: honourably, fairly, without discrimination (without prejudice), always demonstrating high levels of skill and knowledge.*

   Note the role of the College of Policing's *Code of Ethics* (July 2014) in this context.

4. 'Capable' refers to having the required physical fitness and mental resilience to do the job properly.
5. **Statute law** includes Acts of Parliament; **common law** was not written down but was agreed by our ancestors as the expected behaviour of a civilized society, such as laws against theft or murder.
6. Parliamentary Acts (primary) and *subordinate* (secondary) legislation such as orders or regulations.
7. At a magistrates' court.
8. Either in a magistrates' court or at a Crown Court—depending on the seriousness of the offence (for example theft of a little or a lot of money).
9. An 'indictable only' or serious criminal offence, heard before a judge and jury.

10. To be found guilty of a criminal offence a suspect must not only carry out a **criminal act (*actus reus*)** but it must be also proved that the person did so with a **guilty mind (*mens rea*)**.
11. Code C, dealing with *'the detention, treatment and questioning of persons'*.
12. A **police caution** is a formal warning given by a senior police officer to an adult who has admitted his/her guilt.
13. A person under the age of 17.
14. The issuing of a document called a **written charge**.
15. *'**pro bono publico**'*—means 'for the public good' rather than private gain.

## Knowledge Check 10

1. A Fixed Penalty Notice (FPN) under para 1(2)b of Sch 4 of the *Police Reform Act* 2002.
2. Throwing fireworks, trespassing on a railway.
3. Paras 5 and 6 of Schedule 4 of the *Police Reform Act* 2002.
4. Seize drugs.
5. *Criminal Justice Act* 1967, section 91.

## Knowledge Check 11

1. You have the power to require a cyclist to stop, to give you their name and address, and you may give the offender an FPN for riding on a footway.
2. Level 3 fine.
3. Section 87 of The *Environmental Protection Act*.
4. Littering as an offence.
5. You can't issue a PND; this is a level 4 offence.
6. A fixed penalty notice (FPN).
7. Reasonable excuse, registered blind person, owner consents, subsequently disposes properly of the faeces.
8. Failure to give name and address when required (para 1A(5) of Sch 4 of the *Police Reform Act* 2002).
9. ADVOKATE and noted in your PNB.

## Knowledge Check 12

1. Any two of the following offences under the *Licensing Act* 2003:
   1. *Selling or attempting to sell alcohol to a person who is drunk (PND),* **s 141**.
   2. *Obtaining alcohol for a person who is drunk (not PND),* **s 142**.
   3. *Selling alcohol to a person under 18 years (PND),* **s 146(1)**.
   4. *Purchasing alcohol by a child (not PND),* **s 149(1)(a)**.
   5. *Purchasing alcohol on behalf of a child (not PND),* **s 149(3)(a)**.
   6. *Purchasing alcohol on behalf of a child for consumption on relevant premises (not PND),* **s 149(4)(a)**.
   7. *Consuming alcohol by a person under 18 years (PND),* **s 150(1)**.
   8. *Allowing a child under 18 years to consume alcohol (PND),* **s 150(2)**.
   9. *Sending a child to obtain alcohol (not PND),* **s 152(1)**.

2. • a county council,
   • a district council,
   • a parish council,
   • a London Borough Council, and
   • the chief constable of the police force for the area has agreed its inclusion in the list.

3. A designated PCSO under para 3 of S4PRA02 has the same power as a police officer under s 50 PRA02 to require any person s/he believes to have been acting in an anti-social way to give his or her name and address.

4. S/he may await the arrival of a police officer or request the suspect to accompany him/her to a police station.

5. You have the power to require the name and address of a driver who refuses to comply with a traffic direction from a PCSO who is for the time being directing traffic and pedestrians for the purposes of escorting abnormal loads, under s 165(1) of the RTA88.

6. A designated PCSO has the power to require a person whom s/he believes is or has been consuming, or intends to consume alcohol in a designated public place, not to consume that alcohol and to surrender any alcohol or container for alcohol.

7. You can dispose of it according to your Force policy (you can't drink it!).

8. You reasonably suspect the person is in possession of alcohol and that either:

   • s/he is under 18, or
   • s/he intends the alcohol to be consumed by a person under 18 in a relevant place, eg an adult supplying an under-18 with alcohol, or
   • s/he is or has been recently in the company of a person under 18 who has consumed alcohol in a relevant place, eg an adult who has recently accompanied an under-18-year-old who has alcohol.

9. You cannot require a person to remove any of his or her clothing in public other than an outer coat, jacket, or gloves.

10. That you suspect, or have cause to believe, that the person is under 16 years.

## Knowledge Check 13

1. Like a police officer, you have the power to enter and search *any* premises 'for the purpose of saving life and limb or preventing serious damage to life of property'.

2. Section 17(1)(e) of PACE 84.

3. Any place, including vehicle, vessel, aircraft, tent, or moveable structure.

4. You can stop and seize the vehicle under section 59 of PRA2002. 'Careless and inconsiderate driving' are offences respectively under sections 3 and 34 of the *Road Traffic Act* 1988.

5. *Removal and Disposal of Vehicles Regulations* 1986, amended by Statutory Instrument 746 in 2002 (but you knew that, didn't you?).

6. Specifically, you can direct a vehicle to stop, or make a vehicle proceed in or keep to a particular line of traffic. Such powers are normally used in support of traffic surveys, but you can also use such powers for example in directing other vehicles at the site of a road traffic collision.

7. Require name and address.

8. A senior police officer (under PACE, a Superintendent or above, unless in an emergency). The purpose of the check must be 'to locate a witness or suspect in connection with an indictable offence or a person unlawfully at large'.

9. [An] 'object or device (whether fixed or portable) for conveying to traffic on roads or any specified class of traffic, warnings, information, requirements, restrictions or prohibitions of any description'.

## Knowledge Check 14

1. '[W]hilst in the company and under the supervision of a police officer.'
2. Section 44 of the *Terrorism Act* 2000.
3. The person has been arrested; required to wait by a PCSO for the arrival of a police officer; and/or issued with a PND or FPN for a 'relevant offence'.
4. 'Any item or any substance worn on or over the whole or any part of the face or head.'
5. Purpose for which the photograph is taken.

   The use by, or disclosure for any purpose related to:

   • 'the prevention or detection of crime,
   • the investigation of an offence,
   • the conduct of the prosecution,
   • the enforcement of a sentence'.

   Having taken the photograph, the PCSO can retain it but it cannot be used or disclosed except for a related purpose.
6. 'Anything of a non-perishable nature which a person has in his/her possession or under his/her control, which you reasonably believe to have been used in the commission of an offence under s 6 *Royal Parks and Other Open Spaces Regulations* 1997.'
7. Under the *Education Act* of 1996, a truant is 'a child of compulsory school age who is registered and fails to attend school on a regular basis'.
8. 5 years to 16 years.
9. Section 16 of the *Crime and Disorder Act* 1998.

## Knowledge Check 15

1. Fixed Penalty Notice.
2. The person in charge of the dog has a reasonable excuse; or is a registered blind person; or has the consent of the owner, occupier, or authority of the land; or if the person puts the faeces in a suitable receptacle nearby.
3. 30 minutes.
4. To request the suspect to accompany you to a police station.
5. To prevent a suspect from making off.
6. One agreed between a chief constable and a relevant byelaw-making body.
7. A county council, a district council, a parish council, or a London Borough Council.
8. 'That you found the suspect begging for charitable donations in any of the below-named places; or that you found the suspect procuring or encouraging any child or children to beg for charitable donations in any public place, street, highway, court or passage.'

9. Such as a wound or deformity to obtain donations, or 'that the suspect endeavoured 'to obtain donations of any kind under any false or fraudulent pretences'.
10. Summary fine, not exceeding level 3.
11. Para 2A of Sch 4 of the PRA02; the same power as a police officer.
12. Something subjected to legal privilege, such as a letter to or from a solicitor.

## Knowledge Check 16

1. A written authorization by a senior police officer with the consent of the local authority to designate an area and your own Designation under para 4A of S4PRA02.
2. That you had reasonable grounds for believing that the presence or behaviour of that group has resulted, or is likely to result, in any members of the public being intimidated, harassed, alarmed, or distressed.
3. Curfew hours of 2100–0600.
4. 'To prevent children under 16 being in areas without a responsible adult.'
5. Seize and retain until a constable instructs you what to do with them.
6. Members-only clubs. Unless the premises being investigated is an off-licence, the PCSO has to be accompanied by a police officer.
7. Although 'authorized examiners' can test and inspect motor vehicles, they have no powers to stop vehicles in the first place.
8. That the suspect was drunk, behaved in a disorderly manner, and that the place where the person was drunk was a public place.
9. *Criminal Damage Act* 1971 s 1(1) or *Highways Act* 1980 s 132(1), but there is also PRA02.
10. A professional organizer of firework displays, operator of firework displays, firework manufacturer, firework supplier, local authority organizer of firework displays, entertainments' special effects organizer, Government organizer of firework displays, Armed Services organizer of firework displays or pyrotechnics (such as for military tattoos).
11. 'Any device intended for use as a form of entertainment which contains, or otherwise incorporates, explosive and/or pyrotechnic composition, which burns and/or explodes to produce a visual and/or audible effect.'
12. Causing wasteful employment of the police, sending annoying or offensive messages via a network, making false fire alarms.

## Knowledge Check 17

1. Threatening or abusive behaviour.
2. 'A public warning to persons not to trespass on the railway.'
3. Section 56(1) of the *British Transport Commission Act* 1949, 'that the person unlawfully threw, caused to fall, caused to strike at, against, into or upon, any engine, tender, motor carriage, or truck used upon or any works or equipment upon any railway or siding connected to a Railway Board', that the object was likely to cause damage or injury to persons or property, that you made a note of the description of the suspect, that you used ADVOKATE to evidence identification of the person (all the points to prove this time, in case you had forgotten *R v Turnbull*!).

4. Your power of arrest is the same as that of any non-police officer and is called 'arrest without warrant' or 'citizen's arrest'. The person arrested must have committed or be committing an indictable offence.

5. Prevention of injury to self and others, preventing the suspect suffering injury, preventing loss or damage, and preventing the subject from 'making off'.

6. You must make a record of the encounter and issue the person with a receipt.

7. If it is a general conversation, or you are giving directions, looking for witnesses, seeking general information, questioning people to get background to an incident, or issuing a PND.

## Knowledge Check 18

1. National Occupational Standards.

2. In your evidence portfolio, called a Student Officer Learning and Assessment Portfolio or SOLAP.

3. Twelve, then six.

4. By a percentage bar graphic.

5. Because they define what needs to be achieved: you are either competent or you are not (there is no room for 60 per cent competent for example).

6. Elements, 2 to 3 per Unit.

7. In Element 1 usually, but in KUSAB too.

8. Continuous professional development or CPD.

9. Any three from observation of work activity, observation of 'products', ADQs, testimony, explaining a process, written questions, projects, simulation, and role play.

10. People known to the police.

## Knowledge Check 19

1. The National Intelligence Model.

2. The gathering of information designed for action.

3. Information obtained about criminal intentions which criminals do not want known.

4. Acquisitive crime.

5. (1) How does the source know this? (2) Who else knows it?

6. Criminal intelligence is secret information obtained covertly about crimes and criminals, which is sanitized, assessed, and evaluated in order to mount police operations to disrupt, frustrate, or bring to justice, those involved.

7. Tasking and Coordinating process.

8. Using a '5x5x5' report (designed for the purpose).

9. Using a 'tick-box' mentality or a mechanistic approach to intelligence gathering that defeats its purpose.

10. A paid source of criminal intelligence.

11. A Covert Human Intelligence Source (one registered and authorized to be handled as a paid informant).

12. The *Regulation of Investigatory Powers Act* 2000, governing the use of CHIS.

13. The Surveillance Commissioner.

14. Any feature is removed that may identify the source of intelligence.

## Knowledge Check 20

1. The time immediately after first police arrival at a crime scene or incident is of vital importance for the preservation of evidence.
2. First Officer Attending a crime scene—could easily be you in the course of standard patrol.
3. Common Approach Path (to minimize disruption and/or contamination at a crime scene).
4. It might indicate the force used and the point of attack among other things.
5. Edmond Locard.
6. 'Every contact leaves a trace.'
7. '**Traces**' (paint, hairs, fibres, blood), '**impressions**' (fingerprints, footprints, tools, keyboards), and '**intangible data**' (such as that on computer hard drives, disks, or mobile phone data).
8. Because it cannot be disproven scientifically.
9. (1) preserve life and limb, (2) preserve evidence.

## Knowledge Check 21

1. Team Working, Community and Customer focus.
2. By positive and negative indicators.
3. Age, disability, gender reassignment, marriage & civil partnership, pregnancy & maternity, race, religion & belief, sex, and sexual orientation.
4. 2010 *Equality Act*.
5. Eliminate unlawful discrimination, harassment and victimization, advance equality of opportunity and foster good relations between different groups.

## Knowledge Check 22

1. Evidence-gathering during the investigation of offences.
2. Chronological (in time order).
3. Evidence: what you see, hear, touch, taste, or smell.
4. Word for word.
5. **NO** Erasures, Leaves torn out or Lines missed, Blank spaces, Overwriting, Writing between the lines, Spare pages.
6. To record, retain, and reveal.
7. 1976.
8. Significant statements and relevant comments.
9. Guilty action (*actus reus*) and guilty mind (*mens rea*).
10. (1) You do not have to say anything (2) But it may harm your defence if you do not mention (a) when questioned or (b) now something you later rely on in court (3) Anything you do say may be given in evidence.
11. A method of keeping track of physical evidence.
12. It might contain 'relevant material'.

## Knowledge Check 23

1. Sections 1–11 of the *Criminal Justice and Police Act* of 2001.
2. £80.

3. *Police Reform Act* 2002 (it empowers most aspects of being a PCSO).
4. Any two from:
    (a) Suspect does not understand (poor English or too drunk)
    (b) Suspect must be 'amenable' and 'cooperate fully'
    (c) Suspect may have committed two or more related offences
    (d) Suspect is under 16
    (e) Person over 16 commits offence with a person aged under 16
    (f) You are not satisfied with validity of age/identity/address.
5. FPN (1980s).
6. Non-endorsable and endorsable offences.
7. Notice to Owner (of a motor vehicle).
8. One to the police, one to the offender, and one to the Clerk of the magistrates' court.

## Knowledge Check 24

1. An official form (11th in a series) used to record a 'duty statement'.
2. A 'section nine statement' (from s 9 of the *Magistrates' Court Act* 1980).
3. Your collar/badge/PCSO number.
4. Time, day, date, location, PCSO status, and details of other persons present.
5. What a person actually said (verbatim speech).
6. All surnames/family names.
7. A paper clip (not a staple).
8. The Force address or the police station from which you operate. You do not put your own address lest the offender or others use this to target you for retaliation.

## Knowledge Check 25

1. 'Transforming one set of circumstances into another, preferable, state' (Michael Stevens).
2. Because no community is one-dimensional (homogeneous). There are many complex factors within communities and PCSOs have to be adaptable in their approaches to problems within those communities.
3. Any three of public meetings, 'surgeries', mobile police stations, questionnaires, and one-to-one discussions.
4. The physical and social fabric of their neighbourhoods (Home Office Report, 2005).
5. Factors to improve and repair neighbourhoods.
6. An alert review of the dangers or problems in real time and how to deal with them.
7. 'Early and decisive' intervention prevents a problem getting worse.
8. 900.
9. Any three from frustration, inarticulacy, anger, defensiveness, desire to escape, 'under the influence of drink or drugs', guilt (being caught), and fear.
10. When in danger of assault, withdraw.
11. 'Active resistance'.
12. Because if pushed, struck, or rushed, you can step back on to your stronger leg and resist.
13. Fight or flight (or freeze).
14. Dopamine, norephrine, nor-adrenaline, cortisol, and endorphins.

15. Options, Actions, Powers, Risk assessments, and PLAN.
16. Proportionate, Legal, Authorized, Necessary.

## Knowledge Check 26

1. The 'preservation of life and limb' over-rides all other considerations.
2. The risk of severe injury, such as to your back, or a hernia or a rupture.
3. You may yourself become a casualty and exacerbate the original problem.
4. Risk = hazard x likelihood.
5. Generic, specific, and dynamic.
6. Refer the casualty for professional medical assessment.
7. Situation, Plan, Risks, Alternatives, INcrease safety.
8. Weather conditions.

## Knowledge Check 27

1. It is used too generally, like 'society', and can apply to too many different things.
2. As collections of individuals with something in common and a feeling of 'belonging'.
3. Any two from: shared values, outlooks, concerns, origins, ethnicity, and beliefs.
4. 'Home', is the place where we feel most comfortable and most relaxed. But it can also be paradoxically where we can experience most fear or most vulnerability, because this 'home' is where our loved ones are located, where we enjoy our material possessions, where we keep the things which, if not intrinsically valuable, have most significance and 'value' for us.
5. Nearly all of us at some time or other, but particularly the elderly, the frail or housebound, the commuter who works away from the locality in the day, mothers at home with small children, and single parents.
6. Age primarily, but also gender, ethnicity, nationality, and social class.
7. Geographical Information System: giving data on all communities with a geography.
8. The **'available' population** is the people you are likely to encounter on the streets; the **resident population** are those who live in the area, but who might be absent on any given day.
9. National Census website, local estate agents' websites, or Zoopla (incorporating UpMyStreet).

## Knowledge Check 28

1. Belonging, ownership, participation, leadership, mutuality, rootedness, and ties.
2. The belief (often in the face of contrary evidence) that crime is rising, particularly in their location, and they feel threatened and menaced by it.
3. **Gender:** Women are more likely than men to feel that burglary and violent crime have risen; **Age:** Young people worry more about violence and car crime (although men and women in the 65 to 74 age group are most likely to perceive that there has been a significant increase in crime overall); **Ethnicity:** People from non-white ethnic groups are more likely to be concerned about crime than those from white groups; **Location:** Those living in urban areas are more likely to worry about crime that those who live in rural areas; **Accommodation:** Those living in the social

rented sector are more likely to worry about crime than those who rent privately or own their own homes; **Newspapers:** Readers of the 'red top' (tabloid) newspapers are more likely to worry about crime than those who read the 'broadsheets' or 'quality press'.

4. Kershaw *et al* (2008) p 126.
5. Upwards by 8 per cent.
6. 1981.
7. Some crime and disorder incidents function as warning signals to people about the distribution of risks to their security in everyday life. Some crime and disorder behaviours matter more than others in shaping the public's collective perceptions of risk.
8. 'Broken Windows' theory.
9. Expression, content, effect.
10. An authority response that seeks a solution to a particular problem.
11. Because good news stories may get wider distribution and help to reassure people.
12. An Environmental Visual Audit, or 'structured patch walk'.
13. The items listed are not necessarily indicative of a fear of crime within a community, but they do provide examples of things that give people a sense of unease: litter/rubbish strewn around, graffiti—racist/offensive?, vandalism, broken windows/fences, derelict houses, furniture in the garden, drugs paraphernalia, abandoned vehicles, prostitution—cards in the phone boxes, used condoms, 'cruising' cars, large groups of youths hanging about, dog mess, stray animals, broken street lighting—absence of lighting, alcohol debris.

## Knowledge Check 29

1. A means of transmission or communication; in our case between the community and the police through the PCSO.
2. Park authorities, local authority, housing association, education department or education groups in each school such as Boards of Governors, Health, Youth Services, local authority services, such as dog wardens, charities, local businesses, parents, the community itself and its representatives.
3. Community Safety Partnerships (CSPs).
4. The police, local authorities, Fire & Rescue service, the Probation Service, and Health.
5. To 'lead out' of a community its abilities to solve problems rather than imposing solutions from outside.
6. Partners And Communities Together (**nb**: not Police!).
7. Venue, rules, agenda, and chairperson.
8. Police representatives, housing officer, Neighbourhood Watch coordinator, faith leader(s), local business proprietors (or collective groups like the *Lions* or Chamber of Commerce), local councillors, parish councillors, residents' association members, representatives of local charities, school governors, head teachers, local authority officers, local citizens who have some prominent voice in the community.
9. Key Individual Network or contact list.

## Knowledge Check 30

1. 1999 legal inquiry into the death of Stephen Lawrence in 1993.
2. 'Hard to reach' groups require different approaches. They present a challenge to those trying to bring them into the engagement process.
3. Ethnic minority groups, gay and lesbian groups, children and young people, especially those at risk, disabled people, sex workers, victims of crime, homeless people, drug users, the mentally disordered, rural/farming communities, older people, single mothers, poor and acutely economically-deprived people, illiterate people (about 13 per cent of the adult population, lest you think them invisible), domestic violence victims, non-English speakers, those suspicious of the police, refugees, some faith communities, transient populations (for example the travelling community).
4. The term might stereotype a group, excluding rather than including it.
5. Seeing everything from your own fixed individual, cultural viewpoint.
6. Diversity training, cultural awareness booklets, Community Liaison Officers (CLOs), other agencies, support groups, police support groups, the communities themselves, and finally but importantly, *you*.

## Knowledge Check 31

1. The College of Policing.
2. The Professional Standards Department (there is one in every force).
3. Any three from: 1 Honesty and integrity; 2 Authority, respect, and courtesy; 3 Equality and diversity; 4 Use of force; 5 Orders and instructions; 6 Duties and responsibilities; 7 Confidentiality; 8 Fitness for work; 9 Conduct; 10 Challenging and reporting improper conduct.
4. You are expected to conform to expectations of integrity, honesty, fairness, equal treatment for all, and respect for others. As we saw in Chapter 4, you are also expected to observe your statutory duty in upholding the nine protected characteristics under the *Equality Act* of 2010 (or had you forgotten that?).
5. Complaints and internal investigations.
6. When you are required to move from facilitator and sympathetic ear to the community to enforcer of regulations or laws.
7. The balance of probability (not proof beyond all reasonable doubt).
8. The Independent Police Complaints Commission (IPCC).

# References

Note that 'a' and 'b' etc, following a date, refer to more than one publication in the same year with a similar title or the same author. In the body of the text, this is rendered as 'ACPO (1999a)' for example.

ACPO (2005), *Guidance on Police Community Support Workers* (Revised June 2005).

ACPO (1999a), *Major Incident Room standard administrative procedures*, MIRSAP, ACPO.

ACPO (1999b), *The Manual of Standard Operating Procedures for scientific support personnel and major incident scenes*, ACPO.

ACPO/FSS (1996), *Using Forensic Science Effectively*, ACPO/Forensic Science Service.

Adlam, R, and Villiers, P (eds) (2003), *Police Leadership in the Twenty-first Century*, Waterside.

Adler, C, and Polk, K (2002), *Child Victims of Homicide*, Cambridge University Press.

Adler, J (ed) (2004), *Forensic Psychology, Concepts, Debates and Practice*, Willan.

Ainsworth, P (2001), *Offender Profiling and Crime Analysis*, Willan.

Ainsworth, P (2002), *Psychology and Policing*, Willan.

Aldridge, J et al (2002), *Digital Imaging Procedure*, Police Scientific Development Branch, Home Office/ACPO.

Alison, L (ed) (2005), *The Forensic Psychologist's Casebook: offender profiling and criminal investigation*, Willan.

Alldridge, P (2003), *Proceeds of Crime*, Hart.

Arnaldo, C (2001), *Child Abuse on the Internet: Ending the Silence*, Berghahn.

Ashworth, A (2002), *Serious Crime, Human Rights and Criminal Procedure*, Willan.

Ashworth, A (2006), *Principles of Criminal Law*, Oxford University Press.

Baggott, M, and Wallace, M (2006), *Neighbourhood Policing Progress Report*, May, Home Office, Crown copyright.

Barrett, D (2010), *Daily Telegraph*, March 21, available at <http://www.telegraph.co.uk/news/uknews/law-and-order/7487413/160-plastic-policemen-charged-with-crimes.html> accessed 18 December 2013.

Bean, P (2002), *Drugs and Crime*, Willan.

Bennetto, J (2000), 'Sleeping with the Enemy is Clue to a Bent Copper', *The Independent*, 19 May, available at <http://findarticles.com/p/articles/mi_qn4158/is_20000519/ai_n14314433> accessed May 2009.

Billingsley, R, Nemitz, T, and Bean, P (2001), *Informers: Policing, Policy, Practice*, Willan.

Blair, I (2005), 'Response to Daily Mirror allegations', *Metropolitan Police website*; available at <http://content.met.police.uk/News/Sir-Ian-Blairs-response-to-the-Daily-Mirror/1260267672392/1257246745756> accessed 27 July 2014.

Bottoms, A, Mawby, R, and Xanthos, P (1989), 'A Tale of Two Estates' in Downes, D (ed), *Crime and the City*, Macmillan.

Bottoms, A, and Wiles, P (2002), 'Environmental Criminology' in Maguire, M (ed), *Oxford Handbook of Criminology*, Oxford University Press, ch 18.

Bourlet, A (1990), *Police Intervention in Marital Violence*, Open University Press.

Bowling, B (1998), *Violent Racism: Victimisation, Policing and Social Context*, Oxford University Press, especially ch 8 'Policing Violent Racism', 234–84.

Bowling, B, and Phillips, C (2003), 'Racist Victimisation in England and Wales' in Hawkins, D (ed), *Violent Crime*, Cambridge University Press, 154–70.

Brackertz, N (2007), 'Who is Hard to Reach and Why?' *ISR Research Paper*, available at <http://www.sisr.net/publications/0701brackertz.pdf> accessed 29 July 2014.

Brain, T (2003), 'Policing and the Condition of England' (on the changes in relations between police and public over the last 60 years), *Policing Today*, vol 9(4), pp 35–6.

Brand, S, and Price, R (2000), 'The Economic and Social Costs of Crime' Home Office Research Study No 217.

Bridges, I (ed) (2013), *Blackstone's Police Operational Handbook 2014: Law & Practice and Procedure Pack;* Police National Legal Database (PNLD), Oxford University Press.

Brogden, M, and Nijhar, P (2005), *Community Policing: National and international models and approaches*, Willan.

Bryant, R (ed) (2006), *Blackstone's Student Police Officer Handbook*, Oxford University Press.

Bullock, K, and Tilley, N (eds) (2003), *Essays in Problem-Orientated Policing*, Willan.

Burke, R (ed) (2004), *Hard Cop, Soft Cop; Dilemmas and Debates in Contemporary Policing*, Willan.

Button, M (2002), *Private Policing*, Willan.

Byrne, S, and Pease, K (2003), 'Crime Reduction and Community Safety' in Newburn, T (ed), *Handbook of Policing*, Willan, Part III, 'Doing Policing', 286–310.

Caless, B (2007), "Numties in Yellow Jackets": The Nature of Hostility Towards the Police Community Support Officer in Neighbourhood Policing Teams', *Policing*, vol 1(2), pp 187–95.

Caless, B, and Spruce, B (2009), 'Police Code of Professional Standards', ch 2.3 in Harfield, C (ed), *Blackstone's Police Operational Handbook: Practice and Procedure*, Oxford University Press.

Carrabine, E, Cox, P, Lee, M, and South, N (2002), *Crime in Modern Britain*, Oxford University Press.

Clark, D (2004), *The Investigation of Crime: A guide to the law of criminal investigation*, Oxford University Press.

Clarke, R (1999), 'Hot Products: Understanding, Anticipating and Reducing Demand for Stolen Goods', Police Research Series Paper 112, Home Office and TSO.

Clements, P (2006), *Policing a Diverse Society*, Oxford University Press.

Cohen, S (2002), *Folk Devils and Moral Panics*, 3rd edn, Routledge.

Cole, S (2001), *Suspect Identities: A History of Fingerprinting and Criminal Identification*, Harvard University Press.

Coleman, R (2004), *Reclaiming the Streets; Surveillance, Social Control and the City*, Willan.

College of Policing (2014), *Code of Ethics: A Code of Practice for the Principles and Standards of Professional Behaviour for the Policing Profession of England and Wales*; July, Ryton-on-Dunsmore (Coventry): The College of Policing; available at <http://www.college.police.uk/en/20972.htm> accessed 28 July 2014.

Cooper, C (2006), 'A National Evaluation of Community Support Officers', Summary 2006, Findings 271, Research, Development and Statistics Directorate, Home Office.

Cooper, C, Anscombe, J, Avenell, J, McLean, F, and Morris, J (2006), 'A National Evaluation of Community Support Officers', Home Office Research Study No 297, Home Office.

Cope, N, Innes, M, and Fielding, N (2001), *Smart Policing? The Theory and Practice of Intelligence-Led Policing*, Home Office.

Copson, G (2002), 'Breaking the Criminal Families' Cycle: What Works?', *Policing Futures*, vol 1(1), pp 1–10.

Davies, P (2005), 'Consultation Paper on Standard Powers for Police Community Support Officers and a framework for the future development of powers', Home Office.

Emsley, C (2004), *Crime and Society in England 1750–1900*, Longman.

Emsley, C (2005), *Hard Men: Violence in England since 1750*, Hambledon.

Ericson, R, and Haggerty, K (1997), *Policing the Risk Society*, Clarendon.

Felson, M (2002), *Crime and Everyday Life*, Sage.

Felson, M, and Clarke, R (1998), *Opportunity Makes the Thief: Practical Theory for Crime Prevention*, Police Research Series, Paper 98, Home Office, Crown Copyright.

Fitzpatrick, B (2005), *Going to Court*, Oxford University Press.

Forensic Science Service (2006), *Scenes of Crime Handbook*, Home Office.

Forrest, S, Myhill, AQ, and Tilley, N (2005), 'Practical Lessons for involving the community in crime and disorder problems', Home Office Development and Practice Report No 43, 16.

Gaule, M (2003), *The Basic Guide to Forensic Awareness*, New Police Bookshop.

Gilbertson, D (2007), 'Policing Matters—The Road to Recovery after the Riots', *Bernie Grant Memorial Lecture*, available at <http://blog.old-and-bold.info/wp-content/uploads/2012/04/David-Gilbertson-former-DAC-Metropolitan-Police.pdf> accessed 28 July 2014.

Hall, N (2005), *Hate Crime*, Willan.

Harfield, C (ed), (2008), *The Handbook of Intelligent Policing: Consilience, crime control, and community safety*, Oxford University Press.

Harrington, V, Down, G, Johnson, M, and Upton, C (2005), 'Police Community Support Officers: An Evaluation of Round 2 in Kent, 2004/2005', O&D, Kent Police.

Hitchens, P (2003), *A Brief History of Crime: The decline of order, justice and liberty in England*, Atlantic.

HMSO (2005), Criminal Justice and Police Act (ss 1–11), *Penalty Notices for Disorder, Police Operational Guidance*, March 2005.

HMSO (2000), *Regulation of Investigatory Powers Act* (RIPA) (now TSO).

Home Office (2006a), 'Police Community Support Officer: Competency-Based Application Form; scoring key and grading table', April.

Home Office (2006b), 'Summary of Responses to the Consultation Document "Standard Powers for CSOs and a Framework for the Future Development of Powers"'.

Home Office (2014), Road Traffic Offences: Guidance on Fixed Penalty Notices, access at <http://www.cps.gov.uk/legal/p_to_r/road_traffic_offences_guidance_on_fixed_penalty_notices/>.

Innes, M, Fielding, N, and Langan, S (2002), 'Signal Crimes and Control Signals: Towards an evidence-based conceptual framework for Reassurance Policing', a report for Surrey Police, University of Surrey.

John, T, and Maguire, M (2003), 'Rolling Out the National Intelligence Model: Key Challenges' in Bullock, K, and Tilley, N (eds), *Essays in Problem-Orientated Policing*, Willan.

Jones, T, and Newburn, T (2001), *Widening Access: Improving Police Relations with Hard to Reach Groups*, Police Research Series, Paper 138, Home Office Policing and Reducing Crime Unit, London.

Kleinig, J (2006), *The Ethics of Policing*, Cambridge University Press.

MacPherson, Sir W (1999), *Report of an Inquiry into the Investigation of the Murder of Stephen Lawrence*, Cmd 4262.

Maguire, M, Morgan, R, and Reiner, R (eds) (2002), *The Oxford Handbook of Criminology*, 3rd edn, Oxford University Press.

Mason, M, and Dale, C (2008), *Analysis of Police Community Support Officer (PCSO) Activity Based Costing (ABC) data: results from an initial review* (July, Home Office, available from <http://www.homeoffice.gov.uk/rds/pdfs08/horr08.pdf> accessed 1 May 2009).

Mawby, RI (2001), *Burglary*, Willan.

Mistry, D (2007), 'Community Engagement: practical lessons from a pilot project', Home Office Development and Practice Report No 48.

Morgan, J (1990), *The Police Function and the Investigation of Crime*, Gower.

Morgan, J, (1991), 'Safer Communities: The local delivery of crime prevention through the partnership approach' ['The Morgan Report'], *The Home Office Standing Conference on Crime Prevention*. August, available from <http://www.mhbuk.com/reports.aspx?sm=c_b> accessed May 2009.

Morgan, R, and Newburn, T (1997), *The Future of Policing*, Oxford University Press.

Myhill, A (2012), *Community Engagement in Policing*, College of Policing, (NPIA), updated from 2006, and available at <http://www.college.police.uk/en/docs/Community_engagement_lessons.pdf>.

Newburn, T, Williamson, T, and Wright, A (eds) (2007), *Handbook of Criminal Investigation*, Willan.

Nolan, Lord (1995), *First Report of the Committee on Standards in Public Life*, Cmnd 2850-I.

NPIA (2008), *Neighbourhood Policing Programme, PCSO Review* (July 2008).

Paterson, C, and Pollock, E (2011), *Policing and Criminology*, Exeter: Learning Matters, ch 6 'Policing in a multi-agency context', pp 90–106.

Quinlan, P, and Morris, J (2008), *Neighbourhood Policing: The impact of piloting and early national implementation*, Home Office OnLine Report 01/08, available from <http://www.homeoffice.gov.uk/rds/pdfs08/rdsolr0108app.pdf> accessed 16 January 2009.

Read, T, and Tilley, N (2000), 'Not Rocket Science? Problem-Solving and Crime Reduction', Crime Reduction Research Series, Paper 6, Home Office.

Reiner, R (2013), 'Who Governs? Democracy, plutocracy, science and prophecy in policing', *Criminology and Criminal Justice*, vol 13(2), pp 161–80.

Rogers, C (2006), *Crime Reduction Partnerships*, Oxford University Press.

Rowe, M (2004), *Policing, Race and Racism*, Willan.

Sampson, P (2005), 'Criminal Treatment of Community Support Officers', *Daily Mirror*, 11 May, available at <http://pcsos-national.co.uk/mirror.html> accessed 27 July 2014.

Stevens, M (1996), *How to be a Better Problem-Solver*, Kogan Page, 9.

Sutherland, J (2014), *The PCSO Review–An Evaluation of the Role, Value and Establishment of Police Community Support Officers within Cambridgeshire Constabulary*, available at <http://www.rtaylor.co.uk/pdf/PCSO_Review.pdf> accessed 29 May 2014.

Tilley, N (2003), 'Community Policing, POP and Intelligence-led Policing' in Newburn, T (ed), *A Handbook of Policing*, Willan, ch 13, pp 311–39.

Tilley, N (ed) (2005), *Handbook of Crime Prevention and Community Safety*, Willan.

Tilley, N, and Ford, A (1996), *Forensic Science and Crime Investigation*, Police Research Group, Crime Detection and Prevention Series, Paper 73.

Unwin, S (2006), *Police Community Support Officers: A Force For The Future; A Study Into The Training and Employment of Police Community Support Officers,* unpublished MSc Dissertation; Department of Criminology, Leicester University, available at <http://www.national-pcsos.co.uk/JOSSMAN2.pdf> accessed 4 June 2014.

Wadham, J, Mountfield, H, Edmundson, A, and Gallagher, C (2007), *Blackstone's Guide to the Human Rights Act 1998*, Oxford University Press.

Wahidin, A, and Cain, M (eds) (2006), *Ageing, Crime and Society*, Willan.

Wakefield, A (2004), *Selling Security: The private policing of public space*, Willan.

Ward, R, and Davies, O (2004), *The Criminal Justice Act 2003: A practitioner's guide*, Jordan.

Websdale, N (1999), *Understanding Domestic Homicide*, North Eastern University Press.

## Cases and case law

*R v Turnbull* [1976] 3 All ER 549

*R v Heggart and Heggart* [November 2000, CA]

*R v Anthony David Martin* [2001] EWCA Crim 2245

# Index